MULTICULTURAL AND MULTILINGUAL LITERACY AND LANGUAGE

SOLVING PROBLEMS IN THE TEACHING OF LITERACY

Cathy Collins Block, *Series Editor*

Recent Volumes

Multicultural and Multilingual Literacy and Language

Contexts and Practices

Edited by

FENICE B. BOYD *and* **CYNTHIA H. BROCK**
with **MARY S. ROZENDAL**

Foreword by **LISA DELPIT**

THE GUILFORD PRESS
New York   London

KH

Printed in the United States of America

This book is printed on acid-free paper.

Last digit is print number: 9 8 7 6 5 4 3 2 1

Library of Congress Cataloging-in-Publication Data

Multicultural and multilingual literacy and language : contexts and
practices / edited by Fenice B. Boyd and Cynthia H. Brock with Mary S.
Rozendal.
    p. cm. — (Solving problems in the teaching of literacy)
Includes bibliographical references and index.
  ISBN 1-57230-962-8 (hardcover) — ISBN 1-57230-961-X (pbk.)
  1. Literacy—Social aspects—United States. 2. Language arts—Social
aspects—United States. 3. Sociolinguistics—United States. 4.
Multicultural education—United States. I. Boyd, Fenice B. II. Brock,
Cynthia H. III. Rozendal, Mary S. IV. Series.
  LC151.M84 2004
  370.117—dc22

                          2003015737

11/22/04

About the Editors

Fenice B. Boyd, PhD, is Associate Professor of Literacy Education in the Department of Learning and Instruction at the University at Buffalo. She earned her doctorate from Michigan State University in Curriculum, Teaching, and Educational Policy with a speciality in Literacy. Dr. Boyd's research centers on adolescents who struggle with literacy learning and schooling, students' responses to young adult and multicultural literature, and issues related to diversity in classrooms. At the University at Buffalo, she teaches masters and doctoral courses focused on reading comprehension research, adolescent literacy, language arts, young adult literature, and language, literacy, and culture.

Cynthia H. Brock, PhD, is Associate Professor of Literacy Studies in the Department of Educational Specialties at the University of Nevada, Reno. Her primary teaching interests include literacy instruction for children in the middle and upper elementary grades, literacy and diversity, and qualitative methods. Dr. Brock's primary research interests include studying the literacy learning of upper elementary children from diverse cultural and linguistic backgrounds. She also explores how to work with preservice and in-service teachers to foster the literacy learning of children from diverse backgrounds at the upper elementary level.

Mary S. Rozendal, PhD, is Assistant Professor of Literacy Education in the Department of Learning and Instruction at the University at Buffalo. She teaches literacy methods courses that center on instruction for students with disabilities, teacher collaboration in general and special education, and classroom discourse.

Contributors

Martha A. Adler, PhD, School of Education, University of Michigan, Dearborn, Michigan

Nancy Anderson, PhD, Department of Reading, Texas Woman's University, Denton, Texas

Eurydice Bouchereau Bauer, PhD, Department of Curriculum and Instruction, University of Illinois at Urbana–Champaign, Champaign, Illinois

Fenice B. Boyd, PhD, Department of Learning and Instruction, State University of New York at Buffalo, Buffalo, New York

Cynthia H. Brock, PhD, Department of Educational Specialties, University of Nevada, Reno, Nevada

Zoe Ann Brown, PhD, Pacific Resources for Education and Learning, Honolulu, Hawaii

Debbie Diller, MEd, educational consultant, Houston, Texas

Charles W. Fisher, PhD, School of Education, University of Michigan, Ann Arbor, Michigan

Leila Flores-Dueñas, PhD, Department of Language, Literature, and Social Studies, University of New Mexico, Albuquerque, New Mexico

Claudia Christensen Haag, PhD, Lewisville Independent School District, Lewisville, Texas

Elfrieda H. Hiebert, PhD, School of Education, University of Michigan, Ann Arbor, Michigan

Laura Klenk, PhD, Department of Learning and Instruction, State University of New York at Buffalo, Buffalo, New York

Guofang Li, PhD, Department of Learning and Instruction, State University at Buffalo, Buffalo, New York

Laurie MacGillivray, EdD, Division of Learning and Instruction, Rossier School of Education, University of Southern California, Los Angeles, California

Ana Maritza Martinez, MS, Magnolia Elementary School, Los Angeles, California

Gwendolyn Thompson McMillon, PhD, Department of Reading and Language Arts, Oakland University, Rochester, Michigan

Vincent Duane McMillon, MSW, Senior Pastor, St. Paul Baptist Church, Saginaw, Michigan

Mary McVee, PhD, Department of Learning and Instruction, State University of New York at Buffalo, Buffalo, New York

Dorothy K. Moore, PhD, Department of Teacher Education, University of Wisconsin, River Falls, Wisconsin

Elavie Ndura, EdD, Department of Curriculum and Instruction, University of Nevada, Reno, Nevada

Laura A. Parks, MEd, Douglas County School District, Gardnerville, Nevada

Julie L. Pennington, PhD, Department of Curriculum and Instruction, University of Nevada, Reno, Nevada

Elizabeth Rosado-McGrath, MEd, Spring Branch Independent School District, Houston, Texas

Robert Rueda, PhD, Division of Learning and Instruction, Rossier School of Education, University of Southern California, Los Angeles, California

Cheryl Taitague, MA, Pacific Resources for Education and Learning, Honolulu, Hawaii

Judy Wallis, PhD, Spring Branch Independent School District, Houston, Texas

Joan Williams, PhD, Department of Teacher Education, Texas Lutheran University, Seguin, Texas

Foreword

Reading this book took me back to Papua New Guinea, where I conducted my dissertation research. It was there that my nascent theoretical understandings of the role culture plays in education became grounded in irrefutable experience. I remember my own culture shock as I moved into the village and became accustomed to the lack of electricity, running water, and drug stores; as I struggled to learn the language that surrounded me; as I learned to bathe in rivers, cook and "story" around a wood fire, help gather food in gardens, and essentially learn to live and love a completely different lifestyle. The village people patiently and kindly supported my education so that I never felt that my free fall into new cultural territory would result in a disastrous landing.

I was at the village to investigate the results of using the indigenous community language and local culture as the initial language and content of schooling—as the medium for literacy learning and the content of mathematics instruction. The *tok ples skuls* (indigenous language schools), as the new institutions were called, employed teachers who were not necessarily trained in typical teacher education programs, but who were young people from the villages whom the elders determined to be appropriate representatives of the cultural values of the community.

One of the factors that had to be considered prior to the program's inception was the linguistic complexity of the country. There are 700 indigenous languages in Papua New Guinea, few of which had written orthographies. The Summer Institute of Linguistics (SIL), a missionary group that works on developing orthographies and translating religious and other matter into indigenous minority languages around the world, was enlisted to assist. The SIL developed orthographies (working through several regional variations) for six of the languages in the North Solomons Province of the country. They also developed "linguistic-based" phonics readers for teaching rhyming word patterns (like the "Dan can fan the man" readers in English). The village selected teachers, who then received short-course training in how to teach the material using what the developers referred to as "analytical instructional strategies." For example, teachers were instructed to say things to the children such as "If c-a-n spells *can* and f-a-t spells *fat*, then c-a-t would spell *cat*."

A few months after training concluded and school began, I observed in the open-air village classrooms every morning. (School was over by lunchtime so that children could participate in village life.) I watched the young teachers tackle their tasks, but noticed early on that in almost all classrooms, in almost every village, no teacher taught as he or she had been instructed at the SIL training sessions. Instead of using an analytic method of instruction, almost all teachers had students copy sentences written on the big blackboard onto their little blackboards, and then repeat them in unison after the teacher read them. The students did learn to read, as evidenced by assessments I developed later. They had also learned to read and write *tok pisin*, the phonically regular *lingua franca* of the country, through which individuals from different language groups communicate with each other. Interestingly, they had never been taught to read and write this language in the schools, but had "picked it up" in the process of learning mother-tongue literacy.

I was curious about the teachers' instructional strategies. Although a great deal of the area's limited financial and human resources had been devoted to developing the teaching strategies and training the teachers, these strategies and training were not being utilized. Yet, the children were learning.

I gained a greater understanding of the educational mystery as I lived in the village and developed close friendships with village residents. One of the most revealing experiences was teaching and being taught card games. My mother had sent me an UNO game. My friends were anxious to play, so one evening we settled down on the palm-leaf floor of my hut, lit the kerosene lantern, and opened the box. I started by telling them the object of the game and detailing the rules. They were clearly impatient at my explanations. Soon someone said, "Lisa, just pass out the cards, and let's play. You tell us what cards to play." I tried to do as they requested, and we somehow limped through some version of the game.

I began to understand my friends' way of teaching when, 2 days later, they wanted to teach me to play a game they loved. No one ever talked about rules or the object of the game. I was seated at the table with the rest of the players. They assigned someone who wasn't playing to stand behind me and tell me which cards to put down and when.

After doing this for a while, I was supposed to deduce the rules of the game and thus learn to play on my own. I can say that I did not learn as fast as any of the children in the village, but I did eventually learn.

After a few days of thinking about my ineptness in the learning process, I had a "eureka" experience. I figured out what the teachers in the *tok ples* classrooms were doing. The style of teaching and learning in the village was more akin to an apprenticeship, where the learner was supported in imitating the behaviors of the master teacher until they became his or her own. The learner intuited the "rules" through his or her own active thinking rather than being explicitly taught them by the instructor. These strategies were in complete contradiction to the methods taught to the teachers in teacher training, and upon which the program was based. Interestingly, the teachers, without apparently being conscious of what they were doing, had restructured the program to reflect the culture of their students and themselves.

I cannot, of course, speculate what might have happened if the teachers were not from the same culture as their students. Perhaps they would have tried to modify a program that didn't seem to be working— that left their students bored and unresponsive or agitated and unruly. Perhaps they would have shuffled along, like I did in teaching UNO, in some uncomfortable blend of different cultural styles. Or perhaps they would have attempted to teach the program as written, and when the children did not learn, would have assumed that these village children had family problems or were limited in their ability to become literate.

My experiences in Papua New Guinea solidified my understanding of the deep significance of culture in literacy—and any other—learning. Despite a large body of work that supports this perspective, few educators really embrace it. And those who do embrace it seldom really understand the kind of deep community study they would have to undertake to fully incorporate it into their teaching.

A year or so ago, I sat with a superintendent and his cabinet, seeking approval to institute a school reform effort that would focus on improving the achievement of low-income African American children. Although there was some interest in working with us, there was little support for focusing the reform on a particular group (even though the African American students scored at the bottom of all assessments in the district). Some wondered if we were being racist to focus in that fashion. After all, wasn't good teaching good teaching? In the most telling moment, one of the cabinet members looked at me earnestly and tried to explain: "We know it's not what we do in the school. We care deeply about all of our students. We teach exactly the same to all of them. We make an effort to make sure that all classrooms are integrated. All of our students get the same instruction. It has to be the problems these children have at home, not what goes on in school. I think you should probably be trying to work with parents, not with teachers."

"We teach all students exactly the same." "It's the problems these children have at home." Therein lies the problem that we have not understood in the way I had to understand in a Papua New Guinea village. If we truly want to educate all students, we cannot teach them all in the same way. Indeed, that is a great recipe for the failure we currently call "the achievement gap." This book, its editors, and its authors attempt to help us understand this problem. Had it been published when I was in that meeting with the superintendent, I would have sent copies ahead for everyone who was to attend the meeting.

LISA DELPIT, EDD

Contents

Introduction

Constructing Pedagogies of Empowerment in Multicultural and Multilingual Classrooms
Implications for Theory and Practice

FENICE B. BOYD and CYNTHIA H. BROCK

Unequivocally, more students from diverse ethnic, cultural, and linguistic backgrounds are flowing into classrooms all across the United States (Nieto, 1999). Legal immigration between 1980 and 1990 was almost 9 million, equaling the number of immigrants from 1900 to 1910 (Nieto, 1996). In 1994 there were an estimated 9.9 million language-minority students in the United States. The number of students with limited English proficiency, whose lack of facility in English causes academic difficulties, is dramatically increasing. From 1986 to 1992 the number of such students increased from 1 million to 2.5 million. By the year 2020, the number of children in the United States with limited English proficiency is expected to increase to 6 million (Nieto, 1996). Nieto (1996) states, "The largest numbers of new immigrants are now from Asia and Latin America, a marked departure from previous times when they were overwhelmingly from Europe" (p. 189).

Although the number of children from diverse cultural and linguistic backgrounds in U.S. schools is growing exponentially, the ethnic and linguistic makeup of the teaching force in U.S. schools is largely European American. In fact, approximately 90% of the U. S. teaching force comprises European American teachers, primarily women from working- and middle-class backgrounds, who speak only English (Howard, 1999). Clearly, a large and growing mismatch exists between the cultural and linguistic backgrounds of the children attending U.S. public schools and those of their teachers. Given the mismatch between student and teacher backgrounds, and the significant and growing changes in student demographics, questions arise: Does the mismatch between the children and teachers in U.S. schools matter? What might the changing student demographics mean for multicultural and multilingual literacy and language practices? What might all of these changes mean for children in U.S. schools, and for children from diverse ethnic and cultural backgrounds, who are learning to speak English? What knowledge about ethnic, cultural, and linguistic diversity do educators and scholars need to serve students more effectively? The answers to these four questions are complex and just as varied as the statistics we have quoted. Moreover, there is "no quick fix" (Allington & Walmsley, 1995) to what we, as educators, must do to enable all children to be successful literacy and language learners. We elaborate on answers to these questions in the remainder of our Introduction. The chapters in this volume continue to address these questions in more detail.

First, many scholars argue that linguistic and cultural diversity are inextricably linked and include cultural diversity among students whose first language is English (e.g., Delpit, 1988; Moll, 1997; Obidah, 1998; Perry & Delpit, 1998). Obidah (1998), for example, examined African American students' use of what she termed *literate currency* to describe the "multiple and interactive forms of literacy that students and teachers bring into the classroom, and that have a significant impact on the encounters between these two groups in the course of everyday schooling" (p. 51). She argued that African American students' literate currencies are brought into classrooms and the schooling process, but are often ignored by their teachers. The lack of acknowledgment of the diverse and rich perspectives that African American students bring to classrooms is part of a history of sanctioned injustices. Obidah's research reveals a dire need for multicultural reform efforts that go beyond the mere inclusion of culturally relevant literature in classrooms. Educators must find ways to include the knowledge, skills, and dispositions for literacy and language learning that African American students—and students from other cultural backgrounds—bring into classrooms. Similarly, Moll (1997) argued that educators have much to learn from the linguistic and cultural "funds of knowledge" that children bring to classrooms. These challenges suggested by Obidah and Moll call for teachers to remain life-

long learners, because the composition of students has changed historically in this country and will unequivocally continue to change. Clearly,
we have much to learn about the complex cultural and linguistic backgrounds that children bring to classrooms, and how we might structure
schools, and the literacy and language practices within them, to accom-
modate the children.

Second, the changing demographics and the mismatch between children and their teachers both matter, because teachers are often under-
prepared to teach effectively students whose backgrounds are different
from their own (Howard, 1999; Nieto, 1999). Historically, and even in
the 21st century, a one-size-fits-all model for teaching and learning has
been enacted in U.S. schools. This approach involves language practices,
literacy instruction, and literature geared toward the backgrounds and
experiences of middle-class European American children (Connell, 1994;
Jimenez, 2003; Labov, 2003). When children from diverse cultural and
linguistic backgrounds bring different languages, home literacy experiences, and sociocultural backgrounds to U.S. classrooms, educators may
perceive them as being "behind" their mainstream peers in language and
literacy development, because their backgrounds and experiences do not
match mainstream school practices and expectations. As we in the educational community work to sort out ways to educate *all* children in U.S.
schools, we must direct our gaze in the appropriate direction. Our attention should not be directed toward trying "to find out what is wrong
with the children but what can be done to improve the educational system" (Labov, 2003, p. 129).

As an educational community, we *must* follow the lead of scholars
such as Moll, Connell, Obidah, and Labov by attending to ways in
which schools need to be reconceptualized to address issues of linguistic
and cultural diversity; the changing demographics in U.S. schools make
this a necessity rather than an option. If all students are to be taught effectively, educators must recognize, value, and build instruction on the
language practices and life experiences of students from diverse ethnic,
cultural, and linguistic backgrounds (Au & Raphael, 2000). Scholars
(e.g., Hones, 2002) alert us to the urgency of working toward these
ends. Educators at all levels, in all positions, must become aware of the
positive and effective changes that can be made, and have been made, in
some classrooms, school districts, universities, and communities. The
chapters in this book point us in a direction of positive change as an educational community. The chapter contributors draw on their own experiences with teachers, students, and the scholarly literature to provide
concrete and specific suggestions to educators at all levels about ways to
rethink, recraft, reshape, and restructure educational beliefs and prac-

tices to meet the needs of the growing numbers of children from diverse backgrounds in U.S. schools.

SOCIOCULTURAL THEORY AS A CONCEPTUAL FRAMEWORK

In sociocultural theory (e.g., Au, 1993; Au & Carroll, 1997; Au & Raphael, 2000; Moll, 1994; Vygotsky, 1978; Wertsch, 1991, 1998), the lens that we used to conceptualize the organization and structure of this text, a central tenet is that the mind is social in nature (Wertsch, 1991, 1998); that is, the human mind is constituted through, and originates from, language-based social interactions with others. Vygotsky (1978) argued that higher psychological processes, such as those involved in literacy teaching and learning, take place first in social interactions between people, then over time are appropriated within the individual. If educators take seriously this premise, then the social interactions we structure in our school and university classrooms and communities deserve our careful and thoughtful attention, because they serve as the very foundation of learning. The authors of the chapters in this book present a variety of ways to think carefully about structuring social interactions to promote the learning in children from diverse backgrounds. For example, in Chapter 3, Claudia Haag and Joan Williams ask us to look carefully at the ways we use various participation structures in our classrooms to influence the multiple types of interactions. Judy Wallis and Elizabeth Rosado (Chapter 14) take a much broader look at how district-level interactions should be structured to promote teacher and student learning.

Sociocultural theorists also emphasize that language in use plays a central role in mediating our actions as humans. Vygotsky (1978) asserted that human cognition is constituted through meaningful, language-based social interactions. Consequently, the use of language in the context of interactions, and the various analytical ways of looking at that language, become central when considering human learning. Moreover, the ways that discussions are constructed in classroom contexts between students and students, as well as teachers and students, vary in dynamic and evolving ways. Examining carefully the ways that different conversational moves shape encounters between classroom participants impacts the literacy learning opportunities constructed through oral and written language in classrooms (Harré & Van Langenhove, 1999). The chapter authors invited to contribute to this book look carefully at language and how language use impacts children's learning opportunities. For example, in Chapter 5, Nancy Anderson examines the way she structured interactions and used language to impact the learning of an African American child she tutored in an intensive reading intervention. Initially, she was unsuccessful in helping her student to learn to read. Through careful analysis of the language-based interactions she structured during literacy lessons, however, she found a way to reach her student to promote his literacy learning.

An important strength of sociohistorical theory is that it grounds issues pertaining to human learning in social, cultural, and historical contexts (Vygotsky, 1978). This point is significant in contexts in which teachers and children represent different cultural and linguistic backgrounds; a sociocultural theoretical lens calls attention to cultural and linguistic differences. According to Moll and others (e.g., Moll, 1997; Moll & Whitmore, 1993), when educators seek to understand the lives of children and their families from diverse cultural backgrounds, they can better understand the rich cultural and linguistic resources these families bring to schools. Moreover, when educators better understand the cultural backgrounds of the children they serve, they can design classroom instruction that builds on and values these differences. A variety of chapter contributors address this important concern. For example, in Chapter 4, Debbie Diller, a European American teacher, chronicles her struggles and learning as she moved from teaching in a middle-class, predominantly European American school in the Midwest, to an inner-city school in Houston. In Chapter 16, Guofang Li looks carefully and in depth at the literate activities of one Chinese family living in British Columbia, and presents her readers with ways to think about drawing on the home experiences and cultures of children of Chinese heritage. These, and other chapter contributors to this text, demonstrate that viewing children from diverse ethnic, cultural, and linguistic backgrounds as bringing different but rich experiences to the table, rather than perceiving them as deficient, is a crucial first step in the process of changing schools to serve children better. We must stop assuming that these children and their families need to change to serve the often static and outdated institutional needs of schools (Connell, 1994).

These tenets of sociocultural theory have profound implications for facilitating students' literacy learning in multilingual and multicultural classrooms. The ways educators construct classroom communities—including the nature and type of interactions fostered, and the conceptual content constructed—impact what students have an opportunity to learn. This point is exceedingly important for teachers to consider when their cultural and linguistic backgrounds differ from those of the children they serve. Educators must realize that different cultural groups use language to act and interact in different ways, and these different "ways with words" significantly impact children's learning opportunities (Heath, 1983; Philips, 1983).

THE ORGANIZATION OF THIS BOOK

We invited educators and researchers to contribute to this book based on their understanding of research, their reflective pedagogical practices, and their careful attention to students' interests and instructional needs. We have organized the chapters around four overarching, foundational themes in effective literacy instruction for children from diverse backgrounds. These themes include (1) language, text, and context; (2) teacher ideologies and motivation for change; (3) listening to students' voices on issues of diversity and literacy learning; and (4) exploring out-of-classroom influences on literacy learning. Together, the chapters categorized within these themes shed light on how teachers, teacher educators, researchers, language arts specialists, English as a second language (ESL) coordinators, and district-level administrators at all levels might construct meaningful, challenging, and dynamic literacy and language learning communities in multicultural and multilingual classrooms.

Part I, *Language, Texts, and Contexts*, comprises three chapters in which readers are asked to look carefully at the ways they make decisions about using language and texts, and structuring classroom contexts to promote the literacy learning of children from diverse backgrounds. Beginning with Chapter 1, Cynthia H. Brock, Laura A. Parks, and Dorothy K. Moore raise a key question: How do the varieties of languages that children speak and write impact their literacy learning opportunities? The authors address this question by asking readers to engage in a thought experiment that conveys the complexity of language variation. Then, they present scholarly literature to help readers understand language variation and ways that classroom teachers can honor varieties of languages that children speak, while simultaneously teaching children the language of power in U.S. classrooms and society (Edwards, 2003).

Elfreida H. Hiebert, Zoe Ann Brown, Cheryl Taitague, Charles W. Fisher, and Martha A. Adler, in Chapter 2, look at text features and apply them to the design of beginning reading textbooks for English language learners (ELLs). The authors describe the features of current beginning reading texts, review existing research on text features that support language and literacy learning of ELLs, and describe the features of a set of beginning reading texts designed for ELLs. Chapter 3, by Claudia Christensen Haag and Joan Williams, emphasizes that meaningful talk in classrooms enhances students' literacy learning opportunities.

They describe various classroom participation structures and activities—such as read-alouds, art, and drama—that provide venues for ELLs to participate successfully in classroom literacy learning.

Part II, *Teacher Ideologies and Motivation for Change*, consists of four chapters, each of which is a powerful testimony to the impact that meaningfully changing one's beliefs and practices can have on the literacy learning of children from diverse ethnic, cultural, and linguistic backgrounds. The authors tell their readers *why* and *how* they changed their beliefs and practices to improve their students' literacy learning. Chapters 4 and 5 both illustrate how European American educators shifted their thoughts and actions as they worked directly with children of color in specific classroom contexts. In Chapter 4, Debbie Diller writes about her own process of changing her beliefs and raising her cultural awareness as a classroom teacher. In Chapter 5, Nancy Anderson, a teacher–educator, examines how she changed her teaching practices better to meet the needs of an African American child with whom she worked.

The next two chapters take somewhat different slants—with respect to contexts and issues explored—on the topic of teacher ideology and education in multicultural and multilingual contexts. In Chapter 6, Mary McVee, a teacher–educator, examines the provocative personal narrative of Cathy, a European American teacher. Cathy raised an important question in McVee's graduate course: "What can I, as a white teacher, do to be a better teacher for my students who are black?" In addition to addressing Cathy's question, McVee encourages her readers to think about narrative as a tool for exploring complex questions and concerns about issues of diversity and literacy instruction. In realizing her own differences as a black African immigrant to the United States, Elavie Ndura—in Chapter 7—decided to teach her junior high English language arts classes from a multicultural perspective, because she believed that her mostly European American students required a broader educational perspective. Her decision to change her instructional approach came about when she, herself, endured numerous racist and bigoted comments and situations.

We end Part II of this text with Chapter 8, by Laurie MacGillivray, Robert Rueda, and Ana Maritza Martinez, which offers a valuable synthesis of key issues and concerns facing teachers who strive to make meaningful changes in their classrooms. The authors present what they learned from teachers in inner-city Los Angeles about high-quality instruction for poor ESL learners. Their work challenges administrators and educational policymakers to listen to teachers, because they are on the "front lines" in working with children from various socioeconomic and sociocultural backgrounds.

Part III, *Students' Voices on Issues of Literacy Learning and Diversity*, offers readers an opportunity to hear about issues of diversity and literacy from students' perspectives. Traditionally, adult experts in the field—teachers, teacher–educators, researchers, administrators, and policymakers—make decisions about teaching language and literacy. However, authors of the chapters in this section remind us that students' voices must be added to the list of those we consult as we make decisions about fostering the literacy learning of children from diverse backgrounds (Pearson, 1997). The authors of Chapters 9 and 10 consulted adolescent and upper-elementary-level readers and writers about their literacy learning experiences in a variety of contexts. In Chapter 9, Fenice B. Boyd examined one ninth-grade student's literacy learning experiences during a unit centered on multicultural literature. The student examined a videotaped oral presentation to interpret her experiences in the focus unit of study. Boyd argues that listening to students talk about their own literacy learning opportunities offers teachers important insights into instructional decision making. Leila Flores-Dueñas, in Chapter 10, reports the results of a study in which four Mexican American bilingual students responded to literature written by Mexican American and non–Mexican American authors. She illustrates how culturally relevant literature, and meaningful interactions around that literature, can impact positively children's literacy learning opportunities.

The next two chapters remind us, as teachers, that even very young children have much to tell and show us about their literacy learning. In Chapter 11, Eurydice Bouchereau Bauer presents an ethnography of Elena, her daughter, who learned to read and write in English and German simultaneously. Bauer records her daughter's writing development between the ages of 3 years, 10 months and 4 years, 10 months, and highlights how Elena's bilingualism influenced her writing. Laura Klenk, in Chapter 12, describes what she learned from Carmen, a young ELL in kindergarten, that helped her to support Carmen's literacy learning. Woven throughout the chapter is a discussion of the theoretical principles of language and literacy development that guided Klenk's decision making as Carmen's teacher.

Part IV, *Out-of-Classroom Influences on Literacy Learning*, looks at literacy teaching and learning from a variety of different venues. Many scholars have written about the impact of literacy learning in out-of-school contexts (e.g., Hull & Schultz, 2002). The chapters in this section make important contributions to the professional literature pertaining to out-of-school influences on the literacy learning of children from diverse backgrounds. Authors of the first two chapters, both situated in Texas, address ways that state and district mandates and planning can influence—for better or worse—instructional decisions in inner-city schools. Julie L. Pennington begins Chapter 13 by asking "tough questions" about the impact the Texas Assessment of Academic Skills (TAAS) has had on literacy teaching and learning in one inner-city Texas school. Over time, rather than emphasizing the complexity and culture of the students, and seeking to maintain their native languages as much as possible, the school became highly focused on streamlining the curriculum to match the state's objective of passing the TAAS test.

Allington (2002) states, "Few school districts (or state education agencies) seem to have a plan for creating expert teachers. In other words, while most school districts have a long-term plan, and a funding stream, for replacing or rehabilitating the roofs of school buildings, almost none has a plan, or the funding, for developing teacher expertise through professional development activities" (p. 30). This is not the case for Spring Branch Independent School District (ISD) in Houston, Texas. Spring Branch ISD stands out as an example of the kind of instructional planning for which Allington argues. In Chapter 14, Judy Wallis and Elizabeth Rosado-McGrath present the story of how they set out to create a comprehensive, districtwide literacy plan that would place at its heart the needs of all students and teachers in their diverse, inner-city school district.

The authors of Chapters 15 and 16 look carefully inside various cultural contexts—an African American church and a Chinese family—to help readers see the complex literacy practices enacted in these different contexts. We realize that these contexts represent only two of the myriad contexts that influence the lives and literacy of children from diverse backgrounds in our schools. Peshkin (1985) reminds us, however, that careful and thoughtful attention to one context may help us to attend carefully and thoughtfully to other contexts. He writes, "When I disclose what I have seen, my results invite other researchers to look where I did and see what I saw. My ideas are candidates for others to entertain, not necessarily as truth, let alone Truth, but as positions about the nature and meaning of a phenomenon that may fit their sensibility and shape their thinking about their own inquiries" (p. 280). We suspect that the thoughtful work of the authors of Chapters 15 and 16 will help you to "shape your thinking about your own inquiries" into the myriad contexts that influence the literacy learning of children that you may encounter from diverse cultural and linguistic backgrounds.

Chapter 15, written by Gwendolyn Thompson McMillon, a teacher–educator, and her husband Vincent Duane McMillon, a minister, takes readers through a 3-year journey that explores the empowering literacy practices of an African American church in an urban neighborhood. Specifically, they provide a historical backdrop of the literacy practices in black churches, discuss student and teacher relationships, and describe empowering, authentic opportunities provided by the church that motivate students to practice their literacy skills within the church setting. Guofang Li offers another unique and valuable perspective on literacy practices in out-of-classroom settings in Chapter 16. Li studied a Chinese immigrant student's (i.e., Yang Li's) home literacy practices and explored ways his family supported his school literacy learning. In Chapter 17, Cynthia Brock concludes by looking back across lessons learned from the contributors to this volume. As well, she looks ahead to work that needs to be done as we continue to work together to improve the literacy learning opportunities of children from diverse ethnic, cultural, and linguistic backgrounds in U.S. schools.

REFERENCES

Allington, R. L. (2002). *Big brother and the national reading curriculum: How ideology trumped evidence*. Portsmouth, NH: Heinemann.

Allington, R. L., & Walmsley, S. A. (Eds.). (1995). *No quick fix: Rethinking literacy programs in America's elementary schools*. New York: Teachers College Press.

Au, K. (1993). *Literacy instruction in multicultural settings*. Fort Worth, TX: Holt, Rinehart & Winston.

Au, K. H., & Carroll, J. H. (1997). Improving literacy achievement through a constructivist approach: The KEEP demonstration project. *Elementary School Journal, 97,* 203–221.

Au, K. H., & Raphael, T. (2000). Equity and literacy in the next millennium. *Reading Research Quarterly, 35,* 170–188.

Connell, R. W. (1994). Poverty and education. *Harvard Educational Review, 64,* 125–129.

Delpit, L. (1988). The silenced dialogue: Power and pedagogy in educating other people's children. *Harvard Educational Review, 58,* 280–298.

Edwards, P. A. (2003). The impact of family on literacy development: Convergence, controversy, and instructional implications [National Annual Review of Research address]. In J. V. Hoffman, D. L. Shallert, C. M. Fairbanks, J. Worthy, & B. Maloch (Eds.), *52nd yearbook of the National Reading Conference*. Milwaukee, WI: National Reading Conference.

Harré, R., & van Langenhove, L. (1999). *Positioning theory*. Malden, MA: Blackwell.

Heath, S. B. (1983). *Ways with words: Language, life, and work in communities and classrooms*. Cambridge, UK: Cambridge University Press.

Hones, D. F. (2002). In quest of freedom: Towards a critical pedagogy in the education of bilingual youth. *Teachers College Record, 104,* 1163–1186.

Howard, G. R. (1999). *We can't teach what we don't know: White teachers, multiracial school*. New York: Teachers College Press.

Hull, G., & Schultz, K. (Eds.). (2002). *School's out!: Bridging out-of-school literacies with classroom practice*. New York: Teachers College Press.

Jimenez, R. T. (2003). Literacy and Latino students in the United States: Some considerations, questions, and new directions. *Reading Research Quarterly, 38,* 104–141.

Labov, W. (2003). When ordinary children fail to read. *Reading Research Quarterly, 38,* 128–131.

Moll, L. (1994). Literacy research in community and classrooms: A sociocultural approach. In R. B. Ruddell, M. R. Ruddell, & H. Singer (Eds.), *Theoretical models and processes of reading* (pp. 179–207). Newark, DE: International Reading Association.

Moll, L. (1997). The creation of mediating settings. *Mind, Culture, and Activity, 4,* 191–200.

Moll, L. C., & Whitemore, K. F. (1993). Vygotsky in classroom practice: Moving from individual transmission to social transaction. In E. Forman, N. Minick, & C. A. Stone (Eds.), *Contexts for learning: Sociocultural dynamics in children's development* (pp. 19–42). New York: Oxford University Press.

Nieto, S. (1996). *Affirming diversity: The sociopolitical context of multicultural education* (2nd ed.). White Plains, NY: Longman.

Nieto, S. (1999). *The light in their eyes: Creating multicultural learning communities.* New York: Teachers College Press.

Obidah, J. E. (1998). Black-mystory: Literate currency in everyday schooling. In D. E. Alvermann, K. A. Hinchman, D. W. Moore, S. F. Phelps, & D. R. Waff (Eds.), *Reconceptualizing the literacies in adolescents' lives* (pp. 51–71). Mahwah, NJ: Erlbaum.

Pearson, P. D. (1997). Commentary. In S. I. McMahon & T. E. Raphael, with V. G. Goatley & L. M. Pardo (Eds.), *The book club connection: Literacy learning and classroom talk* (pp. 222–223). New York: Teachers College Press.

Perry, T., & Delpit, L. (Eds.). (1998). *The real ebonics debate: Power, language, and the education of African-American children.* Boston: Beacon Press.

Peshkin, A. (1985). Virtuous subjectivity: In the participant-observer's eyes. In D. Berg & K. Smith (Eds.), *Exploring clinical methods for social research* (pp. 267–281). Beverly Hills, CA: Sage.

Philips, S. (1983). *The invisible culture: Communication in classroom and community on the Warm Springs Indian reservation.* New York: Longman.

Vygotsky, L. S. (1978). *Mind in society: The development of higher psychological processes.* Cambridge, MA: Harvard University Press.

Wertsch, J. V. (1991). *Voices of the mind: A sociocultural approach to mediated action.* Cambridge, MA: Harvard University Press.

Wertsch, J. V. (1998). *Mind as action.* New York: Oxford University Press.

Part I

LANGUAGE, TEXTS, AND CONTEXTS

Chapter 1

Literacy, Learning, and Language Variation
Implications for Instruction

CYNTHIA H. BROCK, LAURA A. PARKS,
and DOROTHY K. MOORE

> There is not one thing that is done to, for, with, or against a
> student in school that is not rooted in a political bias, ideology, or
> notion. This includes everything from the arrangement of seats in a
> classroom, to the rituals practiced in the auditorium, to the
> textbooks used in lessons, to the dress required of both teachers
> and students, to the tests given, to the subjects that are taught, and
> most emphatically, to the intellectual skills that are promoted. And
> what is called reading, it seems to me, just about heads the list. For
> to teach reading, or even to promote vigorously the teaching of
> reading, is to take a definite political position on how people
> should behave and on what they ought to value.
> —POSTMAN (1970, pp. 244–245)

In this quotation, Postman (1970) challenges educators to analyze and
critique the ideological underpinnings of literacy teaching and learning.
We concur with Postman's position—power, politics, and ideology are
all central to the work of literacy educators—especially regarding our
work with children who speak varieties of English that are traditionally
marginalized in U.S. public schools and society in general.[1] In this chap-

---

[1] We refer here to the variations of English spoken by those who are learning English as an additional language. For example, this may refer to children whose first languages are Hmong, Spanish, or any other language. It also refers to children who speak African American Vernacular English (i.e., AAVE) as their first language. We are mindful that AAVE is considered to be a dialect by some scholars and a separate language by others (Perry & Delpit, 1998).

ter, we explore ways that politics, power, and ideology impact the literacy and language-related work of educators in U.S. public schools with children from diverse backgrounds, who speak different varieties of English. We address the following question throughout this chapter: How do the varieties of languages that children speak and write impact their literacy learning?

Over a quarter of a century ago, Hymes (1974) articulated some of the many complexities of language use. He argued that

> a person is not adequately described as "speaking English," but as speaking in *some variety of English*, "standard," "dialect," "vernacular," etc.; as speaking in some *recognizable manner*, according to a general *type of situation*, "formally," "consultively," "informally," etc.; or according to some specific *type of scene or genre*, a public lecture, a revivalistic sermon, a bureaucratic decision, etc.; according to some particular *role or relationship*, that of parent, lover, friend, boss, etc. (p. xxiii, emphasis added)

Through these examples, Hymes emphasizes that speakers vary in their use of English according to (1) manner of speaking, (2) choice of speech genres, and (3) roles assumed and enacted between speakers and listeners in conversational encounters. Additionally, conversations occur in communities that are situated culturally, socially, politically, and historically. The use of the conversational norms established in communities—and the variations of those norms—determine, in large part, the voices that "count" in conversational encounters. Hymes's assertions in this quotation merit consideration, because, as he argues, *no* speakers of English speak in some "idealized" or "pure" form of English; rather, *all* English speakers use varieties of English in their everyday acts of communication. *We reiterate: All speakers of English speak a variety of English*. Thus, the notion that there is one standard form of English that all "normal" English speakers write and speak is a myth (Hymes, 1974; Wolfram & Schilling-Estes, 1998).

If you are a teacher or a teacher–educator who works with students learning English as an additional language, you may be thinking, "Yeah, but there *are* significant differences in the ways some of my students write and speak. Do these differences matter, or should I merely ignore the variations in my students' spoken and written English?" We address this question, as well as other pertinent questions, in the following manner within this chapter: First, we ask that you examine your own assumptions about language variation by engaging in a "thought experiment" with us. You may be wondering why we start this chapter by asking you to examine your assumptions and beliefs. We start here, because we believe, with Gee (1996), that our assumptions and beliefs serve as the foundation for our instructional decisions and interactions with children. If teachers have negative beliefs about children, students' learning opportunities suffer (Shannon, 1990). Moreover, unexamined assumptions and beliefs lead to unexamined practices. Consequently, it is worthwhile, we argue, to examine critically our assumptions and beliefs. Next, we draw on scholarly literature to articulate what we mean by language variation. Then, we draw on the work of scholars of language and literacy to talk more about issues pertaining to language, and language variation, by critiquing actual classroom examples of educators working with children from elementary-level classrooms who speak varieties of English. Finally, we present an overview of issues and ideas that merit consideration when educators work with students who speak and write different varieties of English.

LANGUAGE VARIATION: A THOUGHT EXPERIMENT

We present a thought experiment in the form of an excerpt of a conversational exchange between two speakers. This sets the stage for our discussion about language variation. After reading the example, pause briefly to reflect on your own interpretation of the excerpt, including your stance toward both the message and the messengers. After you read the excerpt and answer the questions we pose for your consideration, we'll present our interpretation of the excerpt. We acknowledge that our upcoming interpretation is based on some background knowledge about the excerpt that you don't have.

SPEAKER 1: You ain't got no business walking round these hills, Miss.

SPEAKER 2: Looka here who's talking. I got more business here 'n you got. They catch you they cut your head off. Ain't nobody after me but I know somebody after you.

Consider the following questions pertaining to the conversational exchange:

1. Where do you think the conversation might have occurred?
2. What is the socioeconomic status of each speaker?
3. What assertions might you make about the cultures and social communities of the speakers?
4. What is the gender of each speaker?
5. Describe the historical era in which this conversation took place?

6. In general, what does the language the speakers use reveal about them?
7. What is your attitude toward each speaker? Does your attitude toward the language users matter? Should it matter?
8. What evidence do you draw on to justify your answers to the above questions?

We draw on dimensions of language variation discussed by Hymes (1974), and recognized by other linguists, to render some interpretations of the brief conversational exchange. These dimensions of language include physical and economic context, as well as gender, social status, and historical context.

Physical and Economic Context

When Speakers 1 and 2 mentioned "walking around these hills," you may have suspected that the conversation occurred in a rural setting. It did. You may also have assumed that the conversation occurred in the United States, even though there are certainly many countries with hills in the world, where people speak English. Additionally, the first speaker's use of double negatives and both speakers' use of the word *ain't* may have suggested to you the possibility that both speakers came from a lower socioeconomic class. They did.

What may be less clear from the conversation is the region of the United States in which the conversation occurred. There could be any number of rural regions with hills in the United States, but the first speaker's use of the word *Miss* points us to the possibility that the conversation may have occurred in the South. In the North or the West, it is more likely that a young woman would be referred to as "young lady," or perhaps the statement that ends in *Miss* would have just ended after *hills*, without referring directly to the listener at all.

Gender, Social Status, and Historical Context

The use of the word *Miss* points us to some other useful information as well. We know that the gender of Speaker 2 is female. Moreover, the use of the word *Miss* to address Speaker 2 may tell us something about the relative social status of Speakers 1 and 2. "Miss" could be viewed as a title of sorts. Thus, Speaker 1 may believe that Speaker 2 has a higher social status. The words of Speaker 2 also confirm this assumption. Speaker 2's blatant words, "They catch you they cut your head off," tell us pertinent information about the social and historical context of the words. Obviously, Speaker 1 is in considerable danger and is running from someone or something. We may suspect that law enforcement officers are not after Speaker 1, because even if Speaker 1 were a criminal, he or she would deserve a trial in the United States. Furthermore, even crimes involving capital punishment in the United States have not involved decapitating the convicted. However, historically, in the South, it would have been considered "acceptable" by the law and the established social order of the time to catch and punish slaves in whatever ways the owners deemed acceptable, which might include cutting off someone's toes or chaining his or her feet together. Moreover, the fact that Speaker 2 could look at Speaker 1 and "know" that someone is after her may lead us to believe that Speaker 1 is black and running, and is thus, obviously to Speaker 2, a runaway slave.

The example we have just discussed is an excerpt of a conversation between two characters, Sethe and Amy, in Toni Morrison's novel *Beloved* (1987, p. 78). In the story, Sethe (Speaker 1), a slave, escaped from a plantation in the South and met Amy (Speaker 2), a poor white girl, in the woods during her escape. Sethe was headed toward the North and freedom, and Amy helped her.

Prior to discussing the actual context of the words from Morrison's novel, we led you to some plausible conclusions about the words spoken by Sethe and Amy. Although you undoubtedly would not render all of the interpretations we have suggested, we suspect that at least some of your conclusions about the speakers *could* be similar to ours. By our "read" of the language variety spoken by Morrison's characters, we sought to illustrate how ethnicity, socioeconomic status, gender, and social, cultural, geographical, and historical backgrounds are often inferred from the varieties of language forms we use to represent ourselves. In fact, according to Wolfram and Schilling-Estes (1998), "It is surprising how little conversation it takes to draw conclusions about a speaker's background—a sentence, a phrase, or even a word is often adequate to trigger a regional, social, or ethnic classification" (p. 1).

In our discussion, however, we stopped short of some other essential issues that merit consideration with respect to language variation, and literacy teaching and learning. For example, we hypothesize that some readers might assert that Morrison's characters did not speak a "standard" form of English. For example, Sethe's use of a double negative and both speakers' use of the word *ain't* reflect language choices that may not be considered "standard." Important questions about standards arise. Who decides what constitutes "standard" in terms of a language? What are the criteria by which "standard" is ascertained? By whose authority are "standards" created, maintained, and enforced? If Hymes (1974) is correct that all speakers of English—and, undoubtedly, other languages as well—make vast numbers of "language variation" choices in their daily acts of communication, then we may pose the questions: Are there levels of variation within and across languages and language users? What—or who—distinguishes between levels of language variation choices that are "acceptable" and those that are "not acceptable"? Perhaps most importantly for our purposes, what are the implications of the answers to these questions for children's literacy learning and instruction?

We address some of these important questions by returning to Morrison's excerpt. However, this time we "read" the excerpt in a different manner. We focus now on Morrison, as the author of the language spoken, rather than on the speaking characters. We consider whether background knowledge of language creators impacts our stance toward the language users. Additionally, we consider whether our attitudes toward varieties of language matter.

Clearly, the words that Morrison's characters uttered represent language that varies from "Standard English." However, a host of complex issues arise when we strive to determine whether use of particular languages or varieties of languages matters. For example, as a Nobel laureate in literature, Toni Morrison commands much respect as a speaker and writer. Her social position as a speaker and writer differs greatly from that of her characters, Sethe and Amy. For some readers, Morrison's use of Sethe's and Amy's speech is acceptable; however, if Sethe and Amy were real people, use of their own words would cause them to be stigmatized by some. Consequently, we argue that politics, power, and ideology (i.e., who says what, how, and by whose authority) do matter with respect to the varieties of language we use. Attention to the social, cultural, and historical conditions surrounding the speaking act, or the context, is also important. Why do these issues matter? The answer is, of course, that they engender *real* consequences for *real* people in the *real* world. For example, Toni Morrison earned a Nobel Prize in Literature because of her facility with language. Although the consequences of language use for many children of color in U.S. public schools may be different, to be sure, consequences exist for them, too.

We have asked you to think with us about interpretation and language variation by engaging in a thought experiment. One of our primary goals was to illustrate how we make assumptions—for good or bad—about people's intelligence, background, socioeconomic status, ethnicity, and so forth, based on the language they use. Moreover, the assumptions we make about people influence our actions and interactions with them. These issues matter, of course, when we are educators (and, thus, in positions of power) working with students who may speak varieties of English different from our own. Although heightening our awareness about how we interpret others based on their language use is important in our work with children, so, too, is our understanding of language variation itself. It is to this issue that we now turn.

EXPLORING CONCEPTIONS OF LANGUAGE AND LANGUAGE VARIATION

We begin this section by exploring different linguists' conceptions of the nature of language before we pose a tentative definition of language variation. Many linguists contend that important dimensions of language include phonology, morphology, syntax, semantics, and pragmatics (Chomsky, 1965; Gorrell, 1995; Malmstrom, 1973; Menyuk, 1971; Schlesinger, 1982; Wyatt, 1995). Moreover, language has long been viewed as a tool for conceptualizing and conveying meaning, and for thinking, reasoning, and comprehending (Halliday & Hasan, 1989).

Some linguists (e.g., Chomsky, 1965; Chomsky & Halle, 1968; Goodluck, 1991) view language competence as an innate endowment, with essential linguistic features that develop as we learn and use our native language. Other scholars (e.g., Halliday & Hasan, 1989) emphasize the social genesis and dimensions of language, and view language as a symbol system driven by the need to make meaning in our language-based interactions with others (Cox & Fang, 1997). Effective language use requires competence between and among language users. "Communicative competence," a term coined by Gumperz (1982), refers to the ability to interpret events in contexts and to use speech and gestures to convey and construct meanings with others. Competent language users know how and when to use language to act successfully on—and in—the world. We base our ideas in this chapter on the work of scholars (e.g., Gee, 1996; Halliday, 1993; Wardhaugh, 1998) who advocate the importance of studying language in use in society.

Although there is general agreement among linguists that language is a system of sounds and a combination of thoughts, words, and feelings used for effective communication between people in specific contexts, questions remain about the ambiguous—or nonuniform—manner in which language actually functions within and across contexts (Crawford, 1993; Fillmore, 1997). Like Hymes (1974), more than a quarter of a century before them, other scholars (e.g., Wardhaugh, 1998; Wolfram, Adger, & Christian, 1999), suggest that language variation refers to the nonuniform nature of language. Language, according to Wolfram and colleagues (1999), varies with respect to "sociocultural characteristics of groups of people such as their cultural background, geographical location, social class, gender, or age" (p. 1). Moreover, language variation may also refer to the different ways that we use language in different contexts. For example, when we present a research paper at a conference, we most likely present ourselves more formally than we would when talking with family members at the dinner table. Finally, linguists typically use the term "dialect" to refer to a type of language used by a particular group of people associated with a geographical region or social group (Wolfram et al., 1999).

Wolfram and Schilling-Estes (1998) distinguish between popular viewpoints about dialects and linguists' conceptions of dialects. We draw on their work to present a comparison between the general public's and linguists' conceptions of dialects.

Several themes emerge across the definitions provided here. For example, the general public attaches value or relative worth to the language varieties or dialects assigned to regionally or socially defined groups of people. Linguists, on the other hand, see dialects in a more scientific manner; that is, they explore the different features of speech within and across regionally, socially, and historically defined groups of people. Because of the popular misconceptions often associated with the term "dialect," some linguists prefer to avoid using the term when referring to the ways that language use varies among speakers within and across different language communities (Wolfram & Schilling-Estes, 1998).

TABLE 1.1. Comparisons between the General Public's and Linguists' Conception of Dialects

General public's conception of dialects	Linguists' conception of dialects
"A dialect is something that SOMEONE ELSE speaks."	"Everyone who speaks a language speaks a dialect of the language; it is not possible to speak a language without speaking a dialect of the language."
"Dialects result from unsuccessful attempts to speak the 'correct' form of a language."	All speakers of languages speak dialects; moreover, "dialect speakers acquire their language by adopting the speech features of those around them, not by failing in their attempts to adopt standard language features."
"Dialects have no linguistic patterning in their own right; they are deviations from standard speech."	"Dialects, like all language systems, are systematic and regular; furthermore, socially disfavored dialects can be described with the same kind of precision as standard language varieties."

Note. All quotes are from Wolfram and Schilling-Estes (1998, pp. 7–8).

Consequently, we use the term "language variation" rather than "dialect" in this chapter.

Although we have drawn on the work of respected linguists to pose a tentative definition of "language variation," we are mindful of potential problems associated with definitions of such terms. Scholars such as Foucault (1972, 1978) caution us to be wary of essentialist questions and principles in our work. Rather than asking essentialist questions, such as "What is language variation?", Foucault invites us to consider function-related questions, such as "How does a child's variety of spoken/written language impact his or her literacy learning opportunities in school?" We argue that this shift in questions is worth exploring, because the nature of our questions shapes what and how we explore potential answers.

Changing essentialist questions to function-related questions may shift our focus by changing what we examine and how we perceive language. And perhaps a shift in focus will lead us to useful educational alternatives for serving the children who are traditionally marginalized in our classrooms because of the varieties of language they speak. Thus, although we have posed a tentative definition of "language variation" as a starting point, our primary focus in this chapter is function-related. We are primarily concerned with how the varieties of language that children speak impact their literacy learning opportunities in classrooms. In the next section, we look inside two classrooms to see how the teachers interact with children who speak different varieties of English.

A LOOK AT LANGUAGE VARIATION AND LITERACY LEARNING INSIDE TWO CLASSROOMS

Here, we explore actual interactions involving children who do not speak standard varieties of English in two different classroom contexts, briefly describing each classroom context and sharing examples of how two different teachers have worked with their language learners. We also analyze the instructional practices in each context, with an eye toward exploring what teachers might do to work more effectively with the language learners in their classrooms.

Deng: Learning Literacy in a U.S. Fifth-Grade Classroom

Deng, a Hmong child from Laos, arrived in the United States with his family in time to enroll in the last 30 days of third grade. He then spent fourth grade in a mainstream classroom receiving English as a second language (ESL) pullout instruction, as well as Title I Reading pullout instruction. Cindy, the first author of this chapter, met Deng when he was in fifth grade. His mother had decided that he would not receive any more ESL pullout instruction in fifth grade, and he "graduated" from Title I; consequently, he spent this entire day in his mainstream fifth-grade classroom. That Deng received no language support at this point in his schooling was significant. Scholars (e.g., Collier, 1995) argue that it takes from 5 to 7 years for English language learners (ELLs) to become proficient in English. By fifth grade, Deng was only beginning his second full year in a U.S. school. Thus, it would be several years before Deng would become proficient in English. We take a peek inside Deng's fifth-grade classroom and explore one incident in his literacy instruction.

Mrs. Weber, Deng's fifth-grade teacher, alternated between using basal readers and trade books across the school year. In the spring of Deng's fifth-grade year, Mrs. Weber's entire class read the book *Maniac Magee* by Jerry Spinelli (1990). On May 22, as they did every day while reading the *Maniac Magee* text, students in Mrs. Weber's class were seated on chairs in a semicircle around her in the front of the room. They had been reading the Spinelli text together for 5 days. They had already read that Maniac (a Caucasian boy) moved in with his feuding aunt and uncle when he was 3, after his parents died in a train wreck. Furthermore, Maniac ran away from his aunt and uncle's home at the age of 12, when he could no longer endure their fighting. He then made his way to a town called Two-Mills, Pennsylvania. While there, Maniac bumped into Amanda Beale (an African American girl about his age) and was invited to live with her family when her parents found out that he was homeless.

This 40-minute lesson was typical of the 18 lessons it took for the class to complete *Maniac Magee*. As the lessons began, Mrs. Weber either reminded the children about a key topic or issue they had discussed the previous day, or she prompted them to consider a theme-related issue (e.g., homelessness, loneliness, prejudice). Furthermore, she sometimes identified curricular goals (e.g., comprehension strategies, literary elements) she planned to discuss for the day.

Mrs. Weber read about Maniac diligently helping Mrs. Beale with household chores, such as doing the dishes, mowing the lawn, walking the dog, cleaning his room, and so forth. After reading several paragraphs, Mrs. Weber stopped reading and asked, "Are those all things that kids have to do within a household?" Several students responded in unison, "Nooo," and the class began a 4- to 5-minute discussion about doing chores at home. During this conversation, two children commented about their chores at home, and Mrs. Weber asked them a short series of questions that extended and clarified their initial comments. Additionally, she talked about the importance of children assuming responsibilities around their homes, telling a personal story about doing household chores as a child. The pattern continued throughout the lesson: Mrs. Weber, or a child she selected, read an excerpt from the story; the class discussed the excerpt for several minutes; and Mrs. Weber suggested that they continue reading the story.

Most children anxiously volunteered to take turns reading aloud or to express their opinions as the class discussed segments of the *Maniac Magee* text. This was not true for Deng, however. In fact, never once during any of the 18 lessons pertaining to *Maniac Magee* did Deng volunteer to read or express his opinion during the class discussion of the story. On two occasions across the 18 lessons, however, Mrs. Weber did call on Deng to contribute—one time to read aloud, and another to express his opinion about an event in the story. The excerpt we share occurred when Mrs. Weber asked Deng to read aloud.

In the story, the class read that Maniac accepted a dare from several kids, agreeing to enter Mr. Finsterwald's backyard and stay for 10 minutes. Finsterwald hated kids and was terribly mean to them. All kids in the neighborhood, except Maniac, were terrified of him. Mrs. Weber had just read that a child named Russell was going to time Maniac's stay in Finsterwald's yard. Russell was Maniac's friend and, as such, was very nervous about Maniac attempting this feat. After she read an excerpt from the text, Mrs. Weber asked Deng to read. She began by pronouncing the word *Russell* for Deng, and he started reading the word she had just helped him to pronounce.

DENG: Russell his

MRS. WEBER: throat

DENG: throat too dry to speak rai

MRS. WEBER: Raised his hand

DENG: raised his hand for, from 10 minutes, 15 kid and

MRS. WEBER: possibly

DENG: possibly the universe

MRS. WEBER: held their breath

DENG: held their breath. The only sound made inside their

MRS. WEBER: heads

DENG: head

MRS. WEBER: heads

DENG: heads

MRS. WEBER: Um hum

As this episode continued, Mrs. Weber helped Deng with many of the words in the few sentences that he actually read aloud. There was no discussion about the content and little actual text read. Rather, Mrs. Weber's focus was on helping Deng to pronounce the words in the text. She provided a great deal of assistance—even to the point of making sure that he pronounced the *s* on the word *heads*. This episode was one of the only times Deng ever spoke aloud during any of the 18 whole-group lessons in the unit, and this was not his choice; Mrs. Weber had asked Deng to participate.

As this excerpt illustrates, a child's opportunity for a meaningful and robust literacy experience becomes compromised when teachers focus primarily on the form of language that students speak and ask students to read from texts that are too difficult for them. For example, Deng's engagement with text, teacher, and peers was limited to an embarrassing decoding session that was void of meaning or personal relevance. Clearly, this text was too difficult for Deng, and asking him to read aloud from a frustration-level text was not conducive to promoting meaningful literacy learning for him or his peers (Worthy, Broaddus, & Ivey, 2001).

Additionally, Au (1993) asserts that when teachers focus on correcting children's speech, they run the risk of alienating "children from school learning situations by subtly rejecting their speech. Teachers can discourage children by constantly correcting their speech and by implying [perhaps unintentionally, in many cases] that they know very little" (p. 131). Perhaps, in many cases, when teachers do correct the speech of children, the purpose of such interruptions is not to discourage the children intentionally. Also, as Au emphasizes, and as the previous episode illustrates, by attending to the "correct" form of language rather than to the meaning that can be constructed through language use, children learning English as an additional language may come to believe that form is more important than content.

Our example pertaining to Deng illustrates a classroom practice that is counterproductive to learning for an ELL and his peers. A question that merits consideration is what a teacher should do when working with children in the process of acquiring English, or a more standard form of English. We address this issue in the following section.

Teaching and Learning "Village English" and "Formal English"

Dewey (1916) has suggested that a child's learning environment should "purify and idealize" the existing social customs, while "creating a wider and better balanced environment than that by which the young would be likely, if left to themselves, to be influenced" (p. 22).

Unfortunately, according to Delpit (1995), many learning environments in U.S. classrooms have idealized the existing social customs in which Standard English skills and codes are embedded, while neglecting the rich linguistic traditions that comprise other languages. Often, the wider and more balanced environments that Dewey advocated are overlooked. Au and Raphael (2000) suggest that literacy is a cultural practice involving the families and communities from which our students inherit their first introduction to literacy. The challenge, then, is to help students attain multiple literacies by exploring the literacy customs and practices from which they come, as well as the literacy practices of the dominant culture.

Martha Demientieff, a Native Alaskan teacher of Athabaskan Indian students, demonstrates this ability to celebrate and embrace her students' cultural and linguistic knowledge, while introducing them to the dominant literacies promoted in mainstream public schools. In her practice, Demientieff teaches students who speak and write "Village English"—a nonstandard form of English. Most of Demientieff's native students and their families do not speak or write more standard forms of English. As a result of Demientieff's instructional efforts, her students learn that whereas "Village English" is the norm in their community, there are people in other communities who will look down on them if they cannot also speak and write using other forms of English. Demientieff's students explore the different codes of English as they write words or phrases from their own language onto a bulletin board. The words are then placed under one of two labels: "Standard English" or "Our Heritage Language." Discussing the sometimes subtle and stark differences between these words and phrases, Demientieff exposes these students to the language of a people beyond their village, who speak a form of English that varies from theirs. The students listen to and read the "two ways of saying the same thing" and discuss their preferences— realizing that, many times, the "village way" is "the best way."

Demientieff invites her students to engage in a variety of activities that help them to understand different uses of various forms of English in different contexts. On one day, Demientieff invites her children to dress casually for a picnic. When the students are on the picnic, Demientieff invites them to use Heritage English with one another. On another day, Demientieff's students dress formally for an evening dinner, and she asks them to speak only "Formal English." In this way, students are exposed to variations in culture, language, and location as they are "encouraged to understand the value of the code they already possess as well as to understand the power realities in this country" (Delpit, 1995, p. 40).

We believe that Demientieff's work with her children serves as a powerful model for others who work with students who speak varieties of English that may differ from their own. Demientieff works to strike a balance between honoring and valuing her students and their language, and also helping them to understand other varieties of English. She helps her children to understand that it is not the *right* version of English that they need to learn in addition to their "Heritage Language"; rather, it is the version of English that the power brokers in society may deem appropriate. As Delpit (1995) and de la Luz Reyes (1993) emphasize, we are cheating children of color if we do not help them to understand and learn to use effectively the dominant form of English, because facility with this form of English will impact their educational, as well as employment, opportunities.

KEY IDEAS FOR EDUCATORS

We explore an overarching question in this chapter: How do the varieties of languages that children speak and write impact their literacy learning opportunities? As discussion throughout this chapter has illustrated, tentative answers to this question are complex, multifaceted, and context-specific. Moreover, our tentative answers to this question shape significantly the ways we design our classroom instruction.

One of the key points we seek to make by asking you to engage in the thought experiment is to illustrate Wolfram's point: that even when speakers utter only a few words, listeners make many judgments about them with respect to their intelligence, social class, background, ethnicity, and so forth. Our goal is to emphasize that we, as educators, must (1) identify our own assumptions about students who speak varieties of English that may differ from our own, and (2) exercise caution when we interpret the varieties of languages that our children speak. Variations in the languages spoken by our students do not signal deficiencies in need of remediation. Rather than assuming that we must "fix" the language that our children speak, if they do not speak a "standard" form of English, we would do well to learn from Mrs. Demientieff and realize that our job should be about helping children to learn the discourse of power, in addition to the varieties of language that they speak.

A central point we seek to make in our discussion of linguists' conceptions of language variation is linguists' argument that there is really no such entity as "Standard English"; rather, all speakers of English speak some variety of English. A problem with the notion of "standard" is its implication that anything that sounds different must not be "standard," and must therefore be deficient (Macedo, 1994). The word *standard* is problematic for this reason. Having raised these issues, however, we must realize that those in positions of power in society hold some varieties of

English in higher regard. Consequently, it is imperative that educators help children to learn these varieties of English. Not doing so precludes children's access to positions of power and authority in society.

We have presented several classroom scenarios to illustrate (1) how teachers, such as Mrs. Weber, may unintentionally engage in classroom practices that are not beneficial to children, and (2) how some practices and dispositions can be very helpful to children who speak different varieties of English (as Mrs. Demientieff's work illustrates). The vignette from Mrs. Demientieff's classroom illustrates that ability to work effectively with children whose language may vary from our own requires careful attention to our assumptions about children's language, as well as the ability to help children to appropriate different discourses—while still valuing the variety of English that they do speak. Cummins (2000) reminds us that "underachievement is not caused by lack of fluency in English. Underachievement is the result of particular kinds of interactions in school that lead minority students to mentally withdraw from academic effort" (p. 252).

We end this chapter as we began it—by focusing on the politics of literacy education. As we stated at the beginning, the events surrounding any educational venture are imbued with politics and ideology. A consideration of the politics of language in education directs us to raise questions such as the following: What enduring traditions in classrooms continue to foster practices that marginalize children of particular cultural and linguistic backgrounds? Wolfram and colleagues (1999) purport that language variation is one of the most serious forms of prejudice in society that is still largely ignored. We believe that most educators are caring and ethical individuals who do not deliberately set out to make their students unsuccessful in school. However, as educators, we must examine carefully our assumptions about children who speak different languages and varieties of English. Otherwise, we may inadvertently play a role in promoting in our classrooms the cycle of prejudice and discrimination that Wolfram and colleagues have identified.

REFERENCES

Au, K. (1993). *Literacy instruction in multicultural settings*. Fort Worth, TX: Harcourt Brace.

Au, K., & Raphael, T. (2000). Equity and literacy in the next millennium. *Reading Research Quarterly, 35*, 170–188.

Chomsky, N. (1965). *Aspects of the theory of syntax*. Cambridge, MA: MIT Press.

Chomsky, N., & Halle, M. (1968). *The sound pattern of English*. New York: Harper & Row.

Collier, V. (1995). Acquiring a second language for school. *Directions in Language Education, 1,* 3–14.

Cox, B., & Fang, O. (1997). At-risk readers developing expertise in register switching: Evidence from cohesion analysis. *Journal of Research in Reading, 22,* 143–153.

Crawford, L. W. (1993). *Language and literacy learning in multicultural classrooms.* Boston: Allyn & Bacon.

Cummins, J. (2000). The two faces of language proficiency. In J. Noel (Ed.), *Notable selections in multicultural education* (pp. 244–252). Guilford, CT: Dushkin/McGraw-Hill.

de la Luz Reyes, M. (1993). Emerging biliteracy and cross-cultural sensitivity in a language arts classroom. *Language Arts, 70,* 659–668.

Delpit, L. (1995). *Other people's children: Cultural conflict in the classroom.* New York: New Press.

Dewey, J. (1916). *Democracy and education: An introduction to the philosophy of education.* New York: Macmillan.

Fillmore, L. (1997). Equity and education in the age of new racism: Issues for educators. *Social Justice, 24,* 119–132.

Foucault, M. (1972). *The archeology of knowledge.* New York: Pantheon.

Foucault, M. (1978). History, discourse, and discontinuity. *Salmagundi, 20,* 225–248.

Gee, J. P. (1996). *Social linguistics and literacies: Ideology in discourses.* Bristol, PA: Taylor & Francis.

Goodluck, H. (1991). *Language acquisition: A linguistic introduction.* Oxford, UK: Blackwell.

Gorrell, P. (1995). *Syntax and parsing.* New York: Cambridge University Press.

Gumperz, J. J. (1982). *Discourse strategies.* Cambridge, UK: Cambridge University Press.

Halliday, M. A. K. (1993). Towards a language-based theory of learning. *Linguistics and Education, 5,* 93–116.

Halliday, M. A. K., & Hasan, R. (1989). *Language, context, and text: Aspects of language in a social-semiotic perspective.* Oxford, UK: Oxford University Press.

Hymes, D. (1974). *Foundations in sociolinguistics.* Philadelphia: University of Pennsylvania Press.

Macedo, D. (1994). *Literacies of power: What Americans are not allowed to know.* Boulder, CO: Westview Press.

Malmstrom, J. (1973). *Language in society.* Rochelle Park, NJ: Hayden.

Menyuk, P. (1971). *The acquisition and development of language.* Englewood Cliffs, NJ: Prentice-Hall.

Morrison, T. (1987). *Beloved.* New York: Random House.

Perry, T., & Delpit, L. (1998). *The real ebonics debate: Power, language, and the education of African American children.* Boston: Beacon Press.

Postman, N. (1970). The politics of reading. *Harvard Education Review, 40,* 244–252.

Schlesinger, I. M. (1982). *Steps to language: toward a theory of native language acquisition.* Hillsdale, NJ: Erlbaum.

Shannon, S. (1990). Transition from bilingual programs to all-English programs: Issues about and beyond language. *Linguistics and Education, 2,* 323–343.

Spinelli, J. (1990). *Maniac Magee.* Boston: Little, Brown.

Wardhaugh, R. (1998). *An introduction to sociolinguistics.* Malden, MA: Blackwell.

Wolfram, W., Adger, C., & Christian, D. (1999). *Dialectics in school and communities.* Mahwah, NJ: Erlbaum.

Wolfram, W., & Schilling-Estes, N. (1998). *American English.* Malden, MA: Blackwell.

Worthy, J., Broaddus, K., & Ivey, G. (2001). *Pathways to independence: Reading, writing, and learning in grades 3–8.* New York: Guilford Press.

Wyatt, T. (1995). Language development in African American English child speech. *Linguistics and Education, 7,* 7–22.

Chapter 2

Texts and English Language Learners
Scaffolding Entrée to Reading

ELFRIEDA H. HIEBERT, ZOE ANN BROWN,
CHERYL TAITAGUE, CHARLES W. FISHER,
and MARTHA A. ADLER

> Hop! Hop! Hop!
> Hop, hop, hop on the bed.
> "Stop! Stop! Stop!" said Dad.
> "Not on the bed."
> Hop, hop, hop in the bath.
> "Stop! Stop! Stop!" said Dad.
> "Not in the bath."
> —EXCERPT FROM A FIRST-GRADE
> READING TEXT (Bick, 2000)

When presented with this text in November of first grade, Benito, a native Spanish speaker learning to read in English, read the text as "Harry Potter, Harry Potter." The first Harry Potter movie had arrived in theaters over the weekend, and that morning's classroom sharing time had been devoted to a discussion of the film. Benito was using background knowledge to give meaning to the text, and his excitement was inescapable. However, this particular knowledge and his excitement did not help him read "Hop! Hop! Hop!" Like many first graders, especially those who enter school speaking languages other than English, Benito faces a severe challenge in achieving literacy levels required for full participation in the economic and civic communities of the 21st century (Donahue, Finnegan, Lutkus, Allen, & Campbell, 2001).

In a study of first graders (Hiebert & Fisher, 2002), 40% of the sample, including Benito and most of his English language learning (ELL) peers, did not recognize any high-frequency words in November. If first-grade reading levels predict fourth-grade reading levels and these, in turn, predict high school reading levels (Juel, 1988), Benito has a high probability of being among the 40% of fourth graders in the United States who fail to attain the basic reading level on the National Assessment of Educational Progress (NAEP; Donahue et al., 2001).

Increasingly, large states have relied on textbook programs as the primary intervention for this sizable group of students who are not attaining national standards. However, policies about beginning reading textbooks have outdistanced theoretical and empirical scholarship. The policies of the nation's two largest statewide textbook adopters, Texas and California, have moved in a relatively short time from one end of the philosophical spectrum to the other. In moving from almost exclusive use of literature-based texts to almost exclusive use of decodable texts, an array of other important text features has been ignored.

Recent studies suggest that failure to attend to features such as word repetition rates and the rate at which new words are introduced has made beginning texts accessible only to those first graders who can already read well when they enter grade 1 (Foorman, Francis, Davidson, Harm, & Griffin, 2002; Hiebert, 2001b). For children learning to read from these texts at the same time they are learning to speak and comprehend English, current texts are nothing short of formidable.

The lack of theoretical and empirical foundations for both the design of reading texts and statewide adoption guidelines for textbooks highlights the need for knowledge about the impact of text features on the development of beginning readers. In this chapter, we present a framework for text features and apply it to the design of beginning reading textbooks for ELLs. First, we describe the features of current beginning reading texts. Next, we review existing research on text features that support language and literacy learning of ELLs. Finally, we describe the features of a set of beginning reading texts designed for ELLs.

Several observations will give readers a broader context for these texts, as well as our model of text and its role in reading development. The texts that are presented in this chapter are only part of the entire Network for English Acquisition and Reading Star (NEARStar) program. This multimedia, Internet-based program includes other forms of texts, such as chants and take-home books, as well as virtual trips to worlds where concepts are enriched. Furthermore, these texts are a supplementary rather than a primary reading program. Within the broader primary reading program, teachers read aloud texts with rich literary language (Hiebert & Raphael, 1998). Texts that children read along with a teacher or peers are also critical and likely have different characteristics than the texts of independent reading or teacher read-alouds (Hiebert & Raphael, 1998).

Although a reading program includes texts of many kinds, texts for independent reading cannot be given short shrift, as has been the case in recent decades. A sizable group of children learn to read with the texts of read-alouds and read-alongs. By November of first grade, about 30% of Benito's first-grade cohort had independent reading levels that permitted reading of almost any first-grade text (Hiebert & Fisher, 2002). Another 30% struggled with some texts, such as *Hop, hop, hop*, but were on a trajectory to end the year with sufficient reading skills to make the grade. It is for children such as Benito—the 40% who do not attain basic level on the NAEP, a group in which ELLs are more likely to appear—that the design of texts matters.

CURRENT BEGINNING READING TEXTS AND ENGLISH LANGUAGE LEARNERS

Publishers provide teachers with three types of texts for the instruction of beginning readers: (1) anthologies of large textbook programs, (2) decodable texts, and (3) little books that are shorter versions of the anthologies. Whereas all three types of texts are now offered as part of large textbook programs, the anthologies are the core component, and the little books and decodable books are ancillary components. Samples of each text type from a prominent program are provided in columns 1–3 of Table 2.1.

Table 2.2 presents comparisons of selected text features for a variety of texts. The texts are grouped in four categories: 2000–2001 anthologies, little books, historical anthologies, and the NEARStar program. Each row in Table 2.2 represents an analysis of 10 consecutive texts drawn from the first instructional unit for grade 1. Data in the 2000–2001 category describe the anthologies of the five programs adopted for statewide use by Texas in 2000 (Adams et al., 2000; Afflerbach et al., 2000; Farr et al., 2001; Flood et al., 2001; Scholastic, 2000) and a sixth anthology that was not submitted in Texas (Cooper et al., 2001). These data were reported by Hiebert (2001a, 2001b) as part of a study comparing the texts adopted in 2000 (labeled Study 1A in Table 2.2) with three prior copyrights of Scott Foresman: (1) 1962 (Robinson, Monroe, Artley, & Huck, 1962), (2) 1983 (Aaron et al., 1983), and (3) 1993 (Allington et al., 1993). Data on these three historical Scott Foresman programs are labeled Study 1B in Table 2.2.

Table 2.2 also includes descriptive data on little books (labeled

TABLE 2.1. Examples of First-Grade Texts from Four Programs

Anthology (Scott Foresman, 2000)	Decodable Book (Harcourt Practice Readers, 1996)	Little Book (Sunshine/Wright Group, 1996)	NEARStar		
			Level 1	Level 2	Level 3
Fish Mix	*It's Hot*	*Would You Like to Fly?*	*Jam*	*Classroom Jobs*	*What Are Stars?*
I see one fish. I see two. I see three fish. Will they swim to you? How many yellow fish? How many blue? I see a mix of fish. How about you? Six little fish. They swim like this. One big fish. Its fins go swish!	Tom sat on top. It's hot, said Dot. Come sit on top, said Tom. It's hot. Too hot, said Don. It's not hot here, said Dot. Come sit on top, said Tom. I am hot, said Todd. Come sit on top, said Don. Look! said Tom and Dot.	Would you like to fly in a seaplane? Would you like to fly in a jet? Would you like to fly in a balloon? Would you like to fly in a blimp? Would you like to fly in a helicopter?	I love jam on hot buns. I love jam on cold buns. Jam, jam, jam. I love jam. Jam is on my hands. Jam is on my face. Jam is on my feet. Jam is on me!	We have new jobs in our classroom today. Jan has a new job. Who is Jan today? Dot has a new job. Who is Dot today? Bob has a new job. Who is Bob today? Ed has a new job today. Ed is the cook. Look at Ron!	When you look at the sky at night, what do you see? Do you see many stars in the night sky? What is a star? A star is a big ball of hot gas that gives off light. Stars are far away from Earth.

Note. All texts except for *Jam* are incomplete.

35

TABLE 2.2. Features of Beginning First-Grade Texts

	Unique words/100 words	Average words per passage	% of unique words				
			Singletons	4+ repetitions	High-frequency (100 most frequent)	Phonetically regular (CV and VC patterns)	Multisyllabic
Study 1A: 2000–2001 anthologies							
Harcourt (2001)	21	95	37	37	11	42	18
Houghton Mifflin (2000)	38	76	66	13	7	22	36
McGraw-Hill (2001)	19	115	38	38	11	59	10
Open Court (2000)	21	95	43	34	10	50	12
Scholastic (2001)	21	124	47	28	9	44	18
Scott, Foresman (2000)	21	83	40	35	17	62	7
Study 2: Little books							
Harcourt's Practice Readers	28	49	35	38	29	53	2
Open Court's Decodable Books	24	74	36	35	22	64	8
Rigby PM Plus	11	70	18	68	29	22	26
Sunshine	26	49	50	34	24	21	28
Waterford	21	53	42	35	24	42	12
Study 1B: Historical anthologies							
Scott, Foresman (1962)	10	18	0	100	6	56	6
1983	5	144	5	87	24	31	11
1993	29	79	46	29	9	30	21
NEARStar texts							
Level 1	7	37	0	98	44	34	4
Level 2	10	60	14	63	32	53	2
Level 3	11	91	10	60	35	25	7

Study 2 in Table 2.2). The little books category includes two decodable book programs (Open Court, Adams et al., 2000; and the phonics readers from the Harcourt Reading Program, Farr et al., 2001) and three popular little book programs (Rigby PM Plus, Rigby Education, 2000; the Sunshine books, Wright Group, 1996; and the Waterford Early Reading Program, Waterford Institute, 2000).

The number of different words introduced in a text is one factor that influences a text's accessibility for beginning readers. For 9 of the 11 current programs summarized in Table 2.2, the number of new words introduced per 100 words is within a handful of the mean (22 words). These nine programs show a similar distribution for word repetition. An average of 41% of the unique words occur once, and 35% of the unique words appear four or more times. The patterns for Houghton Mifflin's 2000 program (in which 66% of the unique words occur once) and for the Rigby PM Plus texts (in which 68% of the unique words appear four or more times) vary considerably from the group average and from one another.

The historical analysis showed that between 1962 and 1993, the number of unique words and their pace of introduction increased substantially, whereas the amount of word repetition was curtailed. Prior to 1993, unique words per 100 counts were 10 or lower, and each unique word was repeated 10–20 times in the first instructional unit of grade 1. When programs became "literature-based" in the 1993 copyright, word repetitions fell to three per word and new, unique words were introduced at the rate of 23 per text. Although the Texas-approved texts in 2000 had substantially higher percentages of decodable words compared with texts in 1993, the average number of repetitions and the pace of introducing new words remained at 1993 levels.

The task for entering American first graders in the first decade of the 21st century requires that they sustain a theme across an 83-word text—the average length of the current 11 programs listed in Table 2.2. The typical 83-word text has 18 new unique words (21 unique words per 100), of which almost 8 appear once in the instructional unit. Distributions of words also vary in terms of frequency, interest, and phonetic regularity, depending on the programs that teachers and districts have selected. In some schools, many of the words may be phonetically regular, whereas in others, many words may be multisyllabic.

The obvious questions to ask about these data are as follows:

1. Have entry reading levels of American first graders changed from the early 1980s to make this shift in task a reasonable one?
2. Even if children's entry levels have not changed, do the new task demands reflect beginning first graders' learning rates?

In response to the first question, no wide-scale summaries of the profiles of entering first-grade cohorts exist. Systematic data sets for American grade-level cohorts begin with fourth grade (Donahue et al., 2001), but two studies provide insight into the distributions of a current first-grade cohort. In the first study, Hiebert, Liu, Levin, Huxley, and Chung (1995) assessed a group of 100 exiting first graders from a representative group of American schools. These students had been taught with literature-based programs (similar to the 1993 copyright in Table 2.1), as well as little book programs. At the end of grade 1, 45 children recognized an average of 8 high-frequency words; 23 recognized 25 words, and 32 recognized 57 words from a 60-word list.

In the second study, the one in which Benito participated (Hiebert & Fisher, 2002), assessments were conducted at the end of the first trimester of first grade, the point at which the texts in Table 2.1 should be completed. On a high-frequency word task, 40% of the children failed to recognize any words. The remaining 60% was divided into four quartile groups, with the following mean levels of high-frequency word recognition: quartile 1: 70 (of 80 words); quartile 2: 41; quartile 3: 21; and quartile 4: 10.

Based on the figures in Table 2.2, the first instructional unit of 10 texts will have, on average, at least 32 high-frequency words.[1] The children in the 1st and 2nd quartiles (30%) of Hiebert and Fisher's (2002) sample were fluent with these words. Another 15% (3rd quartile) was fluent with a sizable number of these words. However, for at least 55% of the first-grade cohort in this study (the 40% who read no high-frequency words, and the 15% who recognized an average of 10 high-frequency words), the mismatch between the demands of the texts and their rates of reading acquisition was substantial. Of the ELLs in the sample, 75% were in this latter group.

TEXT FEATURES THAT SUPPORT ENGLISH LANGUAGE LEARNERS' READING ACQUISITION: THEORY AND RESEARCH

In previous articles (Hiebert, 2001b; Hiebert, Martin, & Menon, in press), the Text Elements by Task (TExT) model has been presented as a means for understanding proficiencies required to read beginning read-

---

[1] Based on ten, 83-word texts in which 18 words are unique and 18% of these 18 words are high-frequency words.

ing texts. The TExT model[2] postulates two critical constructs in determining beginning readers' success with texts: (1) linguistic content (e.g., types of words) and (2) cognitive load (e.g., number of different words and number of repetitions per word). Little, if any, of the existing research on the influence of text features on beginning reading development has been conducted with ELLs. In this context, we highlight issues related to text design that may be considered especially suited to the needs of ELLs.

Linguistic Content

The critical linguistic knowledge for recognizing words is evident in three types of words: (1) words that are easy to image and remember because of children's knowledge of, and interest in, the underlying concept; (2) phonetically regular words; and (3) words that occur frequently and often contain irregular letter–sound correspondences. Adding morphemes can change all three groups of words (i.e., inflected endings and comparative suffixes). This review focuses on the earliest stages of reading acquisition, when morphological changes, such as plurals, possessives, and inflected endings, are infrequent.

High-Interest Words

We have chosen the label "high-interest" words to describe words with high meaning, imagery, and concreteness values. Within research on word imagery (Paivio, Yuille, & Madigan, 1968), words such as *democracy* and *stigma* are defined as highly meaningful. What distinguishes the word *democracy* from *Daddy*, *Mommy*, or *trucks* is imagery value and concreteness. Some high-meaning words, such as *democracy* and *stigma*, have neither high imagery value nor concreteness. Words that are highly imagable and concrete, however, are always meaningful (Paivio et al., 1968).

Typical first words in children's speech production fall into the category of high-interest words (e.g., *Mommy*, *Daddy*, *juice*, and *cookie*; Brown, 1973). It is some time before children's speech production includes the inactive verbs and articles that occur with high frequency in written text (Brown, 1973). Similarly, the first words that young readers recognize are often names of siblings, favorite toys, and events (Hiebert,

---

[2] Readers interested in in-depth reviews of the literature that underlies this model are encouraged to explore the references.

1983). In one study, 98% of the words that preschoolers nominated as the word-of-the-day were nouns (Hiebert, 1983).

Words' concreteness and imagery have also been found to influence the speed with which children learn to read these words in school settings. When words that were matched for length and frequency but differed in imagery and concreteness values were presented to kindergartners, Hargis and Gickling (1979) found that the concrete, high-imagery words were learned and retained better than words that were low in these characteristics. In a second study (Hargis, Terhaar-Yonkers, Williams, & Reed, 1988) in which the decodability of words was manipulated along with concreteness and imagery value, high-imagery, decodable words were learned more quickly than other groups of words, including high-imagery, less decodable words. Similarly, Laing and Hulme (1999) found that preschoolers learned highly imagable words more quickly than words with low imagery values.

Despite such findings, high-interest words were used sparingly in the textbooks of American beginning reading instruction for much of the 20th century. The Dick and Jane readers that served as the prototype for beginning reading texts from the 1930s through 1980s were filled with stories of high-interest events to young children, such as playing with friends and pets. However, these high-interest concepts were typically communicated with abstract, low-imagery words. In a story in which Dick, Jane, Tom, and Pete use their shadows to create different characters, characters were described as "big" and "funny" rather than as "cowboy," "football player," or even "shadow" (Robinson et al., 1962, pp. 59–64).

With the shift to literature-based reading programs, publishers turned to texts for beginning readers with predictable text and sentence structures, such as Martin's (1967) *Brown Bear, Brown Bear, What Do You See?* These texts often use an enumerative text structure in which members of a category such as colors or animals (or a combination of the two, as in brown bear or green frog) are introduced serially. Although the same category might be the focus of different texts, publishers have typically chosen texts for anthologies or created little books in which each text enumerates a different set of categories. For example, the other little books of the Sunshine level, from which the third text in Table 2.1 is taken, develop categories such as colors of icing on birthday cakes and meals that a monster might eat, not forms of water transportation. This enumeration of items from different categories accounts, in large part, for the high percentages of single-occurrence, multisyllabic words in Table 2.2.

The few studies conducted on children's learning of words in predictable texts show that most first graders learn few of these words. In a study of children's repeated reading of three predictable texts over 1 month, Johnston (2000) reported that the high-achieving readers retained 19% of the 160 unique words introduced in three predictable books, whereas low-achieving readers retained 4%. Words that the low-achieving readers are not learning include the high-frequency words that appear often but may go unnoticed as teachers and students work on the meaning of the many high-interest words.

For children who juggle the demands of a new language and learning to read and write, the use of English words that represent concrete, familiar concepts in their lives (i.e., food, family members, classroom objects) makes good sense. Words such as *helicopter* and *blimp* (see Table 2.1) make less sense for ELL students. When a large number of words representing unusual concepts appears in beginning reading texts without repetition, such words can be an obstacle for beginning readers in attending to common, consistent patterns in phonetically regular and high-frequency words. An emphasis on a handful of familiar yet compelling categories across a set of texts seems preferable to different categories of items in every text.

High-Frequency Words

Rapid recognition of high-frequency words, such as *here* and *there*, is an essential early step in learning to read and write. In conversation, we use gestures or even objects to convey meaning. In texts, the full meaning cannot be gleaned until these high-frequency words are added. Consider, for example, the difference in meaning of the following sentences:

"The book is on the table."
"Is the book on the table?"
"The book is about a table."

The high-frequency words in these sentences provide the clarification that allows for comprehension.

High-frequency words can be particularly difficult for ELLs to hear and/or read. Many high-frequency words are not phonetically regular (e.g., *the*, *come*); they have meanings that are abstract (e.g., *the*) and ambiguous (e.g., *can*), and they can be homophones (e.g., *be*, *bee*). In addition, some words have similar graphic features that make them very difficult to distinguish for beginning readers (e.g., *the*, *then*, *them*, *when*).

The haphazard presentation of high-frequency words, the *modus operandi* of current texts (whether anthologies, little books, or decodable books), has not increased first-graders' performances on high-frequency word recognition tasks (Hiebert & Fisher, 2002; Hiebert et al., 1995). Furthermore, replacing high-interest words with high-frequency words, a common strategy in beginning reading textbooks of the 1960s through the 1980s, is also likely to be ineffective with ELLs. In oral language programs for ELLs, the meaning of high-frequency words receives substantial attention. Children might be told to "Pick the book up. Put the book down." A similar strategy has not been prominent in beginning reading texts, even though authors of trade books such as *Dog In, Cat Out* (Rubinstein, 1993) show that playful texts can be created around the concepts represented by at least some high-frequency words.

Phonetically Regular Words

Although English has many variations in letter–sound correspondences, English writing is alphabetic; that is, letters—not pictures or other symbols—consistently represent sounds. Children need to become facile in matching letters and sounds early on, if they are to become successful readers of English (National Reading Panel, 2000). The matching of letters and sounds in identifying unfamiliar words depends on learners' ability to distinguish and manipulate the sounds of English, a skill called "phonemic awareness," which is closely aligned to phonics instruction (National Reading Panel, 2000). The National Reading Panel concluded that the most effective phonemic awareness instruction engages children with letters and their associated sounds. Well-designed phonemic awareness and phonics instruction become particularly critical for ELLs. Developing useful programs for ELLs is complicated by the fact that some phonemes in English may not exist in the learner's native language. In some cases, there may be direct conflicts between the sound associated with a particular letter in English compared to the sound associated with that letter in the learner's native language. When a variety of languages are represented in a classroom, these conflicts can be extremely complex. Furthermore, although most native English speakers enter kindergarten with at least a modicum of letter–name knowledge, such as facility with the alphabet song, the written-language knowledge of ELLs may pertain to a different alphabet or representation system. Despite an extensive research base on phonemic awareness and phonics for English speakers, studies of phonemic awareness or phonics knowledge among ELLs are scarce. However, when existing research on native English speakers is examined from the perspective of ELLs, some guidelines for learning to read in English can be suggested.

Identifying unknown words requires children to associate letters with sounds very rapidly, and this skill must be developed early in the process of reading acquisition. Because consonants frequently appear at the beginning of words, knowledge of consonants is a first step in a program that connects phonemic awareness with letter–sound matching activities. Among the 43 phonemes identified as essential for reading (Moats, 1999), 21 graphemes account for the 25 phonemes associated with consonants, whereas 7 graphemes account for 18 vowel phonemes. A group of particularly resilient consonants occurs in the common words of early phonics programs—short vowel words. Treiman, Mullennix, Bijeljac-Babic, and Richmond-Welty (1995) reported that initial consonants are pronounced similarly in 94% of words with simple vowel patterns, and final consonants are pronounced the same in 92% of consonant–vowel–consonant (CVC) words.

Children need to move rapidly from relying on initial and final consonants to the sequential decoding stage in which they produce sounds for the letters in a word in order as in /c/ /a/ /t/ for the word *cat*. To apply this strategy, children need to be exposed to many words with one-to-one letter–sound correspondences for both vowels and consonants.

Unlike the high consistency in consonants, vowels have the same pronunciation in 62% of similarly spelled words (Treiman et al., 1995). When the vowel and the consonant(s) that follows it—the rime—are taken into account, however, consistency increases to 80% in CVC words (Treiman et al., 1995). Wylie and Durrell (1970) reported that 272 rimes with stable vowel sounds are contained in 1,437 words. Within this group of stable rimes, 37 appear in 10 or more words that represent familiar concepts to young children (e.g., *bat, cat, fat, pat, sat*). As children are exposed to rimes, their facility with this larger unit of English orthography and phonology becomes stronger. This process of moving to bigger and bigger chunks of language continues as children move to the reading level that characterizes the end of first grade and the beginning of second grade.

A strategic stance in emphasizing particular phonemes and rimes with ELLs is suggested by research on metacognition. Children who are learning to read in a second language have been found to be more attuned to different sounds in the second language than their peers who speak a single language (August, Calderon, & Carlo, 2000). As Vygotsky (1987) observed, learning to read and to speak a second language is similar to learning scientific concepts. In these "unspontaneous" learning contexts (Vygotsky, 1987, p. 180), learners can use the linguistic and conceptual meanings from their spontaneously learned native language to mediate the learning process. Emphasizing a focused set of consonants or rimes is justified by the greater metalinguistic awareness of second-language learners. Furthermore, Share (1995) has established the presence of a "self-teaching" stance among successful beginning readers.

Children who have a "self-teaching" strategy figure out unknown words by applying knowledge of already taught patterns. Such a self-teaching stance comes about when children are encouraged to generalize their knowledge rather than to focus on memorizing or learning every word, letter, or phoneme.

Cognitive Load

"Cognitive load" refers to the amount of different linguistic information a text requires beginning readers to apply. For proficient adult readers, cognitive load becomes a factor only with an unfamiliar topic, such as a passage on biophotonics poses for nonscientists. For children at the very earliest stages of reading, most written words are unfamiliar. They may recognize an idiosyncratic group of words, such as their names, but these are unlikely to appear in the first texts. In the first-grade text of Table 2.1 (column 1), the title and the first line present five different words: *fish*, *mix*, *I*, *see*, and *one*. Only when children get to the sixth word (*fish*) do they see a word that they've encountered previously in that text.

Unlike adult readers whose cognitive processing is directed to understanding a handful of unfamiliar words or a unique perspective of an author, the cognitive processing of beginning readers is directed at the pronunciation of unknown written words. Once children figure out an unknown word, the assumption is that they know its meaning. In some cases, meanings of the words will not be immediate such as the word *blimp* in the text in column 3 of Table 2.1. For ELLs attempting to pronounce words in a new language and connecting the label for the English word with the label of the concept in their native language, demands on cognitive processing are high. Hence, texts with words that represent familiar concepts are essential.

But to how many high-imagery words can children attend at particular developmental points? How many exemplars of words that share common and consistent letter–sound relationships are needed for children to recognize new words with those patterns? How often do children need to see irregular, high-frequency words for these to become part of instantly recognized reading vocabularies? The research literature provides few answers to such questions. As the review of existing texts reveals, the rate of introducing new words has changed dramatically over the past decades. In the earlier model, three aspects of cognitive load were considered: (1) pacing of new words, (2) repetition of these words in subsequent texts, and (3) the ratio of new words to total words in a text. The formula for cognitive load was summarized in a statement of the New Basic Reading Program of Scott Foresman (Gray, Monroe, Artley, & Arbuthnot, 1956) introducing the first preprimer:

"Each of the 17 words is used a minimum of 12 times in the new *We Look and See*" (p. 48). Unfortunately, research on which guidelines such as these were based was conducted almost exclusively with high-frequency words (Gates & Russell, 1939).

Studies of cognitive loads imposed by texts have been infrequent. One exception is a study by Reitsma (1983), in which midyear first graders and older students with reading disabilities read sentences with target words presented two, four, or six times. For the first graders, but not the students with reading disabilities, the optimal number of repetitions appeared to be four. However, Reitsma's study does not shed light on the number of repetitions required by children at the very earliest stages of reading. All of Reitsma's midyear first graders had received 6 months of reading instruction and were not designated to have reading disabilities.

Despite a limited research base, the factors underscored by Gray and colleagues (1956) cannot be ignored: pacing, repetition, and ratio of new to total words. The uniform application of formulas such as that of Gray and colleagues, however, did not take into account differences in the content of words. All linguistic knowledge is not equivalent in learning to read. Young children typically learn high-interest words more quickly than they learn high-frequency words. Furthermore, words with consistent and common rimes do not require the same number of repetitions as words with less frequent rimes. Juel and Solso (1981) showed that exposure to words that share a rime, such as *man, can, van,* and *tan*, rather than the repetition of a single word, such as *ran*, leads to application to new words with the same pattern.

Because data on the number of rimes or individual letter–sound correspondences that children can assimilate relative to high-frequency and high-imagery words have yet to be reported, we needed to make many choices about cognitive load in designing a beginning reading program for ELLs. As with other aspects of language learning, we assumed that beginning readers require at least some repetition of critical content, and that the pace of assimilating new information required attention as well.

TEXTS THAT INITIATE ENGLISH LANGUAGE LEARNERS INTO READING: APPLICATION

Anderson, Hiebert, Scott, and Wilkinson (1985) described the task of writing engaging and theoretically sound texts for beginning readers as a delicate balancing act. As designers of the NEARStar texts, we found ourselves continually involved in balancing a series of complex trade-offs. On the one hand, we were intent on having texts that would engage children of the early 21st century, whose worlds are full of radios, televi-

sions, compact discs, and videos. On the other hand, we were equally intent on creating texts with critical linguistic information that did not
overtax the cognitive capabilities of young children learning to read and
write in a new language. The texts in the last three columns of Table 2.1
are examples of our attempts to produce both engaging and theoretically
sound texts.

To bring ELLs to the level at which they can participate in typical
reading programs, we developed a three-level curriculum. Each level
consists of 10 lessons, and each lesson provides two texts and a take-
home text. The three sample texts in Table 2.1 come from the middle
lessons of each of the three curriculum levels. Features of the three levels
are summarized in Table 2.2.

Linguistic Content of NEARStar Texts

The NEARStar texts were designed to focus on high-interest, high-
frequency, and phonetically regular words. But even with phonetically
regular and, to the degree possible, high-frequency words, the interest
and familiarity of words for ELLs strongly influenced word selection. All
of the words in the program were analyzed according to the imagery ratings of van der Veur (1975), who rated 1,000 common words on a scale
from 1 (*least imagable*) to 7 (*most imagable*). For the small percentage of
words within the NEARStar program that did not appear on this list, we
used the ratings of two adults to establish imagery values. A majority of
words in all three levels of the NEARStar curriculum have high-imagery
ratings (see Table 2.3). For example, in the Level-1 and Level-3 texts
(columns 4 and 6 in Table 2.3), the words *hands*, *jam*, and *buns* (Level
1) and *star*, *ball*, and *night* (Level 3) have imagery ratings of 6 or higher.
Complying with research showing that children learn highly imagable
words more quickly than less imagable words, the words with the highest imagery values were repeated 10 times, one-third the number of repetitions for less imagable words.

In the NEARStar program, words with low-imagery ratings were
used as little as possible. The low-imagery word group was dominated
by words from the most-frequent-word list of Carroll, Davies, and
Richman (1971). Of the 100 most frequent words, 70 words appear
consistently in the NEARStar program. These words are introduced at
the rate of about one per lesson and appeared an average of 34 times
across the three levels of text. This level of repetition is consistent with
the recommendation of 35 repetitions identified by Gates and Russell
(1939) as necessary for typically developing beginning readers to learn
high-frequency words.

Many high-frequency words were presented in pairs that were

TABLE 2.3. Imagery Ratings of Words in the NEARStar Texts

Type of word	Number of words in entire program	Imagery rating	Frequency rating[a]	Phonetic rating[b]	Number of repetitions	Percentage of word type per level of program		
						1	2	3
High imagery	100	6	6.4	4.3	10	40	32	43
Moderate imagery	98	3.8	4	4	15	38	42	33
Low imagery	65	1.8	1.6	4.5	27	22	26	24

[a] A frequency of 6.4 indicates 640 average in the Carroll et al. (1971) word list.
[b] Phonetic rating is based on scale from 1 (CV pattern such as *me*) to 8 (multisyllabic words).

central to the meaning of texts (e.g., *up–down*, *in–out*, *here–there*, and *can–cannot*). Even when a high-frequency word was not presented in a contrastive pair, the meaning of the word was integral to the text (see, e.g., *on* in the Level-1 text in Table 2.1). By creating texts in this manner, ELLs are given an opportunity both to understand the underlying concepts and to recognize the words.

In the Level-1 texts, high-interest words were chosen to emphasize particular initial and final consonants. Consonants were chosen on the basis of their frequency in written English and potential difficulty for common second-language groups represented among ELL students in the United States. Initial consonant phonemes and graphemes for pairs of target words were chosen for maximum oral contrast. For example, in the contrastive pair *Mom* and *Dad*, the consonant /m/ is made with the lips, whereas the consonant /d/ is made with the tongue behind teeth.

Level-1 texts also systematically introduced selected common rimes, thereby laying a foundation for phonics instruction in Level 2. Of the 50 unique words in Level 1, 23 had common, consistent vowel–consonant (VC) rimes. For example, the high-interest words in the sample text for Level 1 (see Table 2.1)—*jam*, *buns*, and *love*—permit contrasts of three initial and three final consonants. The words—*jam* and *buns*—also contain consistent, common rimes that are the basis for vowel and rime instruction in Level 2.

The Level-2 text sample illustrates our attempt to ensure that children do not overgeneralize rime knowledge by attending to only one group of rimes in a text. In the Level-2 sample, a word with a target rime (*job*) is repeated several times, so that children develop facility with that word. The same rime (*Bob*) also appears in the text. At the same time, words with the same vowel but with different initial and final consonants appear (*Dot* and *Ron*). By seeing vowels with different rimes and initial consonants, children are encouraged to attend to the beginnings and endings of words.

The majority of the words in the NEARStar texts, at all levels, permit students to apply linguistic knowledge that is highly generalizable. The percentage of words that fall into the phonetically regular (CVC) category and high-frequency groups reaches a high of 85% in the second level of the NEARStar texts. This percentage is similar to that for the Open Court decodable texts. Even the Level-1 texts, in which the primary emphasis is high-imagery words as a foundation for children's word recognition, have more high-frequency and phonetically regular words than typical, current programs (78% for the NEARStar Level-1 texts vs. an average of 61% for typical, current programs [see Table 2.2]). The percentage of high-frequency and phonetically regular words in NEARStar Level-3 texts (60%) is approximately the same as the average for the first-unit texts of typical reading programs (61%). The Level-3 texts maintain this level of exposure, while introducing more complex vowels (long to *r*-controlled vowels) that are the focus of phonics instruction at that level.

The low number of unique words per 100 (7 in Level-1 texts compared to an average of 23 for the first units of texts in contemporary reading programs) means that the NEARStar texts give students many opportunities to practice their developing skills with a core group of high-frequency and phonetically regular words.

Cognitive Load of NEARStar Texts

A review of the literature produced few guidelines for establishing the cognitive load of texts for beginning readers. However, we used several design strategies to attempt to reduce the overall cognitive load on beginning readers. In Level 1, where almost every word is a new word for beginning readers, we used engaging illustrations and predictable text structures to mediate cognitive load. However, there were limits on the use of the predictable text structure (see sample texts in Table 2.1). Even at Level 1, children were not expected to identify all of the words in the text from aural memory. Our intention was to use predictable text structure and illustrations to ease the cognitive load but not to permit children to attend only to the illustrations or the aural production of the text.

Including two texts for each lesson also reduced overreliance on aural memory. Both texts used similar words (e.g., *jam* and *buns* in the middle lesson of Level 1, and *classroom* and *jobs* in the middle lesson of Level 2). However, the storyline and text and sentence structures varied sufficiently, so that children could not rely on aural memory exclusively to respond to texts. These strategies kept the number of unique words per 100, on average, to 7 in Level 1 and 11 in Level 3.

The total number of words in a text was also systematically constrained. Fountas and Pinnell (1999) identified total number of words as a distinguishing characteristic of text difficulty in their guided reading levels. Although the total number of words is likely less a factor than the number of different words within a text, the length of the text influences beginning readers' ability to sustain a theme across texts. The total number of words in a text also determines the occasions for repetitions of new and previously introduced unique words. NEARStar texts ranged from an average of 37 words per text in Level 1 to 91 in Level 3. This range meant that texts in Level 1 provided two to three new, unique words each text. In Level 3, students encountered six new unique words, less than one-third the number of new, unique words in the texts of current commercial programs.

A review of the literature on differences in children's learning of words as a function of linguistic content led us to forgo a formula for word repetition, such as that followed by Gray and colleagues (1956). Word repetition was a function of the letter–sound correspondences within the word and the concreteness of the word. At Level 1, concrete words such as *cat* or *dog* were not repeated as often as less concrete and phonetically irregular words such as *what* and *to*. Furthermore, words that appeared later in the program were not viewed as requiring as much repetition as words that appeared earlier in the program. In Level 1, all words were repeated at least four times. When singletons did appear in Level 2, they were of a particular type: words sharing a common, consistent rime that had appeared in numerous other words in the program. For example, once students had had exposure to *can, Dan, man,* and *ran, tan* appeared twice, and *Nan* appeared as a singleton. Fewer singletons and words with two or three repetitions exist in the NEARStar texts than in any current program listed in Table 2.1.

The number of unique words per 100 stays within a range of four words across the three NEARStar levels. At the same time, the program steadily increases the total number of words that students read across the three levels. This increase in the total number of words means that students have an opportunity to apply their linguistic knowledge to steadily increasing text lengths. By Level 3, students are reading texts with approximately the same number of words as texts in the 11 current beginning reading programs (i.e., 80–90 total words). One of the current programs (Rigby PM texts) has relatively fewer singletons and unique words per 100 compared to the other current programs, and the percentage of high-frequency words and phonetically regular words is lower than average. Furthermore, Rigby's percentage of multisyllabic words is near the average of the current reading programs at 18% (compared to 7% for the Level-3 NEARStar texts).

The demands posed by the NEARStar texts on students' recognition of multisyllabic words are substantially lower than those of texts in the current programs. Multisyllabic words constitute an average of 16% of the total words in the 11 representatives of current programs. The percentage of multisyllabic words in NEARStar texts reaches a high of 7% in Level 3. The NEARStar texts provide students with many opportunities to read phonetically regular, monosyllabic words (including words with long vowel and *r*-controlled patterns), providing a solid foundation in applying word recognition strategies.

CONCLUSIONS

The goal of the NEARStar program is to provide ELL students with texts that enable them to be successful with the entry level of currently available beginning reading programs. The design of the NEARStar texts has been grounded in research on linguistic content and cognitive load of beginning reading texts. The texts begin with a set of high-imagery words that pertain to topics of familiar but high-interest content to children. At the same time, these words were chosen to have consistent, common consonant and vowel grapheme–phoneme correspondences. High-frequency words, some of which contain irregular letter–sound correspondences, were regularly integrated into the texts. Whenever possible, these high-frequency words were presented in pairs with contrasting meanings (e.g., *up* and *down*, *yes* and *no*). With this foundational knowledge, Level 2 continued to emphasize meaningful familiar topics, such as the typical activities in classrooms and schools. In Level 2, children were encouraged to develop a self-teaching stance regarding common, consistent, vowel and consonant patterns in English, as exemplified by VC rimes. This linguistic knowledge continued to be extended with meaningful, high-frequency word pairs. In the third and final level of the program, children continued to read words that substantiated earlier phonetic content. They also were exposed to a systematic set of high-imagery words that instantiated more complex phonetic content, including words with long vowels and *r*-controlled vowels.

Throughout the three levels, students are introduced to high-frequency words at the rate of one per text. These words are repeated sufficiently so that, by the end of the NEARStar program, students have been exposed to a core vocabulary that accounts for a substantial percentage of the words that they will read in typical, primary-level texts.

The NEARStar texts, designed specifically for ELLs and other students who face challenges in learning to read, are intended to prepare students to meet the not insubstantial challenge of current beginning reading programs. Initial evaluation efforts document that children respond with enthusiasm to the texts and progress on a faster trajectory than their peers in regular reading programs (Hiebert & Fisher, 2003).

REFERENCES

Aaron, I. E., Jackson, D., Riggs, C., Smith, R. G., Tierney, R. J., & Jennings, R. E. (1983). *Scott, Foresman reading*. Glenview, IL: Scott, Foresman.

Adams, M. J., Bereiter, C., McKeough, A., Case, R., Roit, M., Hirschberg, J., Pressley, M., Carruthers, I., & Treadway, G.H., Jr. (2000). *Open Court reading*. Columbus, OH: Science Research Associates/McGraw Hill.

Afflerbach, P., Beers, J., Blachowicz, C., Boyd, C. D., Diffily, D., Gaunty-Porter, D., Harris, V., Leu, D., McClanahan, S., Monson, D., Perez, B., Sebesta, S., & Wixson, K. K. (2000). *Scott, Foresman Reading*. Glenview, IL: Scott, Foresman.

Allington, R. L., Askew, B. J., Blachowicz, C., Butler, A., Cole, J., Edwards, P. A., Gonzales, G. A., Harris, V., Hutchinson, S. M. C., Morrow, L. M., Sebesta, S. L., Sulzby, E., & Tierney, R. J. (1993). *Celebrate reading*. Glenview, IL: Scott, Foresman.

Anderson, R. C., Hiebert, E. H., Scott, J. A., & Wilkinson, I. A. G. (1985). *Becoming a nation of readers: The report of the commission on reading*. Champaign, IL: Center for the Study of Reading; Washington, DC: National Institute of Education.

August, D., Calderon, M., & Carlo, M. (2000). *Transfer of skills from Spanish to English: A study of young learners*. Washington, DC: Center for Applied Linguistics.

Bick, L. (2000). *Hop! Hop! Hop!*. Parsippany, NJ: Modern Curriculum Press.

Brown, R. (1973). *A first language: The early stages*. Cambridge, MA: Harvard University Press.

Carroll, J. B., Davies, P., & Richman, B. (1971). *Word frequency book*. Boston: Houghton Mifflin.

Cooper, J. D., Pikulski, J. J., Au, K. H., Calderon, M., Comas, J. C., Lipson, M. Y., Mims, J. S., Page, S. E., Valencia, S. W., & Vogt, M. E. (2001). *Invitations to literacy*. Boston: Houghton Mifflin.

Donahue, P. L., Finnegan, R. J., Lutkus, A. D., Allen, N. L., & Campbell, J. R. (2001). *The nation's report card for reading: Fourth grade*. Washington, DC: National Center for Education Statistics.

Farr, R. C., Strickland, D. S., Beck, I. L., Abrahamson, R. F., Ada, A. F., Cullinan, B. E., McKeown, M., Roser, N., Smith, P., Wallis, J., Yokota, Y., & Yopp, H. K. (2001). *Collections: Harcourt reading/language arts program*. Orlando, FL: Harcourt.

Flood, J., Hasbrouck, J. E., Hoffman, J. V., Lapp, D., Medearis, A. S., Paris, S., Stahl, S., Tinajero, J. V., & Wood, K. D. (2001). *McGraw-Hill reading*. New York: McGraw-Hill School Division.

Foorman, B. R., Francis, D. J., Davidson, K. C., Harm, M. W., & Griffin, J. (2002, April). *Variability in text features in six grade 1 basal reading programs.* Paper presented at the annual meeting of the American Educational Research Association, Seattle, WA.

Fountas, I. C., & Pinnell, G. S. (1999). *Matching books to readers: Using leveled books in guided reading, K–3.* New York: Heinemann.

Gates, A. I., & Russell, D. H. (1939). Types of materials, vocabulary burden, word analysis, and other factors in beginning reading. *Elementary School Journal, 39,* 27–35, 119–128.

Gray, W. S., Monroe, M., Artley, A. S., & Arbuthnot, A. H. (1956). *The new basic readers: Curriculum foundation series.* Chicago: Scott, Foresman.

Hargis, C. H., & Gickling, E. E. (1979). The function of imagery in word recognition development. *Reading Teacher, 31,* 870–874.

Hargis, C. H., Terhaar-Yonkers, M., Williams, P. C., & Reed, M. T. (1988). Repetition requirements for word recognition. *Journal of Reading, 31,* 320–327.

Hiebert, E. H. (1983). A comparison of young children's self-selected reading words and basal reading words. *Reading Improvement, 20,* 41–44.

Hiebert, E. H. (2001a, April). *An analysis of first-grade texts: Do the tasks differ across beginning reading programs?* (Research Report 4.1). Honolulu, HI: Pacific Resources for Education and Learning.

Hiebert, E. H. (2001b, April). *State reform policies and the task for first-grade readers.* Paper presented at the annual meeting of the American Educational Research Association, Seattle, WA.

Hiebert, E. H., & Fisher, C. W. (2002, April). *Describing the difficulty of texts for beginning readers: A curriculum-based measure.* Paper presented at the annual meeting of the American Educational Research Association, New Orleans, LA.

Hiebert, E. H., & Fisher, C. W. (2003). *The effects of text characteristics on the reading acquisition of English language learners* (NEARStar Report No. 4.01). Honolulu, HI: Pacific Resources for Education and Learning.

Hiebert, E. H., Liu, G., Levin, L. Huxley, A., & Chung, K. (1995, November). *First graders reading the new first-grade readers.* Paper presented at the annual meeting of the National Reading Conference, New Orleans, LA.

Hiebert, E. H., Martin, L. A., & Menon, S. (in press). The relationship between first-grade anthologies and little books in three conceptually different textbook programs. *Reading and Writing Quarterly: Overcoming Learning Difficulties.*

Hiebert, E. H., & Raphael, T.E. (1998). *Early literacy instruction.* Fort Worth, TX: Harcourt Brace.

Johnston, F. R. (2000). Word learning in predictable text. *Journal of Educational Psychology, 92,* 248–255.

Juel, C. (1988). Learning to read and write: A longitudinal study of fifty-four children from first through fourth grades. *Journal of Educational Psychology, 80,* 437–447.

Juel, C., & Solso, R. L. (1981). The role of orthographic redundancy, versatility, and spelling–sound correspondences in word identification. In M.L. Kamil

(Ed.), *Directions in reading: Research and instruction* (pp. 74–92). Rochester, NY: National Reading Conference.

Laing, E., & Hulme, C. (1999). Phonological and semantic processes influence beginning readers' ability to learn to read words. *Journal of Experimental Child Psychology, 73,* 183–207.

Martin, B. (1967). *Brown bear, brown bear, what do you see?* New York: Henry Holt.

Moats, L. (1999). *Teaching reading is rocket science: What expert teachers of reading should know and be able to do.* Washington, DC: American Federation of Teachers.

National Reading Panel. (2000). *Teaching children to read: An evidence-based assessment of the scientific research literature on reading and its implications for reading instruction.* Washington, DC: National Institute of Child Health and Human Development.

Paivio, A., Yuille, J., & Madigan, S. A. (1968). Concreteness, imagery, and meaningfulness values for 925 nouns. *Journal of Experimental Psychology, 76*(Suppl.), 1–25.

Reitsma, P. (1983). Printed word learning in beginning readers. *Journal of Experimental Child Psychology, 36,* 321–339.

Rigby Education. (2000). *Rigby PM Plus Program (starters, red, yellow, blue, green, orange, turquoise levels).* Barrington, IL: Author.

Robinson, H., Monroe, M., Artley, A. S., & Huck, C. S. (1962). *The new basic readers.* Chicago: Scott, Foresman.

Rubinstein, G. (1993). *Dog in, cat out.* New York: Ticknor & Fields.

Scholastic. (2000). *Literacy place.* New York: Scholastic.

Share, D. L. (1995). Phonological recoding and self-teaching: Sine qua non of reading acquisition. *Cognition, 55,* 151–218.

Treiman, R., Mullennix, J., Bijeljac-Babic, R., & Richmond-Welty, E. D. (1995). The special role of rimes in the description, use, and acquisition of English orthography. *Journal of Experimental Psychology General, 124,* 107–136.

van der Veur, B.W. (1975). Imagery rating of 1,000 frequently used words. *Journal of Educational Psychology, 67,* 44–56.

Vygotsky, L. S. (1987). *The collected works of L. S. Vygotsky.* New York: Plenum Press.

Waterford Institute. (2000). *Waterford early reading program.* Scottsdale, AZ: Electronic Education.

Wright Group. (1996). *Sunshine reading program.* Bothell, WA: Wright Group/McGraw-Hill.

Wylie, R. E., & Durrell, D. D. (1970). Teaching vowels through phonograms. *Elementary English, 47,* 427–451.

Chapter 3

Classroom Language
Inviting All Students to Participate

CLAUDIA CHRISTENSEN HAAG
and JOAN WILLIAMS

Premise: We know students need to talk.
We know this doesn't happen enough.
We know it's more than just language.
What do we do about it?

Let's think about why students need to engage in quality talk in the classroom. If our goal is to promote language, literacy, and cognitive development, we must step back and view what happens in the home long before that child reaches the schoolhouse steps. The interactions between a parent and a child provide a wealth of language opportunities from the very beginning of the child's life. What does that parent do to foster the language and understanding of the child? First of all, the interactions are meaningful. Both the child and the parent are actively engaged in the interplay as the parent listens to, reacts, and expands on the verbal and nonverbal communication of the child. In this setting, the child is encouraged to initiate questions and conversations. He or she is viewed as a competent "meaning-maker" and, as such, is willing to take risks with language (Wells, 1986).

As outlined above, a young child actively participates in making sense of the world through meaningful social interactions. Vygotsky (1978) argued that thought develops through meaningful interactions. In order for non-native English speakers to engage in this language process in English, we must provide the same comprehensible input (Krashen,

1996) that the parent provides for the young child. The language of the classroom that surrounds these children must be not only comprehensible but also invitational.

In our rush to complete the activities of classroom life, we may not stop to reflect on the importance of language in the classroom. Clay (1998) asserts, "We rarely see teachers planning language activities for the sake of extending oral language itself" (p. 208). In the following sections, we present three common, yet often undervalued and untapped teaching practices that foster rich oral language opportunities for all children: the read-aloud, literature dramatizations, and instructional conversations. It is our hope that classroom teachers will thoughtfully consider the power of these strategies and the implications for the English language learner (ELL) in their classrooms.

THE ART OF A GOOD READ-ALOUD

Envision the following: In the classic children's text *Where the Wild Things Are* by Maurice Sendak (1984), Max has just been sent to his room for being a "wild thing." As Max's imagination takes over, he becomes surrounded by a forest and is then whisked away on a sailboat to the land of the wild things.

Just as Max is transported to the land of the wild things, a good read-aloud experience carries young readers to new worlds, where they can feel the spray of the water and taste the salt of the sea. Anything that can cause that much enjoyment can't be educational . . . or can it? Literacy expert and children's author Mem Fox (2001) discusses the power of reading aloud to children. She suggests that conversations around books have been linked positively to cognitive development.

> Reading aloud and talking about what we're reading sharpens children's brains. It helps develop their ability to concentrate at length, to solve problems logically, and to express themselves more easily and clearly. The stories they hear provide them with witty phrases, new sentences, and words of subtle meaning. (pp. 15–16)

According to numerous theorists and educators, the daily practice of reading aloud to students is a foundational piece of a comprehensive literacy program (Britton, 1993; Cochran-Smith, 1984; Heath, 1982; Strickland & Morrow, 1989). Routman's (2000) synthesis of the research contends that a good read-aloud not only brings a true enjoyment of reading but also helps a child become a successful reader by developing a sense of how stories work and how authors write. The power of reading aloud also promotes a rich vocabulary and allows students to make predictions, improve their comprehension, build listening skills, and acquire grammar. Routman asserts that these benefits apply to all populations, including those students who are learning a new language.

These benefits of reading aloud to children correlate well with Krashen's (1983) discussion about language acquisition and the importance of understanding the message. Krashen contends that language is acquired and not learned through grammar-based activities. Children progress in language and literacy development, if the input given makes sense to them.

So how do we use this information to select books for our read-alouds that will help our ELLs develop language and literacy? As teachers choose books for the read-aloud, they must thoughtfully consider whether a book will be comprehensible and find ways to make it so. One consideration is to choose books in which the pictures and the text match. Going back to our example with Max in *Where the Wild Things Are*, as the teacher reads the text in her outstretched hand, so that all can see the illustrations, the author's words are given visual dimension. This concrete vision is especially important for ELLs as they attempt to follow the storyline and comprehend new vocabulary. Books that provide this solid marriage between text and illustrations empower children learning to speak English by providing a "picture dictionary" embedded in meaningful content. Students are able to take away not only a wonderful story but also a new vocabulary.

Another aspect of book selection is to make sure that we share a good variety of books with predictable patterns and repetitive language. In books such as *Hattie and the Fox* (Fox, 1992), an inviting, predictable, and repetitive format helps even the shiest ELLs to chime in easily as they absorb new vocabulary in a risk-free environment. As Wells (1986) emphasizes, language acquisition progresses best when children are encouraged to take risks, experiment, and make mistakes.

Although many teachers realize the importance of read-alouds from a literacy perspective, they may miss the all-important connections between building language and community. Britton (1993) addresses three important processes at work when a teacher reads to the class:

1. Communal experience
2. Experience with the language of books
3. Gaining life experience

First, communal experience allows class members to function as a single group. The emotions evoked during a read-aloud can often transform a diverse group of individual students into a community. These feelings can create a bond within the classroom that allows students the confidence and freedom to become risk-takers.

Second, for the ELL, listening to the English language in its written form expands language acquisition into the academic domain. The experience with the book, how the book is presented, is as important as the read-aloud itself. Britton (1993) notes that a reader's presentation, through the use of gesture and change in tone and voice, can positively affect the students' interpretation of text. In simple terms, the teacher must use voice and gestures to make the book come alive. Third, through reading aloud, the teacher is helping students to gain life experience. In a narrow sense, the read-aloud gives the student the desire to learn to read, but Britton maintains that it is the satisfaction from listening to experiences in books that nurtures the whole child.

During a read-aloud, students are not only building comprehension of literary language, but they are also learning to imagine what it feels like to be within the pages of the book. As Rosenblatt (1978) states in her reader response theory, the story is more than mere words on the page. Students arrive at different interpretations based on their background and experiences. Calkins (2001) relates that the read-aloud is part of the answer in helping children connect and engage in the affective side of reading:

> Our strongest readers open a book and find themselves on a train moving through Russia or listening in panic for some sound behind the fictional door. But when other children read they are not on the train, they are not listening behind fictional doors. They are thinking instead of short vowels and "Whew, what a long paragraph" and "How many more pages are there?" and "What's Pedro doing by the window?" How do we help all children become passionately engaged in the world of the story? How do we help them know what it is to lose themselves in the drama of the story? (pp. 49–50)

Calkins's message is magnified for the ELL student who may be subjected to an inordinant amount of explicit skills and drills, which may take up the majority of their language arts instructional time. Children who learn to view reading as a set of skills and are not given powerful experiences of the "affective" side may never choose to be lifelong readers.

Now, let's contrast two read-aloud scenarios to visualize how the teacher's style affects students' language and literacy experiences.

Scene 1

A group of children is gathered around their teacher as she shares Mem Fox's powerful story *Wilfred Gordon McDonald Partridge* (1991). After reading each page, the teacher asks questions such as the following:

"What does Mrs. Gordon play?" (The organ)
"What kind of voice does Mr. Drysdale have?" (The voice of a giant)
"How old is Miss Nancy?" (90 something)

She calls on students with raised hands and compliments them on their correct answers. She ignores Michael's comment about Miss Nancy's shoes looking like his grandma's. In thinking about this interaction, ask yourself how the students are being invited to participate in this read-aloud experience? Now, let's look at another scene, where the teacher's comments may encourage a different type of student participation.

Scene 2

As a teacher reads through *Wilfred Gordon McDonald Partridge,* she chuckles at the picture showing Wilfred trying to fit through the chicken coop door as he tries to reach for a warm egg. She thinks aloud and comments, "That picture reminds me of the time when my son Cody was 2, and he figured out how to crawl through the doggy door. He crawled out, turned around, and crawled back in, with a big smile on his face."

She allows time for students to talk not only with her but also with each other about their own personal connections to the pictures and the text. As she reads the part where Wilfred hands Miss Nancy his football, his object that is more precious than gold, Luis chimes in, "I'd take my soccer ball." All the children start chattering to one another and to the teacher about what precious possession they would bring to Miss Nancy. After a few moments of sharing and appreciating each other's comments, the class is pulled back to Wilfred's story as the teacher turns the page and starts reading again.

In contrast to scene 1, scene 2 shows how the read-aloud, when made into an interactive experience, allows children to relate their own feelings and connections to the text, which encourages an expanded view by all participants. A read-aloud, in and of itself, is beneficial because of the reasons espoused earlier by Routman (2000). This interactive format, however, expands students' use of language and higher level thinking.

In her study that explored participation during read-alouds and literature dramatizations, Haag (1998) found that the classroom teacher's view of the read-aloud changed over time. Lori, the first-grade teacher in this study, stated:

I used to have the idea that the purpose of having them sit down to read the story was for the activity that was to follow or that I had one goal in mind [for the read-aloud]. Well, I know at the end of the story I want them to take this away or apply this concept to something else and that was it. So all the "Well, I noticed this on this page, and I noticed this on that page" were distracting to me. You know, I'd think, "Oh, that's true, but let's just get through the story," because, I thought, they're going to miss the point. (in Haag, 1998, p. 174)

Lori came to realize that by allowing students to talk about the story and the illustrations, they were taking a more active role in constructing story knowledge and connecting it to their own lives. She also recognized that she had to listen carefully to the children's comments to give appropriate responses. This realization correlates with Wells's (1986) study of preschool children and their home interactions. After examining the interactions of preschool children and their parents in comparison to school interactions, Wells gave the following advice to teachers to help strengthen language and literacy learning for students in the classroom setting:

- Listen carefully to children's responses.
- Try to understand what the children mean.
- Answer children in a language that they can understand.

Haag's (1998) study also revealed two additional insights about the intricacies of the read-aloud event. In viewing the videotapes of the read-aloud events over time, data showed that the ESL learners were spending a vast majority of their time learning *how* to participate. Their nonverbal behaviors showed that the children watched their peers and the teacher closely for clues about what to do during the read-aloud. One of the ELL students in the study often repeated what other students said a moment after they had said it, raised his hand only after watching others do so, and in the beginning weeks, when called on by the teacher, due to his raised hand, looked surprised and gave no response.

The second insight dealt with the teacher's comments about the complexities of the seemingly simple practice of reading aloud to children. The read-aloud, a classroom event that the teacher had almost taken for granted in its simplicity, in actuality became an intricate balancing act. Coded transcripts revealed that Lori and the class were constantly co-constructing story knowledge, which included negotiating the actual message of the story, and analyzing story features and the all-important connections across texts and personal experiences. This new, interactive format caused serious reflection and, at times, disequilibrium for Lori as she began to incorporate a more interactive read-aloud style. She found it a struggle to allow more talk but maintain the flow of the story. After 7 years of teaching, she came to know the complexities, but more importantly, the powerful significance of talk during read-alouds.

THE ART OF DRAMA

How does drama enhance language development and literacy? Many educators have achieved positive effects on children's learning by using drama in a variety of academic disciplines, including language and literacy development (Edmiston, 1993; McCauley, 1991; Pelligrini & Galda, 1993; Wagner, 1988; Wolf, 1995). Drama allows all children, not just the highly verbal child, the opportunity to use both verbal and nonverbal communication to expand their language competence. For the ELL student, drama affords an alternative means to participate actively within the whole group setting in the mainstream classroom. Drama can be particularly beneficial for the ELL student by providing an expanded form of expression (Wolf, 1992). When drama is used in combination with the read-aloud experience, students are given the opportunity to use gestures and body movement to act out the story, and this additional form of response adds another comprehensible layer to the read-aloud. Interviewed by Dillon (1981), drama expert Brian Way relates how the use of drama expands the storybook reading experience, moving it from a two-dimensional presentation to a three-dimensional illumination. The story, through drama, is allowed to become real for students as they are encouraged to bring the words and pictures to life through their own enactments.

Despite the urging of researchers and educators to use drama in the classroom, however, American elementary-level classroom teachers rarely use it on a systematic basis (Stewig, 1984), perhaps because drama may be viewed as an additive to the already packed curriculum. In countries such as England and New Zealand, the arts are seen as constructive processes that are incorporated throughout academic areas. Other areas of concern include management issues and teachers' own experiences with drama. Drama can create "chaos," if not structured correctly, and for this reason, many teachers choose not to use it as a common strategy to foster children's learning. Also, if the only drama format that a teacher has experienced is the common grade-level Open House play presentation, which often takes more than a month to coordinate, practice, and produce, then even the most successful drama event will be relegated to a "once a year" activity.

Despite these possible areas of concern, once you start using drama in your classroom, we think that you'll find it to be a powerful learning tool for ELL students. In the remainder of this section, we show you an informal, yet manageable, framework for using drama as a language and literacy strategy in the classroom. Literature dramatization is one type of drama that affords the teacher a ready-made framework that works well with a diverse group of students in the classroom setting. This informal type of drama, whereby children are encouraged to act out a familiar story using verbal and nonverbal cues, allows students to have a three-dimensional picture of the story and aids in comprehension.

Let's picture one first-grade classroom as the teacher begins using literature dramatizations with her students. Over several days, the teacher reads and rereads a few versions of a classic tale, *The Three Little Pigs* (Galdone, 1984; Marshall, 1989). For each read-aloud, she makes sure that a discussion takes place, and that students discuss story features and compare the texts.

Next, she sets up the dramatization by listing the story characters on the board and allows the students to help construct a retelling of the story to be acted out. The class may combine elements from the two or three versions shared or opt to stay with one version for their enactment. Once the story has been reviewed, the teacher runs through the list of characters and asks students to volunteer for parts. She places students' names beside the characters listed on the board. To allow for full class participation, many of the single parts in the story become group parts. During this particular enactment of the story, there are four wolves and six pigs in each dramatization (this story will be acted out twice).

The teacher then begins to narrate the story, allowing the characters to take their places on stage (pigs behind chairs, which are temporary houses, and wolves lined up on a pretend path leading to the house). Characters are encouraged to chime in with their appropriate lines borrowed from the tale. As they approach the houses, the four wolves chime together, "Little pigs, little pigs, let us come in!" The two pigs per household answer in turn: "Not by the hair of our chinny chin chins!" In these early dramatizations, the storylines are kept essentially intact as retellings but are adapted to allow children to begin to improvise. In this play, for example, the teacher encourages the pigs, who are pretending to be in the three different houses, to decide what their houses are built of as she begins the story. The children talk with each other for a minute, then shout out their house compositions. The pigs in house number 1 shout out, "Bubble gum!" Those in house number 2 shout, "Hearts," and the pigs in house number 3, deciding to stay with the original composition, shout, "Bricks!" Each play takes on its own characteristics, allowing children to make some basic choices, but the storyline stays intact.

In this scenario, the teacher affords all students an explicit format for participating. The children are allowed to borrow whole lines from a common text; they are also able to show comprehension through their nonverbal actions. As the year progresses, and students and the teacher become comfortable with this drama format, the teacher may encourage more improvisation. The role of the teacher as narrator and guide may also be expanded, so that she becomes a character within the drama.

In Haag's (1998) study, the literature dramatizations were evolutionary in nature as they moved from strict interpretations of the storyline to include more problem solving and improvisation. In interviews, the teacher, Lori, related that the dramatizations were becoming an integral part of her curriculum, because they allowed both teacher and students new avenues of participation. The students were naturally moving the dramatizations into the world of content by asking to "act out" science concepts or historical scenes. An added bonus dealt with participation patterns. Because drama was a new strategy for many of her students, Lori gave verbal directives along with gestures and body movements to give students ideas about how they might participate both verbally and nonverbally. These explicit directives allowed all students to understand accepted participation patterns for the dramatizations. Lori also found that the dramatizations allowed her a broader view of students' understandings, and she was pleased to see some of her ELL students show new sides of their personalities by becoming a character.

This "living through" a story may be one of the most powerful feature of literature dramatization, especially for the ELL. In *Wally's Stories*, Paley (1981) discusses a young girl named Akemi, who is just learning English. Akemi, through read-alouds and dramatizations, is able to take chunks of language from familiar stories and use them in her interactions with peers.

What's the best way to begin to use drama as a language and literacy tool in the classroom? Teachers may find it helpful to scaffold the process:

• Start with small but whole texts that have lots of rhythm, rhyme, and repetition. In the beginning, read the entire text, allowing the children to join in as they feel ready to do so. Demonstrate appropriate facial gestures and actions to be used. Text illustrations may also be used to guide students in dramatizing the text. Children may act out all the parts in unison, as in a choral reading, or handle the parts in small groups.

An example of a text that works well for this first drama phase is a cumulative tale, such as *The Little Old Lady Who Was Not Afraid of Anything* by Williams (1986). Students can sit in a semicircle around the teacher as he or she shares the story and encourages them to provide physical actions (stomping feet, shaking arms, wiggling hips) and to chime in on the repetitive lines as they share the appropriate actions.

• Next, allow students to choose their own favorite poems or short stories and work in small groups to create their own dramatizations. Have students decide together on actions, gestures, and voice intonation.

Anthologies with poems that relate to a teacher's current curriculum work well for this phase. Children enjoy getting to choose a poem to present in pairs, small groups, or individually. One example for the Thanksgiving holiday might be to share the poems in Jack Prelutsky's collection, *It's Thanksgiving* (1982) or Virginia Driving Hawk Sneve's collection, *Dancing Teepees: Poems of American Indian Youth* (1989).

• Incorporate writing into the process by creating a common script to use for a choral reading, Readers' Theater, or short play. Both fiction and nonfiction texts may be used for this process. Again, demonstrate the writing process by taking the class through a shared or interactive writing to create the script. Depending on the age level, students may be able to create their own scripts after doing a few dramatizations together as a class.

Fables work well for Readers' Theater scripts, because the stories are short, have simple characters and are easy to dramatize. Arnold Lobel's text *Fables* (1983) works well. The fables are short, humorous, and easily understood by students. Teachers should read aloud several of the fables to familiarize students with the characteristics of fables. Morals should be explained and expanded for younger students, so that everyone understands the lessons learned. After the students are well acquainted with fables, the teacher may have the class vote on a favorite tale that they think would be fun to act out, then demonstrate (using overhead or chart paper) how the text can be adapted into a Readers' Theater script. Students can help the teacher adapt the text through a shared writing format. This co-created text can then be typed and run off for students to practice and present. For older students, the teacher will still need to demonstrate and have the class create a text together as a first step, but he or she can then expand this strategy by allowing students to work in small groups to select, write, and adapt their own scripts for presentation.

• If at all possible, videotape class presentations for students to view, enjoy, and critique. Students enjoy watching their own presentations and also are often their own best critics relative to their use of intonation, phrasing, and pronunciation challenges. The videos also provide an important link between home and school; they may be edited and sent home at the end of the year to show parents how the students' language and literacy skills have grown throughout the year.

The power of drama lies in its ability to place students in different contexts and allow for "thought, feeling, and language beyond those usually generated in typical classroom interactions" (Edmiston, Enciso, & King, 1987, p. 219). However the teacher chooses to use drama as a language and literacy strategy in the classroom, giving clear directives and scaffolding the drama experiences allow both teacher and students to feel more comfortable with the process.

THE ART OF INSTRUCTIONAL CONVERSATIONS

In this final section, we discuss an approach known as instructional conversations, as explained by Goldenberg (1992), who states that the power of this strategy lies in its ability to guide discussions toward expanded opportunities for students' language and cognitive development. Goldenberg describes participation during instructional conversations: "Teachers and students are responsive to what others say, so that each statement or contribution builds upon, challenges, or extends a previous one" (p. 318). Before discussing the elements that make up an instructional conversation, let's take a look at participation patterns in the classroom.

Underlying every classroom conversation, there is a participation pattern. Phillips (1972) describes participation structures as face-to-face interactions in a certain social setting that have their own set of rules, regulations, and responsibilities for the participants involved. In her study with Native American students, she found that during whole-group interactions, in which the teacher does most of the talking from a leadership role, students tend to be silent or embarrassed about participating.

A common language instructional pattern found in classrooms today is known as recitation script or IRE (Mehan, 1979), which refers to the teacher *initiating* an interaction by asking a question, the student *responding*, the teacher *evaluating* the response, then *initiating* another interaction. In an interview with Power (1996), Cazden asserts that the IRE pattern, while useful during direct instruction, is limiting if it is the predominant type of talk found in the classroom.

The following excerpt provides an example of the IRE pattern in a fourth-grade small-group guided reading lesson in a suburban North Texas school. The teacher chosen by the principal and her peers was identified as being an effective instructor in her interactions with ELL students. The group contained five bilingual students (native Spanish speaking) and one native English-speaking student. The students sat in front of the teacher at a horseshoe-shaped table. The material used for the lesson was a test practice packet in preparation for the upcoming state assessment in reading (Texas Assessment of Academic Skills, or

TAAS). The students opened their packets and were asked to take turns reading the passage out loud. The passage was about the characteristics of living things. Table 3.1 presents an example of the classroom language during this guided reading lesson. (This excerpt is taken from a lesson transcript for the whole lesson but is representative of the language patterns throughout.)

The teacher refocuses her students on the information chart and asks leading questions to get them to tell her which living thing has feathers and two legs. No wait time takes place between her posing possible answers to get students to choose an answer from the chart. Students are finally led to the answer, a *robin*.

The teacher shows that community building has taken place as she indicates her interest in their native language and even tries to pronounce the terms. She uses humor as she laughs with the children at her attempts to pronounce Spanish words. The actual discourse, however, reveals little opportunity for the students to participate actively using language to learn. In fact, due to the fast pace of the teacher's questions, little time is given to allow students to reflect and answer in an expanded fashion. Also, students' responses are at times simply ignored, shutting down further participation and clarification opportunities. There is a limited amount of content covered in this interaction, which also limits students' instructional needs. One-word answers are the norm for student participation.

The problem with the language from this reading lesson lies in the lack of participation on the part of the students and a limited engagement with more complex learning. The IRE pattern restricts the discourse of the classroom by its monologic nature (Wells, 2001). By "monologic," we mean that one person is dominating the discussion. Even though the students are involved in the response of the IRE language pattern, talk about information that the students already know is teacher-controlled. Opportunities for interaction and extending students' language, thoughts, and understandings are minimized, especially for the ELL student, if IRE prevails as the primary language pattern of the classroom. Yet this type of interaction is often especially prevalent in mainstream classrooms with ELL students. Verplaetse (1998) describes one example of how content teachers interact with these students on a high school level. She determined that the high school teachers in her study, who were chosen because of their caring, interactive approaches with ELL students, used more directives and asked fewer questions. Verplaetse found that these teachers asked fewer high-level cognitive and open-ended questions. Consequently, the ELL students had fewer opportunities for verbal interaction with anyone in the instructional setting.

Now, let's consider the elements of instructional conversations and

TABLE 3.1. Transcript for Guided Reading Lesson with IRE Pattern

I	T: Let's look at number 4. Which living thing on the chart has feathers and two legs? Ooh, ooh, important words there.
R	S2: Feathers and two legs.
E and I	T: Yes, and what's the other thing, on the where?
R	S1: Chart.
E and I	T: Chart. Let's look on the chart. What has feathers and two legs?
R	SS: (*Other students respond with the same answer.*)
I	T: And what's the other thing, on the where?
R	S1: Chart.
R	SS: (*Other students respond with the same answer.*)
	T: (*Teacher and students look at the chart.*)
E and I	T: Chart . . let's look on the chart. What has feathers and two legs? Dos legs, how do you say *legs* [in Spanish]?
R	SS: Pies!
R	SS: Piernas!
I	T: Juan, tell me.
R	S3: Pies.
I	T: Is that *leg* or *legs*?
R	S3: *Legs*.
R	SS: (*Other students protest this as an incorrect answer, because* pies *means* feet.)
E	T: Oh well, it's OK, it's OK, it's OK. So, two legs. I can't say it anyway.

Note. I, initiate; R, respond; E, evaluate; S1, S2, etc., students; SS, several students; T, teacher.

how they can encourage more language and participation on the part of the students. Table 3.2 divides the elements of instructional conversations into two categories: instructional and conversational.

Notice on the left-hand column of Table 3.2 is a listing of the instructional elements. This is a format the teacher may use as a guide in planning. The teacher selects a theme or idea, figures out how to draw in or build students' background knowledge, and plans for a direct teaching point or two. In this process, the teacher needs consciously to think through how to promote more complex and extended language. Goldenberg (1992) suggests the following invitational phrases:

- Tell me more about that.
- What do you mean by that?
- In other words . . .
- How do you know . . .

- What makes you think that. . . .
- Show me where it says _____. . . . (p. 319)

On the right-hand column of Table 3.2 are the conversational elements. Most teachers are aware that language is important to students' learning but may spend little time reflecting on their own classroom language patterns. This is understandable, considering the incredible demands placed on teachers. Goldenberg (1992) gives teachers a place to start with the conversational elements of instructional conversations. These components call for the teacher to be aware of the nature of the language used during a lesson and his or her role in creating a challenging but nonthreatening atmosphere that allows children to negotiate and construct meaning.

Goldenberg (1992) advises that teachers start small as they begin to use instructional conversations and focus on one or two elements at a time. One way to begin is for the teacher to ask fewer known-answer questions and concentrate on giving to students meaningful responses that lead into further, connected discussion.

So what can the use of instructional conversations look like in the classroom? Table 3.3 presents an excerpt taken from a guided reading lesson in a fourth-grade classroom in a North Texas suburban elementary school. All four students are native Spanish speakers. The teacher, a native English speaker, is also bilingual in Spanish. The book is *Animals Together* (Clyne, 2001), and each student and the teacher have a copy of the book.

As can be seen in the example in Table 3.3, the teacher focuses the children on the theme and invites them to share their background knowledge about the topic. The teacher strives to facilitate the conversation by using fewer known-answer questions, helping to link the children's responses to one another. Direct teaching is evident in two places:

TABLE 3.2. Elements of Instructional Conversations

Instructional elements	Conversational elements
Thematic focus	Fewer known-answer questions
Activation or building of background knowledge	Responsivity to students' contributions
Direct teaching	Connected discourse
Promoting complex language	Challenging, but nonthreatening atmosphere
Eliciting reasons for students' statements	General participation, including self-selected turns

TABLE 3.3. Transcript for Guided Reading Lesson Using Instructional Conversations

T: We've been reading and studying in social studies about working together. Today, we're going to read a book about animals that help each other. In fact, the title of our book is *Animals Together*. How could animals help each other?

S2: One time I read about two fish that helped each other.

T: What did they do when they helped each other?

S2: One fish cleaned the other fish's mouth.

T: And what did the other fish do to help that one?

S2: I can't remember.

S1: I know! When the little fish cleans, the other fish it gets food that way. I read that same book—it's in the basket over there.

S2: Oh, yeah. Now I remember.

T: That was a good connection. Does anyone else have other examples of animals that help each other?

S4: Some animals protect other animals.

T: What do you mean?

S4: Last year, when we went to the zoo in third grade, a lady told us that some animals—I can't remember the names—tell the other animals when another animal is going to get them.

S3: Oh, yeah. Those are called predators.

T: That is a good word to know—*predator*. What exactly is a predator?

S3: An animal that eats another animal.

S4: Like on our field trip to that place in the, the forest. The lady said that the bird eats bugs.

T: Yes, that would be an example of a predator. Let's open our book to page one and read to find out about animals working together. Listen carefully for animal pairs that help each other in some way. (*The teacher begins to read.*)

---

teaching the word *predator* in context and setting a purpose for reading, which is to find out about how animals work together.

So how does a teacher incorporate instructional conversations in her classroom instruction? It might be easier than it appears. A first step would be to choose a text and read it several times to determine key concepts or themes. Then, using the lesson plan for instructional conversations (see Appendix 3.1), work toward including as many of the elements as possible. The next step in the process would be simply to tape-record a lesson. As Cazden (2001) and Paley (1981) have shared in their research, a tape recorder can provide a wealth of information for the language of the classroom. It is not as important for teachers to spend time transcribing the tapes, but by listening to the conversations, their own classroom participation patterns will become visible, allowing them to reflect on whether students are actively involved in using language to learn. As a guide in this reflection, the instructional and conversational elements outlined in Table 3.2 can serve as a rubric (see Appendix 3.2). The classroom teacher can check the elements that are observed, then analyze the language patterns that occur in the lesson. After completion of the rubric, it may be more apparent which elements are beginning to evolve and which can use further development.

CONCLUSIONS

Allington (1994) states that with the ever-increasing pressures for higher standardized test scores, students' opportunities to use language in the classroom are often neglected. The rich context that all students' need is often replaced by decontextualized skills instruction, which places the ELL student at a further disadvantage. This type of skills-based teaching displaces the comprehensible input that is critical for vocabulary and comprehension. That is why it is essential for the teacher to listen carefully to students' responses and also allow alternate formats for students to show their understandings. As Wells and Chang-Wells (1992) assert, "It is in talk through which tasks are defined, negotiated, and evaluated, and by means of which students' participation is monitored and assisted, that students and teachers engage in the dialogic co-construction of meaning" (p. 33).

The following questions may assist teachers in providing richer and more varied opportunities for language development with linguistically and culturally diverse students:

- Do we make explicit the participation patterns of our classrooms? It is of critical importance that the teacher be explicit about how he or she expects students to participate. ELLs often spend a considerable amount of time trying to figure out how the classroom works and, in the process, lose out on meaning.
- Do we adequately demonstrate what language and literacy look, feel, and sound like? Are we giving clear demonstrations, thinking aloud, and selecting books that provide clear images that connect with the text?
- Do we support students' language growth by providing comprehensible input in a variety of settings? We've given three instructional strategies in this chapter that promote understanding for ELL students' mainstream classrooms.
- Are the students able to connect the discussion and readings to

their own experiences? Teachers need to provide opportunities consistently within the school day for students to make and share their own connections to texts and the content of the classroom.

So what does talk have to do with language learning? In classrooms where student language is valued and encouraged, students are actively engaged. These classrooms are buzzing with student talk. The teacher's voice is not the predominant one as students interact in different settings and in various activities throughout the day. These talk-filled classrooms may not be easy to implement, and they certainly take thoughtful planning on the part of the teacher, but the rewards are worth the effort. If thought and language are truly tied together, as Vygotsky (1978) argues, we must work toward allowing our students a variety of opportunities to use language to learn. A student's understanding of what is going on in the classroom must be the primary goal of instruction. We hope that teachers will take another look at the three common strategies in this chapter, and consider language and meaning as foundational pieces of learning.

REFERENCES

Allington, R. (1994). The schools we have. The schools we need. *Reading Teacher*, *48*, 14–29.

Britton, J. (1993). *Language and learning* (2nd ed.). Portsmouth, NH: Heinneman.

Calkins, L. M. (2001). *The art of teaching reading*. New York: Longman.

Cazden, C. B. (2001). *Classroom discourse: The language of teaching and learning* (2nd ed.). Portsmouth, NJ: Heinemann.

Clay, M. M. (1998). *By different paths to common outcomes*. York, MA: Stenhouse.

Clyne, M. (2001). *Animals together*. Littleton, MA: Sundance.

Cochran-Smith, M. (1984). *The making of a reader*. Norwood, NJ: Ablex.

Dillon, D. A. (1981). Perspectives: Drama as a sense of wonder—Brian Way. *Language Arts, 58*, 356–362.

Edmiston, B. (1993). Going up the beanstalk: Discovering giant possibilities for responding to literature through drama. In K. E. Holland, R. A. Hungerford, & S. B. Ernst (Eds.), *Journeying: Children responding to literature* (pp. 250–264). Portsmouth, NH: Heinemann.

Edmiston, B., Enciso, P., & King, M. (1987). Empowering readers and writers through drama: Narrative theater. *Language Arts, 64*, 219–228.

Fox, M. (1991). *Wilfred Gordon McDonald Partridge*. La Jolla, CA: Kane/Miller.

Fox, M. (1992). *Hattie and the fox*. New York: Simon & Schuster.

Fox, M. (2001). *Reading magic: Why reading aloud to our children will change their lives forever*. New York: Harcourt.

Galdone, P. (1984). *The three little pigs*. New York: Houghton Mifflin.

Geisler, D. (1999). *The influence of Spanish Instructional Conversations upon the oral language and concepts about print of selected Spanish-speaking kindergarten students.* Unpublished doctoral dissertation, Texas Woman's University, Denton.

Goldenberg, C. (1992). Instructional Conversations: Promoting comprehension through discussion. *Reading Teacher, 46,* 316–326.

Haag, C. (1998). *Exploring participation in a first grade multicultural classroom during two literacy events: The read aloud and the literature dramatization.* Unpublished doctoral dissertation, Texas Woman's University, Denton, TX.

Heath, S. (1982). What no bedtime story means: Narrative skills at home and school. *Language and Society, 11,* 46–76.

Krashen, S. (1983). *The natural approach: Language acquisition in the classroom.* Hayward, CA: Alemany Press.

Krashen, S. (1996). *Under attack: The case against bilingual education.* Culver City, CA: Language Education Associates.

Lobel, A. (1983). *Fables.* New York: HarperCollins.

Marshall, J. (1989). *The three little pigs.* New York: Scholastic.

McCauley, J. (1991). *The values of "performing text" in reading.* Unpublished doctoral dissertation, Texas Woman's University, Denton.

Mehan, H. (1979). *Learning lessons.* Cambridge, MA: Harvard University Press.

Paley, V. (1981). *Wally's stories.* Cambridge, MA: Harvard University Press.

Pelligrini, A. D., & Galda, L. (1993). Ten years after: A reexamination of symbolic play and literacy research. *Reading Research Quarterly, 28,* 163–174.

Philips, S. (1972). Participant structures and communicative competence: Warm Springs children in community and classroom. In C. B. Cazden, V. P. John, & D. Hymes (Eds.), *Functions of language in the classroom* (pp. 115–134). New York: Teachers College Press.

Power, B. (1996). Testing the fault lines in classroom talk: A conversation with Courtney Cazden. In B. M. Power & R. S. Hubbard (Eds), *Language development: A reader for teachers* (pp. 101–105). Englewood Cliffs: NJ: Prentice-Hall.

Prelutsky, J. (1982). *It's thanksgiving.* New York: Morrow.

Rosenblatt, L. (1978). *The reader, the text, and the poem.* Carbondale: Southern Illinois University Press.

Routman, R. (2000). *Conversations.* Portsmouth, NH: Heinemann.

Sendak, M. (1984). *Where the wild things are.* New York: HarperCollins.

Sneve, V. D. H. (1989). *Dancing teepees: Poems of American Indian youth.* New York: Holiday House.

Stewig, J. W. (1984). Teachers' perceptions of creative drama in the elementary language arts program. *Children's Theatre Review, 33,* 27–32.

Strickland, D. S., & Morrow, L. M. (Eds.). (1989). *Emerging literacy: Young children learn to read and write.* Newark, DE: International Reading Association.

Verplaetse, L. (1998). How content teachers interact with English language learners. *TESOL Journal, 30,* 24–28.

Wagner, B. J. (1988). Research currents: Does classroom drama affect the arts of language? *Language Arts, 65,* 46–55.

Wells, G. (1986). *The meaning makers: Children learning language and using language to learn*. Portsmouth, NH: Heinemann.

Wells, G. (2001). The case for dialogic inquiry. In G. Wells (Ed.), *Action, talk, and text: Learning and teaching through inquiry* (pp. 171–194). New York: Teachers College Press.

Wells, G., & Chang-Wells, G. (1992). *Constructing knowledge together: Classrooms as centers of inquiry and literacy*. Portsmouth, NH: Heinemann.

Williams, L. (1986). *The little old lady who was not afraid of anything*. New York: HarperCollins.

Wolf, S. A. (1992). *Learning to act/acting to learn: Language and learning in the theatre of the classroom*. Unpublished doctoral dissertation, Stanford University, Palo Alto, CA.

Wolf, S. A. (1995). Language in and around the dramatic curriculum. *Journal of Curriculum Studies, 27*, 117–137.

Vygotsky, L. S. (1978). *Mind in society: The development of higher psychological processes*. Cambridge, MA: Harvard University Press.

Lesson Plan for Instructional Conversations

Text:_____ Date:_____

Instructional elements	Conversational elements*
Text-related thematic focus	Fewer known-answer questions
Activation or building of background knowledge	Responsivity to students' contributions
Direct teaching	Connected discourse
Promoting complex language	Challenging, but nonthreatening atmosphere
Eliciting reasons for students' responses	General participation, including self-selected turns

Introduction

During

After

_____

*Adapted from Geisler (1999).

APPENDIX 3.2

Rubric for Examining Classroom Language Using Instructional Conversations

Instructional elements

1. Thematic focus

2. Activation and use of background and relevant schemas

3. Direct teaching

4. Promoting more complex language and expression

5. Promoting bases for statements or positions

Conversational elements

1. Fewer known-answer questions

2. Responsivity to student contributions

3. Connected discourse

4. Challenging, but nonthreatening atmosphere

5. General participation, including self-selected turns

Part II

TEACHER IDEOLOGIES AND MOTIVATION FOR CHANGE

Chapter 4

Learning to Look through a New Lens

One Teacher's Reflection on the Change Process as Related to Cultural Awareness

DEBBIE DILLER

As a teacher, I must constantly change. I must change each year as I get a new group of students. I must change as a new principal is assigned to my school. I must change as I move to a new city and teach in a new school district. I must change as I teach a new grade level or a new curriculum. I must change because change is part of life. Yet teachers, myself included, often resist change.

In this chapter, I focus on the process of teacher change as related to cultural awareness. I begin with some general principles associated with teacher change. Today, working as an educational consultant, I travel the United States helping others to look change squarely in the eye and confront whatever it takes to reach every child in that classroom. In my work, I often see teachers resisting change. Sometimes it's the new teachers fresh out of college who think they know all there is to know. These new teachers do not say that they are resisting out loud, but I can see it in their folded arms and rolling eyes cast about, when they think I'm not looking. Other times, it's the veteran teachers, weary from many years of service, just too tired or discouraged to even think about making yet another change. Occasionally, these teachers even tell me so. I write this chapter to help myself, as well, to understand the change process better.

The majority of this chapter addresses the process of change I went through in relation to cultural awareness as a classroom teacher several years ago. I changed in a way I had never expected. Over a period of time, I changed the way I teach in response to African American students, children with cultural backgrounds very different from my own. I am telling my story of struggle, because I hope it will encourage others to look honestly and openly at their own teaching, their successes and failures, and to help them to make necessary changes to meet the needs of *all* students.

PRESSURE AND TIME

When I think about change, I am reminded of a line from a favorite movie, *The Shawshank Redemption*: "Geology is the study of pressure and time." I believe these two elements, *pressure* and *time*, are essential in any kind of change, human or geological. Change is a process; it can require weeks, months, years, or even generations. Anyone who has tried to change a habit, such as diet or exercise, knows it doesn't happen overnight. It takes awareness, support, and a plan. Sometimes the awareness part itself takes a long time. For example, an overweight person knows he should eat a healthier diet and walk daily. His friends and family urge him to make changes, but for a host of possible reasons, he doesn't make a lasting commitment to doing things differently. Then, one day, he has a heart attack, and the awareness becomes acute. He suddenly has a need to take better care of himself.

This leads us to the *pressure* part of the change equation. Most people don't change just for the fun of it. Change occurs because we have a strong need to do something differently. In the case of the overweight person, the need is physical. If a change isn't made, the person could suffer another heart attack or even die prematurely. Thus, pressure helps to precipitate change.

Is pressure enough to create a lasting change? Probably not. Lasting change takes additional time, support, and a plan. The heart attack victim now must get help from doctors, who give him strategies for eating healthier and exercising. He needs the support of friends and family members, who encourage him to eat better, who take evening walks with him, and who buoy him up for his efforts. He needs help until he can one day perform these new tasks without assistance. Change is affected by our attitude. If we have a positive attitude and really want to change, we are more likely to do so. In the case of the heart patient, a desire to change, coupled with the hope that this change will bring about something positive in his life, help to ensure his success.

What does this have to do with teaching? Everything! It is the same process and the same conditions that bring about change in teaching. How do we bring about and support teacher change, especially related to issues of cultural awareness? Again, time and pressure. Teachers need time and opportunities to work and reflect with one another (Cohen, 2002; DuFour & Eaker, 1998; Lyons & Pinnell, 2001; Robb, 2000; Routman, 2002). The school day can be very isolating for teachers. Teachers rarely interact with other faculty members, except over rushed lunches and forced faculty meetings (Cohen, 2002). Routman (2002) recommends weekly conversations, along with professional study, to facilitate the process of teacher change. Reflective dialogue is critical to a change effort. It gives teachers energy (DuFour & Eaker, 1998).

In a changing world, a healthy school is one in which teachers constantly revisit and renew their purposes, always looking for evidence and feedback about how well they are doing, and honestly examining whether they need to do things differently or better (Hargreaves & Fullan, 1998). A shared vision that all teachers know and care about is needed (Nanus, 1992). Teachers need to know whether and when a fundamental change is needed. It may need to even be in the form of a wake-up call to everyone involved in the organization (DuFour & Eaker, 1998). Again, pressure can be internal or external.

Hope is an important factor in the change process for teachers, too. Teachers who have a strong sense of their own efficacy, who believe they can make a difference in their students, really do. Hope, optimism, and self-belief among teachers are the vital wellsprings of successful learning and positive change. It is individuals who must hope, but it is institutions that create the climate and conditions that make people feel more hopeful—or less so (Hargreaves & Fullan, 1998).

As Cohen (2002) states,

> Any teacher who has spent more than a decade in the profession has already intuited what school reformers have not gleaned in a century of tinkering: lasting and meaningful change does not come from fiats (decrees), whether external or internal. . . . It has to do with how an individual teacher feels about his or her work and how the school perceives that teacher. (p. 533)

Public recognition of individuals is likely to have a positive effect on those teachers that receive it. It also reinforces shared values and vision, and signals what is important (DuFour & Eaker, 1998).

In general, the U.S. teacher population is aging (Cohen, 2002,

p. 533). Veteran teachers often tell me, "If I stand around long enough, the pendulum will hit me in the head. Things are always changing in education." My reply is, "Yes, thank goodness!" I explain that change in fashion doesn't seem to bother too many people. In fact, many of my friends love that kind of change, because it means they can go shopping. I point out that fashions recycle, just like teaching trends. The good news is that fashions come back with new improvements, such as Lycra. I suggest that they see changes in teaching the same way they see changes in fashions, with improvements such as Lycra. There should always be something new and improved that comes from change.

Palmer (1998) identifies two additional factors that contribute to teacher change: relationship building and solitude. He suggests that teachers need to collaborate with other professionals about the diagnosis of students' needs. Teachers also need to attend to their inner voices. He recommends solitude and silence, two factors sorely lacking in the school day. He suggests keeping a journal and finding a friend who will listen.

According to Palmer (1998), self-reflection is essential for a teacher to be successful. He tells the story of Eric, who taught from "an undivided self." He "honored every major thread of his life experience, creating a weave of such coherence and strength that it can hold students and subject as well as self" (p. 15). This is in contrast to others, who, he says, will "distance themselves from others and may even try to destroy them to defend their fragile identities" (p. 16).

The best example of teacher change that I have is my own experience. While meeting as part of a teacher research group over a period of several years, I shared my own struggle with learning to teach children from a culture outside my own and, thus, became more aware of my own change process. One of our members asked me to share the process I went through as I changed the way I think about myself in relation to cultural awareness and teaching. Here is my story.

FROM WASP TO WONDERER

I am a white, middle-class educator who grew up in the northeastern United States in a town with all European Americans. I began my teaching career in a community where the children were from a culture much like my own. I felt very successful as a teacher, so long as I was teaching students from a background similar to mine. In 1994, when I started teaching in a predominantly black school in the South, after being out of the classroom for 13 years, I was worried that my former instructional methods might not serve me as well. I knew these children came from backgrounds with which I had no experience, and I saw the difficulty other teachers were experiencing. After the first week of in-service, listening to other teachers and their troubles, I began to doubt that I could even manage a classroom anymore.

I had been given a choice of any school in the district and had chosen the one with the lowest socioeconomic status and test scores. I wanted a deeper understanding of how to teach reading and knew that the students in this building needed the most help. In fact, a district administrator told me she was looking for the most creative teachers for this particular school. The students there needed something different. I wanted a challenge and certainly got it. It took me months of frustration and failure in trying to reach my students before any real and lasting changes came about in my teaching. And, as I suspected, my first struggles were related to classroom management.

Fortunately, that same year, I became part of the Harvard Educator's Forum, by way of a conversation with a colleague from a private school. She knew from our telephone talks that I was constantly seeking out new ways of thinking about teaching, and she invited me to join the teacher research group to which she belonged. The Educator's Forum included elementary school educators from all around the Houston area, mostly private-school teachers. They met monthly to discuss issues they were interested in learning about and researching. They were not part of a college class or any school district; rather, they met because of their interest in improving their teaching.

I joined immediately, because I wanted to reflect and share ideas with like-minded people. Most of the teachers at my school weren't interested in research. The Harvard Educator's Forum provided the reflective dialogue I craved to help me learn and grow. Our facilitator, Olga McLaren, diligently encouraged us to choose a topic of inquiry and write about our questions and classroom observations. It was through this leadership and subsequent sharing with a group of inquisitive educators, that I began recording my thoughts in a journal and reflecting upon what was happening in my classroom.

At the end of the first day of school, I wrote down things that were going well: "The kids really tuned in when I read books to them. They were mesmerized. I think I'll read a *lot* of books to them. We talked about the books, and it was the one time of day that there was any sense of community, and not just me giving instructions over and over again." I also recorded things that were bothering me: "Our room is crowded and small, and the students seemed to have a hard time listening for directions from their tables."

At the end of the first week of school, I wrote, "I think I want to do a teacher research project on helping kids pay attention." I knew I was having trouble getting and keeping students' attention, but I had no idea at the time that understanding their culture could help me. Thus, a question arose out of something that disturbed and interested me. I was having difficulty engaging the children consistently, so I decided to take a look at how to gain and sustain their attention.

A SEARCH FOR ANSWERS

I went to the library and did a computer search on "attention." What came up was information on "attention deficit." There was little to be found on helping children pay attention. I realize now that what I was really looking for was how to increase student engagement. But much that is available today on brain research was not yet available in professional books and journals for educators. Four years later, when I read Eric Jensen's *Teaching with the Brain in Mind* (1998), I found many suggestions on how to increase student engagement. However, without the benefit of others' research on the brain, my best option was to experiment with a variety of teaching methods. Palmer (1998) says that "experimentation is risky. But if we want to deepen our understanding of our own integrity, experiment we must" (p. 16).

So I tried different ways to get children's attention. When we changed activities, I used clapping signals and tried ringing a small bell. I also taught lessons on how to pay attention. I wrote the steps on the board and demonstrated them:

1. Look at the person.
2. Be still and be silent.
3. Think about what the person is saying.

We practiced the steps involved in paying attention over and over again. These procedures did seem to help. Today, I realize that it was a combination of ritual and novelty that made these things work (Jensen, 1998). I was explicit in my directions and expectations with the children, which helped them to do as I asked. I also know that using structure was important for my students to be successful. Knapp and Associates (1995) identify this as a critical factor for managing high-poverty classrooms.

I also worked at planning activities in which children were gathered in a group on the floor to receive directions. Proximity helped, as did creating activities in which children were interested and involved. For example, when I had children sit close together on the floor by me, I could easily demonstrate something I wanted them to do in groups. I would read aloud a book about spiders, then model how to write about what I had learned. This helped to create community and eliminated some distractions students would have had if they had been sitting at their desks, while I showed them what to do. When I then helped them form groups, and read and write what they were learning about spiders, they flourished. In fact, the whole spider study emerged from their interest in a spider that was hanging from the ceiling in our classroom one morning.

The children were happiest and most productive when they were learning about things that mattered to them. But our spider study almost came to a halt when a neighboring teacher complained to the principal that I was not studying about the farm, like the rest of the grade level. I was called to the office and told not to be a "trailblazer." I was told to teach like everyone else. This could have been a major obstacle in the change process, but a few supportive colleagues, including my teacher research group, encouraged me to follow the lead of my students. I put up a "farm" sign in my classroom, with a few farm books, and continued to teach about spiders.

Student behavior changed and improved temporarily, which gave me hope, but the changes never lasted. As I reflect back, I realize that my focus was on trying to change the children's behavior. I wasn't looking carefully at *my* behavior as the teacher. Nor was I ever encouraged to do so.

THE QUESTION CHANGES

As the school year went by, there were many ups and downs. I celebrated the children's successes but was still plagued with their periodic disruptive, inattentive behaviors, as well as a lack of administrative support. One journal entry read: "It was another *long* day. There were three substitutes in our grade level and will be tomorrow, too. It was very noisy. The kids were tattling a lot, and it was getting on my nerves. We did a new language chart on fall. They did not come up with many observations. It was the least productive chart we've done so far."

Not too long after that, one afternoon, in desperation, I videotaped my class. Notice that I did not videotape *myself*. I took the tape home and watched it. I recorded times, names, and observable behaviors that occurred. Then, I analyzed my notes to see if I could determine patterns of behavior. Time and pressure again. As I listed names and really looked at my children, I noticed for the first time that most of them were African American. I had never really looked that closely before. I had been taught to look at all children as the same. I treated them the same. In my journal I wrote, "Yesterday I taped my class, because I wanted to observe what they were doing. I was so in the thick of things that I could not see the forest through the trees while I was trying to teach. I knew there was a lot of off-task behavior, but I wasn't sure who was doing what." Interestingly, I did not make note of my cultural discovery. I think I was afraid to put this in writing. Miller (1997) refers to members of majority cultures who pride themselves on being "color blind" and "culture blind," and would not dream of discussing issues of race or culture. I would not have called myself proud about being color blind, but I was fearful of admitting this. After all, I had spent most of my life surrounded by people who came from the same cultural background as myself.

THE SEARCH CONTINUES AND A GUIDE IS FOUND

Fortunately, for me and for my students, in my neighborhood, I had recently become friends with an African American woman, Tangye Stephney. We jogged together every morning, and I often shared my joys and frustrations with her. I decided to tell her how I videotaped my class and how I had discovered that most of my students looked quite different than me; in fact, they looked more like her. When I explained that I had tried to treat them all the same, she stopped in surprise and explained to me that I had just found the beginning of the answer to my questions. She told me point blank that my students *were* different from me, and that they wanted me to acknowledge that. What an eye-opener! It was the beginning of a new-vision prescription for me as a teacher. Tangye showed me the need for a new set of eyes, new lenses through which to view my children.

I went to the library, conducted a search, and began to read everything I could get my hands on to learn about teaching African American children. This time, my quest yielded only the disadvantaged literature of the 1960s. Most of the references were government reports written about programs to improve education for the disadvantaged. There were articles on Head Start, and facts and figures about the numbers of African American children living in poverty, but nothing to help me better understand *how* to teach my African American children. I was quite disappointed.

I went to my teacher research group and shared my struggle with them. I told them that I now had a new question: "How can I best teach and meet the needs of my African American students as a white teacher?" They listened with interest, and one teacher in the group shared with me several articles by Lisa Delpit. I hungrily read Delpit's work, beginning with *Skills and Other Dilemmas of a Progressive Black Educator* (1986). I read reflectively, jotting notes in the margins of the articles. In response to this article about process writing, I wrote, "Direct teaching of skills helps black kids, but direct teaching in meaningful contexts. White educators must open the dialogue with black educators to hear what it is that's missing, and to work together to fill in the gap." I moved from there to Delpit's often-referenced *The Silenced Dialogue: Power and Pedagogy in Educating Other People's Children* (1988). After reading it, I wrote, "This is tough. Must abandon your own beliefs and really hear another's point of view. . . . Ask questions about other culture. . . . Seek to understand." I read everything I could find about working with children of different cultures, including Vivian Paley's *White Teacher* (1979), Janice Hale-Benson's *Black Children: Their Roots, Culture, and Learning Styles* (1982), and Kathryn Au's *Literacy Instruction in Multicultural Settings* (1993), for starters. One book led to the next as I searched library shelves and moved from the references in one book to another.

I began to ask Tangye more questions about African American culture. She shared information with me about everything from African American hair to her own reluctance to go to the library. She showed me how to style her daughter's hair and helped me understand how to do the same with the little girls in my class, when they were distressed with a bad hair day. She shared with me that, as a child, she didn't really go to the library and, thus, didn't take her own children. I realized that, historically, libraries were public institutions that were segregated, just like the schools. That made sense when I looked at this issue with my new perspective. I now understood that during segregation, African Americans were pushed away from public institutions, such as city libraries, county hospitals, and many colleges and universities. No wonder some parents still avoid the schools and don't take their children to the library. White people often say, "That happened a long time ago," but, historically, not that many years have passed since the end of segregation.

ACTIONS SPEAK LOUDER THAN WORDS

Suddenly, everything looked different. I realized that Band-Aids matched my skin, but not that of my students. The children in the books I was choosing for them to read did not look anything like them; in fact, they looked more like me. The colors in the crayon box did not represent them well either. I ordered multicultural crayons. Until this point, I was unfamiliar with the theory of cultural discontinuity, or a possible mismatch between the cultures of school and home (Au, 1993). As I became more aware of the ways I interacted with my students, I began to see that I had been teaching them through my eyes only. I looked for picture books that had African American characters and were written by African American authors and illustrators.

In my personal reading, I began to read adult novels by black authors to further improve my new vision. I wanted to learn everything I could about black culture that had been so close, but so far away. One of the first novels I read was *The President's Daughter* by Barbara Chase-Riboud (1994). It was about Thomas Jefferson and his "slave family." I followed with the prequel, *Sally Hemings* (Chase-Riboud, 1992). These were books I found at the public library by chance. As I read, I kept thinking about the African American perspective, not my typical way of looking at things. As my eyes opened, I decided to give Toni Morrison a try. I had read that she was one of the best African American authors in the United States, and I was interested to read from her perspective as well. At first, I struggled with her novels, particularly the dialect she used in conversations among characters. But after a while, I got into the rhythms of her books. I read all of Toni Morrison's books I could find—*Beloved* (1987), *The Bluest Eye* (1970), *Sula* (1974), and *Song of Solomon* (1977). My eyes opened wider and wider in disbelief that people could have been treated so unfairly. Later, I read works of others, such as *The Big Sea: An Autobiography* (1940) by Langston Hughes. I was fascinated with his life journey. These books helped broaden my perspective of looking at the struggle and experience of a group of people about whom I had known little.

To learn more about how best to meet the needs of my students, I began to talk at length with the few African American teachers in my building and learned of their struggles. One told me that she was the first African American teacher to integrate the schools in her district in the 1960s. She shared stories of how she dealt with prejudice and hatred. I had been a schoolchild in the 1960s in a European American town in the northeastern United States, and had no sense of what this teacher had experienced.

One African American teacher, Vickey Tryon, shared her teaching methods with me, and encouraged me to try these in my classroom. She even brought her students to my class and cotaught with me. One afternoon, she taught my children how to play "Zap," a sight-word game she created. We all sat in a big circle. While jazzy music played in the background, we passed the cards around to each other. When the music stopped, each child flipped over his or her card and read the word aloud. A child who could not read his or her word would sit in the middle of the circle. When someone from the circle couldn't read a card, the child in the middle could try to read it and get back into the circle. The children loved the movement, the music, and the challenge. Their bodies moved with the rhythm as they passed their cards. Even if they didn't know a word, they were engaged and paying attention. Before long, practically no one ever moved to the middle. This seemed like such a simple game, but I watched the way Vickey interacted with the children, then modeled her style, her easy give and flow with the children. She was relaxed, whereas, I realized, I had often been tense. They behaved with her like she was someone they trusted. As I learned to do things that they enjoyed and learned, we began to establish a relationship.

Vickey also helped me teach the children spelling words using songs, chants, and movement. She would sing a verse such as *I can spell green, and I can be a washing machine,* and move with the rhythm; then they would echo back to her, imitating her dance. I jumped right in and joined them. It reminded me of the audience–performer style written about by Hale-Benson (1982), much like the responses I heard from the congregation when I had attended Tangye's primarily African American church.

I also increased the ebb and flow of my dialogue with children, encouraging them to give all-pupil responses to my questions. When I read aloud to them, they would all repeat familiar refrains in unison. I no longer insisted on silence or just single children's ideas during read-aloud time, as I often had before. I got them to share ideas with partners by sitting knee-to-knee with a buddy. I watched their faces light up as they gave a thumbs up if they agreed with an answer of a classmate. We sang more, chanted rhymes together, and moved a whole lot more. Vickey said I was beginning to sound like their "mamas," that I was learning their language, and they were connecting with me. This continued over a period of several months.

The problems that had plagued me began to dissipate. The students' attention improved along with their behavior. They began to understand why they had come to this school, and we began to learn together. By the end of the year, I had a clearer understanding of how to work with my African American children, but I still had many questions and a lot more learning to do. I wrote in my journal on the last day of school: "I have instilled in my students a sense of wonder about their world, the skill of observing and looking closely, the joy and love of books and reading, and a quest for information and the knowledge of information sources. We have read together, talked and walked together (sometimes in chaos), thought together, solved problems together, and fussed and fumed together. We were a family. And now we're all moving on . . ."

My journal entry described my work as a teacher/researcher as well. I had a true sense of wonder about my students, I had observed my students carefully and learned from what they taught me, and I had embraced the power of teacher research. I had fussed and fumed, but had kept moving along through it all.

NEW QUESTIONS EMERGE

At the end of that school year, I moved on, too. This time, I took up residence in an even more diverse district, working with new teachers. I had an opportunity to continue to learn, grow, and help others learn to use culture as a teaching tool. Another journal entry from the end of the year sums this up well: "I must work hard to make understanding of other cultures part of my pedagogy." I wanted to relate to the students I taught through acknowledging and respecting their differences and similarities, through choices of literature that reflected their culture and not just mine. I accomplished this by observing the kinds of interactions and activities that best seemed to meet their needs. I wanted to share with other teachers what I had begun to learn about teaching children from diverse backgrounds, children different from me. I also wanted to be cautious about not viewing a group of people as monolithic. All African Americans, like all European Americans, are not alike. Ferdman (1990) reminds us to realize that although there may be commonalities within groups, there may also be significant differences between individuals from the same groups. He writes that culture, by its very nature, is meaningful only with reference to the group, yet it is acted on by individuals.

With this thought in the back of my mind, I continued to read and study, and new questions emerged: How can I help connect home and school language? How can I help teachers learn about observing their students and using elements of culture better to meet students' needs? How should I teach writing to African American children? Are there any different strategies I should use? How can I use my understanding of culture, yet attend to individual needs?

Just like the heart attack victim, it had taken time and pressure to get me to make changes, some small and some large. I had hope that I could make a difference, and I'd found lots of support to help me. Over the course of one long school year, I made huge strides in my thinking. The pressure had been partly external (from the students' not being as successful as I wanted them to be) and partly internal (knowing that I could do better as a teacher). But it had definitely taken pressure.

Why had I changed, while others might have chosen not to in a similar scenario? As I wrote earlier in this chapter, *change occurs because we have a strong need to do something differently.* I had desire coupled with the right conditions for change to occur. I had relationship building and solitude. I had time and opportunities to work and reflect with other teachers through my relationships with Tangye, Vickey, and the Harvard Educator's Forum. This gave me energy and kept me moving forward. The solitude that came through reading, journaling, and reflecting on my own enabled me to teach from "an undivided self." I paid attention to and honored what I was learning not only about myself but also about another culture, which made me stronger as a teacher. I felt a strong sense of hope, optimism, and self-belief. I knew that I could make a difference in the lives of my students. Because I was not in a school system that created the climate and conditions necessary to sustain my hope, I eventually changed school districts. This change in location kept the change process in motion.

REFINING VISIONS: MOVING FORWARD AND EMBRACING CHANGE

In the 8 years following this landmark year, I continued to study and grow. I wrote an article about my experience that was published in *The Reading Teacher* (May 1999). I was invited to speak at state and national conferences about my work. Today, I work in classrooms all around the country, sharing my story and encouraging others to be brave enough to ask tough questions and dialogue with others about possible solutions. I have the privilege of helping teachers make changes in their teaching and in their attitudes toward culture, especially those different from their own.

What do I notice when working with teachers to bring about change? Most importantly, there is an urgency to the need for change today. In complex, rapidly changing times, if you don't get better as a teacher over time, you don't merely stay the same. You get worse (Palmer, 1998).

Change is generally a slow, sometimes painful, process. There is often resistance. Anyone who has ever successfully overcome a deeply ingrained habit such as smoking, not exercising, or overeating can tell you that it takes time, often a long time. Self-reflection is necessary in order to change. Teachers and administrators must often combat deeply ingrained attitudes, as well as habits. Usually, it is pressure that brings this change about. Sometimes the pressure is from outside; other times, it's internal, such as not being able to reach a particular child; at times, it can even come from one's peers.

The old saying "You can lead a horse to water, but you can't make him drink" comes to mind. As teachers confront their own attitudes about culture, as they work in increasingly diverse situations, they will be faced with making decisions. Those teachers that are active observers and reflective problem solvers will be more likely to make changes. Some will change by moving to another career field; others will simply change schools and find a place where they are more like their students; still others will change their views, much as I did. They will get a new perspective and begin to see their students through a new lens. How can we help them?

First, teachers need time to talk with their colleagues at school. Teachers should be encouraged to share their questions and resources with each other. Through regularly scheduled conversations, perhaps weekly, along with professional study, the process of teacher change can be facilitated (Routman, 2002). The Harvard Educator's Forum met monthly in a teacher's home. This same group is still meeting after a decade, but now we meet every other month, because of family and time constraints. I've been involved in afterschool volunteer study groups with colleagues that meet every other week. I've worked with schools to add professional dialogue to the school day, through the addition of a 40-minute meeting once a week for each grade level. This was accomplished by creatively shaving a few minutes daily off music, art, and physical education classes to create an additional block of time for teachers to meet.

Administrators need to spend time in classrooms on a regular basis, and not in an evaluative role, but as cooperative teaching partners (Cohen, 2002). Principals who coteach a reading group side by side with a teacher just once a week can keep their perspective fresh and current to understand what teachers are dealing with in classrooms, looking at culture as well as curriculum.

More training that really helps teachers examine their own attitudes about culture and diversity needs to occur to bring about change. This is probably best accomplished as a school district initiative, to ensure that it happens. Schools are often too burdened at the local level to allocate resources for this important training. One day, as I taught about diverse cultural awareness in Michigan, one teacher shared that her husband, who works for Ford Motor Company, receives regular, on-the-job training about diversity. Their business contracts depend on a full understanding of cultures around the world with whom they deal. Ford Motor Company employees cannot afford to have a cultural misunderstanding; it might cost them as a company.

What a pity that more of our schools do not address the same issues. How many parent–teacher conferences have I witnessed that evolved around cultural misunderstandings? How many interactions have I seen in the hallways between teachers and students that were built around misunderstandings related to cultural differences? After one session on using culture as a teaching tool, one African American teacher told me, "Thank you for having the courage to share your story. If more people would open up and talk about some of these issues, there would be a lot less prejudice in our schools and in this world."

Perhaps this is a simple place to begin. Gather with some colleagues, as diverse a group as you can find, and begin a conversation. Share what's working in your classrooms, and what's not. Come up with a question about culture that's intriguing or disturbing you, and ask for help from persons of that culture. Once you've gathered some information, put it into practice. Roll up your sleeves and take a chance. The pressure of that question, especially one with a bit of challenge, will move you forward, if you truly desire to know more.

Think about getting a new prescription for *your* lenses. Through whose eyes are you currently viewing your classroom? I hope yours is a lens that acknowledges the differences and values of all the children you teach. May you find a new vision as you question, search, and seek out others to help you understand those with cultures and experiences different from your own. Give yourself time. Open up and talk with others, experiment with new ideas, expect change, and watch it begin.

REFERENCES

Au, K. (1993). *Literacy instruction in multicultural setting.* Fort Worth, TX: Harcourt Brace Jovanovich.

Chase-Riboud, B. (1992). *Sally Hemings.* Buccaneer Books.

Chase-Riboud, B. (1994). *The President's daughter.* New York: Crown.

Cohen, R. M. (2002). Schools our teachers deserve: A proposal for teacher-centered reform. *Phi Delta Kappan, 83,* 532–537.

Delpit, L. (1986). Skills and other dilemmas of a progressive black educator. *Harvard Educational Review, 56,* 379–385.

Delpit, L. (1988). The silenced dialogue: Power and pedagogy in educating other people's children. *Harvard Educational Review, 58,* 280–298.

Diller, D. (1999). Opening the dialogue: Using culture as a tool in teaching young African American children. *Reading Teacher, 52,* 820–828.

DuFour, R., & Eaker, R. (1998). *Professional learning communities at work: Best practices for enhancing student achievement.* Bloomington, IN: National Educational Service.

Ferdman, B. M. (1990). Literacy and cultural identity. *Harvard Educational Review, 60,* 181–204.

Hale-Benson, J. E. (1982). *Black children: Their roots, culture, and learning styles.* Baltimore: Johns Hopkins University Press.

Hargreaves, A., & Fullan, M. (1998). *What's worth fighting for out there?* New York: Teachers College Press.

Hughes, L. (1940). *The Big Sea: An autobiography*. New York: Knopf.

Jensen, E. (1998). *Teaching with the brain in mind*. Alexandria, VA: Association for Supervision and Curriculum Development.

Knapp, M. S., & Associates. (1995). *Teaching for meaning in high-poverty classrooms*. New York: Teachers College Press.

Lyons, C. A., & Pinnell, G. S. (2001). *Systems for change in literacy education: A guide to professional development*. Portsmouth, NH: Heinemann.

Miller, H. M. (1997). Breaking the silence. *Reading Teacher, 51*, 260–262.

Morrison, T. (1970). *The bluest eye*. New York: Holt, Rinehart & Winston.

Morrison, T. (1974). *Sula*. New York: Knopf.

Morrison, T. (1977). *Song of Solomon*. New York: Random House.

Morrison, T. (1987). *Beloved*. New York: Knopf.

Nanus, B. (1992). *Visionary leadership*. San Francisco: Jossey-Bass.

Paley, V. G. (1979). *White teacher*. Cambridge, MA: Harvard University Press.

Palmer, P. J. (1998). *The courage to teach: Exploring the inner landscape of a teacher's life*. San Francisco: Jossey-Bass.

Robb, L. (2000). *Redefining staff development: A collaborative model for teachers and administrators*. Portsmouth, NH: Heinemann.

Routman, R. (2002). Teacher talk. *Educational Leadership, 59*, 32–35.

Chapter 5

When "What We Say"and "What We Do" Don't Match

NANCY ANDERSON

> In order to learn, students must use what they already know
> so as to give meaning to what the teachers present to them . . .
> but this possibility depends on the social relationships, the
> communication system, which the teacher sets up.
> —BARNES (in Cazden, 2000, p. 2)

Teachers establish patterns of language use in classrooms, and students take them aboard (Clay, 1998). A problem may arise if taking "academic language" (Cazden, 2002) aboard means unknowingly negating the meanings in a child's life, thus limiting learning opportunities. What we value, believe, and accept as appropriate when we talk in classrooms comprise the norms and expectations of academic language. Our goal must be to build bridges by supporting all students in gaining access to academic language, but the bridge must begin with the child.

Accomplishing such a goal requires careful analysis of our own assumptions and ways of talking in classrooms. If our students, or we, experience frustration when engaging in literacy learning, we, as teachers, need to look in the mirror. Our belief systems surface in our teaching, affecting all learners, but especially diverse language learners', opportunities to learn in our classrooms. Often, we have good intentions and can talk about diversity, but we must make sure that what we say and what we do match: Our students' learning is at stake.

As a teacher educator and University Reading Recovery teacher leader trainer, I tutor first graders and teach undergraduate, master's, and doctoral level courses. I view my work with young children as most valuable in helping me to keep grounded in classroom practices. My interactions with students assist me in my work with university-level preservice and inservice teachers through my successes, and through the humbling experiences I share in this chapter. Here, I illustrate how to maximize the efforts of linguistically diverse children during literacy instruction. First, I put forth the theoretical framework supporting the analysis of my teaching. Then, I connect academic language and classroom discourse patterns to teaching by analyzing two conversations with children. Next, I illustrate how to build bridges for children who may be struggling through our language patterns. Finally, I hope the theoretical and practical implications of my analysis help readers reflect on and change their own teaching.

RELATIONSHIPS BETWEEN LANGUAGE, LITERACY, AND LEARNING

As teachers, it is critical that we acknowledge and seek to understand the relationship among language, literacy, and culture. Children's opportunities to learn in our classrooms and their subsequent achievement intertwine with how we use language as a tool for learning in classrooms. A strong relationship exists among language, conversation, and thought (Bruner, 1983; Clay, 1998; Dewey, 1916; Diaz, Neal, & Amaya-Williams, 1990; Luria, 1981; Vygotsky, 1986). Cognitive development, related to literacy, in this case, significantly affects children's opportunities to use and learn language in school. According to Halliday (1982), three interrelated characteristics of language learning take place side by side, reinforcing each other, and are largely subconscious in the learner: learning language, learning through language, and learning about language.

Learning language means that children, through interaction with others, construct a language system. The constructive process centers on the oral and written symbol systems representing the meanings and functions of our language. While they are learning language, children are also using the symbol system to negotiate existing and emerging understandings of themselves within their world, or learning through language. As children make use of the systems, they develop an awareness of the nature of language and its forms and functions, thus learning about language.

In our schools, learning about language (i.e., parts of speech, phonemic segmentation, genre, etc.) receives primary emphasis. When we unknowingly limit opportunities to learn language, such as developing more sophisticated oral language structures, and to learn through language (talk while learning, as opposed to silent classrooms), children are at greater risk of academic failure. This risk can be compounded if a child enters school and the way the teacher or school uses language to teach (academic language) vastly differs from the home language the children used to learn to talk.

ACADEMIC LANGUAGE

When children begin school, their language competence, which serves them well at home, may not be congruent with academic language, because it is different (not deficient!). For example, a child may not be required to wait his or her turn to speak at home, yet in many classroom settings, children must learn to take turns and raise their hand as an indicator that they have something to say. During the first years at school, children learn academic language or appropriate ways of using language, thinking, feeling, believing, valuing, and acting that lead to acceptance in school (Gee, 1996).

If the ways that children express meaning are not validated through interactions during the transition to school, there is a potential for frustration and withdrawal, resulting in a passive or resistant learner. Although we may cringe when we hear a "creative construction" such as "I gots to use it," we must acknowledge all languages (or ways that children talk) are rule-governed, patterned systems that are generative in nature (De Stephano, 1978).

As teachers, we may not realize why children are hesitant to talk in classrooms, when we have actually perpetuated the difficulty through privileging academic language. Academic language, for example, is entrenched in our talk; it takes a conscious effort to move away from it and explore new patterns. If we rely on one way of interacting with children, we cannot support the range of linguistic diversity present. As a result, our teaching neglects to help children access the meanings in their lives.

We must purposefully vary how we talk to children, according to our observations of children's competencies. Furthermore, we must resist using the label of "low" language simply because the amount of talk is minimal or the language is different from ours. In order to improve our teaching, understanding typical language patterns present in classrooms is critical.

CLASSROOM DISCOURSE

Patterns of classroom language or discourse that frequently surface in talk include initiate, respond, and evaluate (IRE; Cazden, 2002; Mehan,

1979); initiate, respond, and feedback (IRF; Wells & Chang-Wells, 1992); and pseudo-questions (Barns, Britton, & Rosen, 1969). These patterns have a place in our interactions with children but become troublesome when they dominate the interactions. IRE is a three-part structure: initiate (I), respond (R), and evaluate (E). For example:

"Did they catch Dan the flying man?" (I)
"Yes." (R)
"You're right. They did." (E)

When the teacher knows the answer to the question asked, it is a pseudo-question. For example, "What happened after they caught Dan the flying man?" A child might think, "Well teacher, you have read the story, too. Why don't you tell me what happened?"

Wells and Chang-Wells (1992) contend that "evaluation" in the IRE pattern may be changed to "feedback." How teachers respond may not only be evaluative but may also be more an extension of the child's response that also serves as a support for learning the academic language used in schools. For example:

"How did they catch Dan the Flying Man?" (I)
"They catched his feet." (R)
"They did catch his feet and they flew away with him in the air!" (F)

Children who have developed communicative competence congruent with school may easily figure out what the teacher wants when the questions begin. Because of the incongruence, children may become passive in classrooms, thus cloaking their competencies.

"Reconceptualization" may be a pattern of language more supportive in bridging students to academic language (Cazden, 2002). Reconceptualization means that we act as a listener to children's voices, then revoice the child's expressions of meaning. Through the revoicing, children may also expand (Clay, 1998) the response, maintaining the deep structure but rephrasing the surface structure, providing a scaffold and an opportunity to move development forward. Children are heard and validated for their own construction of meaning, thus positively effecting the affective portion of language learning.

COMMUNICATING WITH CHILDREN IN CLASSROOMS

Becoming consciously aware of one's language while teaching supports operating in flexible ways that depend on the unique capacities of individual children. The goal is to tap into the meanings of their lives regardless of perceived deficits. Through my own teaching, I realized I needed really to listen to children to build bridges; I needed to consider *how* I was communicating, in addition to *what* I was communicating.

When two speakers communicate, they cooperate and use what they know about language to make the meaning clear to the listener. Speakers entice listeners to contribute and bring to bear what they know to the conversation. Both speakers and listeners must make sure they have been understood (Clay, 1998). During teaching interactions, "there are several important conditions that apply to good communication making speakers like teachers . . . [and] listeners like learners" (Clay, 1998, p. 14):

Speakers

- The speaker has to get the attention of the listener.
- The speaker has to be sensitive to the listener, observing the listener to look for signs that he or she is understanding.
- The message has to be adapted to the context or situation.
- The speaker has to listen when it is his or her turn to listen.

Listeners

- Listeners judge whether they are getting the message.
- Listeners recognize when meaning has been lost.
- Listeners can let the speaker know the meaning has been lost.
- Listeners can ask for additional information.

I use these characteristics to analyze two conversations. The first illustrates a productive encounter, and the second, a frustration that many teachers may experience.

Example 1

I tutored Kristina, an Anglo American girl, every day at the university for about 5 months. She was experiencing difficulties achieving in a first-grade classroom, was diagnosed with a language disorder, and attended speech class in school and a clinic located in a hospital outside the school. After a month of working with me for about one-half hour every weekday, she and I had the following conversation: In the story *Dan the Flying Man*, Dan flies over the city, taunting the people to catch him. Finally, they catch him, and he takes to the air, with them on his heels. The interaction is quite different than IRE, IRF, psuedo-questions, or even revoicing. I listened and responded in a communicative event in which we were constructing meaning.

NANCY: I like how Dan teases everyone. What do you think?

KRISTINA: (*pause*) Ya, he's laughing at them. (*pause*) He's flying so high, so they can't grab his feet.

NANCY: Well, what about the end?

KRISTINA: I think he wanted them to catch him!

NANCY: I've never thought about that before. Dan must be a pretty smart guy!

KRISTINA: Ya, like me!

This simple interaction contains several important conditions that apply to good communication. Notice how Kristina and I, using these conditions, move in and out of roles as speaker and listener, and negotiate the construction of meaning in ways that are not typical of an IRE or pseudo-question–type interaction. I initiated the conversation with the goal of connecting the meanings of her life to the meaning of the text, thus emphasizing meaning as a critical source of information when reading.

Initially I was the *speaker*, getting her attention by commenting on what I thought about the book, and asking what she thought. Kristina, as the *listener*, acknowledges that she is getting the message by agreeing with me. Then, I turned into a *listener*, when I didn't understand what she meant, by saying that people couldn't grab Dan's feet, when, in fact, in the story, they did. I let her know this by asking her a question to get more information. Then, as a *speaker*, she realized I did not understand her and explained that she thought Dan wanted the people to catch him. As a *listener*, I judged the message. Therefore, I shifted to a speaker and adapted my response to the context and the situation, and followed her lead, saying that I had never thought about it that way before and asserting that he must be a smart guy. Finally, Kristina, as a *listener*, judged that she understood what I meant, and turned into a *speaker* and took the opportunity to tell me how smart she was, taking into account the context. She likely would not say that out on the playground with her friends; this is evidence of her adapting her response to mine.

Example 2

Through my volunteer work at a local school, I was asked to work with Terry, an African American boy, who, after kindergarten and 1 month in first grade, was struggling to learn in his classroom. Terry and I met every morning in his school, and read and wrote together. The following example is from an interaction in which I tried to get him to compose meaningful text while accessing the meanings of his life. My favorite thing to do with children is to compose and to write, so I looked forward to this part of the lesson every day. However, during the first week I worked with him, I had a hard time getting Terry to talk to me:

NANCY: I'll help you think about what to write. What did you do after school yesterday?

TERRY: (*Looks down to the table.*) I don't know.

NANCY: [OK, I thought, maybe if I share something, he will get the idea.] Well, I read this really good book after school. What did you do that was fun?

TERRY: (*Keeps looking down.*) I don't know.

This simple interaction contains several conditions that apply to good communication and clearly illustrates how I did not follow them. Terry and I moved in and out of roles as speaker and listener, attempting to negotiate the construction of meaning. The problem was in my meaning being used, not Terry's. I was asking questions based on the meaning in my life (reading and afterschool or work activities) that was important to me. My questions were based on activities, such as reading after school, that were significant to me. After careful reflection, I realized that I had unknowingly used the patterns of classroom discourse described earlier in this chapter, IRF and IRE. Furthermore, a close analysis of the conversation illustrates how I failed to be a listener.

I began the role of the speaker by getting the attention of the listener, explaining that I would help him think about what to write. Next, as a speaker, I was attempting to adapt the message to the context or situation by asking, "What did you do after school yesterday?" Terry, as a listener, let me know that I was not communicating in a meaningful way to him by turning into a speaker and saying, "I don't know." Here is where the communication breaks down, because, as a listener, I thought I had to get additional information and adapt to the context. The adaptation was sharing what I did after school as a speaker, then asking another question about what Terry did after school. I failed to recognize that the meaning had been lost. Terry, as a speaker, however, was on the ball and let me know again by repeating, "I don't know."

Clearly, the layers of complexity of this interaction reach far beyond just the words. Did the fact that I am Anglo and he is African American influence the interaction? Yes. My goal in this chapter is to illustrate how, through our teaching, to maximize the efforts of all children whom we consider linguistically diverse. Thus, a discussion of race is beyond the scope of this chapter, but its presence is acknowledged.

BUILDING BRIDGES

After the first week of working with Terry, I realized it was critical that I build a bridge for Terry to support his development of a genuine need to communicate and use language. The shrugs and "I don't know" responses would keep him away from valuable language-learning opportunities. I began to take careful notes of our interaction to examine exactly how I was shaping my responses to him. I found this ironic, because I passionately proclaim each semester to my undergraduate students that differences do not equal deficits; rather, the deficits frequently lie in the educator's lack of understandings about language, literacy, and learning (Delpit, 1988).

Could I unknowingly alter interactions with Terry based on his language differences and encourage a passive response? I never overtly corrected or tried to "fix" his language. But was I making an effort to communicate to him that he had something important to say and a reason to talk to me? What follows is how I was able to build a bridge between Terry and me by actively engaging in planned, purposeful conversations. Conversation has the potential to be a "tool" for language learning and developing communicative competence with academic language in our classrooms. Armed with an understanding of the nature of language learning, we may deliberately create opportunities through our language patterns.

Eliciting and Extending versus Questioning

How can we help children learn language, learn through language, and learn about language simultaneously, without unknowingly limiting learning opportunities? If we think about our role as a listener and a speaker using language to extend and shape children's semantic and syntactic systems, we have a place to begin.

It is critical that we acknowledge the competencies of diverse children whose strengths may be cloaked by our assumptions. We can elicit language by convincing the child that he or she has something important to say, and that we are there to listen. Eliciting meaning may be as simple as an invitation to talk about or tell something, rather than asking questions. With passive speakers, we may need to monitor our teaching for *listening* and give the child verbal and nonverbal feedback signaling that what the child has to say is important.

Through analysis of my notes, I realized how typical classroom interactions were interfering with Terry's learning. I realized that I wanted to try to make my practice align more with my theoretical understandings of language and literacy. Consequently, I worked out a plan. I knew that to get Terry to talk to me, I needed to pull him into a meaningful conversation. Reviewing the characteristics of good communication supported the constriction of the plan to convince him that he had something important to say, and that I was there to listen.

My plan meant that I had to elicit language from Terry. Rather than asking questions, eliciting language may be as simple as inviting a student to talk about something or to elaborate on a topic. However, *it is more than simply getting the child to talk*. To elicit language, I needed to send verbal and nonverbal responses signaling that what Terry had to say was important. Therefore, *really listening* to Terry meant that I would have to remain silent to consciously think and see the world through his eyes as he spoke.

How could I convince Terry that I was there to listen? I began deliberately to plan our conversation and monitor my discourse patterns through careful anecdotal records. As I talked to Terry, a little voice resounded in my head, "Doing school won't work here." If I was able to get him to talk through eliciting and listening, I could elaborate and extend the interactions, facilitating his learning.

What follows is an example of how I began to elicit language, listen to Terry, and extend his responses to help him construct meaning. I knew Terry had been to the dentist for extensive dental work, and I decided to approach the composing process with Terry from a different stance, the stance of a listener. I carried out my plan. Sitting next to Terry I began a conversation:

NANCY: Over spring break, I had to go to the dentist and get a root canal. You've been there. Right?

TERRY: Ya.

NANCY: Tell me about your dentist.

TERRY: He stick it in and it hurt.

NANCY: Uhhh, huh . . . (*nodding*).

TERRY: Right there, see (*sticking his finger in his mouth*)?

NANCY: Ya (*nodding*).

TERRY: Where he stick you?

NANCY: The dentist stuck a shiny little pick in the top of my mouth. It didn't hurt. . . . Tell me more about the dentist.

TERRY: He stuck it in. It hurt. My mom make me go and she say, "You don't brush your teeth right."

NANCY: How do you brush your teeth now?

TERRY: My teeth, I brush every morning and night.

NANCY: Go on . . .

TERRY: I go all the way to the top and all the way to the bottom. I wash it off. It's clean.

NANCY: You've told me all about your dentist and brushing your teeth. . . . What could we write about that?

TERRY: I brush my teeth.

NANCY: All right. You also said something about how and why you brushed your teeth. How could we say it so when your friends read your story today, they will know more about brushing their teeth?

TERRY: My mom make me brush my teeth.

NANCY: Oh, really . . .

TERRY: Every day!

(At this point Terry and I wrote the story down together, sharing the pen. After we finished writing the last word, he reread the story and indicated he wanted to add more words.)

TERRY: My mom makes me brush my teeth every day and night. (*We then added the phrase to his story.*)

NANCY: I really think your story will help me remember to brush my teeth.

I elicited language from Terry by starting a real conversation, tapping into what was meaningful in his life (and mine), the dentist. Then, I encouraged his responses by listening and communicating to him that what he had to say was important. "Tell me more" and "Say more" differ from posing a series of questions that often elicit a simple "yes" or "no" answer, or in the child trying to guess, "What is in the teacher's head?" "Tell me more" and "Say more" encouraged Terry to talk more and share meanings about his own life experience of visiting a dentist.

Terry learned language through my response to his talk, although it was syntactically different. For example, when he said, "He stick it in and it hurt" and "Where he stick you?", I responded, "The dentist stuck . . . " and, in turn, Terry said, "He stuck it in . . . " Terry moved in and out of *stick* and *stuck*, which shows evidence of hypothesizing how language works by trying out the structures of language.

I extended and elaborated his responses without negating them or asking another demanding question every time. Terry asked, "Where he stick you?," and I extended his response with more complex sentence structure, without negating his personal structure. Instead of saying,

"Now, Terry, we say it like this: Where did he stick you?", I responded with a more complex structure and vocabulary that carried a message he cared about, because he requested a response. "The dentist stuck a shiny little pick in the top of my mouth. It didn't hurt." As he listened to my response, which was more complex syntactically (prepositional phrases) and semantically (shiny little pick), Terry was learning language, learning through language, and learning about language. I helped him learn to learn language according to school structures but figured out how to meet him half way, by looking in the mirror and questioning myself. In other words, I changed my teaching by building a bridge between Terry and me.

Over time, our conversations became richer, and I saw his competencies emerge. He learned how to "do school," while his classroom teacher and I sought to value what he brought to the table and to let go of my need to "do school." I continue to be humbled by what I need to learn. Now, I realize that no matter how many books I read, or how much theory I talk about, the fuel that fires my learning is to reflect on experiences with children.

IMPLICATIONS: THEORY AND PRACTICE

Talking about something and doing it are two different things. Through the analysis of my teaching, I can implement the theories I espoused in my university classes. My experience leads to three implications and recommendations for reflecting on one's teaching when a child appears passive or is not making progress.

Theory 1

If children fail to respond to instruction in our classrooms, we must first look to ourselves. Too often, when children fail to learn in our classrooms, we seek an excuse or a label. Their differences lead to perceived deficits. I have learned that every child who seems to struggle is an opportunity for me to learn and improve my teaching. As educators, it is our responsibility to build a bridge for the children, so that they can not only celebrate who they are but also see themselves as valued in our classrooms.

Practice 1

Audiotape your teaching during interactions with children whom you perceive as linguistically diverse, and who may be struggling to learn in your classroom. Listen to the audiotape carefully. Analyze how you are talking by thinking about some of the issues I discuss in this chapter that helped me realize the limiting patterns on which I unknowingly relied. Really check on yourself and look for evidence of patterns that may get in the way of learning.

Theory 2

We know, write, and talk about research and theory, but that does not mean we can teach children in ways that reflect those understandings. We may be unaware that our actions and use of language may cause a child's difficulty in our classrooms. We must have mechanisms in place that facilitate self-evaluation and continued learning. You would not go to a doctor who was not current on procedures and research in medicine. As teachers, if we experience ineffective professional development, we may have to figure out how to help ourselves learn and grow. Reading professionally; observing, and being observed by colleagues, then discussing what we see; attending conferences; or taking graduate classes are possibilities. We actually need to watch each other teach and talk about it. After doing all of the above, we actually need to do something about what we discover. *Awareness is not enough.*

Practice 2

Ask yourself some questions:

- How much talk are you doing, and how much talk are children doing? Who is the listener, and who is the speaker?
- How many of the questions you ask are ones to which you already know the answer?
- How do you model for children that you, as the teacher, are listening to them through verbal and nonverbal messages?
- How do you elicit, extend, and elaborate the child's language, while validating the construction of meaning?

Theory 3

As teachers, we must let ourselves be lifelong learners. Too often, we are filled with our own sense of "rightness." The role of learner is difficult, and we may perceive it as a weakness. Quite the contrary, when we allow ourselves to learn from our successes and mistakes, we are truly growing. My growth as a teacher supports the effectiveness of my instruction, resulting in more children becoming literate. *I have learned that the most important goal in learning is not being right; rather, it is understanding.*

Practice 3

After answering each question, *take action*. Move from talking to action. Modify the way you interact with children, and set some specific outcomes that you can review often, with the goal of building a bridge to academic language, while honoring the child's home language.

REFERENCES

Barns, D., Britton, J., & Rosen, H. (1969). *Language, the learner and the school.* Baltimore: Penguin.

Bruner, J. (1983). *Child's talk: Learning to use language.* New York: Norton.

Cazden, C. (2002). *Classroom discourse: The language of teaching and learning.* New York: Heinemann.

Clay, M. M. (1998). *Different paths to common outcomes.* York, MA: Stenhouse.

Delpit, L. (1988). The silenced dialogue: Power and pedagogy educating other people's children. *Harvard Educational Review, 56,* 280–298.

De Stephano, J. (1978). *Language, the learner, and the school.* New York: Wiley.

Dewey, J. (1916). *Democracy and education.* New York: Macmillan.

Diaz, R. M., Neal, C. J., & Amaya-Williams, M. (1990). The social origins of self-regulation. In L. C. Moll (Ed.), *Vygotsky and education: Instructional implications and applications of sociohistorical psychology* (pp. 127–154). Cambridge, UK: Cambridge University Press.

Gee, J. P. (1996). *Social linguistics and literacies: Ideology in discourse.* Bristol, PA: Taylor & Francis.

Halliday, M. A. K.(1982). Three aspects of children's language development: Learning language, learning through language and learning about language. In Y. Goodman, M. Haussler, & D. Strickland (Eds.), *Oral and written language.* Urbana, IL: National Council of Teachers of English.

Luria, A. R. (1981). *Lectures on language and cognition.* Washington, DC: Wiley.

Mehan, H. (1979). *Learning lessons.* Cambridge, MA: Harvard University Press.

Vygotsky, L. (1986). *Thought and language.* Cambridge, MA: MIT Press.

Wells, G., & Chang-Wells, G. (1992). *Constructing knowledge together: Classrooms as centers of inquiry and literacy.* New York: Heinemann.

Chapter 6

On Listening to What Others Say

Narrative as a Catalyst to Uncover Issues of Racial and Cultural Diversity

MARY McVEE

This chapter explores a provocative personal narrative shared during the fifth of 13 class sessions by Cathy, a practicing teacher and participant in a course I taught titled Culture, Literacy, and Autobiography (CLA). In this personal narrative, Cathy raised the question: "What can I, as a white teacher, do to be a better teacher for my students who are black?" Although narrative can be defined in different ways (cf. Connelly & Clandinin, 1990; Labov & Waletzky, 1967; Reissman, 1993), here, I use the term "personal narrative" to refer to a story written and then shared orally by Cathy about her own experience, using a traditional story form of sequenced events, with evaluative comments leading up to a resolution.

From a sociocultural standpoint, Cathy's narrative in both its written and oral forms provided a fixed window into her learning. Within the course, narrative and other forms of discourse functioned as mediational tools to reflect the internalized thought or learning of participants (Gavelek & Raphael, 1996; Vygotsky, 1978; Wertsch, 1991, 1998). In this capacity, narrative acted as a tool to assist Cathy and others in sense-making activities; in turn, narrative can help represent how Cathy and other participants interpreted their surroundings.

It is important to understand that although Cathy's narrative is the focal point of this chapter, as it was for the group's discussion of narratives on this night, it was also part of a larger context of the course and of Cathy's lived social, cultural, and historical experience. Although it is beyond the scope of this chapter to provide a detailed treatment of those macrocontexts, in the following sections, I provide an overview of the discourse and activities that surrounded the introduction and retelling of Cathy's narrative. After a brief introduction to the CLA course and to Cathy, Cathy's learning is explored in four contexts.

The first context is related to the CLA course readings and discussion on the night Cathy shared her narrative in written form. In focusing on the talk that occurred prior to the introduction of the narrative, I show how discussion of course readings and the opportunity to construct and explore topics through discourse allowed Cathy and her peers to begin raising and exploring sensitive topics related to race and schooling (Florio-Ruane, 2001; McVee, 1999); this discussion set the stage for participants to share their own personal narratives about educational experiences.

The second context is the discussion of Cathy's story. This phase of the evening began with my asking participants to read the stories they had written and brought with them on this night, then to discuss these stories. In the context of this discussion, many participants, including Cathy, were prompted to retell their written stories in oral form. In exploring Cathy's learning, I compare the oral and written narratives, and share what meaning participants took from Cathy's story.

Because Cathy's story was left unresolved and open to interpretation, it acted as a catalyst as Cathy continued to explore the question raised by her narrative: What can I, as a white teacher, do better to help black children in my classroom? To further explore this question, Cathy decided to pursue a midterm and final project to help her address her questions about race and schooling. For her projects, Cathy interviewed African American educators about their beliefs and experiences on race, schooling, and literacy. From them, she discerned several different ways to help the children in her classroom. The projects provide the third context for discussing Cathy's learning.

The final context for exploring Cathy's learning is related to an interview conducted 1 year after the course ended, in which I asked Cathy to revisit the narrative she had shared in the CLA course. I conclude that in reinterpreting her own narrative, considering the stories of the educators she interviewed, and in reflecting on other course readings, Cathy took steps to reexamine her stance toward children to help her answer her questions about how best to teach the African American children in her classroom. In so doing, she took a step toward developing a more "culturally relevant pedagogy" that will enable her to teach all children in ways that "capitalize on students' individual, group and cultural differences" (Ladson-Billings, 1994, p. 11).

THE CULTURE, LITERACY, AND AUTOBIOGRAPHY (CLA) COURSE

The CLA course was designed and taught for experienced teachers who are representative of the contemporary teaching cohort in the United States, a cohort in which approximately 90% of teachers are Caucasian, female, and monolingual (Darling-Hammond & Sclan, 1996). As is often noted, the mainstream and middle-class backgrounds of most teachers are increasingly at odds with students who represent myriad cultural, ethnic, racial, linguistic, and class backgrounds. For many white teachers, their own culture is transparent. Rather than exploring how culture frames their understanding of literate practices, schooling, and learning, white teachers focus instead on activities, practices, or programs, and adopt a stance of color blindness in which they emphasize treating all children equally. Many teachers position themselves outside of race and culture, sometimes going so far as to comment: "I don't have a culture." King (1991) refers to this lack of awareness as a state of "dysconscious racism" (p. 337).

The focus of the CLA course was to facilitate teachers' understanding and exploration of culture and literacy, particularly by reading and sharing published and personal narratives to further participants' understandings of issues such as race, class, gender, and literacy. This is important, because teachers often may not realize that their understanding of these cultural constructs mediates their beliefs about children and schooling, and ultimately affects their beliefs and choices in literacy instruction. To assist teachers in their exploration of literacy and culture, I drew on earlier work with teachers' discussions of multicultural autobiography in teachers' book club groups (Florio-Ruane, 2001; Florio-Ruane, Raphael, Glazier, McVee, & Wallace, 1997) and also work using narratives as a means to explore issues of diversity (e.g., Abt-Perkins & Gomez, 1993). Within the course, students read multicultural autobiography and autobiographical fiction; the books read are listed in Table 6.1.

Along with these autobiographical pieces, participating teachers wrote and shared personal narratives about their own educational and cultural experiences. They also read articles and research related to literacy and culture (e.g., Abt-Perkins & Gomez, 1993; Dasenbrock, 1992; Ferdman, 1990; Ogbu, 1992; Soliday, 1994). Typically, we alternated

TABLE 6.1. Books Read throughout the Semester

Date	Author	Title
September 8	Paley	*White Teacher*
September 22	Angelou	*I Know Why the Caged Bird Sings*
October 6	Hoffman	*Lost in Translation*
October 20	Rodriguez	*Hunger of Memory*
November 3	Tan	*The Kitchen God's Wife* (Part I)
November 10	Tan	*The Kitchen God's Wife* (Part II)
November 17	Conway	*The Road from Coorain*

our readings between articles and the autobiographies, focusing 1 week on book club discussions of an autobiography and the following week on a set of articles. Within the course, I acted as both teacher and researcher. I wrote field notes, audiotaped discussions, and collected all written work (e.g., reflective journals, midterm and final projects, narratives, in-class writing) from students in the course.

CATHY: AN INTRODUCTION

Cathy was one of seven participants in this course. Cathy's responses in her writing and her comments in class made it apparent that at the time she entered the CLA course, she had already moved beyond a color-blind approach, in which teachers adopt the stance of treating all students the same. Rather, she had moved toward a color-conscious approach, wherein teachers recognize that cultural and racial differences do matter in educational settings (Cochran-Smith, 1995; Paley, 1979). Cathy had been a teacher for 13 years, and almost all of her teaching experience had been in the primary grades. At the time of the study, she was in her second year of teaching at a charter school affiliated with the Edison Project. One of the "Ten Fundamentals" of the Edison Project is to have "schools tailored to the community" (Edison Project, 1998, p. 7), and in keeping with this philosophy, teachers and children at Cathy's school participated in mini-units called "intensives," where they explored topics related to their community. For example, because approximately 75% of the students were African American, the school devoted time across the school year to the exploration of African American culture and heritage. The remaining 25% of students at Cathy's school were from European American and Latino American backgrounds, and overall, the students had diverse social and economic backgrounds.

Teaching in a school that celebrated racial, cultural, and linguistic differences was new for Cathy. At the beginning of the course, Cathy wrote about her previous experience in another school, where most of the students were African American, and how this contrasted with her current situation. She wrote:

> "At the small, private school where I taught K–2 from 1989 to 1996, the majority of my students were black. I was proud that the students did not seem to notice that they were not all the same color. They never mentioned it, and we never had racial problems. When someone would ask me how many black children and how many white children I had, I could proudly admit that I didn't know, because it never mattered to me." (Journal entry, September 8, 1997)

Cathy commented that this color-blind approach was advocated by the administration at her former school. When she enrolled in my course, Cathy had already completed 1 year of teaching in the new charter school, where the administration encouraged teachers to consider the diversity of their students as a strength on which to draw in their planning and teaching. It is important to be clear that before she participated in the CLA course, read the multicultural autobiographies, and shared her own narratives and listened to narratives of her peers, Cathy had already recognized that she could not be color blind. Unlike the dysconsciousness of which King (1991) speaks, Cathy was aware that color did matter. However, as revealed by her comments in class and journal writings, she still struggled to be color conscious and to be teaching children from diverse cultural and linguistic backgrounds.

In Cathy's journal writings, comments during class, and personal narratives, she continually reflected on her own cultural perspectives. Many of her comments and narratives explore the questions: What can I as a white teacher do to help my students? What does it mean to be a white teacher who works with linguistically and racially diverse students? Her explorations of these questions through discussion, written reflection, and course projects characterized her newly emerging awareness of culture and its ties to literacy.

CONTEXT 1: DISCUSSION OF THE ARTICLE "A GOOD PLACE TO BEGIN—EXAMINING OUR PERSONAL PERSPECTIVES"

On this night of the course, I had assigned students to read "A Good Place to Begin—Examining Our Personal Perspectives" by Abt-Perkins and Gomez (1993), who explain how they began teaching a course called "Teaching Writing to Diverse Learners" by sharing their own teaching stories with their students (p. 193). In the context of the course, the authors and their students—practicing teachers—used writing to explore their experiences, beliefs, and instructional practices of literacy and of multicultural education. I chose to discuss the article during the first part of class to scaffold students' explorations of their own narratives, by providing examples of how several individuals reflected on and analyzed their own personal narratives.

I introduced the article for discussion by noting how the narratives that we would be sharing later in the evening paralleled the process used by the authors. Because our narratives were a means of opening up conversation for us around issues of culture and literacy, they functioned in ways similar to those presented in the article. After this brief introduction, I invited students to comment on what they had read in the article, either narratives or the analysis and interpretations developed by the authors. Cathy, the first to speak, began by commenting, "It is interesting to see the growth of some of these teachers and the changes they made in their teaching and relationships with children." The growth to which she referred involved the teachers' willingness to look at their own experiences and beliefs, and to address difficult issues such as race. In one example from the article, a teacher shared how her only African American student told her that she treated him differently, and that after first becoming defensive, she decided to listen. This ability to listen allowed her to recognize that her own well-meaning efforts were contributing to pain and anger that the student felt over his isolation in the school because of his race. Although being confronted by the student was a painful experience for the teacher, it enabled her to realize that she had to make changes in her curriculum and teaching philosophy. As a result, she changed her writing curriculum to include more collaboration and adopted a stance in which "students knew that race would be talked about" (Abt-Perkins & Gomez, 1993, p. 199).

Cathy stated that even though she worked with first graders, she could do more to help them think about multicultural issues, and in particular, more to help them begin to explore their cultural and racial identities. The following excerpt illustrated Cathy's acknowledgment that teachers need to be aware of cultural issues and their ties to literacy, and that there are also differences between teachers.

CATHY: I'm not gonna be the same as the teacher next door who's black. I'm not gonna respond to the kids the same way. Even if the teacher next door is not black, if the teacher next door is a man, I'm not

gonna respond, you know, the same way. And so that's, that's something to think about. I think, I think that all teachers . . . I think everybody oughta read this. You know, I think we should all be . . .

JAIME: And reflect on it.

CATHY: Pushed to think about that, yeah. That's a good word, *reflect*.

ELLIE: *Reflect*. Where'd you get that word?

Implicit in Cathy's acknowledgment that she did not teach like the
teacher next door was an awareness of her cultural identity as a white,
female teacher. When she said, "I'm not gonna be the same as the
teacher next door who's black. I'm not gonna respond to the kids in the
same way," she was not simply saying that she is white and that the
teacher next door is black; she was acknowledging a difference in teaching styles that may be culturally based. Her statement, "I'm not gonna
respond to the kids in the same way," was a reflection of her role as a
white teacher in a predominantly African American school. She added
that if the teacher next door were a man (which was in fact the situation
in Cathy's school), by comparison, she would also teach differently.
Cathy made the statement that all teachers should read the article by
Abt-Perkins and Gomez and, with Jaime, she co-constructed the idea
that all teachers should reflect on who they are and how this affects their
instructional and literate practices. These comments were further sanctioned by Ellie's repetition of the word *reflect*.

Cathy's comments about culture and reflection, and her willingness
to reflect on her position, served as a model for other participants to begin exploring how their personal perspectives affected their teaching.
For example, Cass shared that, as a teacher who worked with predominantly African American children, she appreciated the story told about
J. D., the first African American student in Abt-Perkins's classroom. As
part of a writing unit, Abt-Perkins interviewed students about their lives
and experiences. When she decided to interview J. D., instead of asking
him the same kinds of questions she asked other students in her class,
she used him to "raise issues about race and prejudice in our society" (p.
194). In this powerful and painful story, Abt-Perkins exposed the mistake she made in using her own power to objectify J. D., and in asking
him to "represent all African American people" (p. 194). Cass identified
with Abt-Perkinss' story and stated that she could see herself making the
same mistake if there were only one minority student in her class.

As the group members continued the conversation, many of them
followed the model provided by Cathy's original reflective comments
about her teaching and began to engage in exploration of their beliefs
about teaching and learning situations in their classrooms. Although

they did not engage in deep reflection, that is, they did not talk for an extended period of time to explore issues from multiple perspectives, they were beginning to think about both their own perspectives as teachers from particular cultural and racial backgrounds, the backgrounds of their students, and how the differences might impact their teaching. As participants discussed the problem at hand, how to teach culturally and racially diverse students when they did not share the same cultural background with them, they focused on their lack of knowledge about communication, culture, and other racial groups. At one point, Ellie challenged both the earlier question and response, by reframing the question in terms of race: "How do we learn about the needs of minority students when we are uncomfortable talking about issues like race?" Questions like the one posed here by Ellie, which address topics such as race, class, gender, sexuality, and so on, are questions we are often taught to avoid in conversation, because they cause disagreement, tension, and confrontation, and can lead to a speaker getting "burned." Such topics have been referred to as "hot lava" (Glazier et al., 2000). In response to Ellie's "hot lava" question, participants' responses moved the group away from further discussion of race.

It is critical to recognize the teachers' willingness to approach "hot lava" issues—even if they did back off from direct examination. Although it would be easy to dismiss these teachers' efforts at exploring their own teaching and the needs of their diverse learners, at best, as superficial and, at worst, as perpetuating institutionalized racism, it is important to consider what these teachers are accomplishing in their talk. As they approach "hot lava" and back off, stating and reframing questions, the teachers begin to seek answers to a practical question: What do I do to help my students with diverse needs? In their discussion of the Abt-Perkins and Gomez article (1993), class members emphasize knowledge differences that exist between the teacher and student, and what can be done about this. This particular theme is powerfully demonstrated in a vignette that Cathy brought to class in response to an assignment asking students to write about an experience in which they felt they were crossing some type of cultural border. Her story is about one teacher's search for answers to the question: What can I, as a teacher of European American background, do to help my students who do not share this background? Cathy's story resonated in powerful ways within the group and, once again, raised the issues of race, culture, knowledge, and the role that white teachers can play in educating "other people's children" (Delpit, 1995). As such, her story caused the group to revisit many of the issues they had begun to explore during their discussion of the article.

Cathy's story, as shared with her classmates, forms the second context for exploring her learning. The following section presents three aspects of Cathy's narrative. After briefly setting the scene, I introduce Cathy's written narrative and an overview of her oral retelling, and the differences and similarities between the written and oral forms. This is followed by an analysis of how Cathy's peers assisted her oral retelling by proposing alternative resolutions or interpretations for her narrative. Discussion of this second context concludes with a reflection on what can be learned through Cathy's retelling.

CONTEXT 2: EXAMINING PERSONAL PERSPECTIVES THROUGH NARRATIVE

Cathy's Narrative: Black Child Placed in Crisis

As we moved into the second phase of class discussion that evening, I asked students to distribute copies of the narratives they had written about their border-crossing experiences. When these narratives were retold, rewritten, and revisited across the semester, they provided me with several snapshots of each course participant's learning and thinking. In general, the narratives provided a workspace in which participants could consider, construct, and reconstruct ideas related to self and other. Specifically, class members could consider what it means to teach in linguistically and culturally diverse settings, and ultimately, examine what it means to view students' linguistic and cultural backgrounds as strengths on which to draw rather than as problems to be mitigated.

We took 15 minutes to read all the short narratives written by class members and jot down questions, notes, or responses. After participants read one another's narratives, I opened the discussion by identifying themes that connected some participants' work (e.g., several class members had written about their experiences as first-time teachers). Class members continued the discussion by commenting on their stories, sometimes offering further information or interpretation, or positioning their stories in relation to others in the class. After approximately 15 minutes of discussion, I asked whether the participants would like to learn more about any particular teacher's story. Several class members immediately asked to hear more from Cathy.

For her narrative vignette, Cathy had written about attending a conference called "Black Child Placed in Crisis."

> "When given the opportunity to attend an out-of-town conference, I happily accepted. The subject of the conference intrigued me, and I was certain that I could learn much that would help me with my at-risk black students at the "Black Child Placed in Crisis" conference.

Being in the obvious minority did not bother me as I looked around
at the sea of black faces around me. However, what did bother me
was the lack of solutions offered by the presenters. I wanted to learn
about tools I could use to better assist the black children in my class.
What I heard in session after session was that there is a problem with
black children in schools, and that something needs to be done about
it. Every presenter said essentially the same thing, but with a different slant according to the title of the session. It seemed more like a
pity party to me. The longer I sat in a session, the more uncomfortable I felt being there. I felt as though the speakers were saying white
people were the reason for the problem. Maybe they were saying
that, and maybe they weren't. But the whole reason I went to the
conference was to learn how I could make a difference in the life of a
black child. I left, sorely disappointed. Later, I told a black colleague,
who also attended the conference, how I felt. She told me about a
part of the Malcolm X movie that seemed to sum it all up. A young,
white coed attended a rally on campus where Malcolm X spoke and
asked him what she could do to help the cause. His answer to her
was: 'Nothing.' "

The high degree of interest in Cathy's story is apparent given the
number of students who wanted to hear more and the rapid, overlapping speech, and comments such as "That was . . . Wow!"; "I wrote
down a question [for Cathy]"; "Talk to us, Cathy!" With this prompting
from others, Cathy retold her narrative, which lasted almost 9 minutes—
an unusually long time for one participant to hold the conversational
floor in our class.

Cathy's oral retelling and her written narrative meet Labov and
Weletsky's (1967) and Labov's (1972) definition of "narrative." Both
contain statements used to *orient* the listener, *complicating actions* that
build the drama, *evaluation* statements that show what Cathy is thinking about the events, and a *resolution* that follows the evaluation and
concludes the narrative. Although both the written and oral narratives
contain all these key elements, there are some differences. Table 6.2 summarizes the key features and differences between the written and oral
versions. Because the text of Cathy's retelling is too long to include here
in its entirety, I quote segments of the retelling in the analysis.

In the oral version, Cathy provides more information about the
conference—where it was held, who attended, why attendance was low,
and summaries of some sessions she and her colleagues attended. In providing this additional information, Cathy repeats and adds more explanation to several statements that orient the listeners to important aspects
of her story. She reiterates that she did not feel uncomfortable being one

TABLE 6.2. Comparison of Cathy's Written and Oral Narratives

Written narrative	Oral retelling
Form	Form
• *Orientation* statements at beginning • *Complicating actions* in the middle • *Evaluation* embedded throughout • *Resolution* in the form of a "flash ahead" (Polanyi, 1985)	• More *orientation statements* (e.g., the reason few white teachers attended, who attended from her school, more description of sessions offered) • More *complicating actions* (e.g., of attending events to build the drama) • More *evaluation* about the conference (e.g., Why aren't they [the presenters] giving me something?) and herself (e.g., Why do I feel this way?) • *Resolution*: Cathy begins to give her resolution but is interrupted midsentence by another participant. Participants offer their own *alternative resolutions* to her story.
Content	Content
Description of attending the "Black Child Placed in Crisis" conference	Description of attending the "Black Child Placed in Crisis" conference, but more details are given (see "FORM," above)
Immediate purpose/function	Immediate purpose/function
To fulfill a course assignment by writing about a "border-crossing experience"	To fulfill a request from her peers to provide more information and details about the experience
Length	Length
285 words	Approximately 1,300 words, 9 minutes
Interpretation/resolution	Interpretation/resolution
Primary: There is nothing that Cathy as a woman and white teacher can do to help black children. *Secondary*: Cathy does not accept that there is nothing she as a woman and white teacher can do to help black children.	*Multiple resolutions from participants*: • Shouldn't blame white people for the problem. • Maybe presenters went to the conference to vent frustrations. • Presenters don't know how to communicate practical advice to white teachers. • Black people want to teach black children in their own schools. • African American educators are telling white teachers they just "don't get it." • As Delpit says, white teachers aren't listening to their black colleagues.

of few white people and repeatedly emphasizes that she had hoped that the conference would provide "tools" that would help her teach the black children in her class. In the oral telling of the story, Cathy also has more opportunity to add evaluative commentary. She does this through direct statements and discourse markers, such as word stress (*italicized* in the following excerpt).

"You know, almost everybody there was black—99% of the people there were black. And I *still* wasn't that uncomfortable until he [a presenter from a private, all-male Muslim academy] got up there and started to speak. And, basically, all he was telling us was what he's doing at his school um, you know, educating them. But all he has is black boys. Well, I can't *do* that. I can't, *I can't create an all black boy school. Look at me.* I wanta know what to *do* with *my* boys, you know. . . . And um, but the two black women that I was with, they weren't so happy either. But they weren't uncomfortable, but they weren't happy with what he was saying."

Throughout the retelling she emphasizes her own position as a white teacher, saying in the excerpt, "Look at me [I'm white and female]." These characteristics exclude her from establishing the kind of environment that the speaker has suggested. Cathy also emphasizes that she needs to know what to do with her boys. Although the speaker made useful suggestions, for example, including more African American history and literature in the curriculum across the academic year, Cathy expressed her frustration, because she did not feel she was learning new things to do. Elsewhere in the oral retelling, she shares how her school mandates "intensives," in which the traditional school curriculum is set aside to teach about issues of culture and heritage. About 75% of the school is African American, and because the staff, many of whom are African American, are dedicated to a curriculum that represents the children they serve, many of these units are Afrocentric in theme.

Cathy's frustration over not being told what to do was especially pronounced in her summary of a session she attended on trying to reach out to families. (Again, stressed words have been *italicized*.)

"[The presenter] was talking about reaching out to the families. And I'm . . . well, that's what we need to do. We need to reach out to the families. But one was worse than the other, because we kept hearing, you know, these families need to be reached out to. . . . And all I kept hearing was these are the bad things that are happening to black children. We need to *do* something about it. But they never said *what to do.* You know, go hug the crack addict whose child is in your class.

Well, OK. Sure, I'll hug her, but then what, you know? And then they still, they still didn't say go out and *do* this and *do* that. You know, and maybe I went with higher expectations than what I should have. Maybe, maybe, the whole conference wasn't about what I expected it to be. But "Black Child Placed in Crisis," I thought, I'm gonna get some tools. I'm gonna, I'm gonna learn some things that I can do with black kids in my class. And I was really disappointed."

Part of Cathy's frustration stems from her evaluation of the conference as a place where she hears about problems facing black children but not about solutions. As a teacher in a school with a predominantly African American student population, she argues that she knows there are great problems facing black children. At one point, she says, "I *know* there's a problem. They didn't have to *tell* me that." Throughout her narrative, Cathy emphasizes that she was "disappointed" in the conference, because, as a "white teacher," she did not feel that she received valuable tools. She asked her African American colleagues who had gone with her, "Why do I feel this way? Why aren't they [the presenters] giving me something?" In response, one of her female colleagues said, "Maybe they [the presenters] just don't know. . . . Maybe they just don't know what, what you can do." The colleague then shared the example of Malcolm X telling the white, female coed that she was excluded from the movement. The comment is vague; it is not clear whether the exclusion of the coed, and, by extension, Cathy's exclusion, is due to race or gender, or both. As she was retelling her story, Cathy began to conclude the oral retelling in the same manner that she ended the written version, by relaying her colleague's revoicing of the position portrayed by Malcolm X, that there is nothing a white woman can do to help the cause. As with the written version, this comment emphasizes that the exclusion Cathy feels is based on race.

Alternative Resolutions to Cathy's Story

Throughout her retelling, Cathy had followed the written form of her narrative very closely. She added further explanation and examples but retold the narrative in a similar sequence and form. The written and oral narratives have assisted her in making sense of her experience and sharing her sense making with the group, as we see in her evaluative comments and in the resolution she presents in the written narrative. However, in the oral retelling, when Cathy reaches the point where she is about to conclude with the same example of Malcolm X, the other participants in the group interrupt her. Rather than accepting her suggested resolution that white people cannot do anything to help, participants offer alternative interpretations, commentary, and questions about the story.

Toni begins this round of alternative resolutions by asking what teachers would do if two kids were "going back and forth." She suggests that she wouldn't let one kid blame the other, but both would have to participate in an agreement or solution. Although she uses an example from a school setting, her meaning is clear, and she finally states directly: "I have a problem if they're saying white people are doing it [causing the crisis for black children] and they [the black presenters] give no solution." Regan, Ellie, and Jaime suggest another resolution: that maybe the presenters were "at a different sort of level of understanding. Like they went there to vent frustrations." Cathy's story and possible interpretations are "hot lava" for all of us. As the course instructor, I participate directly in attempting to shift the conversation to safer ground when I say, "If you take the sort of obvious racial tensions out of it," then talk about parallel research where teacher educators sometimes have difficulty relaying their ideas to teachers. This section of the discussion has the feel of a brainstorming session, in which participants toss suggestions onto the conversational floor, but there is little or no examination of these suggestions. Along with this, the high incidence of repetition, false starts, and halting speech indicate that it is not easy for participants to express their ideas. There is also evidence of the difficulty of this discussion, because participants repeatedly end their turns with the phrase, "I don't know."

Regan, the participant who had read all of Lisa Delpit's work and was the only group participant to have taught in a nontraditional school setting, had taught in Alaska in a program to foster home and school literacy among the Tlingkit Indians. She said, "Maybe they [the African American presenters] think they've been telling them [white teachers] for a while and they're telling, you know, you just don't understand." I picked up on Regan's comment and tied it to the work of Lisa Delpit, and the suggestions made in her article. In "The Silenced Dialogue," Delpit (1988) argues that the experiences and expertise of black teachers are valuable and worth knowing, and that such information is important and helpful for white educators, if the white educators engage in a dialogue and listen to their black colleagues. On this night, the article that we read by Abt-Perkins and Gomez (1993) contained the following extended quote from Delpit:

> We do not really see through our eyes or hear through our ears, but through our beliefs. To put our beliefs on hold is to cease to exist ourselves for a moment—and that is not easy. It is painful as well because it means turning yourself inside out, giving up your own sense of who you

are, and being willing to see yourself in the unflattering light of another's angry gaze. It is not easy, but it is the only way to start the dialogue. . . . We must learn to be vulnerable enough to allow our world to turn upside down in order to allow the realties of others to edge themselves into our consciousness. (p. 193)

Delpit's quote, which we had looked at earlier in our discussion of the article, indicates that it is difficult to "see yourself in the unflattering light of another's angry gaze" and to "allow our world to turn upside down." Mentioning Delpit and echoing the idea that maybe white teachers do not listen to their black colleagues steered the conversation even closer to the "hot lava" topic of racial conflict among teachers. This was not a topic in which participants were willing to engage at the time. Ellie responded to my statement: "It also kinda takes me back to one of the first articles we read, Ogbu's article, and the importance in the black community of the community [itself]." Ellie then began to talk generally about home visits. Other participants chimed in, comparing which schools or programs (e.g., Even Start) required home visits, how home visits are organized, and who had conducted a home visit. Although home visits and fostering home–school connections are important for teachers, Ellie's reframing of the discussion around home visits moved the talk to safer ground, because teachers could focus on the types of visits, the pros and cons of home visits, and so on, without addressing tensions related to race.

What Is Learned through Cathy's Retelling

In sharing her narrative, Cathy had an opportunity to provide further information to orient the listeners and to more fully describe the events at the conference. The form of her oral narrative is similar to that of the written vignette, with statements that orient the listener, complicating actions that build the drama, and evaluative statements that reflect Cathy's feelings about the conference. Both narratives also contain a resolution. In the written vignette, Cathy concluded with the example of Malcolm X, which suggested that she, as a white teacher, could do nothing to help black children. It is clear that this is not a resolution she accepts. Cathy is still teaching in a predominantly African American school. She is still attempting to make sense out of her experience at the conference and to explore issues of self by asking, "Why did I feel that the conference was not helpful? Why was I uncomfortable?" Not only did Cathy reject the resolution written in the vignette, but also she was not satisfied with the resolutions proposed by her classmates. Throughout the CLA course, she continued to explore the question: What can I do as a white teacher to help my black students become successful readers and writers and be successful in school?

Cathy's story opened up opportunities for participants to explore race and culture. However, as evidenced by false starts, halting speech, and moves to reframe the conversation to safer ground, it was not easy for participants to explore these issues. Through narrative, Cathy engaged in the reflection on her own cultural perspective—a type of reflection that she herself advocated earlier in this night of talk, when she stated, "Anybody who's going to work with people of a different race or culture have really . . . [got to think about that]. That's something that somebody needs to put in their head, you know, think about some of these things. We should all sit down and think about . . . where our initial experiences with literacy or education were."

Some readers or listeners will undoubtedly look at Cathy's story and be critical of the emphasis she places on what she can "do" to help her black students. Although it may be easy to criticize her, talking about racial issues is particularly challenging to white teachers, who often see themselves as cultureless beings whose duty is to be "color blind" (Frankenberg, 1993; King, 1991; Paley, 1979). Furthermore, it is important to consider what Cathy does with the narrative she has constructed and how, as a result of having and talking about this experience, she decided to continue exploring issues of race and racism in education.

CONTEXT 3: CATHY'S MIDTERM AND FINAL COURSE PROJECTS AND WHAT SHE LEARNED

For her class projects, Cathy interviewed three African American teachers (one man, two women) at her school and her principal, an African American man with a doctoral degree. In interviewing these educators, she developed a list of questions adapted from Ferdman (1990) to guide her interviews. She asked about the teachers' experiences in school, their socioeconomic class, and family beliefs about education, and how experiences and their views on race affected these teachers and their teaching. Some questions asked were:

- What messages did school communicate to you about your culture and its value?
- What relationship do you perceive between tasks assigned in school and cultural identity?
- How have your own educational experiences affected you as a teacher?
- What part does your race play in this, or does it play a part?

As she conducted these interviews, transcribed, analyzed, and wrote her report, Cathy directly engaged in an exploration of topics related to race, literacy, and schooling.

One of the most prominent themes in Cathy's paper is the idea that teachers can make a difference in the life of a child. She had asked the interviewees about their own educational experiences, and she shared several compelling stories that they told about teachers who had challenged and inspired them, as well as some stories about teachers who were unsupportive. All the interviewees felt that, in their role as black educators, they could talk to black children in particular ways that white teachers may not be able to do. William stated: "I can take a black kid aside and say, 'Look, you're going to have a lot of obstacles, and you can't fall into the stereotypical thing' " (Midterm, p. 7). Another teacher, Kim, observed that a black teacher can walk into a room and, initially, command respect based on his or her color. However, Kim noted that if the students figure out they can walk all over that teacher, they will.

Cathy also was impressed by the ways that the teachers talked about being fair, but not necessarily treating children the same. She wrote, "[The teachers interviewed] do not treat students differently because of race or ethnic background; rather, they treat all students fairly, but not alike. They pointed out that students have to be treated differently with respect to their individual differences as a person. A teacher must look at the whole package" (Midterm, p. 7). Cathy related several stories the teachers shared that demonstrated that they must consider how they respond to students and be careful to have the same expectations for all students. Cathy wrote: "Teachers expect more out of certain students than others, whether consciously or subconsciously" (Midterm, p. 6). In developing this theme, Cathy shared several stories, such as the one told by Doris about her meeting with another teacher, who was white, to discuss a black child who was sleeping during class.

> "I [Doris] told the teacher, 'You can't let her lay her head down in the class. If she's sleeping, how is she going to learn?' And the teacher said, 'I just feel so bad for her, because they're going through a lot and she doesn't have a father.' I said, 'Everyone has a father. Do you mean her father isn't on the scene?' She said, 'Yes, her father doesn't live with them, and she's so tired.' I said, 'So because you feel sorry for her, that means you don't feel she needs to learn? Put your feeling sorry away for this child. Your feeling sorry for this child can destroy her academically. You still need to demand things of her. This may be her only way out. She needs to get what she can get, so she can get out of here.' " (Final, p. 10)

Cathy was also interested in the history that Dr. Abel shared with her about his experiences. Because he was older than the teachers she had interviewed, he had attended segregated schools in the South. In contrast, two of the teachers attended schools in northern cities, and one in a southern, integrated school; though integrated, the student populations in these schools were predominantly African American. Interestingly, Dr. Abel was the only educator who felt that school had really directly shaped his identity. Although he noted the hardships, such as a lack of electricity, poor or nonexistent school materials, and the like, he also conveyed to Cathy how classes in schools he attended were "steeped in Negro history" and taught by black teachers. In her paper, Cathy also related several moving stories that Dr. Abel shared with her about his memories of living in the segregated South (Final, p. 9).

As Cathy talked with her African American colleagues and learned about them, she began to retell their stories in class discussions. As she shared their stories, the new voices and perspectives represented by her colleagues entered our classroom, enriching the discussions that took place. In Cathy's final class presentation, she shared a verbal snapshot of each teacher's beliefs and experiences, as conveyed through their stories. She used her analysis of the interviews and the stories to compose a list of suggestions that these experienced African American educators had for teachers. The form of her written report—case studies followed by an overarching analysis—and her suggestions are remarkably similar to those of Gloria Ladson-Billings in *The Dreamkeepers* (1994), a book that Cathy had not read. Written on a handout that Cathy shared with her classmates, the suggestions for teachers were as follows:

- Respect children for who they are as individuals, regardless of race or culture.
- Challenge *all* students, keeping in mind that many black children are not accustomed to being challenged in school.
- Learn more about the history of other cultures. Read *From Slavery to Freedom* (1994) by John Hope Franklin for accurate information on African Americans.
- Get to know each student as an individual. Become interested in what they [the students] do; attend their games, recitals, performances.
- "Connect" with every child daily. Some children get lost in the hustle and bustle of the day. Speak to each one [student] every day.
- Never give up on any student, no matter how strong the urge, and regardless of how unsupportive the parent is.

- Remember that each child is as precious to his or her parent as your child is (or would be) to you. Remind yourself of this when you are at the height of frustration.

CONTEXT 4: ONE YEAR LATER, CATHY LOOKS BACK AT HER NARRATIVE AND LEARNING

One year after the course was over, I interviewed Cathy to ask her to reflect back on her project, her learning in the course, and the story she had told about the "Black Child Placed in Crisis" conference. To begin the interview, I played Cathy's oral retelling of her story and asked her to comment on it. After listening to a tape recording of her retelling, Cathy shared several insights and changes she had made in her teaching. Based on advice she had received during an interview with her friend William, Cathy made a special effort to establish a relationship with one African American student, Siham, who was "giving me fits in class." William had shared with Cathy how important it was for him to "make a connection with every single one of his kids." Cathy took her student Siham to lunch and visited her several times at home. She explained, "I didn't necessarily use it because Siham was a black child, but because Siham was a needy child."

Fostering these connections with students is a critical aspect of relating to children and in developing a culturally relevant pedagogy. Cathy commented that maybe this was something the presenters had actually tried to share with her at the conference:

> "It could be that in this other one [presentation during the conference] that I went to when they were talking about hugging the crack addict, the mother, and all that kinda thing, maybe that is, is kind of like what my friend William was recommending that we do by making that connection with that child. Making home visits, reaching out, you know. And so I think that maybe, maybe, there was value here [at the conference], and maybe I wasn't seeing it. I just, I was just having a hard time getting through, and maybe that was, I don't know, maybe that was my own attitude. Maybe at that point, I was just miffed and I didn't wanta hear anything else, and I wasn't gonna let anything else reach me." (Interview, January 15, 1999)

Cathy also noted that maybe part of her resistance to the presenters was because "I didn't feel like they were talking to me" and "I didn't speak their language, so to speak." Awareness of this resistance, of not wanting to hear her African American colleagues, was not a part of Cathy's original written narrative or the oral retelling of it in the context of the course. She expressed dissatisfaction with the lack of answers she received, which, in turn, acted as a catalyst to push her to reach out to African American colleagues, and to listen and learn from them. Revisiting the narrative a year later allowed Cathy to identify her own resistance.

As Cathy revisited her story, she reflected on it in new ways, extending her own understanding by using the narrative as a tool. In many ways, revisiting her narrative was representative of interactions that Cathy and I shared during my class. Cathy was willing to use narrative as a tool—a mediational means (Vygotsky, 1978; Wertsch, 1991, 1998) through which she could construct and reflect on her own cultural perspectives. Within this conversation and the course, as a "more knowledgeable other," I assisted Cathy in her use of narrative as a tool by asking occasional questions, and facilitating her telling or retelling of the narrative. As her teacher, I also provided opportunities for her to engage in that exploration by asking her to share her story with peers, to revisit it, and allowed her to design course assignments directly related to the issues she had raised in this one particular narrative.

CONCLUSIONS

In Cathy's case, the written narrative acted as a talking point for discussing issues of race and success in schooling. However, it is critical to acknowledge that it is not simply the narrative that was important. The previous conversation on the night of the course when Cathy shared her narrative and readings supported the inquiry and reflection in which Cathy and the group engaged. Furthermore, although the group's engagement around issues of race may appear superficial, it was a catalyst in Cathy's pursuit of further exploration of the issues. Cathy's interactions both with her classmates and her African American colleagues scaffolded her exploration of racial issues and enabled her to move beyond where she had gone on her own. Through interactions with her classmates, Cathy began to analyze, interpret, and reinterpret her own narrative. The context in which Cathy shared her narrative, and the opportunities provided to retell and revisit, were critical in Cathy's developing awareness of her position as a white teacher. Cathy's pursuit of the stories of African American educators in her midterm and final project extended this exploration beyond the discussions and readings of the course to further explore the question: What does it mean to be a white teacher working with students from linguistically and culturally diverse backgrounds?"

In her final course reflection, Cathy stated that she had "redefined literacy." Whereas she had once viewed literacy as activities of reading, writing, listening, and speaking, she now included culture. She wrote, "I now know that culture is not simply race." Cathy had begun to recognize that a culturally relevant pedagogy involves more than treating all children equally, or as if they are one color. It involved understanding her own cultural and literate practices and those of her students. Although there is still much to learn, Cathy has taken a critical step toward developing a culturally relevant pedagogy in her awareness that race is not the same as culture. Ladson-Billings (1994) has noted one barrier for teachers in developing such a stance: "While it is realized that African Americans make up a distinct *racial* group, the acknowledgment that this racial group has a distinct *culture* is still not recognized. It is presumed that African American children are exactly like White children but just need a little extra help" (p. 9, original emphasis). Cathy stated in her final project that race is not the significant factor in determining a child's success in school. Rather, she wrote, "There is often no relationship between tasks assigned in school and a child's cultural identity," and that teachers must begin to think about these issues. She had begun to take to heart what Cazden and Mehan (1989) admonished teachers to do: "Instead of blaming school failure on student characteristics that the school cannot change, teachers should reconsider aspects of the classroom environment that are within their control" (p. 50).

Narrative can be a powerful tool for teachers such as Cathy to explore questions and concerns they have about issues of diversity and literacy instruction. In telling and hearing stories, teachers are invited to encounter, consider, and transform their beliefs about self and other. However, as with any source of potential learning, the possibility exists that teachers may not use narrative as a tool for transformation. The tool may, in fact, be used to reify their existing beliefs and practices rather than to encourage transformation. Cathy made the choice to continue to explore issues that remain unresolved in her narrative. Thus, her reflection on the narrative, and the narrative's function, as a mediational tool for exploring issues of culture and literacy extends far beyond her construction and interaction around the narrative on this one night of class. Cathy's narrative, the conversation she has with her peers in class, the reading of multicultural literature and research on literacy and culture, and the narratives shared by the African American colleagues she interviews help her create a text through which she explores difficult and controversial issues. This text is a construction zone in which narrative functions as part of the scaffolding in Cathy's examination of beliefs about culture, self and other, and literacy instruction.

Narrative holds forth the potential for Cathy and other white teachers to create alternative texts that explore issues related to culture, self, other, and literacy learning. Such alternative texts can push white teachers toward transformative literacy practices that "force us to confront worlds other than our own, to see ourselves and those we are close to in the stories of others, to address injustices, and to find ourselves changed" (Witherell, 1995, p. 47). Cathy has not yet arrived at the place she has envisioned or enacted the types of transformative pedagogy that Ladson-Billings (1994), Witherell (1995), or other multicultural theorists (e.g., Banks, 1996; Sleeter & Grant, 1999) have advocated. However, it is clear that she has undertaken, and continues to undertake, a journey toward developing a pedagogy that will enable her to teach "other people's children" in ways that "capitalize on students' individual, group and cultural differences" (Ladson-Billings, 1994, p. 11).

REFERENCES

Abt-Perkins, D., & Gomez, M. L. (1993). A good place to begin—examining our personal perspectives. *Language Arts, 70,* 193–202.

Angelou, M. (1970). *I know why the caged bird sings.* New York: Random House.

Banks, J. (Ed.). (1996). *Multicultural education, transformation, knowledge, and action: Historical and contemporary perspectives.* New York: Teachers College Press.

Cazden, C. B., & Mehan, H. (1989). Principles from sociology and anthropology: Context, code, classroom, and culture. In C. Reynolds (Ed.), *Knowledge base for the beginning teacher* (pp. 47–57). Elmsford, NY: Pergamon Press.

Cochran-Smith, M. (1995). Color blindness and basket making are not the answers: Confronting the dilemmas of race, culture, and language diversity in teacher education. *American Educational Research Journal, 32,* 493–522.

Connelly, F. M., & Clandinin, D. J. (1990). Stories of experience and narrative inquiry. *Educational Researcher, 19,* 2–14.

Conway, J. K. (1989). *The road from Coorain.* New York: Knopf.

Darling-Hammond, L., & Sclan, E. M. (1996). Who teaches and why: Dilemmas of building a profession for the twenty-first century schools. In J. Sikula, T. J. Buttery, & E. Guyton (Eds.), *Handbook of research on teacher education* (pp. 67–101). New York: Simon & Schuster/Macmillan.

Dasenbrock, R. W. (1992). Teaching and multicultural literature. In J. Trimmer & T. Warnock (Eds.), *Understanding others: Cultural and cross-cultural studies and the teaching of literature* (pp. 35–46). Urbana, IL: National Council of Teachers of English.

Delpit, L. (1995). *Other people's children: Cultural conflict in the classroom.* New York: New Press.

Delpit, L. (1988). The silenced dialogue: Power and pedagogy in educating other people's children. *Harvard Educational Review, 58,* 280–298.

Edison Project. (1998). *School design highlights* [Brochure]. New York: Author.

Ferdman, B. M. (1990). Literacy and cultural identity. *Harvard Educational Review, 60*(2), 181–203.

Florio-Ruane, S. (2001). *Teacher education and the cultural imagination.* Mahwah, NJ: Erlbaum.

Florio-Ruane, S., Raphael, T., Glazier, J., McVee, M., & Wallace, S. (1997). Discovering culture in discussion of autobiographical literature: Transforming the education of literacy teachers. In C. K. Kinzer, K. A. Hinchman, & D. J. Leu (Eds.), *Inquiries in literacy theory and practice, 46th yearbook of the National Reading Association* (pp. 452–464). Charleston, SC: National Reading Conference.

Frankenberg, R. (1993). *White women, race matters: The social construction of whiteness.* Minneapolis: University of Minnesota Press.

Franklin, J. H. (1994). *From slavery to freedom* (7th ed.). New York: Knopf.

Gavelek, J. R., & Raphael, T. E. (1996). Changing talk about text: New roles for teachers and students. *Language Arts, 73*(3), 182–192.

Glazier, J., McVee, M., Wallace, S., Shellhorn, B., Florio-Ruane, S., & Raphael, T. (2000). Teacher learning in response to autobiographical literature. In N. J. Karolides (Ed.), *Reader response in the classroom* (2nd ed., pp. 287–310). Mahwah, NJ: Erlbaum.

Hoffman, E. (1990). *Lost in translation: A life in a new language.* New York: Penguin.

King, J. E. (1991). Dysconscious racism: Ideology, identity, and the miseducation of teachers. *Journal of Negro Education, 60,* 133–146.

Labov, W. (1972). *Language in the inner city.* Philadelphia: University of Pennsylvania Press.

Labov, W., & Waletzky, J. (1967). Narrative analysis: Oral versions of personal experience. In J. Helm (Ed.), *Essays on the verbal and visual arts* (pp. 12–44). Seattle: University of Washington Press.

Ladson-Billings, G. (1994). *The dreamkeepers: Successful teachers of African American children.* San Francisco: Jossey-Bass.

McVee, M. B. (1999). *Narrative and the exploration of culture, self, and other in teachers' book club discussion groups.* Unpublished doctoral dissertation, Michigan State University, East Lansing.

Ogbu, J. U. (1992). Understanding cultural diversity and learning. *Educational Researcher, 21,* 5–14.

Paley, V. (1979). *White teacher.* Cambridge, MA: Harvard University Press.

Polanyi, L. (1985). *Telling the American story: A structural and cultural analysis of conversational storytelling.* Norwood, NJ: Ablex.

Reissman, C. K. (1993). *Narrative analysis.* Newbury Park, CA: Sage.

Rodriguez, R. (1982). *Hunger of memory: The education of Richard Rodriquez: An autobiography.* Boston: Godine.

Sleeter, C. E., & Grant, C. A. (1999). *Making choices for multicultural education: Five approaches to race, class, and gender* (3rd ed.). Upper Saddle River, NJ: Merrill.

Soliday, M. (1994). Translating self and difference through literacy narratives. *College English, 56*(5), 3–18.

Tan, A. (1991). *The kitchen god's wife*. New York: Putnam.

Vygotsky, L. S. (1978). *Mind in society*. Cambridge, MA: Harvard University Press.

Wertsch, J. V. (1991). *Voices of the mind: A sociocultural approach to mediated action*. Cambridge, MA: Harvard University Press.

Wertsch, J. V. (1998). *Mind as action*. New York: Oxford University Press.

Witherell, C. S., with Tran, H. T., & Othus, J. (1995). Narrative landscapes and the moral imagination: Taking the story to heart. In H. McEwan & K. Egan (Eds.), *Narrative in teaching, learning, and research* (pp. 39–49). New York: Teachers College Press.

Chapter 7

Teaching Language Arts from a Multicultural Perspective
A Junior High School Experience

ELAVIE NDURA

My experiences as a new teacher at Perdy Junior High School (fictitious name) in Arizona, rather than staff and student homogeneity, inspired my determination to teach language arts from a multicultural perspective. As soon as I joined the faculty at Perdy, I quickly realized my differences. I was one of only two faculty members with a doctoral degree. I was the only black person on the faculty. I was an immigrant who spoke English with an accent. My students also quickly realized that I was different. They flooded me with questions, such as "Do you live in a house or a hut?"; "What other languages do you speak?"; "Do you always sound like that, or do you practice everyday?"; "Why does your hair stay in the same place all the time?"; "Why are your hands white on the inside?"; "How can you teach English if you can't speak it?"; "Are you Christian?"; "You are a doctor? So, why do you teach junior high school?" I also quickly learned that my students did not know what to expect of me, a teacher who looked and sounded different. One day, as I presented my accelerated English students with an elaborate plan of how my new classroom management and discipline plan was going to benefit the whole class, without using any punitive strategies, one student asked, "Did you come up with that on your own?"

I soon became aware that my different racial and ethnic background was not a particularly welcome feature in my classrooms. During my first semester, I recorded two direct white supremacist messages written by students. The messages read, "Send all F——ing blacks back to Africa. White power. Long live Hitler." During my third year, I reported to work on a beautiful Monday morning to find my portable classroom door and front wall spray-painted with similar white supremacist messages. Over the 4 years I taught at Perdy, I received several parent messages and complaints indicating that my national origin was not a particularly welcome attribute. On one occasion, I issued a 30-minute detention to a student who repeatedly called the work we were doing in class "stupid" and resisted my efforts to get him productively and positively involved in the lesson. His mother strongly objected to the detention and said, "Here in America, calling a teacher 'stupid' is not a big deal." On yet another occasion, I had a student call her parents to inform them that she had spent a whole class period talking instead of completing her work. When her father called me, supposedly to discuss the incident, his first question to me was "Before we talk about what happened today, where do you come from?" I responded by asking him what my national origin had to do with the incident. He replied, "Maybe that is how you treat children where you come from."

My experiences as a new teacher in the classroom culture just described motivated me to teach from a multicultural perspective to foster positive inquiry and understanding among my students. My first step in the process was to examine the language arts curriculum and figure out ways of presenting content and materials that would open my students' minds and engage them in the discovery and exploration of human and cultural diversity in a constructive manner. I wanted to work within a transformative paradigm not only to empower my students to critically understand the world's realities in a holistic framework, but also to move them and myself to act toward a more accepting, peaceful, just, and liberating world (Toh, 1993, cited in Calder, 2000). This was my responsibility, as a teacher. As Myers and Boothe (2000) argue, today's middle graders must be prepared for life in a multicultural society, because the world is changing. Educators at all levels and in all content areas must recognize their responsibility to teach with a multicultural and multiethnic perspective.

WHAT DOES TEACHING FROM A MULTICULTURAL PERSPECTIVE ENTAIL?

Teaching from a multicultural perspective entails several elements of instruction—not in a linear fashion necessarily, but in ways that are interwoven and overlapping, reflecting an attitude as much as materials and activities. It is moving instruction beyond the prescribed curriculum and involving students in real-life–like activities at the highest levels of critical thinking (Becker, 2000; Collins, 1993; Suhor, 1984; Tama, 1989). A multicultural perspective in teaching is about bringing humanity down to the classroom and recognizing that every kind of knowledge is relative. Teaching from a multicultural perspective is empowering students to examine critically and relate to real issues that affect them and their families every day, and to individually and collectively sort out ways to resolve those issues. Teaching from a multicultural perspective is to approach every unit of instruction with an open mind and a resolve to be true to oneself and to the realities of society.

A multicultural perspective begins with an understanding of the importance of the role that teachers play in shaping students' knowledge, self-concept, and worldview. Through the selection of teaching and learning materials, instructional strategies, classroom interactions, as well as interpretation of the official and hidden curriculum, teachers affect the students' knowledge construction process. They also affect the applications and implications of this process as students grapple with complex societal issues, such as diversity, educational equity, and social justice, as well as basic issues, such as individual differences and attitudes toward other people.

I was aware of the power I had, as a teacher, to impact my students' knowledge construction process when I accepted to teach seventh-grade English language arts in Samba, Arizona. This awareness had grown out of a close reexamination of my own schooling experiences in colonial Africa and my academic preparation in multicultural education. Thus, I understood the challenges and needs of students in today's schools, which are a mirror of an increasingly complex and interrelated world. I understood, as Calder (2000) argues, that students must be able to take a global perspective that challenges social injustice, poverty, and destruction in its many forms and complexities. I understood that the ability to think, feel, and act differently would significantly impact the quality of students' lives (Calder, 2000), and that teaching from a multicultural perspective can help to develop these skills.

Effective instruction from a multicultural perspective requires teachers constantly and creatively to balance their knowledge and understanding of the curriculum and of the cultural environment in which their students are reared. Effective instruction also requires teachers to think beyond short-term objectives to design meaningful and relevant lessons that can positively impact their students' lives. It must be planned and implemented from a multicultural perspective. In this chapter, I discuss the implementation of one lesson within the seventh-grade language arts curriculum at Perdy Junior High School. It focuses on how my students and I analyzed Nicholasa Mohr's "Princess" (1993) to sort out and think through problems with stereotypes.

PERDY JUNIOR HIGH SCHOOL

I had just completed my second year of teaching eighth-grade English language arts and French at Perdy Junior High School, when the principal asked me to join the seventh-grade team the following year. I was excited by the prospects of having one course preparation instead of three but quite perplexed about teaching seventh graders for the first time in my career. I had learned a lot about the school and community dynamics during my first 2 years and felt somewhat comfortable to make and alter instructional decisions.

Perdy Junior High School is one of 13 junior high schools (grades 7–9) in Samba Public Schools (SPS) in Arizona. According to the district's published figures, it houses 1,870 students, more than any other junior high school in the district. The student population at Perdy Junior High School comprises 86% European Americans, 8% Hispanics, 3% African Americans, 2% Asian Americans, and 1% Native Americans. Eighty-five percent of Perdy students live in single-family homes (as opposed to apartments), and 20% live in families headed by single parents. Ninety-eight percent of the Perdy students speak English as their primary language. I taught five seventh-grade classes every day. Each class averaged between 27 and 30 students, representing boys and girls in almost equal numbers.

Perdy opened its doors in fall 1989, and serves the mostly middle- to upper-middle-class families who have populated the new housing developments in northeast Samba for the past 15 years. Overcrowding has pushed many classes into portables located at the back of the main building. The school's A+ banner is proudly displayed in the front entrance glass window to remind both residents and visitors of the school's mission of and dedication to academic excellence. The school employs a mostly white, middle-class faculty.

THE ANTHOLOGY

The main textbook adopted by SPS to fulfill the seventh-grade language arts requirements was *Elements of Literature: Annotated Teacher's Edition First Course* (Anderson et al., 1993), an integrated literature anthology published by Holt, Rinehart and Winston. It is organized around "motif" and genre, but also presents an optional thematic framework, as well as a multicultural connections option. The anthology demonstrates the publisher's great effort to diversify the content and sources of the materials therein. The reading selections are representative of multicultural voices, with writers and experiences from a variety of cultural backgrounds. Together with the mainstream voices of Mark Twain and Ernest Hemingway, the anthology includes, for instance, the Mexican American voice of Sandra Cisneros, the African American voice of Mildred D. Taylor, the Puerto Rican voice of Nicholasa Mohr, the British voice of Rudyard Kipling, and the Jewish voice of Isaac Bashevis Singer. Most of the tasks throughout the anthology require students to identify facts from the readings, to interpret meanings, and to compose creative and critical written responses to selected parts of the readings. The anthology does not, however, challenge the students to identify, analyze, and confront the complex social realities that are uncovered by those representative multicultural voices. For example, "Brian's Song," the saga of white football player Brian Piccolo and his teammate, African American Gale Sayers, is presented as a simple literary play, with no deep societal ramifications.

My main goal was to establish connections between the curriculum and real-life experiences to enable students to reflect on and evaluate critically their acquired knowledge and its impact on their individual and collective attitudes and dispositions. I wanted to teach from a multicultural perspective, and to do so, I had to pay attention to and incorporate the four elements that Ramsey (2000) suggests are required in teaching from a multicultural perspective: (1) incorporation of students' experiences, (2) attention to the learning process, (3) recognition of how culture is reproduced in the classroom, and (4) creative use of conflict as a basis for change.

"PRINCESS": THE STORY

"Princess" is taken from *El Bronx Remembered*, a book by Nicholasa Mohr. The author was born in New York City, is of Puerto Rican descent, and writes stories and novels that take place in her old neighborhoods. Mohr has won several awards for her books.

The story's setting is the Bronx, New York City. The characters are of Hispanic background. A brief overview of the story assists in setting the context. Mrs. Morales moved to the neighborhood with her four children 3 years earlier, after her husband died. The family is on public assistance and cannot make ends meet. To keep food on the table, Mrs. Morales has to buy groceries on credit from Osvaldo and Nereida

Negrón, who own a small grocery store in the same neighborhood. The Negróns have no children, but they have Princess, a little dog on whom they lavish all their affection. One evening as Mrs. Morales prepares to fix dinner for her family, she realizes that the can of beans she bought that afternoon from the Negróns' store is spoiled. She tries to return it in exchange for a fresher can, but the Negróns insist that nothing is wrong with the beans. Exasperated, Mrs. Morales suggests they feed the beans to Princess to prove that the can is fresh. The Negróns agree, and Princess eats the beans. She dies early the next day. The Negróns blame Mrs. Morales and her family for Princess's death. Osvaldo calls Mrs. Morales and loudly accuses her of killing the dog. A heated argument ensues. He requires Mrs. Morales to pay her bill by the end of the week and refuses her any future credit. Mrs. Morales finds another grocery store, farther away, that sells to credit customers. There are no more contacts between the Morales and the Negrón families.

"PRINCESS" AS PRESENTED IN THE ANTHOLOGY

Many educators argue that there are no neutral educational programs or systems (Freire, 1993; Giroux, 1998; McLaren, 1998; Shaull, 1993). Every lesson is a value-laden statement. Literature, and literature-based instruction, is a powerful transmitter of societal overt and hidden messages about people, their environment, and their values and expectations. The lesson, as presented in the anthology, exposes students to a complex web of human relationships defined by who has what, a web that flirts with poverty, single parenthood, socioeconomic status, and, to a certain degree, with race, ethnicity, and their effects on life in the United States.

Yet instead of encouraging students to recognize this complex web and attempt to untangle it, the story and lesson that follow direct them to an easier escape route: Princess, the pet. Students are asked to discuss the role pets play in people's lives, to write a paragraph in which they try to persuade a person who does not have a pet to get one, and to find details that suggest Princess is treated like the child the Negróns never had. The interpretation of the characters and their actions, as constructed by the lesson, is removed from its societal context and confined to the incident described in the story. In other words, the lesson activities and tasks imply a focus limited to measurable, short-term objectives, such as to identify textual facts, interpret textual meanings, and respond to predetermined prompts or actions.

Every lesson has both short- and long-term objectives, whether stated or unstated. Short-term objectives help students pass the test.

They are measurable and, for the most part, non–life altering. Long-term objectives represent what students remember long after the course has been completed, and the test is irrelevant. They impact students' attitudes, self-concept, and worldview. They are for the most part immeasurable and, most of all, life altering. Therefore, when I designed the lesson based on "Princess," I asked myself one key question: What do I want my seventh graders to remember from the lesson 10 years from now? I wanted to design a lesson that had the potential to affect my students' dispositions and attitudes toward themselves and others.

"PRINCESS" PRESENTED FROM A MULTICULTURAL PERSPECTIVE

My main goal in redesigning the reading lesson was to empower my students to read critically and to recognize cultural biases that are often embedded in literature selections. Stereotyping was the bias of focus. The rationale for teaching the lesson from a multicultural perspective was that students were to develop skills that would enable them to detect stereotyping in any type of reading and in their daily social encounters. These skills would enable students to become critical readers, listeners, observers, and actors, capable not only of recognizing stereotypical information but also of countering the development and spread of stereotypes.

Three long-term objectives that would enhance students' critical literacy skills included: (1) developing an awareness of their own cultural stereotypes; (2) recognizing potential stereotypes by placing their interpretation of printed text within a societal context; and (3) developing constructive attitudes that could help to counter the creation and spread of similar cultural stereotypes in their everyday encounters. The prereading, reading, and postreading activities focused on stereotypes based on race, ethnicity, and family structure.

Prereading

After stating the objectives of the lesson, I asked, "What does stereotyping mean?" The students remained quiet, their eyes fixed on me with anticipation. "Raise your hand if you have never heard of the word *stereotype*," I probed. All hands went up. I displayed a transparency with the definition I had adapted from Sadker, Sadker, and Long (1997) and asked the students to write it down. "Stereotyping is showing or talking about a group of people as always doing the same things and behaving in the same way, and not seeing that members of a group are not necessarily all the same. For example, saying that all boys can fix cars or that all Mexicans drive low riders is stereotyping." I then asked the students to think about examples of stereotypes that they had heard at school and in the community and to share them with the class. I affirmed my commitment to opening up this discussion by stating, "It is OK to talk about them." A brief moment of tense silence followed. I probed some more. A few students started whispering to one another quietly when a shy and unsure hand went up. "Girls are dumb," Marcus said hesitantly. The whole class burst into loud laughter.

"That's a good example of stereotyping," I said. "Can somebody explain why it's a stereotype?"

"All girls are not dumb. Many girls are smarter than boys," Jessica responded. I knew the lesson was catching on. Many more examples of stereotypes followed.

"Teachers are mean," Paul ventured.

"That's a stereotype, because Dr. Ndura is nice," John retorted. Then, several students jumped in simultaneously to share experiences with teachers they thought were not nice to them. I had to refocus the class on the task at hand with my usual reaffirming statement. "It's easy to be nice to you," I said. "You are all special to me." They calmed down. Then, I prompted the students to think about racial and ethnic stereotypes. After some hesitation, several students shared the stereotypes that they had learned from their families, the media, and the community:

"Black people are good at sports."
"White people can't dance."
"Mexicans are in gangs."
"My grandma says blacks are lazy."
"Jews are rich. They have diamonds."

I allowed a minute or so for some pretty animated discussion among students to die down, then refocused the class. I explained how important it is to pay attention to and question information that we hear from various sources and read in print, because some of it may spread stereotypes about other people. The students defined and identified stereotypes. I moved to the next step to give the students an opportunity to apply what they had just learned in the prereading activity.

Reading

The objective of the reading activity was to help students recognize potential stereotypes by placing their interpretation of "Princess" within their societal context. After all the students had opened the anthology to the right page, I asked for their full attention: "I want you to read the story carefully and critically. As your read, I want you to find and write down examples of characters' behaviors and actions that are stereotypical, or that are potential sources of stereotypes. Focus on stereotypes based on race, ethnicity, and family structure."

The students were interested, almost excited. This was different. They were going to read, searching for information that was not written anywhere in the text. They immersed themselves in the reading. Even the occasional pen drop was unnoticed. I quietly and slowly strolled among the rows, occasionally glancing at the students' papers, only to see growing lists of things they believed to be stereotypical in the texts. Monica broke the silence, "Dr. Ndura, what is public assistance?" Addressing the whole class, I instructed, "Please stop reading for a moment and listen." Monica had just reminded me that most of the students were from rather comfortable middle- to upper-class families; therefore, the concept of public assistance was not meaningful to them. In the story, the Morales family had been on public assistance since almost immediately after Mr. Morales, the father, died (p. 30). The students paused and listened intently. I explained that public assistance is financial help that the government provides for some very poor families to pay for rent and food. The students resumed their reading and continued to search for examples of stereotypes.

After they completed the reading, the students, in groups of four, compared their notes. Then, I engaged them in a whole-class discussion. I wrote the examples of stereotypes on a transparency as they were shared. Our list included the following examples:

"Hispanics are poor."
"Hispanics don't have cars."
"Hispanic people eat beans and rice all the time."
"Hispanics argue loudly."

Then, I asked the students to think about Mrs. Morales and her family, and how they may be presented in a stereotypical manner. "Yeah, people could say that she is poor because she does not have a husband and her children have no dad," Mike suggested. The class nodded in agreement. Several more examples were added to the list of stereotypes:

"Single moms can't provide for their families."
"Hispanic women have a lot of kids."
"All Hispanic families are on public assistance."
"Hispanic women don't go to work."

We paused. I instructed the students to read over the list individually and quietly. We were ready for the third step.

Postreading

The goal of the postreading activities was to enable students to develop constructive attitudes that could help counter the creation and spread of stereotypes in their everyday encounters. I asked them to review and think about the stereotypes generated in the prereading and reading activities. "Why is stereotyping a problem?" I asked. I instructed the students to write down three problems caused by stereotyping. Then, they discussed those problems in groups. Once again, a class list was generated; it included the following:

"It's unfair."
"Stereotyping makes us not know people."
"It makes all people the same because of their race."
"Stereotyping spreads inaccurate information about people."

Next, I asked the students to discuss what they can do to stop stereotypes from developing and spreading. "Don't believe everything people say about other people," Dan said.

Isabelle added, "When your friends stereotype other people, tell them it's not right."

"We should look for stereotypes when we read and not believe them," Marcus said.

"Maybe try to know people individually," Monica suggested.

The students concluded the lesson with a closure that summarized their learning experiences. They had learned and understood the meaning of stereotyping. The students identified examples of stereotypes in their readings and, possibly, in their everyday social interactions with other people. Most importantly, they had begun to develop strategies that might help break the stereotyping cycle. Teaching the lesson from a multicultural perspective had been a successful attempt to empower students to interpret this piece of literature, and, I hope, other learning experiences, as well as information from various sources, with a critical and essentially multicultural perspective.

TEACHING FOR CHANGE: BEYOND TEXTBOOK PUBLISHERS' GOOD INTENTIONS

I learned several valuable lessons from my junior high school experiences as a language arts teacher. Teaching from a multicultural perspective, as demonstrated in the lesson I described, captivates and engages students. As Marlowe and Page (1999) explain, teaching from a multicultural perspective is liberating for teachers. Instead of focusing solely on what they will do to cover the curriculum, they focus on the ways they can help their students connect content to the most important factors in student learning—students' experiences and prior knowledge. This approach to instruction delivery involves students not just as active learners but also as active members of the community and society. It empowers them to question and challenge the stereotypes and other cultural biases that would otherwise be reinforced by the status quo. It teaches them to look at themselves as cultural human beings and to recognize their own cultural biases. Students do not resent such an opportunity. In my classroom, students welcomed it.

I learned that *Elements of Literature*, like many other language arts textbooks, demonstrates publishers' great intentions to present literature that is multicultural and inclusive. It is not enough, however, to feature selections depicting culturally diverse backgrounds, lifestyles, and ideologies, because there is always the hidden danger of creating stereotypes or perpetuating existing biases. This is especially true with works depicting people of color in the characters and experiences. As Dilg (1995) asserts, although the few students of color present in the classroom may identify with those characters and experiences, the very process of identification has its downside and its own set of psychological and pedagogical challenges that teachers cannot afford to ignore. Consequently, whereas the diversity of the materials must be appreciated, it is essential that they be used critically and creatively to achieve both the short- and long-term objectives that foster positive change, transformation, and lifelong learning experiences.

The case that Hirschfelder (1982) makes against Native American stereotyping applies to many different kinds of stereotypes. When students are exposed to stereotypical information, without any attempt to discredit it, they may grow up discriminating against those who are stereotyped, knowingly or unknowingly. Moreover, students who constantly see their people stereotyped in unfair ways may grow up feeling and acting as if they are not as good as other people. Had I not approached "Princess" from a multicultural perspective, most of my students in this mostly European American, middle-class school might probably have confirmed their stereotype of Hispanics as being poor, and eating beans and rice all the time. My few Mexican American students, on the other hand, might have retreated deeper into their shells, fighting painful feelings of shame and embarrassment. Dilg (1995) argues that when works depicting people of color are discussed in the classroom, students of color become representatives of the population group under discussion. She contends that this may generate awkwardness, embarrassment, or anger, because these students "may be linked by their classmates, however unfairly or unrealistically, with negative characters or characteristics depicted by the writers" (p. 20).

IMPLICATIONS FOR TEACHERS

Language arts teachers have the complex duty of teaching reading, writing, and grammar, as well as elevating the students' critical thinking skills and cultural awareness beyond publishers' grand intentions. They must enable students to become critical readers by encouraging them to activate and draw on their background knowledge; to question, confirm, and judge what they read throughout the reading process (Collins, 1993). Effective teachers assume two essential and complementary roles. They are both curriculum mediators and agents of social change. As curriculum mediators, teachers are responsible for planning and delivering instruction, as well as involving students in tasks in such a way that they meet the district and state requirements for academic success. As agents of social change, teachers must connect classroom learning experiences to the real world. They must prepare the students for something greater and more exacting than chapter quizzes and standardized testing. Effective teachers open their students' eyes to the school's hidden curriculum. They immerse students into the world of cultural diversity that may be unknown to the status quo, or known but silenced. Such teachers teach their students to wonder why, to question, and to challenge. They prepare them to participate in a democratic forum in which critical thinking is central to evaluating issues (Becker, 2000). Effective teachers teach students to become agents for social justice and change. Campbell (2000) contends that schools and teachers play an important role in preparing students for cultural pluralism. Becoming agents for social justice and change will enable students not only to value pluralism as an enriching characteristic of their country and the world, but also to promote mutual respect and understanding among people of diverse cultural backgrounds.

Teaching from a multicultural perspective means that teachers must be culturally aware. Cultural awareness enables teachers to encourage their students to examine the bases of their opinions, assumptions, and the cultural attitudes that shape their perspectives (Calder, 2000). By teaching about "Princess" from a multicultural perspective, I attempted to help my students realize that we are all influenced by somewhat ethnocentric misconceptions that portray members of other cultures according to stereotypes, rather than as the people they really are (Myers & Boothe, 2000). This was an important step in helping my students develop a macrocultural view of the world (Myers & Boothe, 2000), and a beginning step in developing the skills they need to recognize and dispel misrepresentations and unrealistic generalizations about people from different ethnic, socioeconomic, and cultural backgrounds.

REFERENCES

Anderson, R., Brinnin, J. M., Leggett, J., Hamilton, V., Leeming, D. A., & Shihab, N. (1993). *Elements of literature: Annotated teacher's edition, first course.* Austin, TX: Holt, Rinehart & Winston.

Becker, R. R. (2000). The critical role of students' questions in literacy development. *Educational Forum, 64*, 261–271.

Calder, M. (2000). A concern for justice: Teaching using a global perspective in the classroom. *Theory Into Practice, 39*, 81–87.

Campell, D. E. (2000). *Choosing democracy: A practical guide to multicultural education.* Upper Saddle River, NJ: Prentice-Hall.

Collins, N. D. (1993). *Teaching critical reading through literature.* Bloomington, IN: ERIC Clearinghouse on Reading, English, and Communication. (ERIC Document Reproduction Service No. ED 363 869)

Dilg, M. A. (1995, March). The opening of the American mind: Challenges in the cross-cultural teaching of literature. *English Journal*, pp. 18–25.

Freire, P. (1993). *Pedagogy of the oppressed.* New York: Continuum.

Giroux, H. A. (1988). *Teachers as intellectuals: Toward a critical pedagogy of learning.* Westport, CT: Bergin & Garvey.

Hirschfelder, A. (1982). *American Indian stereotypes in the world of children: A reader and bibliography.* Metuchen, NJ: Scarecrow Press.

Marlowe B. A., & Page, M. L. (1999). Making the most of the classroom mosaic: A constructivist perspective. *Multicultural Education, 6*, 19–21.

McLaren, P. (1998). *Life in schools: An introduction to critical pedagogy in the foundations of education.* New York: Longman.

Mohr, N. (1993). Princess. In R. Anderson, J. M. Brinnin, J. Leggett, V. Hamilton, D. A. Leeming, & N. Shihab, *Elements of literature: Annotated teacher's edition, first course* (pp. 28–38). Austin, TX: Holt, Rinehart & Winston.

Mohr, N. (1975). *El Bronx remembered: A novella and other stories.* New York: Harper & Row.

Myers, J., & Boothe, D. (2000). Cultural and language diversity in the middle grades. *Clearing House, 73*, 230–231.

Ramsey, M. (2000). Monocultural versus multicultural teaching: How to practice what we preach. *Journal of Humanistic Counseling, Education and Development, 38*, 170–183.

Sadker, M., Sadker, D., & Long, L. (1997). Gender and educational equity. In J. A. Banks & C. A. McGee Banks (Eds.), *Multicultural education: Issues and perspectives* (3rd ed., pp. 131–149). Boston: Allyn & Bacon.

Shaull, R. (1993). Foreword. In P. Freire (Ed.), *Pedagogy of the oppressed* (pp. 11–16). New York: Continuum.

Suhor, C. (1984). *Thinking skills in English and across the curriculum*. Urbana, IL: ERIC Clearinghouse on Reading and Communication Skills. (ERIC Document Reproduction Service No. ED 250 693)

Tama, M. C. (1989). *Critical thinking: Promoting it in the classroom*. Bloomington, IN: ERIC Clearinghouse on Reading and Communication Skills. (ERIC Document Reproduction Service No. ED 306 554)

Chapter 8

Listening to Inner-City Teachers of English Language Learners

Differentiating Literacy Instruction

LAURIE MacGILLIVRAY,
ROBERT RUEDA,
and ANA MARITZA MARTINEZ

> Today, a student from Chiapas arrived in my class with no paperwork. She was so soft-spoken that I needed her to speak word by word, so I could understand her. She is just one of three new students in my classroom in the last 2 months. So differentiating instruction for me is not about native English speakers and English language learners; it is about individuals, figuring out where they are, and teaching them to be successful and confident readers and writers.
> —A BILINGUAL THIRD-GRADE TEACHER

Too many students are not learning to be successful readers and writers. They are moving into the upper elementary grades as struggling readers. These difficulties in the area of reading and literacy become a burden that affects all of their academic learning. Children of color, children living in poverty, and/or those learning English are grossly overrepresented in the group of unsuccessful literacy students. Important research in the last 15 years can help teachers and principals better meet the needs of children often unintentionally neglected by traditional instruction. Differentiated instruction improves children's chances to become competent readers and writers. In this chapter, we briefly describe some of the considerations involved in making the types of accommodations that can positively impact children's future academic careers.

The basis of our recommendations is work in which we have examined literacy learning in inner-city Los Angeles for several years. Our research has been one of many studies conducted under the auspices of the nationally funded Center for the Improvement of Early Reading Achievement. Recently, we analyzed what we have learned from teachers about high-quality instruction for poor second-language learners. We preface the discussion with a short description of the notion of responsivity, which provides a key theoretical foundation, and underlies the specific practices and guidelines we present later.

VYGOTSKIAN NOTION OF RESPONSIVITY

Sociocultural theory, with roots in Vytogsky's sociocultural theory of mind, emphasizes the social and cultural basis of teaching, learning, and development (Tharp & Gallimore, 1988). In this view, teaching is seen as providing assistance (social mediation) to a learner at a level just above what the learner might accomplish independently. Good instruction that is responsive, then, falls in that space between what the learner can already do alone and what he or she can do with assistance. Teachers can flexibly draw on several means of assisting performance, including modeling, feedback, contingency management, instructing, questioning, cognitive structuring, or task structuring (Tharp, 1993); however, this assistance is always guided by the principle of responsivity. Instruction that ignores what students already know or can do, or that is too difficult, does not represent effective (i.e., responsive) pedagogy. It is therefore important to understand and respond to what children know, and to recognize the knowledge they bring to the classroom. This is especially important given the differences in both the types and the quantity of past mediation that children from different groups have received. It is also important to ensure that simple factors such as language differences do not make instruction inappropriately difficult.

RESEARCH CONTEXT FOR THIS CHAPTER

This chapter is the result of our desire to articulate a bit of what we learned from Latina teachers in some of our recent work, particularly that based on three separate but related studies. These studies include an examination of Latina teachers' memories of learning to read and write, and how that relates to their current teaching practice; a study of the literacy dispositions of students in "high-risk" situations through an analysis of school and home environments; and a study of Latina paraeducators and teachers, and their use of their own cultural knowledge in the classroom.

In the first study (Aguilar, MacGillivray, & Walker, in press; Walker, MacGillivray, & Aguilar, 2001), the purpose was to relate Latina teachers' memories of learning to read and write, the oral and written traditions in which they were raised, and how these related to their current teaching practices. We believed we could learn from them as models of success. The 17 participating teachers were immigrants or the children of immigrants, and taught at schools whose primary populations were Latino immigrants from Central America and Mexico. Most of the teachers were in their 20s and early 30s.

In the second study (Monzó & Rueda, 2001; Rueda, MacGillivray, Monzó, & Arzubiaga, 2001), over a 2-year period, we examined the characteristics of home and community contexts of 21 immigrant Latinos that produced engagement with literacy, as well as those that seemed to foster a value for schooling and literacy. We used a variety of qualitative and standardized measures, and observation methods to document the literacy resources that these children's homes and communities provided for them, as well as the values and beliefs embedded in the activities in which they engaged.

In the final study (Monzó & Rueda, 2003), we conducted a yearlong examination of a 2-year study examining the teaching interactions of 32 Latino paraeducators (eight of whom had gone on to become teachers) working with Latino students during literacy instruction. We conducted interviews and observations with the intent of documenting the participants' cultural knowledge and experiences, and the ways these were used during classroom activities.

DIFFERENTIATING INSTRUCTION

There are many ways to consider differentiating instruction for emergent readers and writers. We strongly believe that problems are situated within specific contexts, much more so than within specific individuals. Therefore, a single approach to varying instruction will not be appropriate for all schools, all teachers, or all children. A basic assumption is that responsive instruction, as defined above, cannot be packaged or scripted ahead of time. Educators must have a repertoire of strategies, so that they can vary their interactions and curricula as needed, but it must always be done with an eye toward students' current levels of understanding and performance.

One theorist whose work has grounded our thinking in this area is Vygotsky (1978, 1987), in particular, his notion of "responsivity." Vygotsky contended that participation in learning activities must be at a level that induces development. He defined this particular level of participation as falling within the learner's "zone of proximal development," the range between the level of difficulty at which individuals can perform independently and the highest level at which they can perform with assistance. Tharp and Gallimore (1988) point out that continuous assessment or monitoring of the learner's level of performance is essential to ensure providing assistance that is responsive to developmental needs. It is the close attention to moment-to-moment activities and responses that parents, often without conscious awareness, carry out with their own children. In essence, responsive instruction is, by definition, differentiated instruction. As the learner moves through the zone, assistance is transformed from interpsychological (from others) to intrapsychological (from self).

Vygotsky (1978) argued that language and writing are cultural tools that have developed through time and serve to mediate the higher mental functions of which only humans are capable. It is through these tools that a more competent other regulates the mental functions of the learner, such that the learner eventually internalizes the process of regulation, using it to guide his or her own mental functions. Expert teachers constantly ask themselves, "How can I get this learner (or group of learners) to the next level of competence or understanding?"

We describe five broad guidelines drawn from our research with teachers, examining the ways they have tried to incorporate the notion of responsivity into their own instructional practices.

Be Responsible for Knowing about Students' Lives

Teachers must learn about their children's lives beyond the school walls. This inquiry can be formal or informal. Teachers can systematically investigate families' worlds. In their work with Latino immigrant families, Moll and Whitmore (1993) used the term "funds of knowledge" to refer to the incredible wealth of typically untapped community wisdom. They involved classroom teachers in examining the highly developed information networks that enabled families to be successful in a variety of areas. The idea is not to re-create students' homes or home lives, but to draw strategically in a way that allows promotion of the teacher's academic goals.

The teachers we worked with used a variety of strategies to tap into this knowledge. Many of the immigrant parents were undocumented workers and feared deportation, so paperwork from the school was viewed as a threat. Even an assignment as seemingly innocuous as a home or parent survey can evoke negative reactions and can be a barrier successful home–school communication. But one teacher has found that her third graders enjoy interviewing their parents about issues such family hobbies and goals. This was her way to replace the traditional "parent survey." Because her students are involved, the process actually leads to building a community in her classroom as families share their results with each other.

Another teacher has invited parents to come to the classroom to share their professions or skills. This strategy is often talked about, but making the parents feel comfortable is critical to success. In this case, one mother brought the ingredients for *horchata*, a sweet, milky drink from Mexico made from rice, and made it with the children. Following the visit, the teacher built on the students' interest, and the class studied recipes students brought in and related them to different cultures and geographies. Other parents presented a variety of topics to the class. By the end of the year, more than 75% of the parents participated in sharing their own knowledge with the students. Although these families are often considered to live in such "at-risk" circumstances that they can contribute nothing meaningful to educational activities, there is often a wealth of knowledge that can be strategically appropriated.

We offer the example of food as a cultural bridge with slight hesitation, because it can so easily be seen as a capstone activity, an end of communication rather than merely a beginning. In his work with Latina paraeducators, Robert Rueda noticed a continuum of cultural interactions (see Figure 8.1). The left end of the continuum is exactly what we are warning against, but the other end of the continuum lies what is most valuable: use of everyday knowledge to further complex learning that encourages a deeper understanding of ourselves and others. So it is not the activity itself, such as sharing food from various cultures, but what comes out of the activity that is valued. The point we want to emphasize is that *appreciating* the cultural knowledge and resources that families and communities bring to school is not the same as *appropriating* those resources for important educational goals and for furthering intellectual development.

Getting out into the community is also a way to develop a better understanding of students' lives. Walking students home, or other impromptu acts, offers insight into children's lives beyond the schoolyard (Orellana & Hernandez, 1999). Teachers and administrators can go for a "print walk" around the neighborhood, noting the types of public messages (from business signs to graffiti), the languages utilized, and the purposes of the text. Rather than asking direct questions about the print,

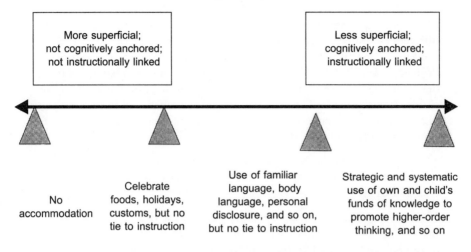

FIGURE 8.1. A continuum of sociocultural scaffolding in instructional settings.

Orellana and Herenandez found that talking with students about their community in general was most beneficial. The students' were interested in the names of their streets, familiar shops, parents' workplaces, and commercial items that targeted them (such as video posters). Surprisingly, they did not engage with most environmental print. Teachers we worked with have also sent home cameras, asking children to take pictures of things they cared about, and then used the photos as points of departure for discussions and writing. These finding suggest the need to put our adult assumptions aside, if we want to learn about children's literacy lives. All of these students live in literate environments, but they do not always easily map onto school activities and curricula.

Expect the Most: Avoid a Deficit Model

It is important that we do not confuse differentiating instruction with lowering expectations. All too often, this is the case, even with well-intentioned teachers. Allington (1983) captured this in a study on the way teachers' lead leveled reading groups. He found that students in the lower-level groups focused less on meaning than the high-level group, and spent more time focused on phonemes. Frequently, with second-language learners, English oral proficiency is confounded with cognitive competence. Similarly, children with different ways of experiencing narrative (such as storytelling) are regularly assumed to lack intelligence.

There is a significant history of attributing diverse childrens' language differences, especially oral English-language differences, to deficits in thinking, cognitive competence, motivation, family values, and so on (Valencia, 1997). Children need high expectations and challenges in order to thrive. It is the kind of experience often seen in classes for gifted children, but much less so in classes for students believed to be at risk for failure. Educators need to figure out what children know, and to use those strengths to move them forward.

Implement Curriculum That Is Meaningful to the Children

Most prepackaged curricula have been created with middle-class, native English speakers in mind. Many of the children that fall outside this group feel alienated when they cannot find images of their own lives and experiences in the curriculum. We must find ways to involve them and their worlds in the day-to-day activities of the classroom, especially those depicted in texts and other written materials.

One teacher with whom we recently worked in a study on reading engagement used issues in the children's lives as the foundation for literacy instruction. In one instance, it began with a conversation that occurred prior to an upcoming election, during a time when there was much public talk about bilingual education. One of the children, Gabriel (a pseudonym), started the conversation with a small group of peers, seemingly to make sense of what he had been hearing in the media and other places outside of school. He said, "On the TV [news] there was a teacher; he was saying to don't speak [sic] Spanish." He asked his teacher about this, trying to make sense of it, to get her answer. Reluctant to give her ideas, so as not to stifle meaningful discussion, she said, "Why don't you ask the children what they think." As was common in this class, she then modeled for Gabriel how to ask the children about their thoughts, and asked the class to think a minute about it. Then, the students began raising hands and offering their thoughts. She assisted Gabriel in facilitating the conversation. What ensued was a group conversation in which the children tried to imagine what the "con" side of the argument might be, as they understood it—why children should not be taught Spanish along with English in school—and discussing a situation in which they saw themselves as speaking two languages. This high-level discussion was strongly facilitated by the meaningfulness of the topic to the students and their families.

In their discussion, the students offered several situations in which they had to know two languages, including their experience that English was required in some stores, Spanish in others. They also discussed the need for English to speak with other urban residents, *los morenitos* (the African Americans). They ended the conversation with comments such as "Why would anyone not want to speak two languages?" and "When you can speak two, why settle for one?" Here, the teacher recognized a chance for the students' to grapple with the negative messages they were hearing around them and to situate the abstract messages in their concrete lives. She was able to promote oral language development, reasoning, analytical thinking, and weighing alternative viewpoints through the mediation she created.

In another instance during social studies, the teacher asked the children to create three-dimensional habitats. Many of the children talked about their overcrowded apartments and the homes they wished to have in the future. Through a variety of literature, such as "A House Is a House for Me," the teacher encouraged the children to think beyond a literal notion of a house as the current place where one lives. The students were encouraged to reflect, look toward the future, and imagine possibilities. As students talked about the difficulties of their present living conditions, many created habitats they would like for the future. And, as always, discussion included the education needed to buy a home. This teacher was able to appropriate the topic to illustrate the importance of school for future career opportunities. These kinds of activities legitimize the children's lives and concerns that are rarely represented in curriculum materials.

Recognize Knowledge of Two Languages and Cultures

Often, students labeled "low" or "struggling" in reading are using language in rich and complex ways outside of school. Specifically, many of these children act as "language brokers," a term coined by McQuillan and Tse (1995). Bilingual students in immigrant families often help monolingual family members interact with the English-dominant environment. This can mean explaining to salespeople what a parent wants, paying bills, and/or translating for doctors and teachers. Literacy brokers learn to be sensitive to cultural and contextual norms when moving between two languages.

Besides carrying the emotional, social, and often the economic burden of critical interactions, these young English language learners (ELLs) often figure out the difficult process of translation and frequently work with a wide variety of genres including bills, receipts, coupons, and legal documents. After spending time in bilingual children's homes and schools, Orellana, Reynolds, Dorner, and Meza (2003) recommended ways that teachers might facilitate literacy instruction in English. Rather than simply reading directions for assignments from worksheets, inviting students to co-create the meaning taps into the literacy and language that some of them use at home. They also suggest asking for texts from home. Using informational materials from the children's lives to study print features (ranging from letter sounds to audience and purpose) increases children's interest, offers a jumping off point for further reading and writing, and importantly, gives insight into the students' worlds.

Another benefit to recognizing children's linguistic backgrounds is a better understanding of students' writing and inventive spelling. Although teachers cannot be fluent in every language spoken in their classrooms, general knowledge about other languages can lead to informative analysis. In particular, creating an atmosphere of acceptance and value for students' primary language and culture is critical. For example, a rudimentary knowledge of Spanish gives teachers specific knowledge of why some students may be using some spelling patterns, such as *ll* for a |y| sound or *b* for a |v| sound. Remembering to reflect on the deeper reasons students may be writing or spelling in a certain way can inform differentiated instruction.

One teacher remembers learning facts in school in El Salvador and having those facts drilled into her. When she has talked with other immigrants, many have shared the same memories. When she arrived in the United States at the age of 9 and was asked to write a story using her imagination, she felt paralyzed. She wondered, "How can I lie?" Now, she realizes that no one had spoken to her about genres. This awareness has led her to integrate genre studies into her language arts program. She knows that for some students, fiction writing is an alien process. Becoming aware of how interwoven cultural beliefs/experiences are with the acts of reading and writing is the first step to a better understanding of the individual processes of our students.

Be Aware of the Default Curriculum: Content and Structure

Some classroom routines and topics are viewed by many as "givens." One very common structural pattern of classroom interactions is teacher–lecture, teacher–question, followed by teacher–conclusion. In these interactional settings, the teacher decides what will be covered and how, and students respond within a narrow band of responses. These types of interactional structures are characterized by a small ratio of student talk compared to that of the teacher. Teachers we worked with remember hating this structure, but many are reproducing it in their own classrooms. This default curriculum is what new teachers see practiced in their schools and represented in most curriculum guides. For many teachers with whom we worked, it was their dominant schooling experience.

Just as there is a default interactional structure, similarly, there is default content. For example, in Los Angeles, many elementary classrooms spend some time focusing on the four seasons. But it is rare to find a tree with orange and yellow leaves in the fall; we only see snow on the peaks of mountains, and the rainy season does not fit neatly into fall, spring, summer, or winter. Holidays can also serve to provide default content as teachers move to become more "culturally sensitive." Many continue to add activities and books void of connections to students' lives. In other words, making a *dradil* every year for Passover is another example of default curriculum. As teachers and principals, we must question and reflect on our curriculum in a responsive fashion, that is, with an eye to the specific learners who will be expected to engage with it. We need the structure and content to work for our students. Also, we need to remember to communicate the reasons for our practices to both our students and their parents.

LOOKING BEYOND READING INSTRUCTION

Differentiating instruction can improve the chances for all children to be successful. But there are some larger societal issues that need to be a part of the conversation. Teachers and principals need society's support. Some overarching factors significantly mediate the impact of instructional accommodations.

Poverty

Edmund W. Gordon, the first director of Head Start, stated, "I think schools can be much more powerful, but I don't think they can reverse all the ill effects of a starkly disadvantaged status in society" (as quoted in Traub, 2000, p. 54). The inequities of our society and the pervasiveness of poverty are recognized in many ways in the mass media. Yet schools are often expected to balance out all inequities. As Traub (2000) wrote in a *New York Times* article, "The idea that school, by itself, cannot cure poverty is hardly astonishing, but it is amazing how much of our political discourse is implicitly predicated on the notion that it can" (p. 52). Although poverty, ethnicity, race, and culture are often used interchangeably, they have complex interrelationships and impact educational outcomes both independently as well as interactively.

In January 2002, President Bush signed into law the No Child Left Behind Bill of 2001 (NCLB). It radically changed the 1965 Elementary and Secondary Education Act (ESEA). The government publicized this act as moving a large amount of money and decision-making powers into the states' hands. With its emphasis on accountability and prescribed teaching methods, NCLB impacts the lives of teachers of English as a second language (ESL) learners. There has been increased attention to preparing students for standardized tests. Prescribed teaching methods often are not sensitive to ESL learners. Although in 2002, $665 million was provided for research on how English learners acquire language skills, many are currently struggling in programs created for English speakers. Importantly, the independent, as well as interrelated, effects of language status and socioeconomic status are not clearly delineated. For example, some students come to school with background knowledge that does not map directly onto school-based texts or literacy activities. But is it a function of poverty that impacts opportunity to learn, or language-based issues, that get in the way of comprehension? Or even cultural factors that impact the out-of-school experiences, beliefs, attitudes, and understandings (about things such as the meaning of schooling)? The answers to these questions suggest quite different ways to address these issues in school, but they are not addressed in current policy and legislation.

As educators, we need to fight both outside and inside the school walls to increase chances of success for children living in poverty. Learning about the economic realities of our children's parents and community issues can enable us to see the complexity between economic opportunities and poverty.

Anti-Immigrant Sentiment and Antibilingualism

Recently there has been both an increase in anti-immigrant sentiment and a move to discourage bilingualism (Valdéz, 1997). One way to examine this issue is to consider the recent initiatives put before Californians and other voters. California seems to be leading a trend that is moving across the country. Arizona, Colorado, and Massachusetts are wrestling with similar bilingual issues.

Proposition 187, which focused on illegal immigrants in 1994, was the first major initiative that caught voters' attention. It made illegal aliens ineligible for public social services, public health care services (unless an emergency, according to federal law), and public school education at elementary, secondary, and postsecondary levels. Various state and local agencies, including schools and specifically teachers, were required to report those suspected of being in the country illegally. The measure was described in the official ballot argument as "the first giant stride in ultimately ending the ILLEGAL ALIEN invasion."

Although the previous proposition was found to be unconstitutional in the courts, 2 years later, Proposition 209 was passed in California. Commonly known as the Anti-Affirmative Action Proposition, among other things, it stopped "the state, local governments, districts, public universities, colleges, and schools from discriminating against or giving preferential treatment to any individual or group in public employment, public education, or public contracting on the basis of race, sex, color, ethnicity, or national origin."

Perhaps the most controversial initiative of all was Proposition 227, commonly known as the Anti-Bilingual Initiative. On June 2, 1998, California voters overwhelmingly approved Proposition 227, an initiative that largely eliminates bilingual education from the state's public schools. Under the California initiative, most limited-English-proficient students are now placed in English-immersion programs, then shifted as quickly as possible into regular classrooms.

Parents, students, and bilingual teachers talk about their feelings of shame even though they knew these propositions were wrong. One teacher vividly remembered an interaction that occurred after the passage of Proposition 227: "My neighbor said to me that it is criminal that our kids are getting Spanish and not getting prepared for junior high. I told her she could come to my class any time and observe during my English language development time."

These larger societal and institutional issues impede children's learning. The environment surrounding discussion of these issues in the media and elsewhere has a significant impact on what students internalize about their native languages and cultures, and their own identities. When students do not feel valued and are encouraged to disown parts of themselves, they are less likely to engage in school tasks.

Lack of Institutional Resources

Most of the schools serving poor children have fewer resources than those in middle- and upper-class neighborhoods (Smith, Constantino, & Krashen, 1996). Smith and colleagues (1996) found that in neighboring communities in Los Angeles, the two low-socioeconomic-scale communities had an average of 0.4 and 2.67 books in the home, compared to 199 for the upper-socioeconomic-scale community. In school, the differences were also vast -47 and 53 per classroom in the low SES community compared to 392 in the higher socioeconomic-scale classroom. We found this in our work. The most recent elementary school in which we conducted research on reading engagement did not have a library until last year. The school later received a library, because the principal obtained a grant. In one large elementary school with about 2,000 students, children in first grade are not able to check out books. In second and third grade, they are able to "check" them out to their classrooms but cannot take them home. The classes visit the library every 2 weeks; visits at other times are not encouraged.

Even though many children have strong family and community networks, and there are advantages to living downtown, the difficulties are numerous. Money for community and police-sponsored programs that once flourished in large cities has shrunk. Drug deals are common in the streets, and crime is high. Safe areas to play outside are almost nonexistent for children living in a downtown apartment, hotel, or shelter. Most importantly, many of the educational opportunities are expensive. We found that many families had not visited the nearby Children's Museum because of high admittance fees. Also, the library was often not used, because the parents were afraid of the fines attached to late, damaged, and lost books. Although these fees may seem miniscule to many middle-class families, they are significant obstacles to these families. Transportation to other areas of town is typically time-consuming and/or cost prohibitive.

There are solutions to these problems, but they need to be long-term and multifaceted. Many corporations are beginning to make positive differences in downtown living conditions. Primarily, this support has come through the schools in the community. Some companies actively encourage their employees to volunteer, as well as offer financial aid. Creating and supporting afterschool and weekend programs offers safe places for children. Another way to intervene is by becoming politically active. Neighborhood organizations, religious groups, and local teacher organizations tend to work on important community issues.

Environmental Hazards

Safety and health issues are rarely discussed problems that decrease children's chances for being successful literacy learners. In our conversations with teachers and their principals, we found they spent a great deal of time and energy fighting for the conditions that exist as a given in many suburban schools. For over a year, one teacher requested to have the vents cleaned in her bungalow because of health reports about the connection between the presence of microorganisms and cancer. Bungalows were also found to lack good circulation, because the only door in the room is closed (due to weather conditions or noise) and many do not have windows that open. Neither issue was addressed in the media until the issue was raised in suburban schools.

The classrooms in these same bungalows were also supposed to be vacuumed *once a month*, though, in many classrooms across the country, once a week is the norm. But even receiving this minimum service was a struggle for some. One teacher had to write several letters to the plant manager informing him that her classroom was not being vacuumed at all. She waited months for action. The plant manager did not report to the principal, so there was not an immediate supervisor on campus. These problems may arise in all school districts, but they are more numerous, and the resolutions seem to take longer, in crowded urban schools. Teachers are busy; having to fight for clean rooms is unacceptable. Students have the right to learn in clean schools.

In suburban schools, parents are more likely to intervene in these kinds of problems. Also, middle- and upper-class parents tend to know more about how to influence the system. For example, they know at what level to complain, who to write, and the tone and content that will most likely get a response. In turn, when parents get involved, problems begin to decrease, because the system wants to avoid the hassle of more complaints. For example, it is worth the effort to vacuum the classrooms every week, because if it does not happen, a parent *might* complain.

It is a mistake to think that most parents in the inner city are less involved in school because they do not care. Possible reasons for not engaging in parent organizations are the same as for parents living anywhere: busy schedules, long work hours, language issues, legal status, and previous negative experiences at school. But more than this, often, there is not a strong parent organization in place. It is easier to move to a new school and participate when there are a variety of ways to get involved: serving on committees, working at fund-raisers, donating services, running for office.

Some inner-city schools do have a high rate of parent involvement; often, it is because they have a strong group of parents with momentum behind them. Also administrators, teachers, and parents have thought more broadly about parent involvement, figuring out ways to invite those with diverse backgrounds and school experiences to participate in their child's learning. Active parent groups address health issues, lack of materials, and many of the other topics we address in this chapter. Inner-city teachers of literacy learners repeatedly refer to parents as a resource in diversifying instruction.

CONCLUSIONS

The teachers we know repeatedly talk about individual students and their relationships with them: Carlos, the second-generation Mexican American who idolizes his college-bound big brother and carries a book everywhere he goes; Lois, a wriggly second grader, who translates Korean into English for her grandparents and hates to write; and a recent immigrant, Maritza, who speaks an indigenous language of Guatemala and follows around *el maestro*. Members of the press write about children en masse, refer to their test scores as raising or falling, and estimate costs to the educational system. Occasionally there is a story about the way inner-city children are being "underserved." It has even become such a permanent problem that a population of our students are even being labeled "underserved," a tacit agreement that the situation will not be changed, at least not in their lifetime.

But the inner-city teachers we talked to are working every day to figure out the best instruction for each child in their class. They seek that special space between what the learner can already do alone and what can be done with assistance to offer responsive instruction. Ongoing education is critical to support teachers in continuing to develop a repertoire of strategies needed for differentiated instruction.

Improving the numbers of successful literacy learners requires actions by multiple groups: teachers and administrators, parents, academics, community leaders, and politicians. Differentiating instruction is not just the job of the teacher. As educators, we need simultaneously to look inward at classroom curriculum and outward at societal issues that impede our students' progress. Practicing the guidelines we have learned from teachers is difficult. Support networks of teachers and administrators are critical for rethinking our curriculum and our role in larger community issues to serve best the needs of inner-city, ESL learners.

ACKNOWLEDGMENTS

We gratefully acknowledge support from the Center for the Improvement of Early Reading Achievement (CIERA), under the Educational Research and Development Centers Program, PR/Award No. 305R70004, as administered by the Office of Educational Research and Improvement (OERI), U.S. Department of Education. However, the opinions and comments herein do not necessarily represent the positions or policies of the U.S. Department of Education, and endorsement by the Federal Government should not be assumed.

We thank the many teachers who have worked with us, sharing their minds and their classrooms.

REFERENCES

Aguilar, J. A., MacGillivray, L., & Walker, N. T. (in press). Latina educators and school discourse: Dealing with tension on the path to success. *Journal of Latinos and Education*.

Allington, R. (1983). The reading instruction provided readers of differing abilities. *Elementary School Journal, 83*, 548–559.

McQuillan, J., & Tse, L. (1995). Child language brokering in linguistic minority communities: Effects on cultural interaction, cognition, and literacy. *Language and Education, 9*, 195–215.

Moll, L. C., & Whitmore, K. F. (1993). Vygtotsky in classroom practice: Moving from indivudual transmission to social transaction. In E. Forman, N. Minick, & C. A. Stone (Eds.), *Contexts for learning: Sociocultural dynamics in children's development* (pp. 19–42). New York: Oxford University Press.

Monzó, L., & Rueda, R. (2001). *Constructing achievement orientations toward literacy: An analysis of sociocultural activity in Latino home and community contexts* (CIERA Report No. 1-011). Ann Arbor: Center for the Improvement of Early Reading Achievement, University of Michigan.

Monzó, L., & Rueda, R. (2003). Shaping education through diverse funds of knowledge: A look at one Latina paraeducator's lived experiences, beliefs, and teaching practice. *Anthropology and Education Quarterly.*

Monzó, L., & Rueda, R. (in press). Professional roles, caring, and scaffolds: Latino teachers' and paraeducators' interactions with Latino students. *American Journal of Education.*

Orellana, M. F., & Hernandez, A. (1999). Talking the walk: Children reading urban environmental print. *Reading Teacher, 52*, 612–619.

Orellana, M. F., Reynolds, J., Dorner, L., & Meza, M. (2003). In other words: Translating or "para-phrasing" as a family literacy practice in immigrant households. *Reading Research Quarterly, 38*, 12–34.

Rueda, R., MacGillivray, L., Monzó, L., & Arzubiaga, A. (2001). Engaged reading: A multi-level approach to considering sociocultural factors with diverse learners. In D. McInerny & S. Van Etten (Eds.), *Research on sociocultural influences on motivation and learning* (pp. 233–264). Greenwich, CT: Information Age Publishing.

Smith, C. R., Constantino, R., & Krashen, S. (1996). Differences in print environment for children in Beverly Hills, Compton, and Watts. *Emergency Librarian, 24*(4), 8–9.

Tharp, R. (1993). Institutional and social context of educational practice and reform. In E. A. Forman, N. Minnick, & C. A. Stone (Eds.), *Contexts for learning: Sociocultural dynamics in children's development* (pp. 269–282). New York: Oxford University Press.

Tharp, R., & Gallimore, R. (1988). *Rousing minds to life: Teaching, learning, and schooling in social context.* Cambridge, UK: Cambridge University Press.

Traub, J. (March 13, 2000). What no school can do. *New York Times Supplemental*, pp. 52–62.

Valdéz, G. (1997). Bilinguals and bilingualism: Language policy in an anti-immigrant age. *International Journal of the Sociology of Language, 127*, 25–50.

Valencia, R. R. (Ed.). (1997). *The evolution of deficit thinking: Educational thought and practice.* London: Falmer.

Vygotsky, L. S. (1978). *Mind in society: The development of higher psychological processes.* Cambridge, MA: Harvard University Press.

Vygotsky, L. S. (1987). *L. S. Vygotsky, Collected works: Vol. I* (R. Rieber & A. Carton, Eds.; N. Minick, Trans.). New York: Plenum Press. (Original work published 1934)

Walker, N. T., MacGillivray, L., & Aguilar, J. A. (2001). *Negotiating higher education: Latina teachers' memories of striving for success* (Research Report No. 3-010). Ann Arbor: Center for the Improvement of Early Reading Achievement, University of Michigan.

Part III

STUDENTS' VOICES ON ISSUES OF LITERACY LEARNING AND DIVERSITY

Chapter 9

In Retrospect

Learning to Learn from Adolescents' Reading Experiences

FENICE B. BOYD

> I really didn't think of anything except that it didn't make
> sense. It wasn't very thought out; I remember that Clogger
> [pseudonym] and I got together just before the presentation,
> and I remember that we were not in agreement. I was thinking
> of things that weren't exactly events in the story; where she
> [Clogger] would relate a theme to events in the story. . . . I was
> also thinking, the presentation sucked because maybe it was
> because I don't really like the themes we chose or I'm not sure.
> . . . The presentation wasn't all that lovely.
>   —LOVE'S RETROSPECTIVE CRITIQUE

The quoted statement was made during a postinterview I conducted with Love on October 5, 2000. Love (a pseudonym selected by the ninth-grade student) watched a video of herself and a classmate working in a small-group context. In the video, the girls were giving a required oral presentation on themes that had emerged from the novel *Shabanu* by Suzanne Fisher Staples (1989; see Table 9.1 for a description of the novel). Listening carefully to what Love said about the presentation, I realized that she was not happy with what or how she represented her knowledge and understanding of the story in the videotape. She said, "The presentation wasn't all that lovely."

I was present in the classroom when Love and Clogger gave their oral presentation on themes they discerned from *Shabanu*. In fact, I videotaped the presentation that Love critiqued. Because I closely ob-

TABLE 9.1. Overview of *Shabanu* by Suzanne Fisher Staples

Life is both sweet and cruel to strong-willed young Shabanu, whose home is the wind-swept Cholistan Desert of Pakistan. The second daughter in a family with no sons, she's been allowed freedoms forbidden to most Muslim girls. Yet her parents soon grow justifiably concerned that her independence and disinterest in "women's work" will lead to trouble.

As tradition dictates, Shabanu's father has arranged for her to be married in the coming year. Though this will mean an end to her liberty, Shabanu accepts it as her duty to her family. Then a tragic encounter with a wealthy and powerful landowner ruins the marriage plans of her older sister, and it is Shabanu who is called upon to sacrifice everything she's dreamed of. Should she do what is necessary to uphold her family's honor—or should she listen to the stirrings of her own heart?

Note. From the book's back cover.

served the body language and uncertainty in Love's voice during the presentation and in my ongoing analysis, I was motivated to learn more about what she thought about the presentation in which she participated. Therefore, I conducted a postinterview 1 year later. After reading and rereading comments in her postinterview, I had several questions:

- What happens when students are encouraged to reflect on their reading experiences of literary texts and instructional activities?
- What strategies might teachers use to learn more about what adolescents think during reading experiences?
- How might teachers use students' insights to inform their instructional practices and assessments?
- As students reveal their understanding (or lack thereof) of stories, how might teachers use that information better to enable adolescents to *read to learn*?

I draw on a literacy event that occurred during the teaching of a unit on various multicultural texts, and Love's retrospective critique of that event 1 year later, to explore tentative answers to my questions. My purpose is to encourage us, as educators, to listen to adolescent readers, so that we become better informed about assessing students' learning relative to reading experiences we structure within the lessons we choose to teach. State- and national-mandated assessments may provide information about students' basic content knowledge and skills. However, standardized examinations convey limited information regarding students' knowledge, skills, and dispositions about their reading experiences and comprehension beyond a literal level of understanding. What I propose here differs from formal (e.g., paper-and-pencil tests) and alternative written (e.g., portfolio) assessments. I am suggesting that when we, as educators, talk with students about their reading experiences in the lessons we structure for them, we gain insightful information that can inform instructional practices. But before I look in depth at what Love's insights might teach us, I explore ideas that many scholars have offered about attending to students' perceptions of their literacy learning experiences in classrooms. I discuss these insights relative to my work with Love.

OVERVIEW OF ADOLESCENTS' PERCEPTIONS OF LITERACY LEARNING

Adolescents bring funds of knowledge (Moll, Armanti, Neff, & Gonzalez, 1992) to literacy learning opportunities that enable them to be successful. Many educational reform movements reveal that educators need to acknowledge what students and teachers (see MacGillivray, Rueda, & Martinez, Chapter 8, this volume) know, and capitalize on their interests and needs to understand what they see as relevant in an ever-changing and evolving world. If educators are to capitalize on adolescents' "funds of knowledge" in a way that enriches their literacy learning experiences, then students need caring and flexible teachers who are mindful of how and when they support students. Such an exchange works both ways when teachers and students feel comfortable in taking risks, revealing what they do not know, as well as what they know and understand to be appropriate learning of content. When students assess their own literacy learning experiences, they can provide us with valuable information for both curriculum materials and instructional goals.

Relative to what you have read about Love thus far, you may have noticed that she engaged in a dialogue with me about what she remembered about the literacy event that occurred approximately 1 year earlier as she watched herself on video. Clearly, in reflecting on her role and responsibility for the presentation, Love remembered engaging in an inner dialogue about what she believed to be appropriate for the presentation. Her thoughts—both during and after the presentation—are not unlike the inner dialogue students have with themselves during reading; that is, as adolescents construct meanings, they move back and forth between reading, writing, speaking, listening, and thinking, to talk with themselves, and with their peers, about the texts they read and larger cultural texts. Larger cultural texts might relate to overarching themes and concepts such as family, survival, socioeconomic conditions, social justice, racism, and how students view their surroundings. The larger cultural texts underlying Love's comments refer to instructional decisions, quality time, and efforts made in executing an assignment. I return to this point later.

Whenever students delve into dialogue, the action implies reciprocity; the dynamic that exists results in transformation, or evolving reality. This is similar to the "poem" described by Rosenblatt (1978). The relegation of significance to the reader, however, only becomes meaningful when we recognize and understand what needs to occur for students to expand their inner dialogue, and to evolve and transform. Students' meaning construction entails comprehension of both texts and the requirements and expectations promoted by teachers. Teachers play a major role in guiding students' interpretations of texts. As noted by Enciso (1997), when teachers expect students to interact with texts and "tell their stories and 'talk back' to literature, we have to learn what constrains and what opens possibilities for such performances" (p. 38). How students develop literary understandings is significant; however, the personal and social connections students make to texts, the reading experiences they encounter, are equally significant. Scholars are challenging teachers to listen to students to better prepare them for literacy learning, and for responsible roles in society. For instance, Broughton and Fairbanks (2003) have recently studied the identity construction of adolescent females within the context of school literacy learning experiences. They state, "By listening to students, teachers can invite them to shape a curriculum suited to their needs and interests, acquire feedback about their literacy experiences, and foster agency through participation in curriculum building and self-exploration with spoken or written texts" (p. 433).

Students' voices and perceptions can provide teachers with valuable information for adaptations and adjustments in instructional decision making. Adolescents *are* participants in their own learning, whether we acknowledge it or not. Sometimes, classroom participation structures might be beneficial to students' learning and understanding. At other times, depending on how lessons are structured in classrooms, students might not acquire additional knowledge and understanding from the lessons in which they participate. When instructional practices are structured for students to learn content, all participants should be invested in what is being taught to maximize learning. However, students are not always invested in their own learning; rather, they may be invested in "getting the job done" (Bloome, 1986; Boyd, 2002). Teachers can encourage students to learn more actively by enabling them to critique themselves as learners, thus making some additional investments in what is learned and how.

SETTING THE CONTEXT TO EXPLORE LOVE'S LEARNING

As the morning bell rings, students saunter into Melissa's (Love's teacher) classroom and sit down. One can hear the locker doors banging loudly as other students rush into the room before the tardy bell rings. Some students look less than eager to be at school. Others, who rush anxiously to their seats, look forward to continuing the reading and discussions about the multicultural texts. Melissa rushes to make last-minute preparations as her students find places to sit at the U-shaped tables and chairs for the next 90-minute block of time in their daily school schedule. The U-shaped arrangement of the tables and chairs gives students an opportunity to look at the faces of 22 peers rather than at the backs of a limited number of heads. Likewise, the U-shaped arrangement allows Melissa to move easily around in a large, open space to speak to all of her students at once, or to come within close proximity to individual students. The space in Melissa's classroom is arranged ideally for developing a literacy learning community in which students have opportunities to interact and make eye contact with each other and with their teacher.

Typical days in Melissa's English language arts class consist of a grammar lesson or a grammar pretest. She informs students that they will not like the pretest, because it will make them feel "stupid," as if they do not know anything. On one such morning, Melissa spent approximately 35 minutes reviewing answers to a grammar pretest and reexplaining what had been previously taught to students. Whenever students gave the wrong answers to her questions, Melissa took several minutes to reteach what they did not know or understand. Other activities included vocabulary development strategies, silent reading, reading aloud, whole-class discussions, and small-group collaboration on culminating activities and projects.

During the 1999 and 2000 fall semesters, I conducted a 6-week research project in Melissa's classroom based on students' reading and responding to multicultural literature. Melissa was my graduate advisee when she studied for her master's degree at a large southeastern university. The research project was conducted at a midsize high school in a suburban community near a large metropolitan city in the southeastern United States (see Boyd, 2002, 2003, for a detailed explanation of the study).

Melissa and I planned a range of lessons and activities to enhance students' learning about multicultural literature. Here, I provide a general overview of the educative events that we planned for her students. Although presented here in a linear fashion, all activities were conducted more in a spiral fashion, winding from the beginning, which entailed a book talk of the multicultural texts, to the ending, which culminated in activities such as presentations of a body biography in PowerPoint. As students became more familiar and engaged in the reading, various activities and, thus, their literacy learning strengthened, intensified, and escalated to enhance their comprehension and perceptions of diverse people and places.

Here's how Melissa and I developed the unit in which Love and her classmates engaged. First, we selected a total of nine different books with different themes and issues. Students were grouped on the basis of the titles of books they chose to read. Second, we designed a variety of journal response themes and small-group projects. For journal responses, students were required to write 10 types of responses including, first impressions of the novel, story conflict, character analysis, background information about the country and culture, description of a setting within the story, a story map, theme(s), response to a related reading, vocabulary words, a cultural log, and an essay on themes, issues, or personal interests that emerged in the story. Third, in small-group formats, students were required to perform a "mini" research study on the country and culture in which the novel was based and develop a PowerPoint presentation. Melissa guided the students by giving them guidelines and suggestions for what to include in the PowerPoint slides. A few examples of what students might include entailed a description of the protagonist, conflict in the story, cultural artifacts, and a book review from students' points of view. Finally, they developed a body biography—a visual and written representation of a student-selected character in the story. Students received extensive guidelines for the body biography from Melissa and me. However, the minimum requirements included an overview of significant events in the novel, motifs significant to a character, original texts composed by the students (e.g., a poem), relevant characters and themes in the story, and three significant speech marks taken from the novel. Students presented their work both to their classmates and to a panel, explaining what they did and why.

Love and Her Perceptions on Reading

Love, a European American female, is a gifted student, reads every day, and is thoughtful in her reflections about her reading and learning experiences. She enjoys reading magazines such as *Teen*, *Seventeen*, *YM*, and *Reader's Digest*, and the local metropolitan newspaper and e-mail messages. Love is "fascinated" by World War II because of her interest in history, and how hatred and inequality, whether due to race or religious beliefs, can become so widespread that people have to endure consequences such as slavery and the Holocaust. She believes in equality for all people regardless of race, cultural background, religious beliefs, and gender.

Love's favorite genres include realistic fiction and Christian books, including *The Holy Bible*. She believes she is a good reader, and says she understands what she reads and has strong comprehension skills. Thus, characteristics of a good reader, according to Love, include possessing good comprehension skills, reading literature that challenges one's thinking and views about the world, having background knowledge of what one reads, reading often, and reading different types of texts. When reading literary texts, Love states that being interested in the lives of the characters motivates her to keep reading. Her best reading experience was when she read *A Tree Grows in Brooklyn* (Smith, 1943), because of the sheer pleasure of reading the novel, the historical nature of the text, and being able to ask her grandmother about events she did not understand.

In addition to her strengths, Love also acknowledges that she has weaknesses as a reader that include reading too fast, not reading different genres, and forming negative opinions about different types of texts before actually reading them. Reading too fast, to Love, means that sometimes, while reading, she does not comprehend or pay attention, because her mind wanders to other things. In forming negative opinions about different types of texts, for example, Love was not accustomed to reading multicultural literature written by and about people from diverse ethnic groups. Sometimes, she made it clear that she did not even want to read about people from diverse backgrounds. Knowing this about herself, she considered not reading widely about other people and cultures to be one of her weaknesses, because it limited her knowledge base and did not foster broader perspectives about society, culture, and literacy learning.

Upon establishing myself as a part of Melissa's classroom community, Love immediately caught my attention. She was always thoughtful about what she said in her written and oral responses to the multicultural literature. In addition, she was courteous to her teacher and peers. I have written about Love elsewhere (see Boyd, 2003), and how she portrayed herself as not shy in admitting that she was "closed-minded" about other people and cultures. Upon reading *Shabanu* (Staples, 1989), however, Love learned that she needed to be more open-minded about diverse people and cultures. I was intrigued by the fact that Love appeared to have a change in perspectives, moving from being uninterested in reading about diverse people (i.e., *Shabanu*), to revealing interest by reading newspapers and magazines articles featuring women in Afghanistan, and using the Internet to research the plight of Middle Eastern women.

Love was always interested in my research in her classroom, as well as what I did at the university where I taught. We talked about both political issues (i.e., racism, prolife and prochoice issues) and the classes in which Love was enrolled at the high school. As a 14-year-old, Love was easy to talk with, and I was impressed with the level of maturity and independent thinking she portrayed. I chose to feature this literacy event in this chapter because Love's insights bring issues to the table on instructional practices and students' literacy learning that need to be addressed, if we expect to listen and "hear" what students have to say.

Presenting Themes as a Literacy Event

As I mentioned earlier, Melissa required all students to write 10 responses to big ideas from the novels they read, one of which regarded themes that had emerged from *Shabanu* (Staples, 1989). Melissa had taught a minilesson on themes earlier, during the morning, using a transparency of themes (see Table 9.2) generated from the novel *The Outsiders* (Hinton, 1967). After the minilesson, students worked in small groups for approximately 20 minutes to generate themes from their own novels, using the themes Melissa presented from *The Outsiders*. After the small-group work, they presented their themes to the entire class, while I videotaped the presentation. Love and Clogger's presentation lasted approximately 10–15 minutes.

I first provide a transcript from the videotape of Love and Clogger discussing themes to portray the literacy event, how Love and Clogger interacted with the teacher during the presentation, and most importantly, what the girls portrayed as themes that had emerged from *Shabanu*. Just before they began, another group had just finished pre-

---

TABLE 9.2. Themes Taken from *The Outsiders* by S. E. Hinton

- *Conflicts arise from misunderstandings of attitudes and values.* Give examples from history, from today's world, and from your own experiences that prove or disprove this statement. Do people have to be the same race, class (wealthy, poor, etc.), or gender (male or female) to share the same attitudes and values?

- *Understanding and kindness can overcome prejudice.* Can you give an example of this happening to someone you know or have heard about? Can you give a definition of prejudice?

- *People are usually not satisfied with what they have.* What are some of the effects of people wanting more in their lives? Can being dissatisfied be destructive? Can being satisfied be destructive?

- *Everyone needs to feel accepted.* Do you agree with this statement? How do people try to gain acceptance? Do any of these ways have negative effects?

- *Loyalty is a necessary quality in human relationships.* What does it mean to be loyal? To whom should you be loyal, and why? Is it ever permissible to be disloyal? Under what circumstances?

senting themes from a different book, but had used themes from *The Outsiders* as a guide. I begin with Melissa acknowledging how well they performed:

MELISSA: OK, good. How about *Shabanu*? What do you have to say about theme? And tell me if I need to put that overhead back on; if you need to refer back up there.

LOVE: The first thing we said was, "Don't assume what you don't know," because, um, when they went to the fair, the [undecipherable] and they saw women, like different kinds of people that, you know, that they didn't know about, because they kind of live by themselves out in the middle of the desert, you know, and they assumed things, and people assumed things about them that really weren't all that true; and so it gave them kind of like a little stereotype; you know, like if they saw another person like that, they automatically assumed that they were like the last one; they may have been mean or they may have been nice, and you know.

MELISSA: I like that.

CLOGGER: OK, the second one [theme] was, "Don't go snooping around. You may find something you'll get in trouble for." When Shabanu went to the *taba* [undecipherable] with [undecipherable], I don't know how to pronounce his name but, um, all among that, she saw all these crowds of people, and her dad told her never go near a crowd of people, but she did it anyway, and she found her dad fighting another man. And he saw her, and she was like, oh no! I'm getting in big trouble now so . . .

LOVE: The third one [theme] is, "Don't compete with others." Only make yourself better, because throughout the book, a lot of people were like [turns to Clogger] you, like that fighting thing, um, and Shabanu and her sister, they compete a lot, but competing with somebody else, it does make you better, but because you realize maybe your weak points, or maybe your strong points. But competing with yourself is better, because then you're not bringing anybody else down, and nobody's bringing you down. You're only making your self-esteem better.

CLOGGER: And some of the rivalries between her sister, um, I mean, Shabanu would soon have. She just had to wait.

Here, Love and Clogger attempt to report themes by reviewing the transparency that Melissa had presented to the entire class (see Table 9.2). In general, themes in stories tend to have broad topics, characteristics, and qualities. As Love and Clogger take turns talking, they present themes that speak to specific scenes and events in the story, and almost in chronological order. A closer look at the themes selected reveals that the girls linked each theme with a specific scenario from the story. For example, Love presents the first theme, "Don't assume what you don't know," and followed with an explanation of an event from *Shabanu*, and an expanded description of striking aspects of the theme, which might include consequences. She states, "To assume something about a person that you really do not know, for instance, might reinforce a stereotype." Melissa encouraged Love, stating, "I like that." Immediately following Love's explanation of the first theme, Clogger provides the second, which is very similar to the first: "Don't go snooping around. You may find something you'll get in trouble for," which, again, is based on a specific event from the story rather than a broad theme. In the next segment of transcript, notice how Melissa directs the students to address the theme of loyalty, and how her question evolves into a conversation about aspects of loyalty to one's culture and roots. Loyalty was a theme Melissa gave students as an example from *The Outsiders*.

MELISSA: Um, what about, you didn't mention loyalty at all?

CLOGGER: Well, we took something from there [themes from *The Outsiders* on transparency]. We took numbers one and five, because those best fit our book. Loyalty would be like, um, Shabanu would have to be loyal to her family in being able to marry someone she's arranged to instead of [undecipherable].

MELISSA: And the customs of their culture. And she wanted to be. She loved her culture, didn't she?

LOVE: But she also loved the desert and being outside, and . . .

CLOGGER: And she didn't even want to become more than she was 'cause they were nomads, and she liked being a nomad. She didn't want to be anything else.

MELISSA: Did you ever get the sense . . . that the people in the city kind of looked down on the nomads?

CLOGGER: Yeah, 'cause they thought . . . the nomads had less than they [people in the city] did, but they're kinda like the Amish people today, because Amish people live out in, you know, forest and they only have one car. They normally just kill animals or their livestock, and they live without any technology.

MELISSA: Electricity, right.

CLOGGER: So they, we think of them [Amish] as low people, because they don't use any of that stuff that we have today that's available to them. It's just their way of . . .

MELISSA: Yeah, their chosen way of life. Yeah, that's a very good analogy actually. I hadn't really thought about that. But, um, I think the, at least Shabanu's family, seemed to be very happy to be nomadic, and um . . .

CLOGGER: . . . And somehow that is better than being somebody who doesn't like themselves, nor their class. 'Cause we're, like I wish I was more than that 'cause, like nomads are *happy* [stresses happy] where they are. They don't want to be anything else.

LOVE: But I think that bein' a nomad kinda gives them a perspective on life, and they appreciate nature more, and they . . . for what they've got, you know? They don't want, they're not materialistic. They don't want . . .

MELISSA: . . . Yeah, they can't be, really, can they? 'Cause then they would have to leave. But you're right, because that forces them to put more emphasis on their family relationships and maybe some of the things that are more important than material things.

LOVE: Yeah, and it makes, it gives things more meaning. Like when they went to the fair and Shabanu got the *chartuse* and the . . . and it was his wife's, and it had all the pretty beads and the colors and stuff. And to us, that would be like just another thing to go in the closet. And then to her, it was really special.

In this segment of transcript, Melissa asked Love and Clogger whether they addressed the theme of loyalty, which was one she provided in the minilesson. One key point to note in Clogger's response is that she answered Melissa by stating that they took themes from the transparency she developed that best fit their book (i.e., numbers 1 and 5), rather than develop themes specific to the novel they read. Because Melissa asked them specifically about loyalty, Clogger attempts to address that theme by giving an example of Shabanu being loyal if she attended to the custom of participating in an arranged marriage. Melissa picks up on Clogger's comment and offers a commentary, stating that Shabanu loves her culture, in reference to arranged marriages. Love, apparently noticing that the conversation is moving toward "young girls accepting their plight in life," reminds Melissa and Clogger that Shabanu also loves nature. In fact, Love had written about how much she admired Shabanu, because she was a nature lover, in one journal response. In addition, Love makes the point that Shabanu, being from a family that raised camels, had a very different perspective on life; she was more in tune with nature than with material things. Love positions herself to speak to the value of what nomads perceive as valuable about life. She argues that Shabanu and

her people were nature lovers. Rather than viewing them as unfortu-
nate because their beliefs and traditions are not familiar, Love implies
that what was valuable to them was meaningful to the nomads. Consequently, Love admires how nomads found meaning in life and nature, as noted in her conversations and journal response entries. This comment comes from Love after she appears to notice that Clogger
juxtaposes the lives of nomads in the Cholistan desert with Amish in
the United States, and when she refers to Amish as "low people," because they live their lives simply. Even though Melissa and Clogger
were taking the discussion to a space in which Love seemed to be uncomfortable, they chime in to support Love. Melissa encourages her,
saying, "So maybe another theme could be something to do with . . ."
"Treasure what you have. It'll make you a better person in the long run,"
Clogger stated, interrupting Melissa's train of thought. Melissa, seemingly
excited by Clogger's newly developed theme, at the same time picks
up where she left off. "Right! Yeah, appreciate, take a look at what
you have and appreciate it. Sometimes people don't look at what they
have until they lose it. Then, when they lose it, they think, like wow,
I had that. OK. That's great." And so Love's and Clogger's presentation
on themes ends. They return to their seats, while the next group moves
to the front of the class to present themes from a different novel, having
used the same themes presented from *The Outsiders* as a guide.

In the next section, I explore Love's perceptions of her presentation
on themes in retrospect approximately 1 year later. Here, she critiques
the videotaped presentation she did with her teammate (Clogger, pseudonym selected by student); the same one I just presented.

Love's Retrospective Critique of the Presentation on Themes from *Shabanu*

On October 5, 2000, I conducted a postinterview with Love. I explained
that the purpose was to acquire her perspective through watching a videotape of a literacy event she participated in 1 year earlier. I asked Love
to stop the video at any point to talk about what she noticed. Like a 14-
year-old, Love wanted to know whether she could watch the videotape
until it stopped, and then talk about it. I explained that I would prefer
that she stop the video at certain points, so that she would not forget
what she wanted to say whenever she noticed something that might need
critiquing. However, she did not stop the video until the segment for
analysis ended. The entire snippet of videotape, which I just presented,
lasted approximately 15 minutes. The following transcript is Love's critique of Clogger and herself.

"I really didn't think of anything except that it didn't make sense. It wasn't very thought out; I remember that Clogger and I got together just before the presentation, and I remember that we were not in agreement. I was thinking of things that weren't exactly events in the story, where she would relate a theme to events in the story. Like where she talked about theme, she would mention a lot of events, where I would talk about a thing that happened, but more of an understanding, feelings or attitudes toward . . . like she mentioned the part of the story about the *chardra* and don't go snooping around, when she [Shabanu] saw her father with another lady. And she mentioned that event, and those weren't really themes to me. Those weren't important, nor what the author was trying to get across. Those were more like rules, but not universal themes of the book. That really was all that I was thinking, but I knew that I was annoyed, because we only had four themes, and we each had two. I didn't think hers were very well thought out, but maybe they were important to her or relative to the themes, but I'm sure to her they were. My themes didn't seem very explanatory, but I don't think that's what I'm looking for; I don't really know. I can't think of how to say this; they kinda, let's see, they were good, I thought, but maybe I could have gone in depth more. A lot of them were themes that everybody's book had. That may have been because Mrs. Richardson [Melissa] gave us like five themes, and told us to choose which ones. Whereas . . . like if she wouldn't, I just think because they were all the same, I didn't feel the need to explain. Just like if you're told, 'Out of these five adjectives pick three of them,' and you choose red, brown, and big, you don't have to explain as much, because they understand; you've already explained those adjectives. But if I would've had to choose my own, I would have chosen themes that were more personal to my book. I was also thinking, the presentation 'sucked' because, maybe it was because I don't really like the themes we chose, or I'm not sure. I didn't have very good speech etiquette. I was like playing with my hair, scratching my face. Maybe because I was in an uncomfortable situation, I could just like . . . [playing with her hair as she critiques her body language from the video] so the presentation wasn't all that lovely." (October 5, 2000)

IN RETROSPECT, WHAT CAN WE LEARN FROM LOVE?

Earlier, I posed four questions as I reread Love's comments in her post-interview: What happens when students are encouraged to reflect on their reading experiences of literary texts and instructional activities?

What strategies might teachers use to learn more about what adolescents think during reading experiences? How might teachers use students' insights to inform their instructional practices and assessments? As students reveal their understandings (or lack thereof) of stories, how might teachers use that information better to enable adolescents to read to learn? In the remainder of this discussion, I answer these questions to encourage us, as educators, to adjust our instructional directions and purposes when students critique their own literacy learning and collaborative activities.

As Love watched the video of Clogger and herself, she observed specific areas of performance she believed to be problematic during the presentation. One such area was how they selected themes from *The Outsiders*, which Melissa used as a guide, and matched those to specific events from *Shabanu*. Love implied that events in the story of *Shabanu* did not necessarily mean that they were themes, and that themes from *The Outsiders* did not necessarily link with overarching themes in *Shabanu*. Love distinguished her thinking about themes from that of her teammate by acknowledging that even though she and Clogger looked at events, she was trying to connect the events to more of "an understanding" of feelings and attitudes to get to "universal themes." It may have been helpful for Love and Clogger to look at events from their story, then craft "universal themes" versus looking at themes from *The Outsiders* and matching those with *Shabanu*.

To work closely with Love in this study and focus on what she really acquired from the presentation on themes required additional time and effort. Teachers of course, do not always have the time to spend one-on-one with each and every student they teach. However, as an alternative assessment for instructional purposes and to make adjustments in instruction, teachers might encourage students to write brief reflections to understand better the nature of their reading experiences of literary texts and instructional activities. Or students might engage in a *self-assessment* of what they learn from reading a text, engaging in collaborative activities with peers, and from small- and whole-group discussions and projects (see Appendix 9.1). At the end of this unit on reading and studying multicultural literature, Melissa and I required students to respond to a self-assessment related to what they learned from reading about teenagers from other countries and cultures. It consisted of seven questions. Examples of issues included questions about which activities students found helpful and which were not, and students' contributions to the overall learning community.

Another strategy that might be beneficial for Love, Clogger, and their peers would be for the teacher to conduct a minilesson on themes (e.g., definition, description) before looking at specific themes from a story. According to Cullinan and Galda (1998), "A theme is a central, unifying idea. Often a theme is the reason authors write in the first place: A story allows them to say what they want to say. Many stories have several interwoven themes. Interpretation of themes varies among readers, with each student internalizing the theme in an individual way" (p. 15). Tunnell and Jacobs (2000) offer a similar definition of theme, with examples: "The central idea of the story is the theme: friendship, coming-of-age, sibling rivalry, coping with the death of a pet, and adjusting to a new town, to name a few" (p. 16). One theme that Love and Clogger might have explored in their presentation of themes is coming-of-age, because Shabanu was dealing with the tensions of following and honoring Muslim traditions; at the same time, she had been allowed freedom and independence not usually afforded to young Muslim girls.

Finally, as Love noticed, the appropriation of the themes her teacher selected from a different novel (i.e., *The Outsiders*) was problematic. Melissa modeled a lesson on how to identify themes, which was beneficial to the students. But rather than appropriate their teacher's themes, students might develop a method of finding themes specific to their reading. When this method is appropriately executed, students then reveal what they think about the book, rather than mapping onto "premade" themes. Students would be thinking about their book rather than looking for ways to fit readily available themes to it.

Love engaged in dialogue about her literacy learning opportunities in this literacy event. Her memory about the activity was clear, yet the videotape enabled her to recall more details about the specific discussion, as well as her body language (i.e., playing with her hair). As Love engaged in a conversation with me about what she remembered and noticed, it was clear that she participated in the activity but did not necessarily agree with what she was doing. Perhaps teachers and all educators can better encourage students both to participate and to invest in what they present. Consequently, when students invest in literacy events and activities in which they participate, they invest in their own literacy learning.

REFERENCES

Bloome, D. (1986). Building literacy and the classroom community. *Theory Into Practice, 25,* 71–76.

Boyd, F. B. (2002). Conditions, concessions, and the many tender mercies of learning through multicultural literature. *Reading Research and Instruction, 42,* 58–92.

Boyd, F. B. (2003). Experiencing things not seen: Educative events centered on a study of Shabanu. *Journal of Adolescent and Adult Literacy, 46,* 460–474.

Broughton, M. A., & Fairbanks, C. M. (2003). In the middle of the middle:

Seventh-grade girls' literacy and identity development. *Journal of Adolescent and Adult Literacy, 46,* 426–435.

Cullinan, B. E., & Galda, L. (1998). *Literature and the child* (4th ed.). New York: Harcourt Brace.

Enciso, P. (1997). Negotiating the meaning of difference: Talking back to multicultural literature. In T. Rogers & A. O. Soter (Eds.), *Reading across cultures: Teaching literature in a diverse society* (pp. 13–41). New York: Teachers College Press.

Hinton, S. E. (1967). *The outsiders.* New York: Viking Press.

Moll, L. C., Armanti, C., Neff, D., & Gonzalez, N. (1992). Funds of knowledge for teaching using a qualitative approach to connect homes and classrooms. *Theory Into Practice, 31,* 132–141.

Rosenblatt, L. (1978). *The reader, the text, and the poem: The transactional theory of literary work.* Carbondale: Southern Illinois University Press.

Smith, B. (1943). *A tree grows in Brooklyn.* New York: Perennial Classics.

Staples, S. F. (1989). *Shabanu: Daughter of the wind.* New York: Knopf.

Tunnell, M. O., & Jacobs, J. S. (2000). *Children's literature, briefly* (2nd ed.). Upper Saddle River, NJ: Merrill.

APPENDIX 9.1

Self-Assessment Questionnaire

Directions: Please write a thoughtful and complete answer to each question.

What do you think about the novel you read? Explain.

What did you learn from reading your novel? Explain.

Which activity or activities helped you to develop a better understanding of your novel?

Describe what you learned while collaborating with your peers on the
_____ activity.

Describe what you did to contribute to the learning of your classmates.

What would you do to improve this project next time? Explain.

Chapter 10

Reader Response, Culturally Familiar Literature, and Reading Comprehension

The Case of Four Latina(o) Students

LEILA FLORES-DUEÑAS

When I was a child, I loved school. I tried to please nearly all of my teachers, did all of my homework, made good grades, scored well on standardized tests, and spoke up in class. My father was an officer in the army, and my mother was a teacher at the same elementary school my siblings and I attended. Of my public schoolteachers, all but one of my elementary teachers and two of my secondary teachers were of northern European American ancestry and probably held middle-class values. Most of my classmates, daughters and sons of military officers, were from similar ethnic backgrounds as my teachers, with the exception of maybe one or two African Americans, Japanese Americans, newly arrived German immigrants, Mexican Americans, and Korean Americans, who went to school with me in our rather large classrooms.

The literacy curriculum, as we moved from state to state during my elementary school years in the 1970s, seemed to be fairly similar, which made it easy to adjust to the next school. There was a focus on spelling and grammar, as well as on decoding and answering questions at the end of stories. Reading instruction consisted of whole-class read-alouds from the *Dick and Jane Stories* (Gray, Artley, & Arbuthnot, 1940–1970) in round-robin fashion. Then, the class broke up into high, medium, and low groups to practice decoding and reading comprehension skills from basal readers. Next, we went to centers to answer questions written on color-coded, leveled cards in the Standardized Reading Assessment (SRA) program box. Once a week, we read and discussed events and stories from the *Weekly Reader* and *Highlights* magazines, and after recess, the teacher held story time and read books by Dr. Seuss, as well as titles such as *Curious George* (Rey, 1941), *The Real Mother Goose* (Wright, 1994), *Velveteen Rabbit* (Williams, 1983), and *Paul Bunyan* (Kellogg, 1994). All stories that I recall reading in elementary school sounded like and dealt with issues that I imagined were part of my classmates' daily lives. They weren't the kinds of stories that my dad and my *tío* Noé used to tell about *La Llorona* or *Las Malinchitas* at our ranch in Mexico, but they were the kinds of books that we had on our shelves at home.

In the secondary grades, the same was true. Most of the books and literature I read were written from the same European American perspective. Even though I enjoyed reading in general, the older I got, the more I wondered why I was not thrilled by the books that I had to read, like most of my school counterparts seemed to be. I suspect that as time went on, I must have internalized my disinterest as something wrong with me. For example, when we would return to school in early fall and the teacher would ask the titles of books we had read over the summer, I seemed always to be ashamed that I had not read more. This feeling of inadequacy was further exacerbated in high school, when my teachers continued to introduce more and more of what I now see as culturally and linguistically distant texts, such as works by Shakespeare, Chaucer, and Dickens. Of course, I realize that some of my other classmates probably felt the same way.

What was wrong with me? I wondered why I was so disinterested in reading books such as *The Scarlet Letter* (Hawthorne, 1965), *The Great Gatsby* (Fitzgerald, 1952), and *The Grapes of Wrath* (Steinbeck, 1972). Although I was able to read all those stories and even test well on their content, why was I so disengaged when I read them? Why did I grow to like them less and less? For years, I pondered these questions and never came up with any acceptable answers for myself. I just accepted that maybe I was not as smart as I thought or was often told. I knew that this insecurity had to be affecting my comprehension of even "good" literature in a negative way, and would later show up on my college entrance exams, when my mathematics scores exceeded my seemingly high verbal skills.

Looking back, there were just a few books that I really sunk my teeth into during my junior high school years. They included *Anne*

Frank: Diary of a Young Girl (Frank, 1952), *Summer of My German Soldier* (Greene, 1973), and *A Separate Peace* (Knowles, 1985). These stories sounded natural to me, unlike so many of the other novels we had to read, which were contrived, with an overabundance of description. In addition, perhaps the recurring themes of adversity and difference in these "interesting" texts also attracted me.

As time went on, I went to college and did well in my studies. During those years, some of the books that I read for pleasure included *Jaws* (Benchley, 1974) and *Sophie's Choice* (Styron, 1979), both of which I read after seeing the movies. Even though I was absorbed in those books and others, I still had no faith in reading for my beginning College English classes. I was constantly tested and would have to have the "right answer." As expected, all my English literature classes, again, required the class to interact with the same kinds of texts I had to read in high school. Running through my head were the same old questions: "Why was I so detached from these stories?" "Why did 'they' always have to use the same kind of literature that came mostly from England?" "What made that kind of literature so much better than our own from the United States?" These questions continued throughout most of my university studies and even into my children's literature classes in teacher education.

Once I graduated from college, I became a bilingual education teacher in an inner-city school district. During that time, I read mostly the newspaper and young adult literature to plan for my fifth-grade curriculum—none of which, was multicultural. Nevertheless, as time went on, most of my reading took place during my classroom's sustained silent reading period, because my school required that I read silently with my students. I began reading novels such as Maya Angelou's (1969) *I Know Why the Caged Bird Sings* and James Baldwin's (1985) *Go Tell It on the Mountain*. I don't know how those multiethnic books got into my hands, but they did, and they made a big difference in my self-confidence as a reader again. With those two volumes, something wonderful had begun. The struggles of identity, justice, and equality were all topics I was required to know at my family's dinner table. I could relate to those books, finally.

Those two books renewed my faith in myself as a reader. They gave me a taste of what was good or "quality" literature for me. The following year, I moved to another state and district, and started off the school year reading the newspaper, while my first graders were adjusting to sustained silent reading. During the 2 years I spent teaching in that district, I began reading mysteries by and about feminist women. I thought that they were interesting, but not as great as books by Maya Angelou.

Another great book I recall reading from that time was Dostoyevsky's (1958) *Crime and Punishment*. Although the character's names were hard to remember, the text was a healthy challenge, and I loved it. It was the type of book that I could live through, and feel all the fears and hopes of the characters. However, once I finished it, I did not pick up another novel; instead, I only read academic articles that my astute principal slipped into the faculty's mailboxes, addressing education of English language learners (ELLs). Once again, I loved academic reading. Why I floundered so much in my feelings about certain genres of text became an interesting question for me, and for my teaching.

The following year, I went to graduate school. Back to my comfortable academic reading, I still did not embrace reading novels in my spare time. Every now and then, I read a short mystery, but reading novels for sheer enjoyment was basically still on the back burner. During my second year of graduate school, my partner wanted to share literature discussions with me and suggested that I read a book written by a Chicano writer, Rudolfo Anaya, titled *Bless Me, Última* (1972). I had never heard of any Chicana(o) writers and was doubtful that I even wanted to read the book, but I said that I would try.

Wow! Once I got into Chapter 2 of that book, I had to finish it! I had never read anything like it! I was amazed at how I read, never thinking about my comprehension, my speed (it was going so fast), or whether I was bored. In other words, not using my metalinguistic awareness was uplifting! The text sounded like people in my extended family. It had code switching in Spanish and English, which is always great fun when you know two languages and can put your thoughts together so cleverly. I couldn't believe my eyes. It was amazing! I could hear the sounds of the characters and see the landscape. I understood at such a profound level that I had to read more stories like this or about *mi gente*.

The next book I read, Isabel Allende's *Eva Luna* (1995), reflected a Latina's passion for life and love. Next, I read Allende's *House of the Spirits* (1984), replete with magical realism that mirrored stories told by old-timers in my family's village in Mexico. I also read Amy Tan's *The Kitchen God's Wife* (1992), Sandra Cisneros's *The House on Mango Street* (1984) and *Woman Hollering Creek* (1991), and Villaseñor's *Rain of Gold* (1991), all of which helped me to see how these writers used forms of oppression as a gateway to honest and provocative material for their books.

The list of books I began reading, and continue to read, help me to understand what my family talked about, and that how we communicated was of value and useful in the development of my voice as a teacher. If culturally relevant literature had been a motivator for me to read more, and if I had gained a healthier literate identity (Langer, 1987) about my reading abilities, then what might happen to younger readers who read about things they knew? That was the question that guided the following study.

CULTURALLY AND LINGUISTICALLY DIVERSE STUDENTS AND READING

So there I was some 20 years later, sitting on grade-level committees, planning the same curriculum that I had experienced as a child for my own students. As I planned with other nonbilingual teachers, I often questioned how my Latina(o) and African American students would be able to understand books that I was not interested in as a child, such as some of those found on the Newbery Award book list. Even though I had an inner conflict about what was seemingly "quality" literature for "all" children, I stayed quiet and acted as though the core literature that my well-intentioned colleagues had selected was suitable for all students. Of course, as most bilingual and English as a second language (ESL) teachers are taught, I would be the one teacher on my grade level who would go out of my way to make the "connections" for my students. I was also worried about the other students who had exited from bilingual and ESL programs, and were now attending all-English classrooms, where those connections most likely did not take place on a regular basis.

With these Latina(o) students in mind, I have focused this chapter on the personal stories and narratives that four fifth-grade Mexican American bilingual learners can contribute to our understanding of their experiences with reading in English. It is my hope that by listening to their voices and responses, educators can learn how better to serve these children.

In the remainder of this chapter, I tell you about a study in which four Mexican American students responded to literature that was part of their regular classroom curriculum (written by non–Mexican American authors), and selected literature by Mexican American writers who were not part of their classroom libraries. My goal in this study was to understand how the students responded to these different texts and the role that cultural familiarity played in their text comprehension.

READER RESPONSE AND CULTURALLY AND LINGUISTICALLY DIVERSE LEARNERS

During my years in graduate school and more recently, through my university teaching and research experiences, I have searched for studies and theories in literacy education that explain what might be going on when minority children respond to reading culturally unfamiliar texts in the classroom. I have found that reader response theory can partially explain what might be going on with these readers.

One of the most famous names associated with reader response theory is Louise Rosenblatt. In her book, *Literature as Exploration* (1983), she centers her thoughts on the idea that personal experiences shape readers' literary experiences and must therefore be taken into account as teachers interpret how readers' understand literary text. In other words, Rosenblatt encouraged us to look more deeply into students' reading responses to consider the idea that not all readers understand stories in the same way. Rosenblatt explains that the meaning of the text does not exist exclusively within the text, nor is the text's meaning solely in the reader's mind; rather, it is where the text and the person's personal and literary experiences come together to make sense in a particular context. Thus, it is within this "transaction" that reading (comprehension/meaning) occurs. Therefore, it follows that the more a reader's personal experiences match the experiences reflected in the text, the greater the comprehension for the reader.

So what does all this theory mean for culturally and linguistically diverse students', who often have very different personal experiences from those characters portrayed in the literature they read in our schools? This mismatch can mean that they may respond or interpret the story differently from what the author or teacher expects of the reader. Or worse, there may be a breakdown in comprehension that causes the reader to focus more attention on simple tasks, such as decoding, performance, or pronunciation of individual words, rather than on the meaning the text evokes. According to Rosenblatt, such conflicting responses can also be examined to help us understand more deeply the reader's comprehension of the text. Rosenblatt (1978) began to distinguish between the ways that readers interpreted text, indicating that readers often take two different stances toward the text.

According to Rosenblatt (1978), within these stances, readers focus their attention on understanding a text in an *efferent way* (reading for information) or in an *aesthetic way* (experiencing a text as primary). Or they may take on the characteristics of both, while still favoring one stance over the other. The *efferent* stance is taken when the reader focuses on seeking and retaining information from the text itself (to answer consequent questions on worksheets or at the end of chapters, or on tests, etc.). It is the efferent stance that educators have traditionally modeled for students to adopt during reading activities in the classroom. This approach inherently implies that there is one interpretation of the text, which can only be found within the text. Encouraging students to find one meaning for each text reflects an only-one-answer approach (based most often on the teachers' manual or "basic" interpretation) to teaching reading. Although knowing the "facts" of a story is a necessary part of reading comprehension, it is limiting to teach from this single approach, because it may prohibit students from fully engaging with the texts they read. In addition, efferent reading also maintains educators' ignorance of the many creative interpretations and personal experiences these students can bring to a text.

Unlike the efferent stance of responding to literature, the *aesthetic* stance is taken by readers who focus attention on not only the concepts that the words of the text represent but also what they experience as they bring personal experiences to their understanding of the text during the reading. In the aesthetic stance, readers' ideas and feelings are prompted by the text, so that readers experience a new text. Rosenblatt (1978) suggested that using a more aesthetic approach to teaching literature may be more beneficial to students, because it may provide better opportunities for them to bring forth their personal experiences while reading the text, thus allowing the full transactional nature of reading comprehension to take place. To this, I add that text choice matters, and that these transactions can perhaps be better understood by examining the role of cultural and experiential familiarity, and its relationship to text comprehension.

Analyzing Latina(o) students' stances toward literature can perhaps help us to understand the role of literature selection in text comprehension. In the following sections, I analyze the writings of four Mexican American bilingual students as they respond to a classroom curriculum of reading literature by European American authors and supplemental stories by Mexican American authors.

THE SCHOOL AND THE STUDENTS

The school I selected was in an inner-city, low-socioeconomic-level elementary school (early childhood through fifth grade) located in a large city in central Texas. It was a "typical" Mexican American *barrio*, or neighborhood, school located in a segregated urban area of the larger city. The school housed a total of 531 students: 73.4% Hispanic (predominantly of Mexican descent), 16.9% African American, and 9.6% other (European American, Asian American, and Native American). It also served 247 limited-English-proficient (LEP) students in bilingual education and ESL programs.

Four students, Sonia, José, Rosalinda, and Alfredo were selected to participate in the study. All of these students were exited from bilingual programs and were completing all academic work in English in the fifth grade. At the time of the study, the students had passed the standardized Texas Assessment of Academic Skills (TAAS) in the fourth grade and were considered to be "average" or "above average" by their teachers. These students were interviewed, and after much questioning, seemed to have similar views of themselves as readers and writers. They said that they liked reading but "weren't really good at it," so they did not read for enjoyment. They each confirmed the desire to become better readers in English and expressed interest in learning more about their own reading problems. In addition, all four students worried about how they sounded while reading, and about their understanding of what "they [the text] want you to know."

Sonia, a tall girl who often wore overalls, had long black hair with stringy bangs, and red glasses. Her classmates referred to her as "smart, tomboy-like." She was often the one student who raised her hand first in class and had many of the "right" answers. Her Latina teacher described her as being "smart, funny, and a good student" who was always prepared for class. Often outspoken in her class and in our afterschool study meetings, Sonia had much to say about what she read. She was angered by texts and would argue about the texts' content and how they were written. At the time of the study, she did not read for enjoyment, only for a "reading record" that earned her class points for a schoolwide book reading competition.

José was also in Sonia's class. In his teacher's interactions with him and me, it was clear that she did not always appreciate José. She often mentioned that he was "lazy, a street kid with baggy pants and slicked hair, who rarely gets his work done." On several occasions, I observed José keeping to himself and asking no questions of his teacher or his classmates. He rarely read for pleasure, because he did not "like the kinds of books they have at school." He read out loud with Standard English pronunciation when it was his turn, and when he had to answer questions, he was often correct. He was quiet in class, used few words to express himself, and did his work at a minimal level, but, again, it was nearly always correct. Although José did not interact much with others in his classroom, he was very interactive in our study sessions.

Rosalinda and Alfredo were in another fifth-grade classroom, just down the hall from Sonia and José. Rosalinda, a newer immigrant from Mexico, was considered "shy and quiet, always giggling and boy crazy" by her Latina teacher. On various occasions, Rosalinda expressed that she was a "poor reader," because she thought that she did not "sound right" when she read aloud in class (most reading was done aloud in both classes). In other words, her perceived pronunciation problems affected how she saw herself as a reader and communicator. Au and

Kawakami (1991) refer to these kinds of perceptions of oneself in literacy activities as having an influence on one's ownership of literacy. Rosalinda also worried about "not having the right answer" after reading in class, or when turning in homework. This fear, or not meeting these school expectations, greatly affected how Rosalinda saw herself as a reader. At the time of the study, Rosalinda said that she loved reading picture books to the children on the stairs of her inner-city, neglected apartment complex. Other than those books, she did not read chapter books for pleasure.

Alfredo, the most recently arrived immigrant of all of the students, had been working in all-English classrooms for only 1 school year and was making A's and B's in all subjects. Often labeled the "class clown," he was always smiling and trying to make others laugh. In terms of his literacy learning, he always did exactly as he was told: "Read the passage below and answer the questions" (TAAS practice played a major role in students' reading in class); however, he did not participate in the fifth-grade reading competition. In fact, he did very little, if any, outside reading for pleasure. According to his mother, that year he did read one or two books he had gotten from a school book fair, as well as lots of advertisements that came in the mail. These he read to his toddler sister.

STUDYING STUDENTS' RESPONSES TO LITERATURE

This analysis is part of a larger, yearlong study that took place with the students, their parents, and teachers (see Flores-Dueñas, 1997). For the purposes of this chapter, I analyze the types of stances the students took as they responded to their classroom literature (written by non–Mexican American and Mexican American authors) during 20 afterschool focus group sessions. Each session consisted of the following procedures: (1) Students read a story silently, then (2) retold the story in writing, and (3) discussed the story in a focus group interview. For each procedure, students read the story silently and at their own pace, returned the copy of the story to me, then began retelling the story in writing. Once they finished these written retellings, they joined the group to engage in conversation about the story and about their own reading comprehension of the text for that day. I used the written retellings as a catalyst to promote rich discussions about the literature, because this procedure provided the students with an opportunity to formulate their thoughts, so that they could participate in authentic exchanges (Martínez & Roser, 1995). I took field notes, audiotaped the focus group interviews, and transcribed the content of the audiotapes. I analyzed the data collected according to Rosenblatt's (1978b) notions of the efferent and aesthetic stances she believed readers took as they respond to particular texts. In the next section, I share what I found within these students' written and oral responses to selected stories.

TAKING AN EFFERENT STANCE
TO CLASSROOM LITERATURE

Analyzing the students' responses to stories that were part of the classroom curriculum provided a context for my understanding how the students might interact with such texts on a regular basis. In this section, I analyze and reveal how the students' responses to their classroom literature were essentially efferent in nature. In the case of the four participants, the state-adopted and grade-level approved classroom curriculum, as well as books in the classroom library, were almost exclusively written by non–Mexican American authors. Although the majority of these authors seemed to have values that reflected the dominant culture, there were a few stories and plays by African American authors on the shelves, as well as a few library picture books by Mexican American authors in the children's desks.

In analyzing the students' written retellings and their conversations in response to their classroom literature, I focused on the content of their contributions rather than on the structure of language and/or spelling, because I was interested in the constructs that the students grasped from the text. Although I do mention form in some of the examples, my primary intent is to understand why students took a particular stance to retell their stories.

Using Textbound Details

As I analyzed the students' written retellings of the non–Mexican American literature, one of the themes that emerged was the students' recall of small bits of information to retell the entire story. These small bits of information, or details of the story, were nearly always events that came directly from the text, and were reflective of students' comprehension of only a few events of the story. For example, as indicated in Figure 10.1, José responded to "With a Way, Hey, Mr. Stormalong" (Cohn & Schmidt, 1993), a tall tale about a giant sailor and his extraordinary experiences on a ship at sea. This tall tale inherently required the reader to have an abundance of cultural and linguistic knowledge related to the context and the topics of the text. In this case, to understand the meaning of the text, the reader had to have background knowledge of nautical, geographical, and historical life in New England.

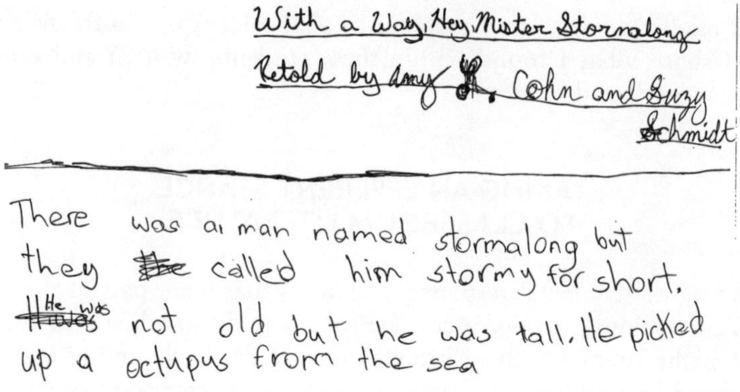

> *With a Way, Hey, Mister Stornalong*
> *Retold by Amy L. Cohn and Suzy Schmidt*
>
> There was a man named stormalong but they ~~be~~ called him stormy for short. ~~He was~~ not old but he was tall. He picked up a octupus from the sea

FIGURE 10.1. José retells "With a Way, Hey, Mr. Stormalong" (Cohn & Schmidt, 1993).

As José responded to the text, he wrote only a few sentences about simple details that seemed directly related to the text. Rosalinda and Alfredo responded similarly. Sonia, on the other hand, used details but also took one event (a fight the main character had with an octopus) she remembered and cleverly used it as the main idea in retelling the whole story. For example, she states, "He [Stormy] was so tierd [sic: tired] that they had to replaes [sic: replace] him with another person on the ship." Making a new story out of one event in the story was perhaps used to mask her lack of understanding of the text. Figure 10.2 shows how Sonia recalled details to make up a new story.

In the group's discussion about "With a Way, Hey, Mr. Stormalong," similar patterns revealed that the students took an efferent stance in response to this text. For example, I asked, "What do you think about this text?" There was little response until the students started talking about the problems they had with the text. Again, the comments were text-bound. In the following transcription, the students describe many of the diversions they made in their minds as they read and tried to make sense of unknown vocabulary. They shared their thoughts about various misunderstood words and what they did to redirect their thinking to stop themselves from concentrating on the unknown vocabulary.

LEILA: What do you think about this text?

JOSÉ: . . . when it says, "The captain looked at the ledger and said, 'You're able-bodied, all right.' "

SONIA: I was gonna say that.

ALFREDO: I didn't understand *ledger.*

JOSÉ: You are able to be a body? (*laughter*)

LEILA: You didn't understand *ledger* or *able-bodied*? OK, so what did that do to you when you kept reading?

ALFREDO: We kept on reading, and while we were reading, we kept on thinking about that word.

ROSALINDA: It just makes me think about something else.

ALFREDO: I thought the story was about a storm.

SONIA: Like the word *fathoms*—it makes me feel like the Phantom of the Opera.

LEILA: Phantom of the Opera?

JOSÉ: I saw *fathom*, and then it reminded me of *The Phantom of the Opera*; that's when I went into that book.

If one were to use such a text to evaluate José's or the other students' retellings of this text, some teachers might view the reading level as "below grade level" or as "at risk," since the children had such low comprehension. I submit that each of the four students experienced low comprehension with this text because they did not understand the cul-

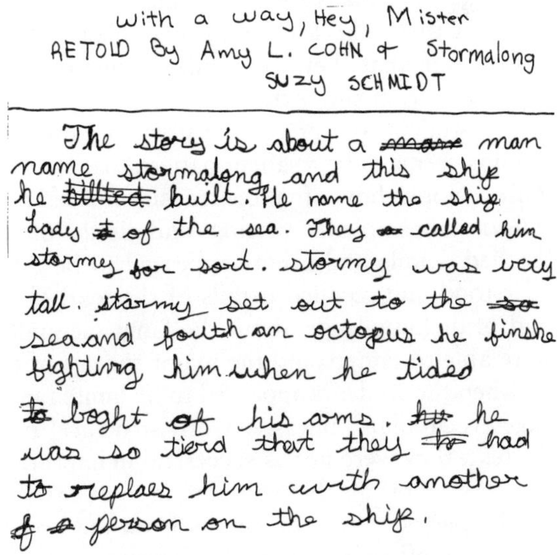
With a way, Hey, Mister
RETOLD By Amy L. COHN & Stormalong
SUZY SCHMIDT

The story is about a ~~man~~ man name stormalong and this ship he ~~billted~~ built. He name the ship Lady ~~#~~ of the sea. They ~~a~~ called him stormey for sort. stormey was very tall. stormy set out to the ~~sa~~ sea and fouth an octopus he finshe fighting him when he tided to boght ~~of~~ his arms. ~~he~~ he was so tierd that they ~~to~~ had to replaes him with another ~~f a~~ person on the ship.

FIGURE 10.2. Sonia retells "With a Way, Hey, Mr. Stormalong" (Cohn & Schmidt, 1993).

tural context or have the vocabulary they needed to fully understand the comical nature of this tall tale. Out of all of the stories we read from the students' classroom curriculum, this text seemed to be the most difficult and the furthest away from readers' background knowledge.

Using Textbound Recounting

One classroom text that the students seemed to enjoy was *Where the Red Fern Grows* (Rawls, 1961). Their satisfaction with this book was revealed in their discussions once they had finished their written retelling. Upon examination of their retellings, all four students had responded similarly, recounting in a step-by-step manner the events of the story. Their reconstructions also seemed to demonstrate that they were able to retell the story with ease.

Although the students' reconstructions seemed to be recountings of small pieces of information, this was for them an accomplishment, because they had expected this text to be "boring, like most other American chapter books," and expressed that they rarely felt that they understood novels the teacher assigned. In Figure 10.3, Alfredo's recounting in his lengthy retelling is very much like the text. He tells the reader what happened first, next, next, next, and so on, by using the word *then* over and over again. Although this may seem like a long listing, with this text (unlike the student's responses to "With a Way, Hey, Mr. Stormalong"), Alfredo and the other students were able to make sense of the text in a coherent manner. For these ESL learners, being able to recount in order was a very positive sign that they were indeed comprehending and remembering large ideas from the text.

Although each student interpreted the story in a different way, this notion of recounting seems to be a salient pattern that runs through each student's responses. Notice how often the transition word *then* is used in this text. In analyzing the students' writings and discussions, the number of students' recalled details and events appeared to be related to how much they understood and recalled details of the text. With this story, the students had prior knowledge about the language and/or events of the text and were able to understand the major themes of the story. On the other hand, when the students appeared to be limited in their knowledge of language (vocabulary, phrases, word structure) or experiences expressed in the text, they were not as successful in interpreting the content or the characters' emotions. Nonetheless, in most cases, the students appeared to recall specific events or details from the text to retell the story, which mirror an efferent response to literature.

Of all of the non–Mexican American texts that the students read, *Where the Red Fern Grows* (Rawls, 1961) seemed to capture their interest,

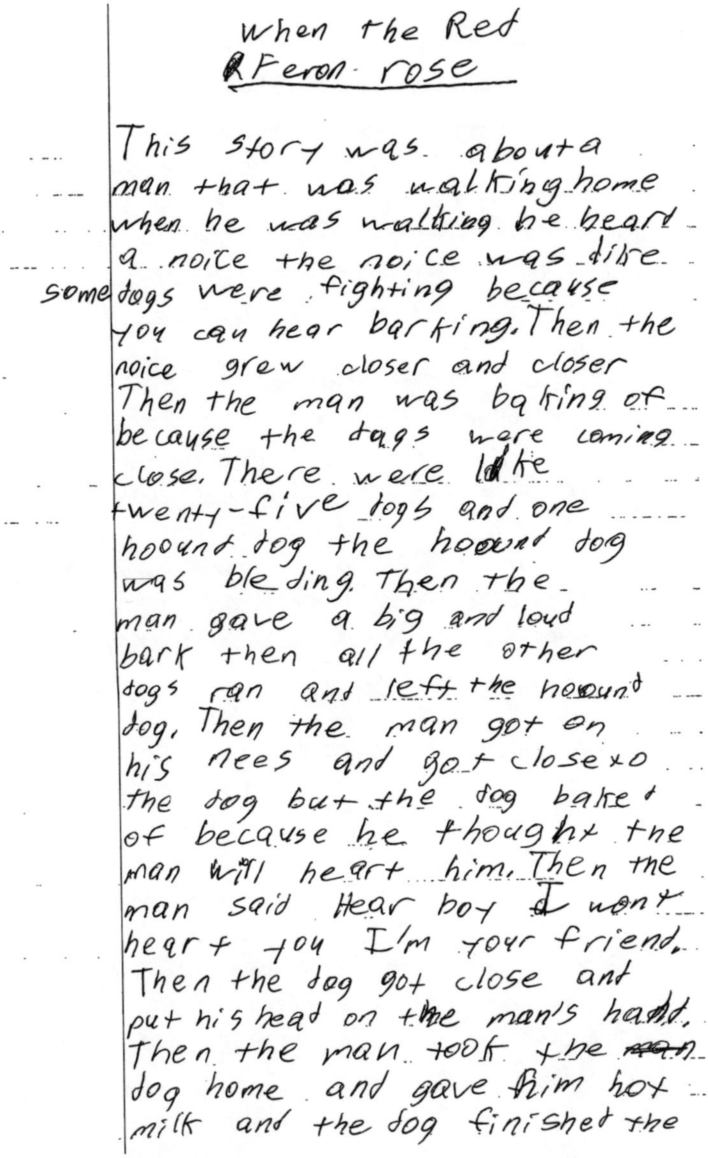

when the Red
R Feron rose

This story was about a
man that was walking home
when he was walking he heard
a noice the noice was like
some dogs were fighting because
you can hear barking. Then the
noice grew closer and closer
Then the man was baking of
because the dogs were coming
close. There were like
twenty-five dogs and one
hoound dog the hoound dog
was bleding. Then the
man gave a big and loud
bark then all the other
dogs ran and left the heound
dog, Then the man got on
his nees and got close to
the dog but the dog baked
of because he thought the
man will heart him. Then the
man said Hear boy I wont
heart you I'm your friend.
Then the dog got close ant
put his head on the man's hadd.
Then the man took the man
dog home and gave him hot
milk and the dog finished the

(continued)

FIGURE 10.3. Alfredo retells Chapter 1 of *Where the Red Fern Grows* (Rawls, 1961).

milk. Then the man gave
him meat and the dog
finished all the meat in
the house. Then the man
went to the store to buy
more meat for the dog.
The man told the dog
that he could lease at
night so that night
the man opened the door
so the hoound dog could
leave. Then the dog left
and Then he looked back.
Then the man waved goodbye.
Then the dog kept walking
throug the rain, storm, snow.
But the dog was thisty
and hungry. Then the man
said that he woued live
the gate open incase if
the dog comes back
from his trip. But the
man grabed logs put it
in The chimnny but withe
the lights turned off
he got 1matche and turned
it on so he can turn on
the fire. When the dog got to his house
he liked his masters
hand and his master gave
him food and something
to drink then the dog
was happy to be home
with his master.

FIGURE 10.3. (continued)

because they understood it. The students claimed to understand it the most and to like it best. They stated that they liked it because it was interesting. In the following dialogue, I asked them why they found this story interesting. In response to my question, Sonia did not tell me why the book was interesting; instead, she told me what the story was about. After this, the other students also contributed the events that they recalled from the story. The conversation reflects Rosenblatt's notion of an efferent response to this story, because it was mostly completely storybound.

LEILA: So what do you think about the story?

SONIA: I thought it was interesting.

LEILA: How come? Interesting, why?

SONIA: It talks about a dog like . . . It's about this man that he, he's at this place and he finds this dog, then when he, he, when the dog leaves, the man said that it reminds him of when he was in his boyhood, then, then he said that when he was going in the house he saw, he found some wood. He started a fire and then, and the man said that he saw these two, two, two dogs. I think that reminds him of his childhood.

LEILA: OK, did you like the story?

SONIA: Yes.

LEILA: How come? 'Cause, just because it was about a dog?

SONIA: No. It's interesting. I just like it.

LEILA: OK, tell me about how you felt about the story, everyone.

ALFREDO: I hated when like four or five dogs were fighting the dog.

LEILA: How come, Alfredo?

ROSALINDA: 'Cause he didn't belong there.

ALFREDO: He was from another uh . . . town.

LEILA: He was an outsider?

ALFREDO: Then there was this man that was walking. He heard all these noises and he knew that there were dogs fighting, but he didn't pay much attention. Then the noise came closer and closer. Then he saw this dog.

LEILA: Okay, stop there. José . . .

JOSÉ: He saw several dogs fighting and . . . he, he, he got the dog before the . . . I forgot what they're called. They're gonna pick him up, like they're gonna' pick up a dead dog if he didn't do nothing, if didn't do something about it.

In this discussion, all of the students are involved in telling what the story was about. They appear to be very interested in participating in the discussion, because they all have something to contribute to the conversation. The story started out with a dog fight that was very exciting. Most of the students understood this part. This was the only story in the non–Mexican American literature to which the students reacted in this way.

TAKING AN AESTHETIC STANCE TOWARD MEXICAN AMERICAN LITERATURE

In this section, I use the term "Mexican American literature" to describe culturally authentic (Bishop, 1993) literature written by Mexican American authors. It reflects the daily nuances, language, and experiences of living in a Mexican American community, as portrayed by the author. Some of the authors I used in this study wrote about their experiences in these communities with a mostly English text, then substituted a few words in Spanish. For example, in the story "El Sapo" (Rice, 1994), the author does this in sentences such as the following: "Let's go look for some more *sapos*!" The Spanish word *sapos* means "toads" in English. According to Barrera, Ligouri, and Salas (1993), writing *sapos* instead of "toads" would most likely "provide important cultural grounding" and be representative of how language is used in the author's community.

When responding to the Mexican American stories, the students seemed to interact with the content and the characters in the texts rather than just recall text-direct information about them. In other words, the students seemed to bring their own knowledge and experiences to their discussions about these texts. Rosenblatt (1978) identifies these types of interactions with texts as *aesthetic* responses to literature. In my analysis of most of the students' writing samples and discussions, it appears that they were able to retell the story in writing as if they understood what the main characters were experiencing through the course of events in the text. Although these ESL learners did not use conventional punctuation, grammar, or spell correctly, it was evident that they had made personal connections to the meaning of the texts. These personal connections turned into personal, aesthetic responses, because they were able to express their ideas in their own ways.

As the students retold the Mexican American stories in writing, they occasionally grappled with new vocabulary and information, just as they did with any other stories; however, with this literature, no information was so foreign that they did not understand the main ideas and the depth of the characters in each story. In fact, the students consistently demonstrated that they were able to use their prior knowledge of language, ideas, and writing, as well as their own living experiences, to understand, express, and support the main themes of the stories.

The students also demonstrated that they were able to retell the stories at a fairly high level, which might be a consideration for educators and parents, who have historically been taught that the only "quality" literature is that deemed canonical literature. For example, most of the writing samples illustrated that the students were able to retell coherent stories that had a beginning, a middle, and an end. They recalled main ideas of the story and supported them with details, while sequencing events. Incidentally, they had much more intelligible and profound responses to this literature than to the classroom stories.

Drawing on Personal Knowledge for Comprehension

Throughout nearly all of the retellings of the Mexican American literature selections, the students seemed to understand the main themes and events of the story. As they retold some of these stories in writing, however, they appeared to focus on certain aspects of the texts, while still telling what happened in the story. These foci often became visible in the form of details that students provided about particular aspects of the text. In the next section, I describe the various ways that the students seemed to connect with particular parts of the stories.

On some occasions, the students appeared to relate to particular characters in the stories. For example, in Rosalinda's retelling of "El Sapo," she appears to relate to the character Berta. In Figure 10.4, Rosalinda elaborates and demonstrates that she understands Berta's role in dealing with the two younger boys. For example, midway in her writing sample, Rosalinda begins to discuss the story, with many details about Cousin Berta. She recalls how Cousin Berta let the boys stay up until midnight, and that it was she who gave the boys permission to go out in the rain. Rosalinda also recalled the smell of the tamales that Cousin Berta made to calm David and Roger down, so she could tell them a story that would scare them.

Incidentally, in Rosalinda's personal life, she was the oldest of four children and had many responsibilities with her younger siblings. In an interview, her father informed me that she was the one who helped her mother cook, clean the house, babysit, and read to her younger brothers and sister. In our discussions, Rosalinda also stated that she was interested in reading books from the "Babysitters Club" series, because she

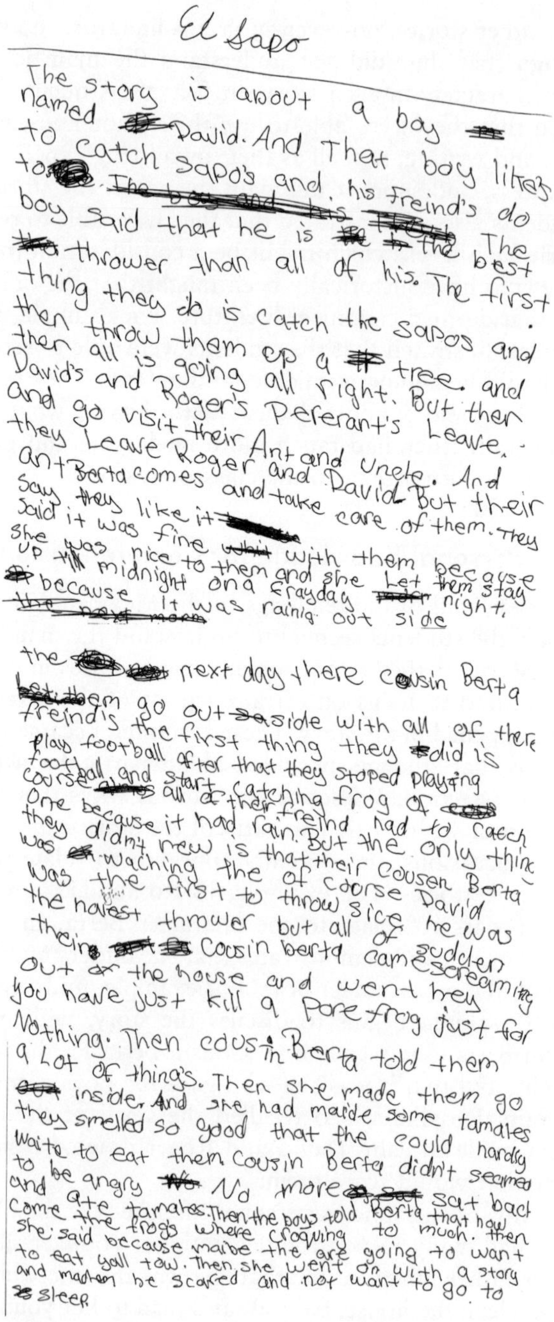

El Sapo

The story is about a boy ~~is~~ named ~~te~~ David. And That boy like's to catch sapo's and his freind's do ~~too. The boy and his~~ boy said that he is ~~te the F. Cate The~~ best ~~to~~ thrower than all of his. The first thing they do is catch the sapos and then throw them up a ~~tr~~ tree, and then all is going all right. But then David's and Roger's Pererant's Leave. And go visit their Ant and Uncle. And they Leave Roger and David But their ant Berta comes and take care of them. they saw ~~they~~ like it ~~ii~~ said it was fine ~~what~~ with them because she ~~was~~ nice to them and she Let ~~them~~ stay up till midnight on a erayday ~~toir~~ night. ~~to~~ because it was raing out side ~~the next more~~

the ~~blaw~~ next day there cousin Berta ~~let them~~ go out ~~as~~side with all of there freind's the first thing they ~~did~~did is play football after that they stoped playing football, and start catching frog of ~~cose~~ course ~~as~~ all of their freind had to caech one because it had rain. But the only thing they didnt new is that their cousen Berta was ~~a~~ waching the ~~th~~ of coorse David was the first to throw sice he was the holest thrower but all of their ~~suff he~~ Cousin berta came screaming out ~~of~~ the house and went hey you have Just kill a pore frog Just for Nothing. Then cousin Berta told them a Lot of things. Then she made them go ~~out~~ inside. And she had maide some tamales they smelled so good that the could hardly waite to eat them Cousin Berta didn't seamed to be angry ~~No~~ No more ~~sat~~ sat back and ate tamales. Then the boys told berta that now come the frogs where Croawing to much. then she said because maibe the are going to want to eat yall tow. Then she went on with a story and maby be scared and not want to go to ~~to~~ sleep

FIGURE 10.4. Rosalinda retells "El Sapo" (Rice, 1996).

liked taking care of children. She also liked playing "teacher" with younger children in her apartment complex.

Rosalinda's response to this text focused on the role of the older female caretaker; such was not the case, however, in the boys' retellings of this text. In the following example, José tells his own story by centering on the main character, David. In fact, he demonstrated his ability to tell creatively his reconstruction of "El Sapo." In Figure 10.5, he illustrated how his interest in this story enabled him to use his knowledge of writing and storytelling. For example, he used particular skills to make the story interesting, such as punctuation, expressive language, and dialogue, and to walk the reader through the events of the story and make the characters seem genuine. Throughout this retelling, he used this approach over and over again by recalling and using dialogue that the characters used. In addition, José was able to draw on his knowledge of storytelling, which is evident in the way he sequenced the events of the story and described the characters' reactions. For example, José enables the reader to visualize how frightened David and Roger feel at the end of the story, when he tells how the boys look at each other.

Deconstructing Social Issues

Another way that the students used their personal knowledge to comprehend the literature they read was to focus primarily on particular events the authors described in the stories. For example, after reading "Tito, Age 14" (Bode, 1989), Alfredo recalls various events in the story that he later reveals as his own concerns about living in his own community. In Figure 10.6, Alfredo recalls how Tito's parents talked with him about ignoring drugs and not "hang[ing] out with gangs," how Tito's father had lost his bakery, how "other people saying [say] that Mexicans can't do anything," and that "Tito said that he would show thoes [those] people that they were [w]rong." I attribute Alfredo's focus on these events as part of his true interest in the issues that Tito discusses in the story.

On several occasions, Alfredo mentioned the importance of making choices about drugs and student gang membership. His interest in these topics became very apparent in our focus group discussion about this story. During this conversation, Alfredo revealed his own use of alcohol and cigarettes, and, by doing so, convinced the other students to confess their experiences with these substances. In addition, Alfredo's family had also endured many economic hardships in both Mexico and in the United States. This became apparent to me in the interview I had with his mother, when she told me about losing her job and the family problems that resulted from that event. Finally, Alfredo wrote about how Tito was going to show Americans that they were wrong

El Sapo

There's a boy who use to catch sapas a lot. His name was David. Nobody could throw a sapo as far as him. He would get a sapo that was the size of his palm. he would let the frog's legs stick out between his fingers then he would throw it every body would say EEEEEE! oooo-oo! They would use sapos to play catch. They would shoot 'em with their BB guns. The sapos would get between the two yellow lines in the high way 107. The sapos' neck would pop out and the shot 'em. They used sapos for many things. There dad and mom went to Sanantonio The stayed with their prima. The trough a sapo and it landed. I didn't make a noise because it was dead. cousin Berta came out and told them why they killed that a sapo. They said it was just a sapo. She told them to put the sapos back in the charco. David said, "Even the ones in the box." Berta said what box She looked in the box and they were the small sapos. She told them to put those, too. They put them back because she looked pretty when she was angry. They went in the house she said when they were asleep the sapas wher going to kill them. They laughed. They told them about the time the sapos killed a baby.

Then they looked at each other and they were scared. But when they went to sleep they closed the windows and there was still a whole under the door. They went to sleep. They sleped well.

FIGURE 10.5. José retells "El Sapo" (Rice, 1996).

about Mexicans. This is not surprising, because these students appear to be aware of their cultural differences, and their parents often discuss how to get ahead in this country, as Alfredo's mother had expressed to me.

Other stories provoked similar discussions about social issues that the students endured on a regular basis. For example, in retelling *The House on Mango Street* (Cisneros, 1984), Sonia inferred that the main character, Esperanza, "wants to live in a(n) elegent (elegant) house so she won't be asame (ashamed) to show the house to her friend." In no part of Cisneros's text, is the notion of shame mentioned; however, Sonia believes that Esperanza must feel this way. When Sonia had completed the retelling in writing, she wrote a separate, personal reaction to the story. She stated:

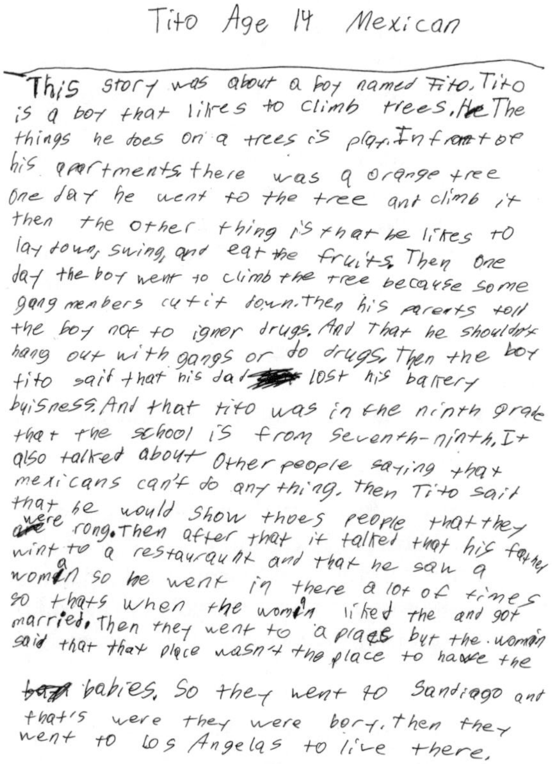

Tito   Age 14   Mexican

This story was about a boy named Tito. Tito is a boy that likes to climb trees. He The things he does on a trees is play. In front of his apartments there was a orange tree One day he went to the tree ant climb it then the other thing is that he likes to lay down, swing, and eat the fruits Then One day the boy went to climb the tree because some gang members cut it down. then his parents toll the boy not to igner drugs. And that he shouldn't hang out with gangs or do drugs. Then the boy tito said that his dad lost his battery buisness. And that tito was in the ninth grad that the school is from seventh-ninth. It also talked about Other people saying that mexicans can't do any thing. then Tito said that he would show thoes people that they were rong. Then after that it talked that his family wint to a restaurqunt and that he saw a woman so he went in there a lot of times so thats when the women liked the and got married. Then they went to a place but the woman said that that place wasn't the place to have the babies, So they went to Sandiego ant that's were they were bory. then they went to Los Angelas to live there.

FIGURE 10.6. Alfredo retells "Tito, Age 14" (Bode, 1989).

"Why I like this story is because it('s) about a familly [sic] and I like
story(ies) about familly [sic]. Also because it talks about a family
that moves and when I was in the thirde [sic] grade I moved to three
diffren't [sic] schools and I still stayed in thirde [sic] grade. I went
with Mis(s) Etone, Mrs. Cantu, and Mrs. Celedon."

Sonia was able to relate this story to her personal life experiences. In our
focus group session, Sonia told our group about these events, and about
having one teacher after another in one school year. She contributed
many thoughts about being poor and expressed what appeared to be anger and frustration about how society viewed poor people.

Another story, *Eleven*, by Sandra Cisneros (1991) provoked similar
responses by the students. For example, they seemed to understand
Esperanza's powerlessness to speak up when the teacher put the un-
claimed red sweater on her desk. Although they did not describe "powerlessness" in their response, the students still seemed to understand why
the main character responded the way she did.

In some of the students' retellings of the Mexican American stories,
they appeared to take complete ownership of the texts they read by re-
constructing the stories as a storyteller would do for an audience. On
these occasions, the students appear to use all that they know about
writing, stories, and characters' feelings. In these writing samples, the
students walk the reader through the events of the tale by using expressive language, transitioning words, and precise timing to make the story
come alive for the reader. For example, Rosalinda demonstrates her storytelling ability in her retelling of *Eleven* (Cisneros, 1991).

In reading Rosalinda's reconstruction, it is clear that she ties the
major themes of the story to feelings of the main character in the story.
She does this by telling what the character is thinking as she interacts
with her teacher. Rosalinda is careful to use details, such as the following:

"When she wanted to say something the teacher turns around and
goes to give the Math page. The girl just said in a Low voice it's Not
mine. Then when the other children are working in math she is over
there in her desk thinking how is she going to get rid of the sweater.
At last she move's [sic] the sweater at (to) the eadge (edge) of her
desk. . . ."

In addition, Rosalinda appears to invite the reader into a particular context, such as a regular school day "in science" and "math." Using these
details, she places the reader squarely in the middle of the classroom and
makes the events realistic.

In responding to *The House on Mango Street* (Cisneros, 1984), by relating their personal experiences of feeling inadequate to the group, the students inferred that they knew what the main character was feeling. For example, in the following lengthy yet telling dialogue, Sonia expresses how she relates to the character by telling her own story of moving from school to school when she was in the third grade. The other students chime in with their own stories, and the conversation seems to take off, revealing extreme sensitivity on the part of the students. This conversation took place immediately after the students had written their retellings of the story:

LEILA: How did you like *The House on Mango Street*?

SONIA: I liked it because it talks about a family that moves a lot. 'Cause when I was in third grade, I moved a lot and I moved to three schools and I was still in third grade.

LEILA: What was so hard about moving a lot?

SONIA: That I'd leave my friends behind. So my mom, in one year I was in one school, she told me not to make friends because then we had to move.

LEILA: Wow, yeah, I moved a lot too when I was a kid. So tell me, how do you feel about the story?

ALFREDO: Good, but I hated the last part, because they went to Mango Street and the girl said to someone where they lived and they said "over there," and the girl didn't want to live there.

ROSALINDA: They made her feel like she was nothing.

Later in the conversation:

LEILA: Do you think is good to read stuff like this?

JOSÉ: Yes.

LEILA: That talks about being poor?

SONIA: I can relate to it.

ROSALINDA: It makes you remember things that you think about—your life.

JOSÉ: Maybe we think about what he's thinking.

This discussion continued, illustrating the vast range of students' awareness and emotions about their socioeconomic status, and about living in their particular communities. In this narrative, the students appear to be very conscientious and caring individuals, who can express themselves well. This literature selection sparked so many thoughtful personal insights and responses to difficult issues that were important in these students' lives.

DISCUSSION

In general, the students interacted with the Mexican American texts by bringing their own personal experiences to the discussions about the stories. These personal responses clearly indicate that the students took an aesthetic stance to nearly all parts of these stories. They also seemed to be able to infer information from the texts, because they understood the main themes, events, and feelings of the characters.

From the retellings and subsequent discussions about these texts, it was obvious that the students identified with the Mexican American texts in many ways. For example, they consistently mentioned characters' names that sounded Mexican or Spanish. The students expressed that it would be good to find books with names that sounded Spanish, because they would be more interested in reading them. They respectfully identified with the author, as if he or she were the same gender as the student reading the texts. They tried to recall the names of authors of Mexican American texts, because they seemed to identify with the story content in some way and because they wanted to find other books by the author.

In addition, during the discussions, the students interacted with the texts in rich and insightful ways. They consistently demonstrated that they understood the experiences of the characters by sharing similar stories in their own lives. The students also brought their personal experiences of living in their communities and homes to the discussions about the Mexican American texts. They revealed their understanding of living in communities similar to those of the characters portrayed in the texts.

Finally, their retellings of the Mexican American literature revealed that they understood what was happening in these stories; they appeared to have adequate social, cultural, and linguistic background knowledge to construct meaning from the texts. In their retellings, the students demonstrated that they were able to recall and support the main idea of the story with a significant amount of written details. Their writing samples were significantly longer and contained more depth than those that they wrote about the non–Mexican American literature. In these retellings, the students connected with particular characters, depending on their personal experiences. For example, Rosalinda provided the reader with a perspective of the character, Cousin Berta, who cooked and took care of her younger cousins—similar to Rosalinda's experiences with her younger siblings. We also saw how José utilized what he knew about good writing to retell *El Sapo* as a storyteller would. Using his own creative writing skills, he was able to reconstruct a vivid story to make the characters seem realistic. Sonia was able to use inference skills to reconstruct meaning from the *The House on Mango Street*. She understood what the story was about and was able to relay her personal feelings about this story during the focus group discussion. Alfredo demonstrated that he understood the stories and was able to employ what he knew about good writing.

REFERENCES

Au, K. H., & Kawakami, A. J. (1991). Culture and ownership: Schooling of minority students. *Childhood Education, 67*(5), 280–284.

Barrera, R. B., Liguori, O., & Salas, L. (1993). Ideas literature can grow on: Key insights for enriching and expanding children's literature about the Mexican American experience. In V. J. Harris (Ed.), *Teaching multicultural literature in grades K–8* (pp. 203–241). Norwood, MA: Christopher Gordon.

Bishop, R. S. (1993). Multicutural literature for children: Making informed choices. In V. J. Harris (Ed.), *Teaching multicultural literature in grades K–8* (pp. 37–54). Norwood, MA: Christopher Gordon.

Flores-Dueñas, L. (1997). *Second language reading: Mexican American student voices on reading Mexican American literature.* Unpublished doctoral dissertation, University of Texas, Austin.

Langer, J. A. (1987). A sociocognitive perspective on literacy. In J. A. Langer (Ed.), *Language, literacy and culture: Issues in society and school* (pp. 1–20). Norwood, NJ: Ablex.

Martínez, M. G., & Roser, N. L. (1995). The books that make a difference in story talk. In N. L. Roser & M. G. Martínez (Eds.), *Book talk and beyond: Children and teachers respond to literature* (pp. 32–42). Newark, DE: International Reading Association.

Rosenblatt, L. M. (1978). *The reader, the text, the poem.* Carbondale: Southern Illinois University Press.

Rosenblatt, L. M. (1983). *Literature as exploration* (4th ed.). New York: Modern Language Association.

ADULT, YOUNG ADULT, AND CHILDREN'S LITERATURE

Allende, I. (1995). *Eva Luna.* New York: HarperCollins.

Allende, I. (1984). *House of the spirits.* New York: Bantam.

Anaya, R. (1972). *Bless me Última.* New York: Warner.

Angelou, M. (1969). *I know why the cages bird sings.* New York: Bantam.

Baldwin, J. (1985). *Go tell it on the mountain.* New York: Laureleaf.

Benchley, P. (1974). *Jaws*. New York: Ballantine.

Bode, J. (1989). Tito, age 14. In *New kids in town: Oral histories of immigrant teens*. New York: Scholastic.

Cisneros, S. (1984). *The house on Mango Street*. New York: Vintage.

Cisneros, S. (1991). Eleven. In *Woman hollering creek*. New York: Vintage.

Cohn, A. M., & Schmidt, S. (1993). With a way, hey, Mister Stormalong. In A. L. Cohn (Ed.), *From sea to shining sea: A treasury of American folklore and folk songs*. New York: Scholastic.

Dostoevsky, F. (1958). *Crime and punishment*. New York: Bantam.

Fitzgerald, F. S. (1952). *The great gatsby*. New York: Simon & Schuster.

Frank, O. (1952). *Anne Frank: Diary of a young girl*. New York: Doubleday.

Gray, W. S., Artley, A. S., & Arbuthnot, M. H. (1940–1970s). *Dick and Jane stories*. New York: Scott, Foresman.

Greene, B. (1973). *Summer of my German soldier*. New York: Dial Press.

Hawthorn, N. (1965). *The scarlet letter*. New York: Bantam.

Kellogg, S. (1994). *Paul Bunyan*. New York: Scholastic.

Knowles, J. (1985). *A separate peace*. Upper Saddle River, NJ: Prentice-Hall.

Rawls, W. (1961). *Where the red fern grows*. New York: Bantam.

Rice, D. (1994). El Sapo. In *Give the pig a chance*. Houston: Bilingual Press.

Rey, H. A., & Rey, M. (1941). *Curious George*. New York: Houghton Mufflin.

Steinbeck, J. (1972). *The grapes of wrath*. New York: Viking Press.

Styron, W. (1979). *Sophie's choice*. New York: Vintage.

Tan, A. (1992). *The kitchen god's wife*. New York: Ballantine/Ivy Books.

Villaseñor, V. (1991). *Rain of gold*. New York: Dell.

Williams, M. (1983). *Velveteen rabbit*. New York: Holt.

Wright, B. (1994). *The real Mother Goose*. New York: Scholastic.

Chapter 11

Parallel Development of Writing in English and German

EURYDICE BOUCHEREAU BAUER

A great deal of research in the area of young children's writing (i.e., Bissex, 1980; Ferreiro & Teborosky, 1982/1996; Schickendanz, 1990) reveals "children's growing awareness of the relationship between oral and written language and their knowledge about print" (Seda & Abramson, 1990, p. 380). These studies suggest that children must reconstruct and reconceptualize the written system and make it an object of knowledge to make it their own (Ferreiro, 1986, 1996, as cited in Moll, Sáez, & Dworin, 2001).

Ferreiro and Teborosky (1982/1996) were the first to identify a progressive sequence of levels through which young, Spanish-speaking 4-, 5-, and 6-year-old children move on their way to becoming proficient writers. Young children move through these levels in the following way:

Level 1: Children use curved or straight lines to represent print.
Level 2: Children's writing reflects conventional letters and a fixed number of characters to a word.
Level 3: Children use sound for the different characters; each character represents a language sound, usually a syllable.
Level 4: Children engage in more alphabetic writing.

Kamii, Long, Manning, and Manning (1986) replicated part of Ferreiro and Teborosky's study (1982/1996) with English-speaking children. They found that 4-, 5-, and 6-year-old English-speaking children move through the same developmental levels as the children in Ferreiro and Teborosky's study. The only variation in the findings was at Level 3. Ferreiro and Teborosky found that students use characters to represent syllables, whereas Kamii and colleagues found that the English-speaking children use each character to represent individual consonants.

Bus, Sulzby, de Jong, and de Jong (2001) have added to the discussion on developmental levels found in young children's writing. They examined the writing development of 4-, 5-, and 6-year-olds, and found that the children used a variety of scribbles, well-learned elements (i.e., names), and nonphonetic and invented spelling. Baseline data with the older children did not reveal the use of more invented spelling. When children were encouraged to use their phonetic-based alphabetic knowledge, they increased their use of inventive spelling. However, the children continued to use earlier forms of writing, along with invented spelling. The authors hypothesized that until young children fully comprehend and integrate a particular form of writing, they will continue to write using all the forms at their disposal. In fact, young children's mixed use of the previously mentioned forms of writing may assist them in writing longer stories.

Yaden (as cited in Stahl & Yaden, in press), in his study of 100 four-year-old, Spanish-speaking children in the United States, found that they exhibited developmental levels similar to those of students in Ferreiro and Teborosky's (1982/1996) study. However, similar to results in the Bus and colleagues study, they found that young children's understanding of a particular form of writing does not limit their use of less sophisticated forms. For example, approximately 25% of the students in Yaden's study used one graphic to represent a syllable, and 6% understood that individual letters in their name represent a smaller unit of a spoken word than a syllable. These students continued to use less sophisticated written forms in conjunction with graphic forms representing syllables and phonemes.

Most of the research on bilingual's writing has been done with limited-English-proficient (LEP) students. Edelsky's (1986, 1989) research increased understanding of writing by young bilinguals. She questioned the fallacies associated with learning to write in a bilingual context, namely, that children need to speak a language before they can develop literacy in that language, and that they must follow a fixed sequence for learning to take place. In general, it can be said that the research on young bilingual children's writing development across both languages is quite limited. From the small body of research that exists (i.e., Cukor-Avila & Hadaway, 1986; Brisk, 1985; Schwarzer, 1996; Seda & Abramson, 1990) we know the following:

1. These students show a greater disposition to code-switch during oral communication than in their writing. The code switching that occurred there was triggered by social factors.
2. If these students are allowed the opportunity to explore writing in both languages in a supportive environment, they do so.

Although research on LEP students' writing development across their two languages is limited, even less is known about how writing develops for young simultaneous bilinguals. Simultaneous bilinguals are children raised from birth with two languages. The need for attention to this area of research is great given the increasing number of bilinguals in the United States (National Center for Educational Statistics, 2001). Understanding how young bilinguals at the emergent stages of biliteracy development approach a written task, and the influence of the two languages on their writing development, will impact researchers' approaches to exploring how LEP students approach writing. Currently, we know that Spanish speakers may use individual graphic symbols to represent syllables instead of individual sounds (Ferreiro & Teborosky, 1982/1996); however, we do not have a working model of how children, for example, who speak Spanish and are in the process of learning English make use of both languages.

In this chapter, I report on one simultaneous bilingual's writing development from the age of 3 years, 11 months to 4 years, 10 months. This chapter highlights the type of writing in which the child engaged, her general writing development, and the influence of bilingualism on her writing development.

METHOD

This research is part of a larger longitudinal study focusing on the biliteracy and language development of Elena, a young bilingual (English/German), from the age of 2 years to 5 years, 6 months. The study is a single-case ethnographic study. This chapter focuses on Elena's writing from the age of 3 years, 11 months to 4 years, 10 months. During this period, Elena attended a halfday preschool and was at home in the afternoon with a German-speaking day care provider.

The primary participants are Elena; her father, a native German speaker; her mother; the researcher, an English-dominant speaker; and her German-speaking caregivers. Elena's father spoke only German to her; her mother, only English; and her German caregiver, German. All the adults spoke English with each other.

Data collected for this study included Elena's writing samples from both home and school. Some of the home samples include notes to a family members, stories, and labeling of pictures Elena drew. The school writing samples, primarily copies of pages the teacher had given the students, were later excluded from analysis, because they did not provide insight on Elena's emergent writing development. The examples did show that Elena was able to copy what had been given to her. The few written samples not prescribed were later analyzed. Handwritten notes on each writing sample that explained the context for the writing were also included for analysis. In all, 107 writing samples were collected from January to December 1999.

As part of the analysis, all writing samples were read and reread, and categorized according to type of writing, the person who interacted with Elena relative to the writing, the type of help she received during the writing activity, the audience for the writing, language use, spelling, and the content of Elena's writing.

RESULTS

Types of Writing

Analysis of the type of writing in which Elena participated revealed that some of it represented the writing of single letters–words–sentences, with instances of random single-letter writing and scribbling. Elena also attempted to write single letters sequentially, as in writing the alphabet.

Some of her writing samples resulted from her own exploration of writing, when she was alone in her room. Other samples were written when an adult was in the room, but there was no adult engagement in Elena's writing. At times, the writing was a direct result of a parent or caregiver helping her write a word. Often, this involved the adult stretching the word (i.e., /c/ /a/ /t/) for Elena, so she could hear the sounds in the words.

Format for Writing and Audience

Elena's writing was typical of that of most children her age; that is, she wrote letters or cards for close family members. She would also write messages to her family. Periodically, Elena wrote a few sentences she called a "story"; lists, such as grocery lists; and what she wanted to get as presents from her parents. Elena's writing was primarily intended for her family and close family friends in the United States. However, she did, on occasion, write to her grandparents in Germany and her daycare provider.

Writing Development

Elena used single letters to represent words. This occurred to a greater degree earlier in the year than later. This type of writing occurred far less on or after May 1999. For example, in the following examples, Elena uses each letter to represent an entire word. The only exception was when she wrote her name: L F ELENA D F DHL [love from Elena, is this thank? dank you for this heart, love] (March 3, 1999). It is clear that her name represents a different type of writing (i.e., known element). She had experimented numerous times with her name and was able to write it using standard spelling. It is also important to note that this type of writing, in which one letter represents an entire word, was more prevalent when Elena attempted to write an entire sentence or phrase.

Typical of other writers her age, Elena used fewer vowels in her writing at the beginning of the year. In the following example, we see that she often represented the beginning, middle, and end of a consonant sound in each of the words (i.e., DG [dog] (January 2, 1999); KTS [katze = cat] (January 2, 1999); KRSTFR [Christopher] (January 2, 1999); GST [gesagt = said] (April 30, 1999). This type of writing was typical when she wrote individual words. The use of vowels in her writing appeared with greater frequency during the second half of the year. For example, Elena wrote the following words when writing messages to various people: geBN [geben = give] (June 18, 1999); bEGINNG [beginning] (August 30, 1999); DANKE [danke = thank you] (September 9, 1999); LAIDIBOG [ladybug] (October 2, 1999).

In general, Elena captured what she heard in the words (i.e., Pla [play] (January 29, 1999); LIBE [liebe = dear] (September 9, 1999); BDRFLI [butterfly] (October 2, 1999); cadplr [caterpillar] (October 2, 1999). Her increasing ability to sound out words and to represent them phonetically was supported by the adults around her. They would often enunciate the words for Elena and stretch them out for her as she wrote. By the end of the year, Elena was stretching out the words and attempting to represent all the sounds she could hear.

The social construct supporting her emergent writing skills can be understood in terms of the nature of the interactions of adults with Elena relative to her writing. At the same time that Elena was engaging in these types of writing explorations, she was also developing good decoding skills in reading. She was reading approximately at the first-grade level in both languages as she approached her fifth birthday. Just 2 months before her fifth birthday, she wrote a note for her mother. It is a good illustration of what she did in her writing and of what she knew about language and writing. She wrote:

For mom
stor mom
i lik wn u hag mee i lik wen u kis mee i l wen u ar wsc mee
elena

[Star mom, I like when you hug me, I like when you kiss me, I like when
you are with me. Elena—December 20, 1999]

Although her mother appreciated the kind gesture, she found it fascinat-
ing that many of the words that Elena spelled inventively were words
that she consistently, and readily, recognized when reading. After Elena
read the note, her mother asked her which words she would write differently now that she had written the note and had a little more time to
think about the way the authors of her books would have written the
words Elena wrote. Her mother suggested that Elena visualize the
words; that is, to imagine a line that she had read recently, in which that
particular word was used. After doing this for each of the words, Elena
came up with the following: "I like when you heg mee. I like when you
kiss me. I like when you are woth me." This example shows that Elena's
initial drafts were not a true indicator of her overall writing performance. The simple nudge by her mother elicited a level of writing performance that was not anticipated by either Elena or her mother.

Influence of Bilingual Factors on Elena's Writing

On closer examination of Elena's writing, it appears that she utilized her
knowledge of both of her languages when writing. She tried to generalize certain letter–sound pairs across the two languages:

ECH [ich = I] German—from English (e.g., each) (June 18, 1999)
leb [liebe, dear or love] German—from English (e.g., leave) (April
   25, 1999)
FRAND [friend] English—from English (e.g., sand) (August 31,
   1999)
mee [me] English—from English (e.g., see) (December 20, 1999)
Cst [kennst = know] German—from English (e.g., comedy) (Febru-
   ary 13, 1999)

In the first example, we see that Elena used what she understood about
English sounds to help her write *ich* [ich = I]. In German, the initial
sound in the word sounds like a short *i*. She represented it using the long
sound for the letter *e* in English. In the second example, she used the letter *e* in English to create the long *e* sound written as *ie* in German. In
both examples, she used the name of the letter to represent the *e* sound.

The third example reveals what Elena already knew about word families, that is, that the sound /and/ is created by using *and*, and she extended that understanding to the word *friend*. The fourth example reveals that she also understood that two *es* make the long /e/ sound in English. The last example, again, shows her use of English to represent German sounds. In English, it is permissible to use a *c* at the beginning of a word to represent a hard /k/ sound. By contrast, German words with a hard /k/ sound at the beginning typically start with a *k*. German names and borrowed words (i.e., Latin words) may start with a *c*. However, in these cases, the letter *c* must be followed by an *h* to create the /k/ sound. We can say, looking at the above examples, that Elena attempted to write German words the way they sounded in German, using English sounds.

It should be noted that Elena seldom code-switched in her writing. When she did, it was often one word in the sentence, and the code switch maintained the syntactical nature of the sentence. For example, in the earlier example, in which Elena wrote L F ELENA D F D H L [love from Elena. Danke (thank you) for this heart, love] (March 3, 1999), we see her substituting the word *danke* for the words *thank you* in English. It is interesting to note that the single word *danke* in German represents what is said in two words in English. Elena appeared to be aware of this, because she did not attempt to write *danke you* in her sentence.

Another interesting aspect to Elena's writing is that she seemed to have some level of awareness that some English and German words sound alike but are spelled differently (i.e., *house, Haus*). However, when asked to take a second look at her writing and to try to spell the words the way she had seen them in her books, those words having close ties, such as *house/Haus*, were the last to be changed. Some of Elena's code switches in her writing occurred intrasentencially and reflected these types of words.

There is a match between Elena's audience and the language she used in her writing. The only exception is one example in which she wrote to the German caregiver in English. When she attempted to write to a German-speaking person, she typically wrote in German. For example, in a computer message to her grandmother in Germany, Elena wrote, "Oma, leb oma leb opa Lea oma ek wl an gshek" (Oma, Liebe Oma, Lieber Opa, Liebe Oma ich will ein Geschenk) (April, 25, 1999) [Grandma, dear grandma, dear grandpa, dear grandma I want a present]. Again, we see the same type of spelling patterns discussed earlier.

It is also apparent from the data that Elena explored the different sounds across the languages. For example, she wrote *liebe* as *libe* and *later* as *lebe*. Her knowledge about what makes the long /e/ sound in German was still in flux.

When all of Elena's writing is taken into account, it is apparent that she preferred to write in English. Sixty-four percent of her writing analyzed here was in English. She also code-switched in her writing (28%). German is seen only in 8% of her total writing. When alone, Elena did not write in German at all; alone, she wrote in English most of the time (81%). She did periodically code-switch in her writing (19%).

CONCLUSIONS AND IMPLICATIONS

The code-switching patterns found in Elena's writing were similar to those found in her reading (see Bauer, 2000). Her code-switching patterns were systematic and revealed Elena's working understanding of German and English. Given her age, it is not surprising that much of this understanding was still emerging. In general, Elena tended to stay in the basic syntax with which she started, and her code switches were appropriately placed.

These findings also fit with the general data on code switching. According to Saunders (1988), children tend to code-switch because of the language of the conversational partner, because they are able to access one word in one language faster than in another language, and because of the topic of the conversation. It appears that in a number of situations, Elena code-switched because she could retrieve a word faster in one language than the language in which she was writing. However, if we stop here in our understanding of what Elena did when she wrote, we would be overlooking some key issues.

I have argued (see Bauer, 2000) that spontaneous, oral code switchers are well aware of their specific use of code switching, as well as its occurrence in their communities (Poplack, 1988; Sankoff & Poplack, 1981; Scotton, 1983), and extrapolate that readers, too, have specific uses for code switching in their reading (Muysken, Kook, & Vedder, 1996). I would extend this premise to writing as well. Elena made clear how her knowledge of the two languages influenced the spelling in her writing. Her examples reveal a complex understanding that extends beyond what she could convey in words to adults.

Another aspect of the data that is consistent with other research studies is how context and the interlocutor influenced Elena's writing. This fits with what we know about young bilinguals. Literacy, like all language acts, is socially constructed, and the bilingual influences the context in which he or she is. The type of assistance that Elena received from the adults who interacted with her undoubtedly shaped her emergent understanding of how to approach and represent ideas in writing. However, as Wells (1989) and Wolf (1990) suggest, children eventually learn through these socializing processes how to exploit their linguistic abilities to serve their communicative and intellectual goals. Certainly, we see Elena using her written language skills to garnish gifts from her grandparents, and to gain affection and attention from her mother.

Findings from this study also support Yaden's (as cited in Stahl & Yaden, in press) and Bus and colleagues' (2001) findings that young children between the ages of 4 and 6 use a mixed repertoire of written forms, even when they are aware of phonetics. Elena, like many of the children in these findings, used all she knew about written forms in both languages to communicate her ideas on paper. The lengthier the piece, the greater the likelihood that Elena would use single letters to represent whole words; a single, consonant letter to represent the sounds at the beginning, middle, and end of a word; and inventive spelling to represent her understanding of individual phonemes.

These findings overlap with Yaden's findings in yet another way. Yaden found that students' knowledge of letter names was not a strong indicator of their choice of written forms during writing. In fact, he suggests that the best way to understand what students know about written forms is through "clinical interviews." Although no "clinical interviews" were conducted with Elena, she participated in ongoing discussions about writing with various individuals. In part, through these discussions, I was able to discern Elena's intent and strategies. These findings have implication for research conducted with young children that merely collects their writing, with the intent of representing students' understanding of writing and its development. Both this and Yaden's studies seem to suggest that more is needed to understand fully these young bilinguals.

Although this study highlights several points regarding what young simultaneous bilinguals might do when writing in both of their languages, other issues related to the development of biliteracy must be addressed. This study shows that if we want to promote biliteracy in the fullest sense, especially in the area of writing, we have to allocate the same amount of attention to biliteracy as we do to reading. In retrospect, it is apparent to me that we did not support Elena's writing to the same degree we supported her reading. In particular, Elena was left to write in German, if she chose to do so. This latitude was not given to Elena's reading. She was supported to read not just in English, but in both her languages. Although no specific decision was made to promote English writing, the result is that Elena did little writing in German. This has real consequences for teachers attempting to develop bilingual writers through a bilingual program. The same attention and opportunities must be given to both languages. According to Moll and colleagues (2001), "Becoming literate in two languages . . . implies that not only the acquisition and development of a set of skills or abilities but how children become competent in a range of practices or uses of literacy constitute the experience of living and going to school in a bilingual community" (p. 447). Studies such as this one will extend the view that to understand biliteracy is to understand discourse and literacies not found in monolinguals.

REFERENCES

Bauer, E. B. (2000). Code-switching during shared and independent reading: Lessons learned from a preschooler. *Research in the Teaching of English, 35*(1), 101–130.

Bissex, G. (1980). *Gnys at wrk: A child learns to write and read.* Cambridge, MA: Harvard University Press.

Bus, A. G., Sulzby, E., de Jong, W., & de Jong, E. (2001). *Conceptualizations underlying emergent readers' story writing* (CIERA Report No. 2-015). Ann Arbor: University of Michigan, School of Education.

Cukor-Avila, P., & Hadaway, N. L. (1986). *Composing in two languages: A bilingual child's response* (Report No. ED280288). Paper presented at the annual meeting of the National Social Science Association, San Antonio, TX.

Edelsky, C. (1986). *Writing in a bilingual program: Había una vez.* Norwood, NJ: Ablex.

Edelsky, C. (1989). Bilingual children's writing: Fact and fiction. In D. M. Johnson & D. H. Roen (Eds.), *Richness in writing: Empowering ESL students* (pp. 165–176). New York: Longman.

Ferreiro, E. (1986). The interplay between information and assimilation in beginning literacy. In W. H. Teale & E. Sulzby (Eds.), *Emergent literacy: Writing and reading* (pp. 15–49). Norwood, NJ: Ablex.

Ferreiro, E. (1996). The acquisition of cultural objects: The case of written language. *Prospects, 26*(1), 131–140.

Ferreiro, E., & Teborosky, A. (1996). *Literacy before schooling.* Portsmouth, NH: Heinemann. (Original work published 1982)

Kamii, C., Long, R., Manning, M., & Manning, G. (1986, April). *Spelling in kindergarten.* Paper presented at the annual meeting of the American Research Association, San Francisco.

Moll, L., Sáez, R., & Dworin, J. (2001). Exploring biliteracy: Two student case examples of writing as a social practice. *Elementary School Journal, 101*(4), 435–449.

Muysken, P., Kook, H., & Vedder, P. (1996). Papiamento/Dutch code-switching in bilingual parent–child reading. *Applied Psycholinguistics, 17,* 485–505.

National Center for Educational Statistics. (2001). *Condition of education, 2001* [Online]. Available at: http://nces.ed.gov/pubsearch/pubinfo.asp?pubid=200172

Poplack, S. (1988). Contrasting patterns of code-switching in two communities. In M. Heller (Ed.), *Code-switching: Anthropological and sociological perspectives* (pp. 217–244). Berlin: de Gruyter.

Sankoff, D., & Poplack, S. (1981). A formal grammar for code-switching. *Papers in Linguistics*, *14*, 3–45.

Saunders, G. (1988). *Bilingual children: From birth to teens*. Clevedon, UK: Multilingual Matters.

Schickedanz, J. (1990). *Adam's writing revolutions: One child's literacy development from infancy through grade one*. Portsmouth, NH: Heinemann.

Schwarzer, D. (1996). *Parallel development of writing in Hebrew, Spanish and English in a multilingual child*. Ann Arbor, MI: UMI Dissertation Services.

Scotton, C. M. (1983). The negotiation of identities in conversation: A theory of markedness and code choice. *International Journal of the Sociology of Language*, *44*, 115–136.

Seda, L., & Abramson, S. (1990). English writing development of young, linguistically different learners. *Early Childhood Research Quarterly*, *5*, 379–339.

Stahl, S., & Yaden, D. B., Jr. (in press). Development of literacy in preschool and primary grades. *Elementary School Journal*.

Wells, G. (1989). Language in the classroom: Literacy and collaborative talk. *Language and Education*, *3*(1), 6–11.

Wolf, D. P. (1990). For literate lives: The possibilities for elementary schools. In C. Hedley, J. Houtz, & A. Baratta (Eds.), *Cognition, curriculum, and literacy* (pp. 121–136). Norwood, NJ: Ablex.

Chapter 12

Supporting the Silent Second-Language Learner

A Professor Learns from a Kindergartner

LAURA KLENK

> Our tutoring session was over and I escorted Carmen back to
> her kindergarten class. A few steps from the classroom door,
> Carmen stopped and turned to me, grinning broadly. "Pink,"
> she exclaimed, pointing to a flower embroidered on her
> sweater. "Green," she continued, pointing to another, and then
> "Orange." Carmen's twinkling dark eyes glanced shyly upward
> to catch my delight and approval before she slipped quietly
> back into her class.
>
> —FIELD NOTES, MID-DECEMBER

To the principal and teachers at Cityview Early Childhood Center, a
bilingual inner-city school, little Carmen[1] was an enigma. The second of
five siblings in a trans-migratory Puerto Rican family, Carmen had
undergone a standard language evaluation during the kindergarten
screening process. This evaluation was unsuccessful, because Carmen
refused to respond to either English or Spanish prompts. Her mother reported that both Spanish and English were spoken at home, but without
Carmen's participation in the evaluation, it was not possible to determine her dominant language. Her older brother, Carlos, was repeating

---

[1] Pseudonyms are given for the participant and school name.

kindergarten at Cityview; he had been evaluated as language-delayed and had failed to meet grade-level expectations the previous year. Because school staff believed that Carmen might struggle with the same difficulties as her brother, she was assigned to begin the school year in a Spanish-only rather than a bilingual class.

In early October, her teacher reported that Carmen was still not speaking either to her or to other children. Carmen's receptive language seemed to be fine, but it was possible that she followed the actions of her classmates through the daily routines. Mainstream American culture values expressive language. As teachers, we often judge children not only by what they say but also how well they say it. A child like Carmen makes us uncomfortable, in part because her silence means that we cannot evaluate her progress. Was Carmen learning the alphabet? Could she count? Did she know color words? If she completed worksheets correctly, was it because she understood the directions or because she copied the child next to her? In addition, research from sociolinguistic and cognitive perspectives (Snow & Tabors, 1993) indicates a strong correlation, even a reciprocal relation, between oral language and literacy acquisition. Watson (2001) summarizes this perspective: "It is that forms of oral language associated with literacy can be orally transmitted and, once acquired, facilitate the acquisition of literacy-related skills and success in formal education" (p. 43).

The relation between language and literacy is more complex for young children who are learning English as a second language (ESL). Our understanding of these complexities is still developing, but it is clear that specific *patterns* of support for both the first and second language, along with the *continuity* of support across home and school contexts, may have either positive or detrimental effects on language and literacy acquisition (Tabors & Snow, 2001). The more teachers know about how language is used at home, the more effectively they can plan for school support. In Carmen's case, which is not atypical, very little was known about the ways Spanish and English were used in her home.

Concerned that Carmen was not learning in the Spanish-only class, the principal and teachers transferred her to a bilingual classroom, where they hoped she would be more willing to speak. Several weeks passed and Carmen was still not talking. At this time, in early November, I offered to volunteer in the kindergarten program. I had recently moved to the city and was interested in meeting teachers who might want to participate in a collaborative research project in early literacy. Cityview was the primary school in my neighborhood—a historically Italian section of the city that now included a growing Hispanic community. My offer to volunteer was welcomed by the principal and kindergarten teachers, and soon I was meeting Carmen in the school library once a week for 30- to 40-minute tutoring sessions, which lasted until the end of the school year in mid-June.

I audiotaped these tutoring sessions and kept brief field notes of our activities, filling in details from these field notes as I transcribed the tapes. In addition, I photocopied all written pieces and drawings produced by Carmen. One purpose for collecting these artifacts was to compile a record of Carmen's development over time; another was to help me assess my interactions with her. Although I am bilingual, my second language is not Spanish, and I began our association with serious doubts about my ability to be helpful.

In this chapter, I describe the different ways I engaged and supported Carmen in language and literacy activities. To begin, I describe my initial, awkward attempts to engage Carmen in conversation. I then focus on how I used opportunities for storybook reading and emergent writing to facilitate Carmen's development of print concepts and written language structures, and how I came to realize that what I thought were simply good, emergent literacy activities were in fact rich opportunities for oral language development. Woven throughout the chapter is a discussion of the theoretical principles of language and literacy development that guided my decision making.

ESTABLISHING RAPPORT AND ELICITING EXPRESSIVE LANGUAGE

My first conversations with Carmen centered on familiar objects and people. I commented on her colorful clothing and the bright accessories that decorated her ever-changing hairstyles. I engaged Carmen in a guessing game, pointing to decorations (kittens, flowers, balloons, etc.) on her sweaters. "This flower is orange. Where is the green flower?" Soon Carmen joined the game, whispering answers that were barely audible. She was not always accurate, but she responded appropriately with color names. The anecdote that opens this chapter marked a turning point in my work with Carmen: It was the first time she spoke to me without a prompt, borrowing from a now well-rehearsed "Guess the Color" game. Carmen was becoming a risk taker with language; that she was learning to identify colors and color names was also a sign of progress in the kindergarten curriculum.

Math skills, such as counting and demonstrating the concept of quantity, are also important in the kindergarten curriculum, and I brought counting games and number flash cards to our sessions. In the following excerpt, Carmen was shown a set of cards with the numerals 1 to 5. I turned over one card at a time to see whether she could recognize the numbers in random order.

LAURA: OK, Carmen, tell me about these numbers.

CARMEN: (*whispering*) I can't say the numbers.

LAURA: Let's try this one.

CARMEN: One.

LAURA: I thought you couldn't say the numbers! What's this one?

CARMEN: Two?

LAURA: It sure is. How about this one?

CARMEN: Five?

LAURA: How about this one?

CARMEN: One?

LAURA: Close, three. How about this one?

CARMEN: Four.

LAURA: That's right! And this?

CARMEN: Five.

In this transcript, note that I maintained a stance of *confident expectation*; that is, I did not verbally acknowledge Carmen's lack of confidence but rather forged ahead: "Let's try this one." At the same time, my own language may have confused Carmen, because I asked repeatedly, "What's this *one*?" A better choice of words would have been, "What's this *number*?" I did not always catch such confusions, but by listening to the transcripts, I realized the need to be more deliberate in my choice of words.

Along with color and counting games, I engaged Carmen in social rituals that often mark conversations between adults and children, such as asking about her family, her birthday, or her age, as in the following excerpt:

LAURA: How old are you?

CARMEN: Carmen.

LAURA: How *old* are you? I know your *name* is Carmen. Are you 5 years old?

CARMEN: Just nice.

LAURA: Yes, you're just nice. And I think you're 5, and Carlos [her brother] is 6.

Carmen understood from my intonation that I was asking her a question. After repeating the question and getting no response, I elaborated, awkwardly: "I know your name is Carmen. Are you 5 years old?" Carmen gave another response that, once again, indicated she was familiar with the question, "How are you?" From this brief interaction, I could tell that Carmen was learning to respond with an appropriate sense of language pragmatics.

Those of us who work with young children often assume that 5-year-olds have acquired the language to respond to such ritualistic questions, but for ESL learners, even these routines must be practiced. Each new experience becomes a language lesson, as seen in the following excerpt, as Carmen inspected the contents of my book bag:

CARMEN: Look!

LAURA: What is this? What do we call this?

CARMEN: This. Bag.

LAURA: It's like a bag, because we put things in it. It's called a *folder*.

CARMEN: Folder?

LAURA: What is in the folder?

CARMEN: Folder.

LAURA: What else?

CARMEN: A paper.

LAURA: What do you call it?

CARMEN: This.

LAURA: What is it like?

CARMEN: Umm...

LAURA: It's like a *pencil*, but it's a *marker*.

Each new item that Carmen encountered required a name—a manila folder, writing utensils, and many others. Although our exchanges here were still not smooth, Carmen was obviously listening carefully and repeating words that I used. As the weeks passed, she would repeatedly ask, "What's this?", as she pointed to ceiling tiles, electrical outlets, the water sprinkler, bookshelves, or the pencil sharpener. And Carmen eagerly emptied my book bag each week to make new discoveries, as in the following transcript from mid-February, when she received what may have been her first Valentine's Day card.

Carmen: Look, a paper. Another paper.

LAURA: What do you think is in there?

CARMEN: What's in there?

LAURA: What does it look like?

CARMEN: Hmm.

LAURA: This is called an *envelope*. You have to open the envelope.

CARMEN: Oh. It's not open.

LAURA: You can tear it open.

CARMEN: That's not open.

LAURA: Still not coming open?

CARMEN: Broken.

LAURA: (*assisting*) That's OK. You can tear it. That's how you get envelopes open.

CARMEN: Ohh! My brother has this.

LAURA: Do you know what it is?

CARMEN: (*Labels the picture.*) Cat.

LAURA: There's a cat in the picture. It's a *card* for Valentine's Day. It says, Valentine. Do you know what a *Valentine* is? It's a friend. A Valentine is a friend. But who is it from? You can turn it over. From . . .

CARMEN: Here.

LAURA: (*pointing to the print*) That's my name. My name has an *L*. Laura.

CARMEN: Laura.

LAURA: (*Reading, pointing to print*) Valentine, big *V*, Valentine, You're Adorable.

CARMEN: Adorable.

LAURA: That means you're pretty. Can you read it with me? (*Points word by word.*) Valentine . . .

CARMEN: (*Echoes.*) Valentine . . .

LAURA: You're . . .

CARMEN: (*Echoes.*) You're . . .

LAURA: Adorable.

CARMEN: (*Echoes.*) Dorble.

LAURA: Say "Adorable."

CARMEN: (*Repeats.*) Adorable.

Here, the social pragmatics of receiving holiday cards provided another language lesson. I began to use opportunities such as this to emphasize basic print concepts. I had not deliberately planned for this "going-through-the-book-bag-routine" to become an instructional activity, but, clearly, that is what happened. Vocabulary development evolved as a major focus of these sessions.

The transcripts shared thus far reveal how our conversations evolved over time, and they demonstrate Carmen's curiosity with respect to language learning. Although I devoted time each session to alphabet and counting activities (along with the book-bag routine), I always brought a collection of children's books and writing materials. I believed that storybook reading and reenactments would further promote vocabulary development, and I wanted to document Carmen's responses to emergent reading and writing tasks. In the next section, I trace Carmen's engagement in emergent writing.

EMERGENT WRITING AS A FORUM
FOR EXPRESSIVE LANGUAGE

From the developmental perspective known as "emergent literacy," children begin learning to read and write from their first encounters with print (Teale & Sulzby, 1986). Even scribbles or "pretend readings" are considered legitimate expressions of literacy in early childhood, as young children strive to make sense of print and the enterprise of reading and writing. Carmen was no exception. Her writing did not progress neatly in a stage-like manner from prephonemic to phonetic, but followed what Sulzby (1989) and others have documented: that children develop a repertoire of writing forms and move back and forth across these forms, depending on task demands. Thus, a child may segment sounds to produce phonetic spellings in a list one day, and employ cursive-like scribbles to compose an original story the following day. Simultaneously, and unexpectedly, these activities proved to be a rich context for generating expressive oral language.

I kept my book bag stocked with paper, markers, crayons, pens, and pencils. Carmen began each session by emptying the bag, exploring new items, and choosing the utensils she wanted to use that day. Writing was her favorite activity, especially writing on the chalkboard. Most of her stories consisted of primitive stick figures that represented members of her family. Just as constructive play with blocks, clay, toy cars, and so on, is often accompanied by expressive language, Carmen narrated her stories as she drew.

Dyson (1993) has eloquently documented the language of young children as they negotiate multiple layers of social worlds in their story-telling and writing. For Carmen, writing was also a sociocultural process; in Dyson's words, she employed outer (preconventional) signs to express inner meanings. Unlike the children studied by Dyson, Carmen was not negotiating her story with peers. I was present, but as she wrote, Carmen often appeared oblivious to my presence. I did not interrupt her monologues, or ask her to elaborate. In the first example, Carmen's narration of her family portrait (early March) can be described as labeling and commenting on the illustration:

> "The three little kids. This, this, this is a nose. That's on the head. They got ear, they got ears, a big ear and a little ear. I wanna make my sister. And me. And my brother." (From transcription, early March)

There is no plot or setting in this story, yet Carmen reveals the importance of her family in her social world. Three months later, in early June, she composed another family-centered story: Once again, she drew simple stick figures, but this time she added names, action, and dialogue:

> "My little brother look happy now. Joenito cried and my mommy said, 'Crybaby.' He likes his mommy and a house. I play my dolls and my little sisters. My sister have juice and potatoes, and she spit. Mommy say, 'That wasn't spitting, that was raining!' (From transcription, early June)

Throughout these narratives, Carmen was experimenting with vocabulary, grammar, and the pronunciation of words. She also experimented with various forms of preconventional writing, including cursive-like scribbles and the letters in her name. The *m* from her name figured prominently in some of these writing samples. Carmen gradually began to search for print forms to copy: She sorted through alphabet cards and examined book titles, identifying the letters in her name. During other sessions, she copied letters and words, both on paper and on the chalkboard.

By the time the school year ended, Carmen had grown confident enough to assume the role of teacher. One day, after cleaning the chalk-board with an eraser, she announced: "And something else we got that we can do. Read a book and take it home." Then, Carmen began copying letters from the title of a book. As she wrote on the board, she continued to "talk like a teacher":

> "Every day, every night something. Something else. Say 'came to you.' Do you come to me? Dear, what's letter is this? Do you come to me? Every night."

When her "lesson" was over, Carmen had copied most of the letters from the title, albeit from right to left, and with some randomness in the order:

ymmotdnarapta (*Tommy and Sara*)
DNFRES (*Friends*)

The variety of preconventional print forms seen in Carmen's work follow a typical developmental progression of emergent writers and spellers. The *form* of her writing varied, from scribbles to random letters, and eventually to copying from environmental print. These changes indicate that Carmen was becoming increasingly aware of print (Gentry & Gillet, 1993). With respect to the *content* of her writing, Carmen primarily created stories in the *expressive mode,* what Temple, Nathan, Temple, and Burris (1993) describe as "purely and simply self-expression through words" (p. 129). Expressive writing is marked by spontaneity, a conversational tone, and a strong sense of the writer's voice. Above all, Carmen employed writing in personally meaningful ways to share her own experiences, and to "try on" the role of an important adult figure (her classroom teacher).

Fillmore (1991) in her now-classic model of second-language acquisition, asserts that social processes are a crucial component of language learning. In her words, these processes are "the steps taken by learners and TL [target language] speakers to create a social setting in which communication by means of the target language is possible and desired" (p. 53). For Carmen, opportunities for emergent writing created a context in which she was able to practice speaking English in a naturalistic, conversational style. In addition, I was able to observe a level of social competence in these sessions that Carmen was unable to display in a classroom with 22 other children. I think that writing may have distracted Carmen from whatever concerns she had for speaking. The examples given here provide evidence of the reciprocal relation between language and literacy (Watson, 2002).

Carmen did not stray far from familiar topics while engaged in writing. She told numerous anecdotes involving her parents and siblings. These were "safe" topics for her. I believed that introducing storybook reenactments would expand the scope of her language learning in other ways; that is, by hearing storybooks read aloud, and through reenacting these stories on their own, children hear and begin to internalize the structure of written language, which provides a strong and necessary foundation for conventional, independent reading (Doake, 1985; Meek, 1991, 1996; Sulzby, 1992). In addition, storybooks often introduce children to unfamiliar vocabulary, thus preparing them for meeting new words when they begin to read from print. For all of these reasons, I included storybook reading as an essential component of my weekly sessions with Carmen. In the next section, I describe her language use in the context of this activity.

ACQUIRING THE LANGUAGE OF STORYBOOKS

The book bag that Carmen poked through each week always contained an assortment of picture books, nursery rhymes, wordless books, and English and Spanish stories. As with her written compositions, Carmen transposed her own family into storybooks. One of her favorites was a beautifully illustrated board book titled *Field Animals* (Greeley, 1984). Each picture in this 12-page, wordless book features a pair of field animals (voles, gophers, rabbits, etc.). Carmen was intrigued by the intricate, realistic drawings of these animals, and she named each pair "Carmen" and "Carlos." As with her first original compositions, Carmen's reenactment of this picture book consisted of labeling and naming each animal character. Whereas some wordless books lend themselves to dramatic story reenactments, this book did not; the pages consisted of animal portraits, without any action. To engage her in more elaborated written language forms, I read at least one picture storybook to Carmen each session. *Are You My Mother?* by P. D. Eastman (1960) became her favorite. This story contains a universally powerful theme for young children: A baby bird is separated from its mother and goes on a search to find her. As you will see, Carmen responded with strong emotions—in fact, with some agitation—to the reading of this story.

Doake (1985) describes several "participation strategies" employed by adults and children in joint storybook readings. These include "echo reading," in which the child repeats words and phrases after the adult, "mumble reading," in which the child "mumbles" along with the adult reader, and "completion reading," in which the adult pauses to allow the child to fill in repetitive or familiar phrases. After reading the story to Carmen at least twice, I began encouraging her to "read with me." In Table 12.1, I present the actual text of the story in the left column. In the center column is a transcript of a joint reading with Carmen from mid-February, in which she engaged in completion reading for the first half of the story. The transcript in the right-hand column occurred 3 months later; this time, Carmen produced an independent reenactment. During the weeks between these reenactments, more subtle changes were noted as Carmen gained familiarity with the story, and with telling it in English. I have selected these two transcripts to reveal the extent to which her language progressed over the course of several months.

TABLE 12.1. Carmen Reenacts *Are You My Mother?*

Are You My Mother? Text[a] (Eastman, 1960) Page		Carmen's reenactment, mid-February: "completion reading"	Carmen's reenactment, late May: "original reenactment"
[L:	Can you read it with me? *Are you my mother?*	C: Are you my mother? [echo reads]	The story is the little mommy. . . . *The little mommy and the kid?* OK, *go ahead.* The mommy and the kid, the little kid.
1	A mother bird sat on her egg. The egg. . . . *Do you remember what the egg did?* It jumped! "Uh oh," said the mother bird. "My baby bird will be here. He will want to eat." *You just pointed to the egg. What did the egg do?*		
2	"I must get something for my baby to eat," she said. "I will be back." The egg . . .	C: jumped	The momma's got a egg. When the baby comes out he get mm, mm, mm **PT** The little baby went rubbin,' rubbin,' rubbin,' moving and moving around. The baby went here, she got tummy ache, no, she got tummy ache. **PT** And the mommy's fly away! **PT**
3	It . . .	C: jumped	gettin' food
4	and jumped and jumped. Out came	C: jumped	and then moving and moving and moving and K-crack! **PT**
5	the baby . . . bird. "Where is my mother?" he said. He looked for her. He looked up. He did not see her. He looked down. He did not see her. "I will go and look for her," he said. So away he went. *What's gonna happen?*	C: out	The little baby said, Mommy? Mommy where are you? **PT** And he was just get out of the egg, the broken egg, and he jump in here. **PT**

228

#		C:	PT
6	Down out of the tree he went. Down, down, down. It was a long way down.	C: He fall. [Carmen traces lines on the page with her finger to show the baby bird falling down]. PT	And that's what he says, not up or down. PT And he really looked and he flied and he jumped away. PT
7	The baby bird could not fly. He could not fly but he could walk. "I will go and find my mother," he said. He did not know what his mother looked like. He went right by her. He did not see her. He came to a ...	C: cat	Don't have to be mommy, he's coming with mommy and he really up and look up PT and he's coming.
8	"Are you my mother?" he said to the kitten.	C: No	Seein' at mommy PT And he said, "You're not my mommy." PT
9	The kitten just looked and looked but didn't say anything. The kitten was not his mother, so he went on. Then he came to a hen. "Are you my mother?"	C: No, no	Every day having the same [ ]. PT
10	he said to the hen. The kitten was not his ... mother. The hen was not his ...	C: mother	
11	So the baby bird went on. "I have to find my mother," he said. Then he came to a dog	C: dog	
12	"Are you my ... "	C: his mother	Here, he's not my mommy, not my mommy, not my mommy. He's not my mommy either.
13	he said to the dog. "I am not your mother. I am a ... dog," said the dog. *Read it with me.*	C: his mother	
14	The kitten was not ...	C: his mother	*(continued)*

229

TABLE 12.1. (*continued*)

Are You My Mother? (Eastman, 1960) Page Text[a]	Carmen's reenactment, mid-February: "completion reading"	Carmen's reenactment, late May: "original reenactment"
15 The hen was not . . .	C: his mother	
16 the	C: dog not his mother	And **PT**
17 so the baby bird went on. Now he came to a . . . cow	C: cow. Eating the grash.	he said, "mom," and the cow said, "I'm not your mom." **PT** He talks. And hmm, the baby said, "Huh, which my mommy go?"
18 Unhmm the cow is eating the grass		
19 "Are you my mother?" he said to the cow. "How could I be your mother? I am a . . ."	C: Are you my mother?	Ooh. [ ] be here. And they really really hurt.
20 The kitten and the hen were not his . . .	C: cow	The cows not her, his mom, or the dog is not his mom or the chick, what's this?
21 The dog and the cow were not	C: mother	**PT** *That's a chicken.* No. *Hen.* Hen, and a hen, a hen, is not her him his mommy, and a kitty's not her, her, his mommy and was his mommy go. Maybe my mommy is getting some lunch for me. My, my tummy is groaning, my tummy ache is groaning. **PT**
22 Did he have a mother?	C: a mother C: No!	And where is she my mom go? **PT**
23 "I did have a mother," said the baby bird. "I	[*Carmen listens to the rest of the story.*]	
24 know I did. I have to find her. I will. I WILL!"		

230

25 Now the baby bird did not walk. He ran! Then he
26 saw a car. Could that old thing be his mother?
27 No, it could not.

28 The baby bird did not stop. He ran on and on.

29 Now he looked way, way down. He saw a boat.
30 "There she is!" said the baby bird.

31 He called to the boat, but the boat did not stop.
32 The boat went on.

33 He looked way, way up. He saw a big plane.
34 "Here I am, Mother," he called out.

35 But the plane did not stop. The plane went on.

36 Just then, the baby bird saw a big thing. This
37 must be his mother! "There she is!" he said.
38 "There is my mother!"

39 He ran right up to it. "Mother, Mother!
40 Here I am, Mother!" he said to the big
41 thing.

42 But the big thing just said, "Snort." "Oh, you are
43 not my mother," said the baby bird. "You are a
44 Snort. I have to get out of here!"

And where is she my mom go? PT

And the little kid went just look around, down and he really be scared now. PT And he said Mommy, Mommy, that's look like my mommy.

What's that? *What is it?*? Plane. *That sure isn't his mommy.* PT

And a little kid went oh, oh, oh. And up and up. PT

And a lit- same. A little kid said but that isn't his mother. That, this is catching him. *What is that thing?* I don't know. PT

I think, is that the Snort? Yeah, but it's not his mommy. PT

(continued)

231

TABLE 12.1. (*continued*)

Are You My Mother? (Eastman, 1960) Page Text[a]	Carmen's reenactment, mid-February: "completion reading"	Carmen's reenactment, late May: "original reenactment"
		Got lot of [] Who put that back there? [ ] And one day, all day long was [ ]. Gets big teep. *Ooh, big teeth.* [ ] thought it was a monster in there. And he said, Mommy you in there? And got big teeps, and he's trying to get the rocks. Put 'em in there and he worked, whoo whoo whapsh. **PT**
45 But the baby bird could not get away. The Snort		
46 went up. It went way, way up. And up, up, up		
47 went the baby bird.		
48 But now, where was the Snort going? "Oh, oh,		He was getting there, **PT** and really worked.
49 oh! What is this Snort going to do to me? Get		
50 me out of here!"		
51 Just then, the Snort came to a stop.		Scared, scared, and jumped over the thing. The little kid is really scared. **PT**
52 "Where am I?" said the baby bird. "I		And that's what he say. "Mommy, what's in there?
53 want to go home! I want my mother!"		Wanna come home." He had to come home **PT**
		or mommy will get sad. Woop, you don't go over
54 Then something happened. The Snort put that		there and he better go home or mommy get sad, and
55 baby bird right back in the tree. The baby bird		found him **PT**
56 was home!		
57 Just them the mother bird came back to		and he say "Mommy!" He got to save him, she got to
		save him. **PT**
58 the tree. "Do you know who I am?"		
59 she said to her baby.		

232

60 "Yes, I know who you are," said the baby bird.
61 "You are not a kitten. You are not a hen. You
62 are not a cow. You are not a boat, or a plane,
63 or a Snort! You are a bird, and you are my
64 mother."

And he's just getting a worm for him. And he fall down. He fall down. *Where did he fall?* There! *Look at that.*

And he found Mommy. That's Mommy. And that's the end. **PT**

65 [Reads end pages] and that was mommy, too. Mommy was big upset and the little kid is really being really really saved. *Really really saved, yep.* And that's the end. *Thank you very much. You did a lovely job.* I like that story.

Note. L, Laura; C, Carmen; **PT**, page turn; [ ], unintelligible speech.
a Laura's comments are in italics.

In the first reenactment (center column) Carmen supplied words and phrases at the end of sentences. She paid careful attention to the illustrations, even tracing action lines with her finger (line 7), as if to experience the baby bird's fall from the tree in a more kinesthetic manner. By the time Carmen reenacted the story on her own in the second transcript (right-hand column), she had heard the story six more times. Then she was able to produce a story similar to the original text. She employed some structures of written language, such as dialogue carriers ("he said," "the baby said") to set off characters' speech. Carmen was able to reenact nearly verbatim a repetitious scene (line 20), and she used more vocabulary from the story. For example, she hesitated on the word *hen* in line 21, and started to say *chicken*. I repeated the word *chicken* to affirm that this was a good choice, but Carmen recalled the actual text and corrected me!

This evidence of written language indicates that Carmen was not merely memorizing the story; she was beginning to internalize the syntax, vocabulary, and conventions of written language. Overall, however, this reenactment displays primarily oral language, or the language of conversations. Carmen reenacted most of the episodes, but her language was abbreviated and contextualized; that is, without the illustrations, a person listening to the story would not fully understand the plot. There are also numerous indications that Carmen was a second-language learner. Carmen struggled to match pronouns with characters (lines 20–22), and she referred to the baby as "she" in the first few lines, later switching to "he." Carmen engaged me in the story, as if in a conversation, at times. Such dialogic asides also mark an "oral" reenactment.

It is interesting to note that Carmen never referred to the characters in this story as birds: They were always the mommy and the little kid. In part, I believe that this indicates the powerful emotional response that Carmen had to this story. It is also possible that she still did not quite distinguish between make-believe and true stories. In line 17, Carmen remarked in an aside to me, "The cow talks." And a few weeks earlier, Carmen gave the following explanation of the mother bird feeding her baby:

CARMEN: It's getting it.

LAURA: What is the mother bird getting?

LAURA: It's a *worm*.

CARMEN: Worm.

LAURA: What's the worm for?

CARMEN: For the kid.

LAURA: What's the kid going to do with it?

CARMEN: Eat it. But the, but the, but the, but the mom, but the momma don't eat the worm, just eat spaghetti. The, the, the kids eats worms, but the kids throw it.

Carmen wants this story to make sense: In reality, a little kid, or a mommy, for that matter, would not eat worms. Carmen's affective response to the story is also seen in her repeated mentions of the mother's sadness, the fear of the little kid, and, in her conclusion to the story, when she declared that "the little kid is really being really, really saved."

A common thread that recurs in this account is that Carmen made steady, and very real, changes in her language. The language Carmen used to tell stories, whether or not she was reenacting a storybook, became increasingly sophisticated. She still had not achieved performance measures by the end of kindergarten, but Carmen definitely had found her voice.

For children like Carmen, who come from homes in which storybook reading is probably not a daily ritual, the importance of teacher read-alouds cannot be overstated (Dickinson, McCabe, & Anastasopoulos, 2002). The experience of reenacting stories in her own words provided another context in which Carmen could be engaged in both practicing a second language and learning the structure of written language. Along with writing and other conversational routines, these experiences framed our social interactions and allowed Carmen to take increasing control over her language.

DISCUSSION

Even as Carmen began to talk during our one-to-one sessions, her long and continued silence in class remained a mystery. I learned from colleagues and previous research that young ESL learners often go through a "silent" or "nonverbal period" (Gibbons, 1985; Saville-Trioke, 1988), in which receptive language develops much more rapidly than does expressive language. In addition, children watch, listen, and silently rehearse the new language to gain a degree of mastery over it (Tabors & Snow, 2001). During this silent period, it is considered desirable that children not be pressured to speak. It is possible that by focusing her attention on writing and reenacting a familiar storybook, Carmen was able to use and experiment with English in ways that were within her comfort level, or zone of proximal development (Vygotsky, 1978). She demonstrated the desire to learn and communicate in English, a trait that Fillmore (1991) and others have consistently identified in ESL learners. She was curious about new words and frequently asked to be told the name of objects she found either in the classroom or in a book.

In early childhood classrooms in which teachers feel pressured to meet high academic standards, opportunities for rich experimentation with language may be supplanted by instruction focused on achieving narrowly defined aspects of literacy development. It is important to remember that ESL learners can benefit richly from opportunities to create original stories, to dramatize or reenact familiar stories, and to role-play (e.g., to "play teacher" or to engage in various dramatic play centers). Not only do these activities lead children into conventional reading and writing, but, as I learned from the time I spent with Carmen, such opportunities are also fertile ground for language learning.

REFERENCES

Dickinson, D. K., McCabe, A., & Anastasopoulos, L. (2002). *A framework for examining book reading in early childhood classrooms* (Technical Report No. 1-014). Ann Arbor: University of Michigan, CIERA.

Doake, D. B. (1985). Reading-like behavior: Its role in learning to read. In A. Jaggar & M. T. Smith-Burke (Eds.), *Observing the language learner* (pp. 82–98). Newark, DE: International Reading Association and the National Council of Teachers of English.

Dyson, A. H. (1993). *Social worlds of children learning to write in an urban primary school*. New York: Teachers College Press.

Eastman, P. D. (1960). *Are you my mother?* New York: Random House.

Fillmore, L. (1991). Second-language learning in children: A model of language learning in social context. In E. Bialystok (Ed.), *Language processing in bilingual children* (pp. 49–69). New York: Cambridge University Press.

Gentry, J. R., & Gillet, J. W. (1993). *Teaching kids to spell*. Portsmouth, NH: Heinemann.

Gibbons, J. (1985). The silent period: An examination. *Language Learning, 35*(2), 255–267.

Greeley, V. (1984). *Field animals*. New York: Peter Bedrick Books.

Meek, M. (1991). *On being literate*. London: Bodley Head.

Meek, M. (Ed.). (1996). *Developing pedagogies in the multilingual classroom: The writings of Josie Levine*. Staffordshire, UK: Trentham Books.

Saville-Troike, M. (1988). Private speech: Evidence for second language learning strategies during the "silent" period. *Child Language, 15*, 567–590.

Snow, C. E., & Tabors, P. O. (1993). Language skills that relate to literacy development. In B. Spodek & O. N. Saracho (Eds.), *Language and literacy in early childhood education* (pp. 1–20). New York: Teachers College Press.

Sulzby, E. (1989). *Emergent literacy: Kindergartner's write and read*. Ann Arbor:

Regents of the University of Michigan and the North Central Regional Educational Laboratory.

Sulzby, E. (1992). Assessment of emergent literacy: Storybook reading. *Reading Teacher, 44,* 498–500.

Tabors, P. O., & Snow, C. E. (2001). Young bilingual children and early literacy development. In S. B. Neuman & D. K. Dickinson (Eds.), *Handbook of early literacy research* (pp. 159–178). New York: Guilford Press.

Teale, W. H., & Sulzby, E. (Eds.). (1986). *Emergent literacy: Writing and reading.* Norwood, NJ: Ablex.

Temple, C., Nathan, N., Temple, F., & Burris, N. (1993). *The beginnings of writing.* Boston: Allyn & Bacon.

Vygotsky, L. S. (1978). *Mind in society: The development of higher psychological processes.* Cambridge, MA: Harvard University Press.

Watson, R. (2001). Literacy and oral language: Implications for early literacy acquisition. In S. B. Neuman & D. K. Dickinson (Eds.), *Handbook of early literacy research* (pp. 43–53). New York: Guilford Press.

Part IV

OUT-OF-CLASSROOM INFLUENCES ON LITERACY LEARNING

Chapter 13

Teaching Interrupted

The Effect of High-Stakes Testing on Literacy Instruction in a Texas Elementary School

JULIE L. PENNINGTON

We do practice [for the TAAS test]. I do expect them to do well. And yes, we do TAAS homework, so they become familiar with the format of the test. [The TAAS test is] not quite like literature circle, where we sit down and discuss what is going on in the book and whether you agree or disagree. No, there is a right answer and so it's very different and you just have to train [your students]. I hate to say that, but you have to teach them how to take a test.

—DELORES

When a state proposes to align literacy instruction and assessment through a criterion-referenced standardized test, how does that test influence teachers' views regarding children's literacy development? How does high-stakes testing affect the way teachers teach reading? Eight educators at Elena Elementary School, a predominately Latina, urban school in Texas, answered these questions. I did not initially pursue high-stakes testing as a research question; I merely sought to explore the teachers' general definitions of literacy. Yet high stakes testing became a driving force in data collection as the study progressed and became tightly centered on literacy, as defined by the teachers, when state educational policy altered the assessment of literacy at Elena Elementary School.

In this chapter, I share ways the teachers at Elena plotted the course of the literacy instruction of their students. During the study, it became clear that the reading program at Elena had gradually eroded into a simplified view of teaching reading and writing. Rather than emphasizing the complexity and culture of the students and seeking to maintain their language as much as possible, the school became highly focused on streamlining the curriculum to match the state's objective of passing the Texas Assessment of Academic Skills (TAAS) test. Elena's literacy goals were narrowed by the state's accountability system as the teachers' definitions of literacy became aligned with those of the state. Teachers first portrayed TAAS as a time-intensive interruption in their daily teaching practices, but as our conversations continued, they depicted TAAS as a highly pressurized event in the spring that guided their entire year. They ultimately described TAAS as an inadequate measure of literacy for their students. The complexity of the teachers' definitions of literacy prior to TAAS and their constructions of the children's reading abilities during the study provided a glimpse into how high-stakes testing shaped instruction and teachers' beliefs about teaching reading in one Texas elementary school.

ELENA ELEMENTARY SCHOOL

Elena Elementary School was my home school for 14 years. I student-taught there in 1987, and except for one year of teaching first grade in Fresno, California, I remained on staff until 2002. My teaching positions at Elena were varied; I taught first grade, multiage first and second grade, and multiage fifth and sixth grade. My last 5 years at Elena were spent as a Reading Recovery teacher. Over the years, literacy instruction at Elena followed the flows of national movements, such as the Whole Language movement, and the notions of balancing literacy in the classroom, but no development had greater influence on the literacy instruction at Elena than the state accountability system of Texas.

With a predominately Latino (93%) population, Elena Elementary was defined by the Federal government as a Title I school by virtue of the high number of Spanish-speaking students and the low socioeconomic status of the community. Situated within a Latino neighborhood that was extremely stable during my tenure there, Elena had a high level of parental involvement; many of Elena's parents had attended the school, and a strong relationship existed between the community and the school.

LITERACY INSTRUCTION AT
ELENA ELEMENTARY SCHOOL

Over time, the high-stakes accountability system greatly altered the instructional focus at Elena Elementary School. When I arrived in 1987, teachers were utilizing the traditional basal reading program provided by the state-adopted textbook. They worked their way through the reading series, using the workbooks and ability-grouping the children. During this time, Elena Elementary had a strong bilingual program that emphasized developing literacy in both English and Spanish. The campus was geared toward supporting the school's community through its commitment to bilingual education. Within a few years of my arrival, the teachers on campus began to seek outside resources to enhance the school literacy program. The State of Texas supported a site-based decision-making model, and Elena teachers were allowed to form study cadres to explore areas such as literacy and bilingual education. Teachers attended workshops and wrote a grant to buy trade books for a new campus bookroom. A Dual Language Grant supporting English and Spanish literacy was also approved, and teachers and administrators labored to transform Elena into a school open to innovative ideas. Teachers' professional development was extensive in the areas of literacy and second-language acquisition. The school district was supportive; a balanced literacy program was defined as a campus goal, and teachers designed their instructional day around the goals of balancing quality literature with extensive word study and phonics.

By 2001, the TAAS test served as the primary measure of the literacy abilities of Texas children. The State of Texas was no stranger to utilizing standardized tests as measures of student progress, but during the late 1990s, the TAAS test evolved into a significant component of a strengthened accountability system. In 1997, Governor George W. Bush implemented a statewide initiative designed to improve reading in the state. The new accountability system set goals for reading achievement through standardized test scores. To meet the state's goal of having all children reading by third grade, third graders in Texas were expected to pass the TAAS reading test.

High-stakes testing can be distinguished by the ways that schools, teachers, and students were placed under a punishment or reward system tied to achievement. Test scores were used to rank schools, and monetary rewards were dispensed to administrators of high-performing schools. Schools lacking high success rates on the TAAS were reorganized and subject to curricular and staffing changes based on their unacceptable scores. The Texas accountability system was clearly defined:

TAAS standards for reading, writing, and mathematics

- For a campus or district rating of *Exemplary*, at least 90% of "all students," and students in each group meeting minimum size requirements, must pass each section of the TAAS.
- For a campus or district rating of *Recognized*, at least 80% of "all students," and students in each group meeting minimum size requirements, must pass each section of the TAAS.
- For a campus or district rating of *Academically Acceptable*, at least 55% of "all students," and students in each group meeting minimum size requirements, must pass each section of the TAAS.
- Those districts (or campuses) not meeting the standard for *Academically Acceptable* or higher are rated *Academically Unacceptable*. (Texas Education Agency website, http://*www.tea.state.tx.us*)

Early on in the implementation of the state's new accountability system, Elena Elementary School received an unacceptable rating. This event was a catalyst for many changes that slowly altered the school's approach to literacy instruction. The unacceptable rating was the result of teachers giving the test to many of the English language learners (ELLs) to see how they would fare. The diagnostic use of the TAAS by Elena Elementary School was a mistake, and the staff underwent an intensive review of all teaching practices through a supervised audit by the Texas Education Agency. Elena's history of performing at an adequate level on the previous state standardized tests had placed the school in a comfortable position. Elena's teachers did not necessarily strive for high-test scores because of their use of multiple data sources to document reading progress. Teachers were well-versed in many forms of literacy assessment, such as informal reading inventories, running records, and writing samples, prior to the state's emphasis on TAAS, and student growth in reading was evident in the data collected by the school through means other than standardized tests.

During my study, Elena had approximately 631 students and had maintained an acceptable TAAS rating. This rating meant that the school was not considered to be in need of remediation but was expected to improve its rating status and progress to the next level. Elena remained at the cusp of this acceptable rating and, in spring 2002, moved up, into the "recognized" category.

METHODS

Because of my familiarity with the school and the historical background of literacy instruction there, I found it useful to couch my research within an ethnographic theoretical method and framework. My critical ethnographic view (Foley, 1995; Trueba, 1993; Wolcott, 1994) into the practices and views of the teachers was conducted through a series of interviews with teachers, my coworkers, ranging from grades 1–6, and included an assistant principal, the campus literacy specialist, and a special education teacher. Four of the participants were Latino and four were white. My unique positioning as both peer and researcher allowed me to spend extensive time on site and use my relationships with my coworkers to bring their voices to the foreground and to let the teachers guide me. In Texas, the cacophony of voices related to the accountability system rarely includes the stories of teachers and their classrooms. In this chapter, I present the stories of the teachers at Elena as essential in the dialogue surrounding high-stakes testing.

Interviews initially centered on reading and writing teaching methods, assessment, and teachers' perceptions of the literacy of students' families. Clandinin and Connelly (1995) have explained three desires teachers have to make sense of their teaching lives, relative to their personal lives:

1. The desire to tell stories as a form of meaning making.
2. The relationship of telling stories to others as an active construction of meaning that moves experiences into educative areas.
3. The reflective aspect of storytelling that alters past experiences into new interpretations.

I encouraged storytelling in my dealings with the teachers, so that our ways of interacting during the study would remain similar to our past interactions. This method proved to be the most natural way to approach data collection and maintained consistency in our relationships.

Over time, the power and influence of the TAAS reading assessment became clear. Most of our conversations about everyday life in the classroom began to revolve around stories about the TAAS test. Elena was a campus with an exceptional staff, highly educated in the area of literacy. Many of the teachers I interviewed had completed master's degrees in reading and/or attended extensive professional development in the area. The school focused on developing strong literacy programs that emphasized practices such as guided reading workshops (Fountas & Pinnell, 1996) and literature study groups. Elena's teachers were well versed in various models of literacy instruction and evaluation. Their thoughts regarding TAAS testing and reading instruction became a major theme of data collection and analysis. All of the teachers were given the opportunity to review and revise their interview transcripts and were apprised of the findings of the study. As I shared the findings on the influence of TAAS on instruction, they all agreed that the skills tested on TAAS had become the first priority in the literacy goals of the school community.

TAAS AS AN INSTRUCTIONAL GOAL

By 2001, TAAS was a large part of the teachers' instructional strategies, and it became embedded in their literacy goals. This was evident, because every teacher and administrator in this study mentioned TAAS mastery as the primary objective for the students at Elena. Dolores, a third-grade teacher with 15 years' experience, explained how teaching her students to pass TAAS was one of her top three literacy goals for her students:

> "My views on literacy? Number one is to have my students love reading; number two, to help them read so they can love reading and do it on their own, and I hate to say this but, number three, to master the TAAS objectives. It is just part of reality, and I know that when TAAS is on, a TAAS monster takes over, because I'm competitive. I want my students to reflect what I've done in the classroom. It's a matter of pride, and I hate that, because sometimes your ego gets in the way of what's best for the students."

Dolores described a view shared by the teachers I interviewed. TAAS was a required part of literacy assessment in Texas. Regardless of other curricular concerns, TAAS was the state's ultimate measure of reading achievement. Not only were the students' reading abilities measured by TAAS, teachers' efficacy was also evaluated by the annual test. Although the teachers had extensive knowledge about how to teach literacy, and a multitude of books and resources at their disposal, the powerful nature of high-stakes testing in reading affected their teaching methods in several ways. In the next section, I share how teachers reacted to the pressure of TAAS, how TAAS narrowed the curriculum, and how teachers felt it necessary to teach to the test.

TAAS PRESSURE

Each year, the pressure became more intense regarding Elena's TAAS scores. TAAS was viewed as the sole indicator, by the state, of student and teacher achievement in reading. Katia, a fourth-grade teacher for 2 years, conveyed how she and her students felt the day of the test:

"The kids were burned; well, no, the kids were OK, because I think I made it OK for them. I took on all the pressure for them. I cried. I vomited. I had headaches. I did everything, and they were excited. They were looking forward to TAAS day, because my husband made tacos for them. We made a whole TAAS breakfast. It was a big deal for that day to come, and everyone was so excited about it. On the inside, I was the one going through all the chaos."

Katia describes how the immense pressure of the test affected teachers and students alike. Each year, the stakes were higher. By 2003, any third grader not passing the reading portion of the test would be retained. TAAS results were published in the newspaper. Teachers' appraisals reflected their students' performance on the test. The Elena staff promoted pep rallies the week before the test. Teacher training was extensive, and practice materials were purchased. Teachers were expected to improve their students' scores each year. The high-stakes nature of TAAS encouraged rewards and punishments based on student performance. Rewards at Elena were pizza parties and trips to the local water park for the children. Whereas teachers' names and scores were circulated and used for teaching evaluations, administrators and schools received awards through publicity. TAAS rewards and practice materials had become so pervasive that one Texas lawmaker felt it necessary to propose a bill. A school district employee or any other person may not give to a student a material award that: (1) is based on the student's performance on an assessment instrument administered under Subchapter B; or (2) is in any other way related to an assessment instrument administered under Subchapter B (Texas Legislature Online, 2001). TAAS was the primary goal for administrators, schools, and teachers because of the high-stakes nature of the accountability system and the pervasive fear of failure. Material incentives for success, unheard of prior to TAAS, encouraged students at Elena to find specific answers on the test for rewards rather than to read multiple texts for enjoyment and learning. Dolores, a third-grade teacher, discussed her reaction to the importance of the test. "[TAAS] loses sight of the fact that these are children and, at the third-grade level, it is much more crucial because it's the first year that they have to tackle this kind of task. I mean, it's your score too; what your kids make is what you make. It's hard on parents, it's hard on teachers, and it's hard on kids."

Dolores also provided an example of how she critically evaluated the TAAS as not necessarily being what she might think of as best for her students, yet it was one of her top three focus areas in literacy. Teachers at Elena had learned the importance of the TAAS test and struggled to improve the performance of their students. The experience with an unacceptable rating in the past created at Elena an understanding of the importance of the accountability system based on TAAS scores. Throughout the conversations with Elena's educators, there was a constant thread of acknowledgment that TAAS was a reality, coupled with the uneasy feeling that TAAS was not an adequate goal for reading instruction. Every teacher, regardless of position or grade level, felt the pressure of the test, and every teacher believed that the emphasis on TAAS narrowed the curriculum focus.

NARROWING THE CURRICULUM

In the past, Elena teachers and the administration worked to design literacy education around Guerra's (1998) notion of literacy as practice. Literacy as practice can best be described as "a socially constructed and highly contextualized activity. Literacy is [not] considered a singular, monolithic, or universal entity; instead, scholars who take a practice-oriented perspective contend that there are many literacies in any society serving multiple and culturally specific purposes" (p. 57).

Elena Elementary School had developed a literacy program aligned with the community. Bilingual literacy was emphasized via the Dual Language Grant. Teaching methods were varied, and teachers used many forms of assessments to understand better their students' language strengths and build on them. Materials used in literacy instruction ranged from state-adopted textbooks and trade books, to sharing literacy from the community in the form of oral stories and writings. Teachers were focused on meeting the needs of their students and being knowledgeable enough in their profession to seek out various resources related to literacy.

Over time, Elena teachers struggled to find ways to ensure that the school's ratings would improve, and their teaching strategies became narrowly focused on TAAS. With only so many minutes in each day, teachers and administrators began to make decisions emphasizing TAAS practice. TAAS trainings, practice materials, and test-taking strategies became a large part of the daily curriculum. Although only grades 3–6 were required to take the test, teachers at all grade levels understood the importance of preparing students for the TAAS. Devin, a 15-year veteran, former prekindergarten teacher, and current first-grade teacher, shared her thoughts on the influence of testing on curriculum and teaching methods:

> "When it comes down to testing, that kind of changes the perspective a bit, because what ends up happening is—it's not a suggestion any

more. It's more of a requirement, so I think that teachers start feeling like, 'Oh, OK, they want the kids to know their letters, then I'll teach them the letters.' Then what happens is that program starts becoming more watered down. It changes what we're doing . . . Now that we know we have [the test]. I keep thinking, well, am I going to start getting little practice booklets? Am I going to get little practice materials to prep them for this? That starts changing the perspective of your curriculum, if you know you've got something else that you're accountable for here."

The influence of TAAS on the curriculum was profound. Devin illustrates how tested reading objectives were clearly laid out in practice booklets, and teachers were prepared to alter their instruction to address those objectives directly. Even though the basic skills, such as letter recognition, were taught prior to TAAS, in the pressurized atmosphere, only the skills targeted by the test were addressed in the classrooms. The TAAS reading objectives were not novel. Texas had always required specific state standards for reading. The difference was in the narrowing of the scope of the curriculum. With TAAS becoming increasingly important, teachers became tightly bound to the testing criteria and conservative in their instruction. Teaching the objectives on the test provided more of a guarantee for success than depending on any other reading methods with wider scope and sequences of literacy skills. Bob, a sixth-grade teacher and 24-year veteran, relates the way that TAAS required low-level reading skills:

"[TAAS] is a little body of skills. As far as TAAS is concerned, it's eight little skills or six, or whatever it is, and if you can do six, you're a literate person. You can be a TAAS whiz. That's the kind of people we're developing? It is sad that literacy has become that."

All of the educators with whom I spoke relayed similar views. TAAS was not considered to require a high level of literacy. Teachers were quite critical when it came to evaluating TAAS as any type of reading assessment. Many arguments were made supporting the idea that the TAAS test consisted of reading skills all students should be able to do, but in their daily teaching practices, teachers felt bound to teach test-taking skills specifically. TAAS, to the teachers at Elena, was little more than a measure of *whether* the children could read or not. TAAS did not provide teachers with helpful information on how to assist children in developing their reading skills beyond the format of the test. Natalie, the campus literacy specialist, with 18 years of classroom experience, described how the information on the TAAS was not adequate for teachers, because the test did not provide valuable information to inform their teaching:

> "The test itself, I don't have a problem. I do not have a problem with the way the reading test is done. It's a reading passage. The questions are fine. A child who is literate at his or her grade level should be able to do that. It doesn't give very good information to the teacher. First of all, most of the teachers know going in whether the child is going to pass or fail the test. They don't need the test to tell them, especially at third grade. I have a lot of experience at third grade; it didn't give information about what the child was doing, whether it was oral reading they were having problems with, or decoding, or whether it was a comprehension problem, or they don't have the vocabulary. All it measures is whether they can answer questions about the passage."

Although TAAS was not a diagnostic tool for teachers, because of its limitations in assessing reading, it still had the power to guide instruction as a result of the power of the accountability system. The state's system appeared to work, in that it gave the state a way to measure whether children were reading or not. The state's call for ensuring that all children read by third grade, as measured by TAAS, was clearly meeting the assessment needs of the state, even if it was somewhat useless in the teachers' opinions. When asked if TAAS measured reading, Katia concurred with Natalie. Both teachers believed that any child reading at grade level should pass the required TAAS objectives, and they both discounted the value of TAAS as an informative way to illustrate a child's reading proficiency. Katia said:

> "No, I don't think TAAS measures reading. . . . It wouldn't be a true reflection of what they know in reading. I think it would be lower, because I think what TAAS does is teach them how to take a test. Here at this school, anyway. We don't teach them how to read for information. We teach them how to take the test. I can say that, at this school, I am teaching so that the kids can pass that test, teaching them how to pass it. I'm not teaching them to read the passages and understand them. I'm teaching them how to find the information and take shortcuts, so that they don't end up brain dead halfway through the test because they've read and reread."

Katia refers to the ideas other teachers mentioned as they described the TAAS test. Their opinions centered around the ideas that TAAS was not a true reflection of the children's literacy. Teachers viewed TAAS as a separate form of reading that had to be specifically addressed through explicit test-taking instructional methods. Bob explained the limited scope of the test: "The only TAAS question that even gets any where near [critical thinking] is inference. [The TAAS is] regurgitation."

TEACHING INTERRUPTED: TEACHING TO THE TEST

Katia expressed frustration with how much time she had to spend teaching directly to the test, forgoing her regular reading instruction:

> "[The test] got in the way of me being able to pick up my reading [instruction] the way I wanted to. [My] independent reading program came *after* [the test] was over. . . . Unfortunately, the [trade] books were always shafted and put aside; it was ridiculous how testing was just consuming everything."

The teachers perceived TAAS to be a unique genre of reading. Because the needs of the state became focused on getting the children to read well enough to pass the test, the teachers complied. This is similar to what Guerra (1998) describes as "literacy as institution." Literacy as institution presumes that "learners have to be provided with the necessary scaffolding and are judged on their ability to meet certain institutional expectations" (p. 56). As the state focused on having all children reading by the third grade, it also settled on set criteria to evaluate them via the TAAS test, and teachers followed suit.

Madaus (1991) writes, "How do teachers teach to the test? The answer is relatively simple. Teachers see the kind of intellectual activity required by previous test questions and prepare the students to meet these demands" (p. 230). Once teachers were familiar with the test requirements, they began to teach to these requirements, and scores continued to improve. Penny, a special education teacher for 6 years, with a masters' degree in literacy, described how some children had been conditioned to read for TAAS:

> "You see them, the kids who are in the TAAS classrooms. Sometimes you can spot those kids that are in the classroom for TAAS work, because you give them that TAAS [practice] and they are underlining, circling, numbering, and doing all of this. They've got those strategies down, but they don't know quite what to do with all of them. But you can see the ones you've taught do this, and the teacher's [saying], 'I'm going to be walking around with a clipboard. If you're not doing these things, I'm just going to mark it on my little [sheet], and those of you who did it get a pizza party.' "

The idea that children were taught to underline specific sections or words as they skimmed test practice passages, then were rewarded for it with pizzas, was common. The "TAAS reading program" unofficially sanctioned the use of TAAS practice materials and teaching for mastery of those behaviors. Teaching to the test became an art and a way of teaching that required specific coaching for teachers. Teachers working with students in the grades tested by TAAS were closely monitored and coached to ensure that they were using the practice materials and teaching test-taking strategies. Teachers who had proven their teaching abilities by having their class score well on the test were not watched as closely as new teachers or those having trouble with their test scores. The principal sent the literacy specialist to assist most novice teachers in their TAAS preparation. Katia explains how another teacher was required to coach her in TAAS preparation:

> "Maria does it [teaches teachers on campus how to pass TAAS]. She is one of those teachers who, if you've made time for them, will come, and you observe them, and they'll come and teach your kids how to pass the TAAS. Even the principal, the first year that I was doing it, asked me, 'Are you making the kids read the passage before they answer the questions?', and I said, 'No,' and she said, 'Don't do that. *Make sure that you're not making them read.* You need to teach them how to find those answers. You need to teach them to find the answers so they can pass.' "

During Katia's first year of teaching, the principal wanted to make sure that her children passed. Although Katia was a recent university graduate and specialized in reading instruction, she was pressured into teaching the children to "find the answers" and "not read the passage." It was too important to risk allowing her to teach reading; she was supposed to teach the children how to take the TAAS. As Bob mentioned, reading and "TAAS reading" were defined by the teachers at Elena as two distinct types of reading, with "TAAS reading" being a lower level of activity. This can be compared in some ways to what Apple (1986) describes as intensification that may cause teachers to " 'cut corners' by eliminating what seems to be inconsequential to the task at hand" (p. 42). A seemingly simple answer to Elena's need for TAAS recognition, intensification actually resulted in lower literacy expectations for students and frustrated teachers.

Intensification was evident when teachers at Elena began to teach to the test and disregard other activities. Apple (1986) predicts that this atmosphere may lead to what he terms "intellectual deskilling, in which mental workers are cut off from their own fields and again must rely even more heavily on ideas and processes provided by experts" (p. 42).

Teachers at Elena began to depend on the TAAS test for measuring reading achievement rather than on the multiple measures they used in the past. Katia felt that her integrated reading and writing program suffered at the hands of the TAAS practice she was required to do by the school's administration. Being a fourth-grade teacher put her in a highly stressful position, because her students had to take the reading, writing, and math tests. Caroline, a third-year teacher with experience with first and fifth graders, shared her thoughts about the pressures of seeking success, and how she differentiated between teaching reading and teaching children to pass the TAAS test:

> "There's that pressure to want your kids to do well on the test, and you want them to pass the test. There's that focus on this is what they need to know on the test, and then, at the same time, the test is basic skills that they should have anyway. I think that a lot of the way we go about teaching the TAAS and the pressure of the TAAS doesn't really make that environment a natural learning environment for the students. I think that it's too high pressured. If you get these right, then you get rewarded; if you don't, then you're punished and set apart from the rest of the world. . . . It's a hard thing to have to have in your classroom, that pressure. But I do feel that there was a lot of push [to pass the TAAS], and a lot of it wasn't natural reading. I didn't think that the kids were learning, and I didn't think that they were learning to be better educated, or to be better students, or to be better members of society. I thought that they were learning so they could pass the test."

Teachers and administrators learned quickly that the primary goal was to teach the children to read enough to pass the test. These teaching behaviors are closely aligned with what Haladyna, Nolen, and Haas (1991) call "test pollution." Test pollution can be characterized as "teaching test-taking skills, promoting student motivation for the test, developing a curriculum to match the test, preparing teaching objectives to match the test, presenting items similar to those presented on the test, using commercial materials specifically designed to improve test performance, and presenting before the test the actual items to be tested" (p. 4).

Teaching to the TAAS test became refined by teachers in several ways. The Elena campus began to utilize the TAAS pretest materials in early fall as a guide to test-taking ability, and the teachers regrouped children based on their pretest performance. One way that classroom teachers dealt with the pressure was to construct ways to organize the children into groups according to their abilities on the TAAS practice tests. Teachers tended to teach to the students on the verge of passing.

Students who were exceptional or performing on grade level were placed in groups, and the students who did not pass the practice tests and did not read on grade level were either placed in special programs or grouped within classrooms to receive extra TAAS practice. Bob described this form of tracking:

> "The trouble with TAAS is that TAAS is what you call a mastery test. So if you're teaching to TAAS at your grade level, you're only doing half of your class. The other half is sitting there with not a clue and unable to do it, because we only have a 70% pass rate. If you are into TAAS and are taking the 'TAAS Bible' and using it, and trying to do it all year long, then you are only teaching half of your class. So the other half, who are not going to pass, and who are not up to that level, are out. There's only half of the middle that really knows what they are doing."

Bob describes how the students who received the most instructional attention were the ones perceived to have a chance to pass the test. This tendency for the teachers to categorize children according to their ability to pass the TAAS simplified reading instruction. High-performing students believed to have the ability to pass the test were not an issue. Low-performing students were sent for TAAS tutoring or referred to special education, and the middle group of students, those who were thought of as capable of passing the TAAS, became the focus for most teachers. This tracking occurred in various ways. Teachers grouped students within their classrooms, with some teachers working with other teachers to regroup students across grade levels to focus instruction on the skills needed for TAAS. Ability groups were formed according to which TAAS objectives students needed to master. The stakes were high, and the freedom to alter reading instruction to help students pass, in any way, was embraced. This idea was magnified throughout the school district, as explained by Natalie:

> "I think the teacher shortage is being affected now by TAAS, more so because evaluations are being so closely tied to TAAS, and because of the pressure. The stress of high-needs schools and high-needs kids is so dramatic that teachers are getting out as fast as they can. It's going to get worse. I see very dedicated, experienced teachers who are counting their years to retirement or trying to go to a school that's easier, because we have a hard job. We have a really hard job."

Teachers at Elena school did "have a really hard job," and in some ways the TAAS test made it easier. Due to the fear that the students would be unable to pass TAAS with the "regular" reading instruction models, teachers at Elena began to spend greater amounts of time rigidly defining "TAAS reading" and prioritizing the teaching of "TAAS reading" over their regular literacy activities. Rather than worry about teaching high-level skills using multiple materials and methods, teachers became increasingly dedicated to finding out more about the test and how to help children excel on the TAAS. The teachers slowly succumbed over the years to the stress created by TAAS, and aligned instructional goals and methods to the test despite their concerns. All of the education, knowledge, and beliefs the teachers possessed about the definition of literacy and how to teach students to be literate became reprioritized because of the high-stakes assessment model. The effects of the TAAS test, as it was used in Texas, were closely linked to a simplified curriculum, and the subsequent classification and categorization of children based on their TAAS scores. The teachers and administrators at Elena began to use the TAAS test to organize classroom instruction, special education referrals, and the bilingual program in ways never used before.

At Elena, deep within a Latino community, where the billboards were in Spanish and the halls of the school were covered with Spanish and English bulletin boards, the influence of the community seemed to be disappearing within the school's walls. The dual language program faded out, with sighs of relief from many teachers, who felt that it required too much work and interfered with TAAS. Elena schoolchildren were hurriedly moved into English reading to pass the state tests in English. Procedures and attitudes changed toward literacy, and the teachers' views were reflections of the overall emphasis the district and state placed on the TAAS test and its lack of specific attention to all aspects of reading assessment. Elena teachers were merely enacting their world as they felt they should in response to the broader goals of the policy community. Ultimately, this resulted in shaping the literacy goals for the students at Elena into what Scribner (1984) describes as functional literacy.

FUNCTIONAL LITERACY AS A GOAL FOR THE STUDENTS AT ELENA

> Reading is information. Reading is survival. It's survival because, if you can't read, you can't read street signs. You can't read any important documents.
>
> —KATIA

The teachers' views and the state's goals for the Latina children at Elena came together in a way that created an atmosphere of survival coupled with low reading expectations for students. There was an implied resignation by the teachers that the children needed to read just well enough to pass TAAS. The state set TAAS mastery as a goal, and the teachers and school complied. This idea of maintaining strong test scores was an indicator of the school's tacit acceptance of a functional view of literacy (Scribner, 1984). Functional literacy is "the necessity for literacy skills in daily life . . . on the job, riding around town, shopping for groceries" (p. 8).

To survive in the accountability system, the teachers and students had to perform well enough to rate as "acceptable." The state's call to have all children reading by third grade was an attainable goal, and the teachers rose to the occasion, but for many students in other schools, reading well enough to pass TAAS was the minimum goal. Critical thinking and creative interpretations of text were their true goal. Penny, a reading specialist and special education teacher, shared her thoughts on the ways TAAS guided teachers' definitions of functional literacy goals for the children at Elena:

> "Literacy is functional. Especially at the level at which I'm working with kids here. Literacy is functional. Many of these children, I hope, will one day attain the level we have, but I don't really see that as a valid goal right now. We went on a field trip and [one of my students asked,] 'Can I eat in the bus?' and I said, 'Read number 4.' He looked up and read number 4, which said, do not eat and drink on the bus. That's what I want my kids to be able to do at least at the bare minimum. I want them to be able to read menus and signs, and fill out a job application and stuff. So literacy is functional for me."

Functional literacy (Scribner, 1984) was seen by the state and thus, the teachers, as an indicator of reading achievement. The message for which schools were held accountable for children passing the test was clear, and the standards also implied that if all children could pass the test, they could read. A passing score reflected how the state and the teachers began to agree with Guerra's (1998) conception of "literacy as entity," according to which "it is institutionally possible to help people become literate" (p. 52). Through its implementation of state policy, Elena Elementary School became the institution, or instrument, of literacy. Therefore, the characterization of "literacy as institution" as defined by TAAS accountability criteria enabled the school to survive. Another way that the new construction of literacy illustrated Guerra's "literacy as institution" metaphor was evident in the idea of "the capitalist-oriented approaches [that] recommend literacy as a currency that makes it possible for members of the society to buy their way to success"

(p. 55). Success on the TAAS brought rewards in the form of pizza parties for students, job security for teachers in evaluation documents, and public kudos for administrators. To continue to promote the idea that schools could make all children literate, institutions, such as the State of Texas, narrowed and simplified the focus and definitions of literacy. Once the teachers acquiesced, and aligned their goals with the state and focused on helping all children pass TAAS, the scores at Elena Elementary School improved. Logically, then, the children at Elena were meeting the goal of the state, as measured by TAAS; they were clearly capable of reading.

Elena was ahead of its time before the accountability system began to abbreviate the bilingual program, the focus on teacher education, the commitment to the community, and the contributions of its culture. It was becoming more difficult for teachers to seek out knowledge other than that advocated by the state. Apple (2001) also prophetically describes the road Texas appeared to be taking to educate its children and control its teachers:

> Under the growing conditions of regulated autonomy, teachers' actions are now subject to much greater scrutiny in terms of process and outcomes. Indeed, some states in the United States not only have specified the content that teachers are to teach, but also have regulated the only appropriate methods of teaching. Such a regime of control is based not on trust, but on a deep suspicion of the motives and competence of teachers. And this will be policed by statewide and national tests of both students and teachers. (p. 51)

By 2002, any school in the Elena school district not performing well on TAAS was subject to the superintendent's reorganization plan. This plan dictated one reading program for all students, and its use was required of all teachers. Teachers were instructed to teach reading for 90 minutes a day, without interruption, and had permission to use only a districtwide, designated reading program and materials.

Literacy assessment changed in the state, and subsequently at Elena. Many of the teachers and administrators understood that the TAAS test measured everything—the effectiveness of a teacher, a principal, a school, and the entire school district. The teachers had learned from their past experiences of being audited that nothing else about Elena was weighted with such importance; nothing else meant as much to the district and the state as the TAAS scores. The school district did not measure Elena's special education program, bilingual program, or community involvement in ways similar to the assessment of literacy through TAAS. These endeavors were maintained and recorded for documentation purposes, but they were not given priority in the accountability system and, subsequently, were not a top priority for many of the teachers. Although they saw the limitations in the state's accountability system, the teachers at Elena believed they should take the time to teach explicitly to the TAAS test. And, though they resented the TAAS test and did not see it as valuable, the teachers focused on it as the goal of the state and were rewarded. TAAS scores at Elena gradually increased each year as teachers moved into TAAS practice activities and away from their previous reading methods. It was assumed that the children should be coached in TAAS practice, and the rising test scores reinforced this assumption. The institutionalization of literacy at Elena was complete.

As students at Elena school learned to pass the TAAS test with greater success, teachers' attention turned to maintaining the school's acceptable rating status, and, in 2002, they achieved the status of being recognized by the state in all areas. Elena was one step away from being an exemplary school, the highest achievement the state of Texas bestows upon its schools, its teachers, and its principals. Yet Elena was becoming a reflection of the changing culture and goals of state policy. Once defined by multiple and complex views, such as the culture of the community, the development of children literate in English and Spanish, and a teacher population open to diverse learning theories and new ideas, the school's standards were quickly eroded by the streamlining and simplifying of goals required by the TAAS test. This was a prime example of literacy as institution (Guerra, 1998). The state of Texas and the teachers at Elena viewed the Latino children through a lens that emphasized the literacy goals of the institution over those of the community in which the school resided. Guerra's notion of "literacy as practice," in which the sociocultural aspects of literacy are seen as a priority, was noticeably absent in the rhetoric of the state accountability system and the recent teacher discourse.

CONCLUSIONS

Guerra's (1998) idea of literacy as practice typifies the philosophy at Elena Elementary School prior to the high-stakes accountability system:

> An individual's literacies vary according to the personal and social circumstances of his of her life, so everyone is considered literate in certain situations and not in others. The goal, from this perspective, is not to master a particular form of literacy, but to develop ones' ability to engage in a variety of social practices that require us to operate in a plethora of settings and genres to fulfill different needs and goals. (p. 58)

The Texas accountability system pressed the teachers at Elena into one monolithic view of literacy and left the students and teachers little opportunity to build on the existing literacies of the community. These findings have many implications. I conclude with the notion that teachers' voices need to be heard. During a time when the No Child Left Behind Act seeks to reinforce and strengthen the role of standardized tests in reading assessment, teachers' stories must have a place. Hillocks (2002) quotes George W. Bush's testing plan, presented during his presidential campaign:

> We will praise and reward success and shine a spotlight of shame on failure. . . . Without testing, reform is a journey without a compass. Without testing, teachers and administrators cannot adjust their methods to meet high goals. Without testing, standards are little more than scraps of paper. Without testing, true competition is impossible. Without testing, parents are left in the dark. (p. 9)

Teachers need a voice to disseminate their professional knowledge to administrators, policymakers, and the public. An important factor in the prevention of teaching to the test is to encourage teachers to join the battle against high-stakes testing. Many times, when teachers spoke out against the role of high-stakes testing as educational accountability, it was assumed they were attempting to circumvent the evaluation of their performance, when, in reality, teachers knew that testing was an inadequate measure of reading. All too often, administrators and policymakers attended to improving test scores and assumed that children were receiving better reading education, when higher test scores only indicated that more teachers had become adept at understanding the test and had learned to teach accordingly.

Rather than creating pressure that encourages an environment conducive to constructing literacy as a pragmatic tool for survival, assessment of reading should explore multiple indicators. Even as TAAS was touted as a measure of how the state's children were reading, Elena teachers held the view that the TAAS test was not able to provide them with information detailed enough to guide instruction. Because of their extensive knowledge base about reading assessment, Elena teachers had the ability to see the faults of the system. Yet they believed they had no recourse, even though they had used various informal reading assessments in the past. Teachers understood the difference between measures of reading performance on a standardized test and measurements of reading behaviors over time, in ways illustrative of students' reading strategies and comprehension.

As high-stakes accountability became a reality in 1997, Elena Elementary School became more influenced by outside forces. TAAS cannot be named as the sole cause of any of these changes, because alteration of the focus of literacy instruction may have occurred without the impact of accountability. However, it can be said that, in 2001, passing TAAS was the most important goal at Elena. Prior to the TAAS test, Elena operated under a philosophy shaped by the principal, the teachers, and a community open to various methods of instruction and assessment. Elena chose to embrace a love of reading and a high level of engagement by the children. Teaching children to read under the pressure of high-stakes testing was stressful, and the teachers at Elena worked to provide the best for their students under tremendous pressure. The confining nature of the state polices proved to be overwhelming, as Dolores expressed in her thoughts concerning the state's goals for her students during our final conversation:

"[So the students] are our worker ants? We want our worker ants to be able to problem-solve, and these are the problems that we want them to solve, and this is the way that the problem will be worded? You know, is this real life? And then we want them to be able to pull things from texts, and this is the information we want them to pull. And these workers, in order to be good workers for us, must be able to do the following skills. That scares me. So is that what public schools are going to become? We're going to be the feeders to this industry and this industry and this industry? Or are we really going to create quality citizens who can make decisions on their own, and who will have a chance to make those choices? I don't want worker ants. My babies are not worker ants. They are thinkers. But the TAAS says, 'Don't think. Don't question. Just do it.' And to that I say, 'No, no. You better question. You better question, even me.' I tell [my students], 'You have every right to question.' "

REFERENCES

Apple, M. W. (1986). *Teachers and texts: A political economy of class and gender relations in education.* New York: Routledge and Kegan Paul.

Apple, M. W. (2001). *Educating the "right way": Markets, standards, God, and inequality.* New York: Routledge/Falmer Press.

Clandinin, D. J., & Connelly, F. M. (Eds.). (1995). *Teachers' professional knowledge landscapes.* New York: Teachers College Press.

Foley, D. E. (1995). *The heartland chronicles.* Philadelphia: University of Pennsylvania Press.

Fountas, I. C., & Pinnell, G. S. (1996). *Guided reading: Good first teaching for all children.* Portsmouth, NH: Heinemann.

Guerra, J. C. (1998). *Close to home: Oral literate practices in a transnational Mexicano community.* New York: Teachers College Press.

Haladyna, T. M., Nolen, S. B., & Haas, N. S. (1991). Raising Standardized Achievement Test scores and the Origins of Test Score Pollution. *Educational Researcher, 20*(5), 2–7.

Hillocks, G., Jr. (2002). *The testing trap: How state writing assessments control learning.* New York: Teachers College Press.

Madaus, G. F. (1991). The effects of important tests on students: Implications for a national examination system. *Phi Delta Kappan, 73,* 226–231.

Scribner, S. (1984). Literacy in three metaphors. *American Journal of Education, 93,* 6–21.

Texas Legislature Online. (2001). Available: http://www.capitol.state.tx.us/tlo/77R/billtext

Trueba, H. T. (1993). Culture and language: The ethnographic approach to the study of learning environments. In B. J., Merino, H. T. Trueba, & F. A. Samanigo (Eds.), *Language and culture in learning: Teaching Spanish to native speakers of Spanish* (pp. 26–44). Washington, DC: Falmer Press.

Wolcott, H. F. (1994). *Transforming qualitative data.* Thousand Oaks, CA: Sage.

Chapter 14

Fostering Systems of Support for Teachers and Students

JUDY WALLIS and ELIZABETH ROSADO-McGRATH

> What makes me hopeful . . . is our infinite capacity for
> inventing the future, imagining things otherwise.
> —MEIER (1995, p. 184)

Today's educators face many challenges as they prepare students for the future. They work in an atmosphere of constant change and reform, while trying to sustain the energy, enthusiasm, and hope necessary to accomplish the work of educating our children. We have watched as many of our colleagues have grown weary of imposed educational reforms that tend to focus on the structure of an organization rather than the culture. We must acknowledge the fact that teachers work within a very complex context (Hargreaves, 1994). Today's educators lead demanding lives in which competing agendas and ideas often create a confusion that obscures the very essence of why they became teachers. For example, some reforms emphasize that there are "right" programs, "correct" methods, and "perfect" materials. We have seen teachers' energies depleted and have shared their frustrations and confusions (Graves, 2001). Both the seasoned veteran and the eager beginner have become entrapped in contexts in which isolation and competition are the norm (Palmer, 1998). Additionally, changing demographics, combined with high-stakes testing, have further compounded the complexities of the settings in which teachers work.

Educators whose assignments involve working with students for whom English is a second language often become the most isolated from their colleagues. Furthermore, they are culturally worlds apart from the students they teach (Freeman & Freeman, 2001). With increasingly rapid demographic changes occurring in U.S. schools, most districts have not been able to keep up with the challenges these changes present, and they often lack a network of support available to the teachers within the schools.

What follows is a story of how we—the language arts administrator and the bilingual/English as a second language (ESL) administrator—set out to create a comprehensive literacy plan or process that not only places at its heart the needs of all students in our system but also places teachers there. Our story takes place in a large, urban district, with approximately 31,000 students and more than 2,000 teachers. The cast of student characters in this story is diverse. One-third of our students are English language learners (ELLs), and approximately one-third are recent immigrants. The students speak more than 40 different languages, with the vast majority being native Spanish speakers. As in all good stories, a problem drives the plot and its interaction with the characters and the setting. In this story, the problem presents itself in a familiar way in the changing demographics at both the national and local levels.

During the school year 1998–1999, 4,416,580 ELLS were enrolled in U.S. public schools. This represents a 27.3% increase in enrollment over the 1997–1998 school year. Furthermore, the General Accounting Office reported a shortage of between 100,000 and 200,000 bilingual teachers. This is representative of a much larger, nationwide shortage of teachers—estimated at 2.0–3.5 million in the next decade (Barron & Menken, 2002).

As in the stories across the nation, the complexion of our district didn't always look the way it does now. As recently as 15 years ago, Spring Branch Independent School District (ISD) was largely a suburban, Anglo, middle- to high-income district. Students arrived well prepared to "do school." Their middle-income backgrounds matched the expectations and culture of district schools. When these rapid demographic changes began, both teachers and students were unprepared.

In our years in education, we had individually come to the realization that an effective organization is one in which shared values are identified, articulated, modeled, promoted, and protected (DuFour & Eaker, 1998). We knew we wanted to create a culture within our district that would perpetuate shared values and practices about literacy education, learning, and teaching. We wanted to create a place where teaching was more than just a job. We knew that human connections were an essential requisite to renewed energy and efficacy. The resolution to the problem we faced in our story—creating a place where students could learn and grow—would only be realized if we also created a culture that supported and nurtured the professionals.

We know from a plethora of research that systems theory (Senge, 1990) holds an answer. If we are to support and sustain teacher development, we must create an infrastructure, or system, and culture that place teachers at the heart of the organization. Michael Fullan (2001b) notes that "educational change depends on what teachers do and think—it's as simple and complex as that" (p. 115). With the deteriorating conditions in which teachers must work, the need to identify ways to support, sustain, and create capacity within the teaching force is essential. Necessarily, we must place teachers at the center of our work. In fact, Cohen (2002) suggests that after decades of school reform, it is time to create "teacher-centered" schools. He argues that school reform has "paid little attention to the work of the teacher, the one critical player who makes the biggest difference" (p. 532).

Teachers are at the heart of Figure 14.1, which illustrates their many roles within the educational context. Support for these complex roles must come from the infrastructure created by the educational lead-

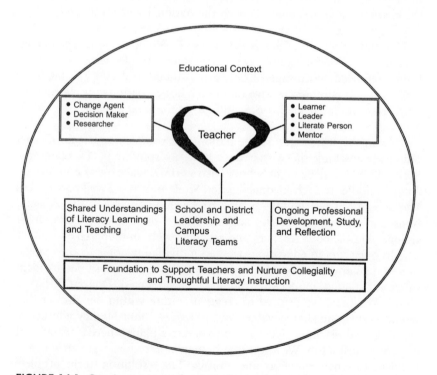

FIGURE 14.1. Creating systems of support for teachers within a literacy program.

ership. In creating high-quality contexts in which teachers to play out their roles, the leaders must provide the necessary opportunities for teachers to acquire knowledge and increase their understanding of their role in the change process (Fullan, 2001a). Furthermore, the organization must create spaces in which teachers have time for purposeful learning and dialogue. Figure 14.1 outlines the kinds of support required to achieve effective and thoughtful change.

One of the most critical dimensions in creating organizational capacity requires that educators spend time developing shared understanding about literacy learning. Effective teaching requires that educators spend time together to think about and discuss the theories and beliefs that undergird their teaching practices. Because teaching cannot be reduced to mere technique, and the language and terms we use to describe pedagogy are often ambiguous, we must create time in which teachers tease out the nuances of practice. Routman (2002) suggests that "even the best professional development may fail to create meaningful and lasting changes . . . unless teachers engage in ongoing professional dialogue to develop a reflective school community" (p. 32).

A second dimension in supporting thoughtful literacy instruction is leadership—both at campus and district levels. Effective leadership provides the support that is critical to sustain positive change. A recent study (Bender-Sebring & Bryk, 2000) suggests that successful principals are inclusive and facilitative in their leadership style, maintain focus on student learning, manage in efficient ways, and achieve a balance between pressure and support.

Moreover, at the district level, clarity of focus is essential. Often, district-level administrators play an interpretive role, helping teachers see how the entire literacy process and program fit together. Furthermore, they support and nurture teachers' reflective needs and professional growth. Both district- and campus-level administrators serve as mentors for teachers so that all engage in the kind of apprenticeship that allows professionals to grow in their craft. Palmer (1998) suggests that this relationship between colleagues resembles "an ancient human dance, and one of teaching's great rewards is the daily chance it gives us to get back on the dance floor" (p. 25).

Ongoing professional development, study, and reflection serve as the third foundational component a district must put in place. Sarason (1990) has suggested that it is virtually impossible to create and sustain productive learning for students when the same rich learning contexts do not exist for adult learners. To accomplish this, the organization must recognize that professional development is more than certificates and teachers meeting district requirements for annual professional development hours. When done well, this final dimension becomes not only a mechanism for retooling, refining, and extending professional growth, but it also serves to nourish the soul of the professional and initiates feelings of efficacy and renewal. In his book, *The Energy to Teach* (2001), Graves explains that often our energy comes from unanswered questions and then passes from "the unanswered question to the joy of knowing and explaining" (p. 69). Providing both time and space for teachers to examine unanswered questions and to consider the many paradoxes teaching presents is one of the most significant gifts a district can offer teachers. Darling-Hammond (1997) stresses that we can transform and redesign institutions only when we invest in individual and organizational learning. The power of reform rests in our willingness to accept this maxim.

We must interject one note of caution, however. A system must look carefully at its professional development, making sure that the learning opportunities weave a coherent message about teaching and learning. It is attention to this aspect of the system that results in the creation of a highly successful professional learning community. As leaders, we must make explicit how each learning opportunity connects to the literacy education of students. When we fail to make the message clear, we risk leaving teachers confused and uncertain.

In our district, we formed a group called the Literacy Round Table to work toward developing shared understanding among the professionals who had district responsibilities and touched teachers and students in their work. The purpose of the Literacy Round Table was to provide a time and place for district literacy leaders to share beliefs and vision about the kind of literacy instruction we wanted for all district students and teachers. We intentionally included the people who had general responsibility for language arts, specific program responsibilities such as bilingual, ESL, early childhood, and special education, and other individuals who provided safety net structures for students. What was striking about the first meeting was that we had never before all been at the same table at the same time, concerned with one goal: to support the ongoing teaching and learning of literacy in our district.

Goodlad (1984) and others have noted a common theme that often stands out in schools. In what he labeled as "autonomous isolation," he noted that there is little exchange of ideas and practices between groups of educators. Some have characterized the condition in which educators work as learning impoverished for both teachers and students (Rosenholtz, 1989). So teachers often become trapped in their own development. They are given neither the opportunities nor the encouragement to grow. Hargreaves and Fullan (1998) note that "professional learning must be made integral to the task of teaching, with time for it built into the system and ongoing commitment to it regarded as a basic professional obligation" (p. 49). Senge (2000) suggests that schools are often organized on fragmented specialization. This view is based on an Industrial Age assumption that knowledge arises in separate categories and contexts. Certainly, this was true for us. Ours was a context fraught with all of the obstacles mentioned in school reform literature. We set out to construct a view of what we wanted literacy to look like in our district, then to create a structure that would support this vision. Over a number of meetings and e-mail discussions, we finalized a model (Figure 14.2) that captures not only the instructional features individuals wanted for our students but also addresses the supports teachers need in their work. One of the most interesting and lengthy discussions we had in creating this was about how to characterize it. So often, we refer to what we do as a "program." However, the group, *not* wanting to communicate a lockstep way of teaching, decided to label the model as a *process*. This model is the result of many hours of discussion and negotiation.

FACETS OF THE PROCESS

This model (see Figure 14.2) became know as the Spring Branch Comprehensive Pre-K–12 Literacy Process. Its function is to capture the complex interrelationships of each of the components necessary to ensure thoughtful literacy instruction. As we prepared and designed the model, we were influenced by the work of our colleague, John O'Flahavan. Each facet is critical and serves as a reminder when we meet to reflect, plan, and problem-solve as administrators and teachers.

Formative and Summative Assessment

Living in an era of high-stakes testing and accountability, the Literacy Round Table needed to find ways to infuse our process with thoughtful formative and summative literacy assessments that would guide teachers and administrators in planning, monitoring, and guiding instruction. We created a system of assessment that included both informal and formal measures. Furthermore, we developed a district database in which teachers could enter students' reading progress throughout the year.

   This database has become a rich resource that is used by district and campus administrators to monitor our students' literacy progress, and by teachers to identify group and individual student needs. We have also begun to study the data for patterns and trends that might reveal how best to transition second-language learners, support our students throughout the school year, and provide professional development targeted for teachers administering assessments and analyzing data. For example, we

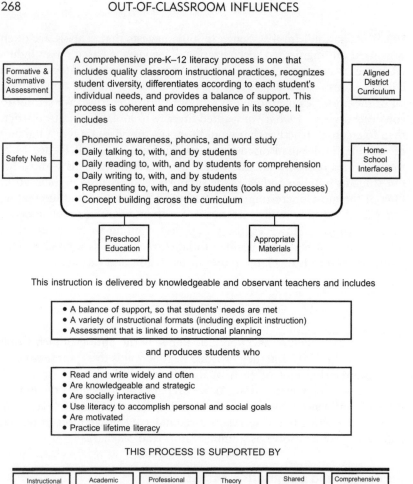

This instruction is delivered by knowledgeable and observant teachers and includes

- A balance of support, so that students' needs are met
- A variety of instructional formats (including explicit instruction)
- Assessment that is linked to instructional planning

and produces students who

- Read and write widely and often
- Are knowledgeable and strategic
- Are socially interactive
- Use literacy to accomplish personal and social goals
- Are motivated
- Practice lifetime literacy

THIS PROCESS IS SUPPORTED BY

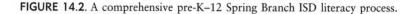

| Instructional Leadership | Academic Coaching | Professional Development | Theory & Research | Shared Language, Understanding, & Vision | Comprehensive Literacy Program Evaluation |

FIGURE 14.2. A comprehensive pre-K–12 Spring Branch ISD literacy process.

are using district reading data to create trajectories of growth as students acquire literacy skills in their second language. As we work with teachers, we are creating opportunities for conversations and inquiries about how best to support students acquiring a second language.

Safety Nets

Several members of our Literacy Round Table worked within district safety net programs that provided support for students. The group agreed that quality literacy instruction includes multilevel, short- and long-term safety nets that reflect the goals of the comprehensive literacy process and address students' varying needs. The members discussed how to identify or create *short-term* safety nets that include student modifications, small-group or individual literacy support, and second-language transition. We also recognized the need for *long-term* safety nets, such as dyslexia support, special education, and alternative interventions and environments. We agreed that the use of safety nets would be most effective with continuous and ongoing monitoring and assessment. Furthermore, we agreed that we must work to boost collaboration between teachers in student support roles and classroom teachers.

Preschool Education

It was during the conception of this model that the district was preparing to move toward districtwide implementation of a fully funded prekindergarten program for all Spring Branch ISD students. The Literacy Round Table leaders believed that quality literacy instruction begins with access to preschool experiences and includes a strong emphasis on oral language and concept development. The committee, recognizing that children learn through social experiences and play, also agreed that literacy should be infused into all activities. Additionally, the group strongly believed in the notion that students' home experiences need to be respected and valued as a foundation for all learning.

Appropriate Materials

As the Round Table members discussed the diverse needs of students, we realized that teachers were often restricted by a lack of appropriate resources and materials to use in differentiated student instruction. One complication was that teams within schools often purchased materials for individual-classroom or grade-level use. Because these materials were not kept in a central location, teachers in other grade levels had little access to them. This resulted in a shortage in some situations and duplicate resources in others. We began to address this problem in a variety of ways. Schools have been encouraged to create literacy libraries, where all materials are kept in one location. In fact, we invited an outside consultant to work with each elementary campus to create schoolwide instructional collections of books to support all students. By pulling books together in one location, it was easy to see materials were inadequate. By identifying these gaps, schools are able to better address their needs during the budgeting process. One way we provided assistance from the district level was to apply for and use grant funds to build more comprehensive arrays of instruction materials from which teachers can select.

We were able to use Goals 2000 funds (titled Academics 2000 in Texas) to add fiction and nonfiction English and Spanish materials to ensure that teachers had adequate resources to meet students' individual and small-group needs.

Home–School Interfaces

We knew that quality literacy instruction must bring the home, the community, and the school into partnership to achieve mutual respect and a reciprocal flow of information. Our students come from homes in which parents speak many different languages. Our goal was to recognize and celebrate this diversity, and we wanted to identify ways to ensure that we built on the cultural capital our students possessed. One way we reached out to families was to extend school library hours. District librarians and teachers created warm and welcoming evening programs for the whole family. Some schools bought board books and puzzles for young siblings accompanying the families when they came to school. Computer labs were often opened to parents to work on general equivalency diploma (GED) preparation.

As we worked with schools across the district, we recognized that the more we tried to familiarize ourselves with the unique needs of each school's students and their parents, the more we could create social connectedness and trust between the home and school communities. Studies show that when schools work together with families to support learning, young people "tend to succeed not just in school, but throughout life" (Putnam, 2000, p. 303). As educators, we must understand the relationship between literacy learning and the social practices in classrooms and schools. Luis Moll (2000) posits that we can better connect to our students by studying the diversity of life in households and using this awareness to better address the needs of students.

Aligned District Curriculum

At the time the Literacy Round Table began to meet, one of the district's initiatives was to align the curriculum and address coherence within the literacy education of our students. Whereas that process would provide consistency between grade levels, it was clear that teachers also needed a shared understanding of the state and district standards and student expectations. This continues to require ongoing dialogue within and between grade levels on campuses and across the district. In addition, we have created a multilevel approach to professional development to support teacher learning. We discovered that teachers need to discuss not only learning objectives but also to share understanding of pedagogical practices. For example, teachers often said that they used guided reading as a way to teach reading, but when asked to explain what they did within a guided reading lesson, they often described very different teaching practices. The focus was more about cosmetic or surface features than about more critical aspects, such as the balance of teacher support and student responsibility.

PROCESS SUPPORT

The members of the Literacy Round Table set out to determine the infrastructure necessary to support this comprehensive reform process. Educational reform includes a plethora of theories and initiatives that often lack a vehicle to make lasting change a reality. Sweeney (2003) points out that unless we address the organizational changes and necessary supports, teachers are often left to carry on alone. This increases obstacles and challenges, and reduces the hope that real systemic reform ignites.

Instructional Leadership

Strong leadership at the school and district levels is crucial to provide the continuity and support teachers need in their work. Johnson (1996) found that influential leaders focus on three types of leadership: (1) pedagogy and learning, (2) securing resources and building coalitions, and (3) using resources to supervise, support, and plan. As members of the Literacy Round Table, we knew we would need to address each of these three functions to realize our vision. Because the plan hinged on strong professional development that included consultants, coaches, and classroom support, in addition to resources such as literacy materials, garnering support from the superintendent, and other district leaders was crucial. We were also aware that principals would play a key role in ensuring that the district process was being implemented as designed.

Academic Coaching

One of the foundations supporting the process was academic or instructional coaching. The members of the Literacy Round Table knew that campus-based, professional development through ongoing modeling was necessary. We believed that students' success would be enhanced as staff were encouraged to engage in reflecting, planning, and problem solving as members of a professional community. In addition to providing demonstration lessons, coaches could provide feedback and support as teachers attempted and implemented new instructional practices. Furthermore, the campus literacy coaches would assist in setting up literacy teams, establishing literacy libraries for each campus, and providing the necessary initial leadership that would be required. Because the coaches would not have their own classroom, they would be positioned to provide the kind of modeling, coteaching, and support that teachers deserved.

We discussed one additional aspect of coaching, knowing that we must be dedicated to the growth of literacy coaches by providing them ongoing professional development. They needed access to professional development that would connect them with sound ideas and key leaders in the field of literacy. However, even though each coach was a member of the larger district community, each represented campuses that faced unique needs. Our role included supporting the coaches as they selected the appropriate time and strategies to implement new ideas and practices at the campus level.

Professional Development

We approached professional development in two specific ways by using long-term consultants and a multilevel professional development plan. We selected several consultants with theories of learning and action (Fullan, 2001b) congruent with our view of literacy and learning. These consultants provided on-site support to help teachers connect their theories of learning to their instructional practices. In this way, we had a better chance to build capacity successfully and increase the quality of literacy instruction. These consultants have been partners with us for the past 3 years. Their work with us focuses on writing instruction, schoolwide literacy change, and reading.

In addition, we approached district professional development using a four-pronged approach (Figure 14.3).

1. We established a partnership with a local university and began providing a master's degree program in language arts. We developed courses that built on one another, so that we provided a coherent and comprehensive course of study. The activities and assignments connected directly to teachers' classrooms, giving them instant contexts in which to apply their new learning. Course instructors often made themselves available to demonstrate instructional strategies right in the classrooms of the teachers taking the courses.

2. We created core sessions from the topics included in the university program. For example, we created a 4-day balanced literacy institute that would either enhance or lead to the university courses.

3. We created short 2- to 6-hour courses teachers could attend after school or in the summer. These sessions were more narrowly focused. For example, a session might explore a topic such as guided reading.

4. We developed an offering we labeled on-demand professional development. These courses could be requested by a campus and were based on individual campus needs. Campus-based literacy coaches were involved in every aspect of professional development.

Theory and Research

Quality literacy instruction has its theoretical foundation in a broad-based body of research. Part of our professional development and curricular planning includes engaging *all* professionals in careful study of

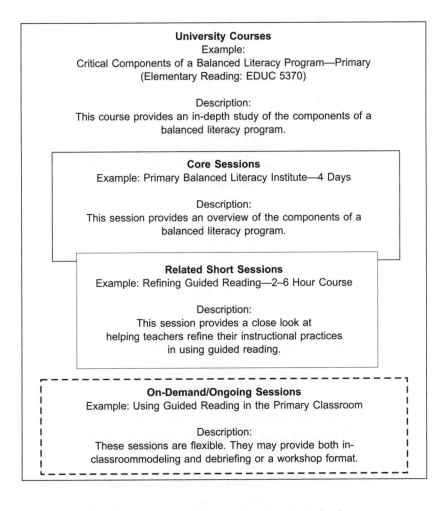

FIGURE 14.3. Creating alignment in professional development

research and policy decisions that affect our literacy practices. Literacy Round Table members, literacy coaches, and teachers study to stay grounded in research that suggests best practices. With the advent of the No Child Left Behind legislation, effective January 2002, we have been cognizant of how our practices must be based on quality research in theory and pedagogy. We draw from a breadth of literacy research, so that all our practices are based on sound premises and theories, sharing professional articles and books regularly in our meetings with the Round Table and the district literacy coaches. They, in turn, engage their school colleagues in discussions and inquiry projects. Often, campus literacy teams decide on particular areas of study that match individual school needs. Reading and reflecting as colleagues play integral roles in the success of our students.

Shared Language, Understanding, and Vision

If students are to be successful, our instructional practices must be based on shared understanding of what constitutes effective literacy instruction. We have identified several approaches to accomplishing this goal. One practice involves holding biannual literacy summits, where literacy teams from across the district come to learn, share, and refine their practices. A second way we are working toward shared understanding is by identifying common language to describe our teaching practices and the terms we use. For example, we created classroom posters that list and define the cognitive strategies threaded throughout our district curriculum pre-K through grade 12 and writing posters clarifing the language we use to discuss the characteristics of successful writing. We know that our students' learning is enhanced when parents, teachers, administrators, and community members use shared terms understood by all to describe literacy beliefs and practices.

Comprehensive Literacy Program Evaluation

One of our current goals is to identify ways to assess the effectiveness of our teaching practices. We are creating ongoing, multifaceted formative and summative evaluation practices, including a comprehensive district reading database that captures information about students' development and differentiated instructional opportunities. Furthermore, we are engaging in observation of classroom practices, monitoring teachers' implementation of the district's curriculum, and measuring the impact of professional development. Principals and other program administrators use walk-through checklists to determine ways that classroom instruction reflects how teachers implement new learning into their instructional practices. Campus literacy coaches meet regularly. As district administrators, we recognize that changes in instructional practices are a result of continuous evaluation of each of these areas.

Once we began district conversations as Literacy Round Table meetings about our comprehensive program, we discovered that we had a variety of different understandings about second-language learners and how they acquire literacy. Many of our colleagues perceived differences between our literacy process and programs that supported our students for whom English is a second language. As we continued to work on new ways to support both teachers and students, we created the model in Figure 14.4.

The issue of access was identified as a distinguishing characteristic of differentiated instruction for second-language learners. For us, access issues are defined as knowledge of pedagogy, linguistics, and cultural and linguistic diversity (Menken & Antunez, 2001). Our plan to ensure that all stakeholders understand the relationship between instructional strategies for all students and the necessary differentiation for ELL students includes an increase in professional development opportunities in the following areas:

Knowledge of pedagogy for second-language learners

- Understanding the role of native language literacy/content in students' first language

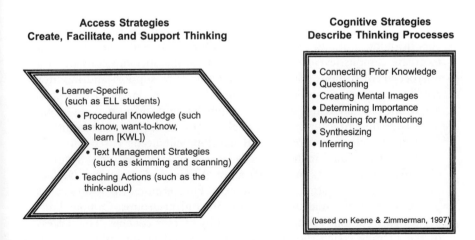

FIGURE 14.4. Creating access and scaffolding instruction.

- Understanding the role of native language literacy/content in students' second language
- Understanding bilingual and ESL methodology

Knowledge of linguistics

- Psycholinguistics
- Sociolinguistics
- First- and second-language acquisition
- Contrastive language structure in students' first and second languages

Knowledge of cultural and linguistic diversity

- Implications of theory, models, research, and policy
- Instructional foundations for ELLs
- Studies that focus on multiculturalism, cultural diversity, and cross-cultural issues
- Awareness of communication regarding parent and community involvement

It is our belief that by specifically defining "access strategies," teachers and administrators will provide professional development for all teachers including those who work with second-language learners.

THE ROLE OF LITERACY TEAMS

As we mentioned earlier, a key component to ensuring that change occurs in thoughtful and meaningful ways for all students and teachers is to create campus-level literacy teams, whose membership consists of a microcosm of campus educators. Their role is to support and monitor the literacy program and connect their school to the larger district literacy team. Literacy teams act as a campus-based decision-making group to provide direction for teachers, analyze data to determine program effectiveness, determine professional development needs based on data, identify instructional material needs based on data, analyze scheduling of grade levels for maximum instructional time, and problem-solve factors that may affect student achievement. Furthermore, the team's focus is to ensure equity in achievement for all student groups. Campus literacy teams are initially organized and led by literacy coaches. The success of the literacy coach, however, is often dependent on guidance from district-level curriculum staff about roles, responsibilities, and support in his or her own professional growth.

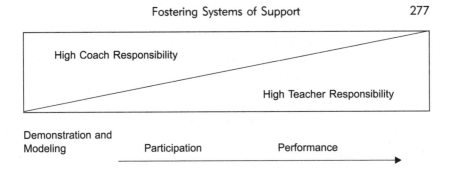

Demonstration and
Modeling   Participation   Performance

FIGURE 14.5. Gradual release model.

SUPPORTING CHANGE

Often, school reform utilizes packaged programs and generic professional development. However, we have learned that just as we support our students as they learn and grow, we must also support professionals. We use the gradual release model shown in Figure 14.5 (Pearson & Gallagher, 1983) to support not only our students but also campus literacy coaches.

We recognize that to support well, we need to spend considerable time in schools to understand better the unique needs of campus literacy coaches and their individual schools. We see ourselves in dual roles as district administrators—to be both coaches and supporters. In a true learning community, we recognize that we must be prepared to act on these roles at different times. Above all, we must establish relationships built on care and concern. Transformation occurs only when we work with others in an atmosphere of authenticity and respect. Only by supporting coaches as they assist teachers can we achieve the vision of the Literacy Round Table.

CONCLUSIONS

Although we don't have all the answers, we do know that our hope for positive educational change lies in our corporate work. Our chapter ends unlike a typical story, in which a resolution occurs; our story continues. We live the story each day in the hope that the lives of both our students and teachers are enriched by our work. At the beginning of the chapter, we referred to Michael Fullan's words: "Educational change depends on what teachers do and think—it's as simple and complex as that" (2001b, p. 115). We know that touching the lives of teachers—

placing them at the heart of our work—is the way to provide all students with the kind of rich literacy instruction they deserve, and the only way to bring about lasting educational change.

REFERENCES

Barron, V., & Menken, K. (2002). What are the characteristics of the bilingual education and ESL teacher shortage? *Ask NCELA, 14*.

Bender-Sebring, P., & Bryk, A. (2000). School leadership and the bottom line in Chicago. *Phi Delta Kappan, 81*(6), 440–443.

Cohen, R. M. (2002). Schools our teachers deserve: A proposal for teacher-centered reform. *Phi Delta Kappan, 81*(6), 532–537.

Darling-Hammond, L. (1997). Reframing the school reform agenda: Developing capacity for school transformation. In E. Clinchy (Ed.), *Transforming public education: A new course for America's future*. New York: Teachers College Press.

DuFour, R., & Eaker, R. (1998). *Professional learning communities at work: Best practices for enhancing student achievement*. Reston, VA: Association for Supervision and Curriculum Development.

Freeman, D. E., & Freeman, Y. S. (2001). *Between worlds: Access to second language acquisition* (2nd ed.). Portsmouth, NH: Heinemann.

Fullan, M. G. (2001a). *Leading in a culture of change*. San Francisco: Jossey-Bass.

Fullan, M. G. (2001b). *The new meaning of educational change* (3rd ed.). New York: Teachers College Press.

Goodlad, J. I. (1984). *A place called school: Prospects for the future*. New York: McGraw-Hill.

Graves, D. H. (2001). *The energy to teach*. Portsmouth, NH: Heinemann.

Hargreaves, A. (1994). *Changing teachers, changing times: Teachers' work and culture in the postmodern age*. London: Cassell.

Hargreaves, A., & Fullan, M. (1998). *What's worth fighting for out there?* New York: Teachers College Press.

Johnson, S. M. (1996). *Leading to change: The challenge of the new superintendency*. San Francisco: Jossey-Bass.

Keene, E. O., & Zimmermann, S. (1997). *Mosaic of thought: Teaching comprehension in a reader's workshop*. Portsmouth, NH: Heinemann.

Meier, D. (1995). *The power of their ideas: Lessons for America from a small school in Harlem*. Boston: Beacon Press.

Menken, K., & Antunez, B. (2001). *An overview of the preparation and certification of teachers working with limited English proficient (LEP) students*. Washington, DC: National Clearinghouse for Bilingual Education.

Moll, L. C. (2000). Inspired by Vygotsky: Ethnographic experiments in education. In C. D. Lee & P. Smagorinsky (Eds.), *Vygotskian perspectives on literacy research: Constructing meaning through collaborative inquiry* (pp. 256–268). New York: Cambridge University Press.

Palmer, P. J. (1998). *The courage to teach: Exploring the inner landscape of a teacher's life*. San Francisco: Jossey-Bass.

Pearson, P. D., & Gallagher, M. C. (1983). The instruction of reading comprehension. *Contemporary Educational Psychology, 8*, 317–344.

Putnam, R. D. (2000). *Bowling alone: The collapse and revival of American community.* New York: Simon & Schuster.

Rosenholtz, S. J. (1989). *Teachers' workplace: The social organization of schools.* New York: Longman.

Routman, R. (2002). Teacher talk. *Educational Leadership, 59*(6), 32–35.

Sarason, S. B. (1990). *The predictable failure of educational reform: Can we change course before it's too late?*. San Francisco: Jossey-Bass.

Senge, P. M. (1990). *The fifth discipline: The art and practice of the learning organization.* New York: Doubleday.

Senge, P. M. (2000). *Schools that learn: A fifth discipline fieldbook for educators, parents, and everyone who cares about education.* New York: Doubleday.

Sweeney, D. (2003). *Learning along the way: Professional development by and for teachers.* Portland, ME: Stenhouse.

Chapter 15

The Empowering Literacy Practices of an African American Church

GWENDOLYN THOMPSON McMILLON
VINCENT DUANE McMILLON

For years, educational researchers have attempted to address the academic difficulties that African American students experience in U.S. classrooms (Fordham, 1988; Gilbert & Gay, 1989; Hale, 1982; Heath, 1983; Irvine, 1990; Ogbu, 1995). These children have been called culturally deprived, genetically inferior, educationally disadvantaged, and at risk, ultimately locating the problem within African American children and families. Researchers have attempted to develop ways to improve the success rates of African American students despite the persistence of academic underachievement (Delpit, 1995; Edwards, Pleasants, & Franklin, 1999; Hopkins, 1997; Ladson-Billings, 1994; Lee, 1991; Taylor & Dorsey-Gaines, 1988). The paradigm shift toward a more sociocultural view of literacy exemplifies the value that researchers have begun to place on out-of-school literacy experiences, and the influence that these experiences may have on in-school literacy learning and development. Some of these important out-of-school practices can also inform school personnel concerning specific ways to improve classroom instruction.

A sociocultural theory of learning and development (Luria, 1976; Scribner, 1985; Vygotsky, 1978; Wertsch, 1985) focuses on the ways learning takes place within cultural contexts and addresses the importance of looking beyond the classroom to examine institutions that may influence children's classroom learning experiences. In recent years, several researchers have emphasized the importance of considering the literacy practices of outside institutions to understand the literacy crisis within the classroom (Edwards et al., 1999; Heath, 1983; McMillon & Edwards, 2000; Purcell-Gates, 1997; Resnick, 1990). In her groundbreaking study comparing the literacy practices of mainstream and nonmainstream communities, Heath (1983) discusses the importance of studying all the environments within a community, including "ways of living, eating, sleeping, worshiping, using space, and filling time" (p. 3), to understand the entire process of literacy acquisition and development. Purcell-Gates (1997) further emphasizes this point:

> When we seek to understand learners, we must seek to understand the cultural contexts within which they have developed, learned to interpret who they are in relation to others, and learned how to process, interpret, or decode, their world. (p. 5)

As African American researchers, we believe that much of this processing, interpreting, and decoding for many African American children is often done through lenses developed in the context of the African American church.

The African American church has historically taught African Americans successfully, but its voice is often excluded from the conversation concerning the effective education of African American students (McMillon, 2001). One reason for this exclusion may be the scarcity of documentation addressing this issue. Although some researchers have reported on African American church history (e.g., Baldwin, 1991; Billingsley, 1992; Frazier, 1963; Meltzer, 1964; Montgomery, 1993; Mukenge, 1983; Nelsen & Nelsen, 1975; Nelsen, Yokley, & Nelsen, 1971; Sernett, 1975; Smith, 1988; Washington, 1984), theology (Burkett, 1978; Cone, 1989, 1997; Copher, 1993; Felder, 1991; Hopkins, 1994), culture, and the overall environment within the African American Church (Franklin, 1997; Freedman, 1984; Lincoln & Mamiya, 1990; Myers, 1991; Shade, 1989), few studies have focused on educational aspects of African American churches (Cornelius, 1991; Hale, 1994; Kunjufu, 1984; McMillon, 2001; McMillon & Edwards, 2000; Ward, 1998). Specifically, little is known about literacy practices within the African American church environment. Although it has been accepted as an influential institution, the African American church has not been considered a resource for educators (Edwards, Danridge, McMillon, & Pleasants, 2001; McMillon, 2001; McMillon & Edwards, 2000).

Conducting research in the context of the African American church can provide educators with information concerning the educative processes utilized in a learning environment in which many African American students are considered successful (McMillon, 2001). This information can assist teachers of African American students by illuminating possible points of connection through which schoolteachers may find creative ways to help students negotiate the cultural boundaries of their various learning environments. Additionally, by conducting research in the church environment, we hope to promote the idea of investigating students' cultural environments outside of school to identify ways to connect with students inside the classroom.

In this chapter, we report on a journey we undertook for a 3-year period, during which we conducted an ethnographic study of the empowering literacy practices of a Midwestern, mainstream Protestant, African American church in an urban neighborhood. As members of an African American church, we recognize that although the church is the most influential institution in the black community (Edelman, 1999; Franklin, 1997; Frazier, 1963; Freedman, 1984; Lincoln & Mamiya, 1990; McMillon, 2001; Mukenge, 1983; Nelsen & Nelsen, 1975; Smith, 1988; Ward, 1998), it has not been invited into the conversation concerning the best ways to educate black children. We believe that it is critical for educators to become knowledgeable about their students' cultural values and beliefs to develop creative connections for their students that build on knowledge acquired from valuable out-of-school literacy experiences. Thus, we wrote this chapter not only to provide information for teachers about African American students who participate in the literacy practices of an African American church but also to challenge educators to seek information proactively on all of their students' cultures by looking beyond the classroom to identify effective points of connection between their students' out-of-school and in-school literacy learning.

This chapter is divided into four sections. The first section provides a brief history of the church and discusses the black theological perspective on which many values and beliefs are based. The second section describes the setting of the specific church in which the study is conducted. One of the recurring themes in the study was the closeness of the members within the church community, which is discussed in the third section. In this section, we present examples of the caring concern shown by teachers and students, and discuss specific ways that the church provides cultural capital for its members. Finally, the fourth section explicates the authentic ways that literacy skills taught during formal church classes are utilized, while children participate in the religious practices of Youth Sunday worship service. This chapter is organized to help readers understand the empowering impact that the church has had in the lives of many African Americans—past and present.

THE HISTORICAL CONTEXT
OF THE AFRICAN AMERICAN CHURCH

> "For what do I go to this far land which no one has ever reached? Oh, I am alone! I am utterly alone!" And Reason, that old man, said to her, "Silence! What do you hear?" And she listened intently, and she said, "I hear a sound of feet, a thousand times ten thousand and thousands of thousands, and they beat this way!" He said, "They are the feet of those that shall follow you. Lead on! Make a track to the water's edge! Where you stand now, the ground will be beaten flat by ten thousand times ten thousand feet." And he said, "Have you seen the locusts how they cross a stream? First one comes down to the water-edge, and it is swept away, and then another comes and then another, and then another, and at last with their bodies piled up a bridge is built and the rest pass over." She said, "And, of those that come first, some are swept away, and are heard of no more; their bodies do not even build the bridge?" "And are swept away, and are heard of no more—and what of that?" he said. "And what of that—"she said. "They make a track to the water's edge." "They make a track to the water's edge—." And she said, "Over that bridge which shall be built with our bodies, who will pass?" He said, "The entire human race." And the woman grasped her staff. And I saw her turn down that dark path to the river.
> —OLIVE SCHREINER, "Dreams" (in Thurman, 1973, p. 6)

Olive Schreiner's parable encapsulates the great sacrifices made by the forefathers of today's African American children in the intense struggle to become literate, empowered, and liberated. The inhumane oppression of slavery failed to strip blacks of their indelible desire for liberation and equality for their children. Through the years, African and African American forefathers have offered their bodies to build bridges that make a track to the water's edge. They were beaten, lynched, and raped, but, as a race, they withstood these degradations, while they continued to voice explicitly a demand for physical, economic, and educational liberation for themselves and their children. These martyrs, depicted in Schreiner's parable, were frequently members of African American churches—an unlimited source of human capital and empowerment. As indicated by Marian Wright Edelman (1999), the African American church has provided "lanterns" to help its children "see" more clearly as they pursued their various paths or journeys to freedom and success.

When studying children, or assessing the current status of a group of people, it is extremely important to consider their history—the historical events, people, and institutions that may have influenced their present state (Elder, Modell, & Parke, 1993; Vygotsky, 1978). One must understand the culture, cultural values, artifacts, beliefs, and idiosyncrasies of a group of people to understand the people within the culture (Heath, 1983). African Americans have a somewhat gruesome history in the United States. Slavery, segregation, discrimination, and all the ideologies that served to cripple them across the years have no doubt affected many generations. However, an institution was created from a combination of beliefs, and was specifically designed to meet the multifaceted, complex needs of African Americans in the United States—the African American church (Lincoln & Mamiya, 1990). When developing educational strategies for African American students, the time has come for educators to consider the influence that literacy practices within the African American church may have on in-school literacy learning and development.

What Is the African American Church?

To begin to grasp its influence on literacy learning and development, it is necessary to first understand what the African American church is to African American people. It has *no* counterpart in the United States. The separation of church and state does not exist for most African Americans, because they believe that religion plays a significant part in *every* aspect of their lives. Broadly conceived, the African American church is often represented as the most successful and influential institution in the African American community. As such, many metaphors have been used to describe the African American church. Historically, it has taken the leadership role in the community by serving as the *mouthpiece*, the *advocate*, and the *defender* (Proctor, 1995). The African American church has always been the *clearinghouse* for the community. Whether the issues were social, political, or economic, the African American church has been the place where conversations occurred, ideas were shared, problems were solved, and actions were taken (Nelsen & Nelsen, 1975). To African Americans, the church is not just a place of worship. It is a *safe haven* for wounded spirits, a *firm foundation* for unstable families, and a *fortress* in a community that is constantly under attack by outsiders trying to promote their own agenda by attempting to exploit the weaknesses of others (Mukenge, 1983). The African American church is the only institution that African Americans own and control, without having to answer to *outsiders* (Freedman, 1984). It is one of the few institutions that endured through slavery. After worshiping with their masters, slaves secretly attended their own church, an *invisible institution* located in the backwoods of plantations, or in their own slave quarters, where they would hear a *liberation gospel* that taught them that God created all men to be equal (Montgomery, 1993).

The African American church continues to be the place where African Americans go to receive encouragement, reaffirmation, and validation. It is the *mother womb* of black culture (Lincoln & Mamiya, 1990). It has given birth to schools, banks, insurance companies, and low-income housing; it has nurtured young talent for musical, dramatic, and artistic development (Lincoln & Mamiya, 1990). E. Franklin Frazier's (1963) description, *nation within a nation*, represents the multiple levels of involvement of the African American church in the black community. An old cliché that is well known in the black community states that "anything worth anything came out of the black church." Within the numerous metaphors used to describe the African American church, there lies the opportunity to discover how the positive, empowering atmosphere of the church affects literacy, teaching and learning inside and outside the church environment. To learn how the church can support the learning of African American children, it is first necessary to understand what they are taught in this setting.

The Black Theological Perspective

The African American church is a place where theological perspectives are taught and developed. Theology is the study of man's beliefs about God. When a group of people has similar beliefs, those beliefs facilitate the development of a sense of community among them (Frank & Yasumoto, 1998). Because of the dehumanizing way that most blacks were brought to the United States, they shared a common slavery experience, and many brought African religious beliefs and practices that had similarities. These commonalities among blacks created a unique "social location" from which to develop a cohesiveness that would continue to unify them forever (Weems, 1991). Renita Weems, an African American Vanderbilt theologian, asserts that social location is past experiences, values, and beliefs from which a person develops his or her perspective. This perspective becomes the foundation of his or her decision-making process. In an effort to develop strategies for survival, slaves created a black theology that met their needs based on their social location. This black theology was the impetus that compelled black men and women to separate from white Christian churches and start their own church—the African American church. Although slavery no longer exists, black theology continues to thrive and is the foundation on which African American churches are built today.

Black theology is a liberation theology (also called a *liberation gospel*) (Cone, 1989; Felder, 1991; Hopkins, 1994; Moyd, 1995; Proctor, 1995) based on three goals: (1) fighting racial discrimination; (2) building black resources; and (3) an undaunting, unrelentless faith in freedom. First, fighting racial discrimination refers to efforts to restructure the power relations between blacks and whites in the United States. Much energy is spent on attacking restrictions caused and imposed by the white-male-dominated power structure. This goal intertwines religion and politics in the African American church and "is identified with black self-determination for political power, claiming one's space" (Hopkins, 1997, p. 5). As previously stated, there is no such thing as separation of church and state in this context. In fact, the African American church was birthed in response to oppressive political strife.

Second, building black resources refers to the church's commitment to building black people, institutions, and movements. This goal is associated with the cultural beauty of blackness and self-identity. The church has invested much time, energy, and other resources focusing on the arts. Many famous musicians, actors, and singers first performed in the African American church setting. African American churches spearhead numerous community and economic development programs in an attempt to build black institutions. Also, the African American church has been, and continues to be, a resource of human capital for movements that strive to improve the status of blacks in this country, including the National Association for the Advancement of Colored People (NAACP) and countless other organizations.

Finally, an unrelentless faith in freedom has been the bricks and mortar that cemented the African American church together for centuries. Black people's belief in their own destiny of freedom has always been based on the unique African American interpretation of the Christian Bible. The core message of the Christian Bible and the lived experiences of African Americans are uniquely similar, in that they both exemplify the struggles of the poor and demand justice, equality, and liberation for all. The very existence of the African American church has been based on the three aforementioned goals and the belief that it is God's divine will to continue to pursue attainment of these goals. Thus, pursuit of these goals has shaped the belief and values systems within the context of the African American church, which affects the beliefs and values of its members.

When children attend African American churches they learn from explicit and implicit teachings of values and beliefs. They attend classes and participate in activities that teach them to process and interpret their world according to the African American church values system, which becomes internalized after continuous exposure. These values are learned and reinforced socially, politically, psychologically, spiritually, and economically. Therefore, African American children, many of whom attend African American churches, have a unique, preestablished frame of reference from which to build (in the case of a teacher who understands their culture) or as a source of cultural interference (if their teacher is uninformed).

As *insiders*, African American researchers familiar with the values and beliefs taught in the context of the church, we were privileged to conduct an uninhibited investigation of the literacy practices of a Midwestern African American church. This case study illuminates experiences that contribute to the development of a unique frame of reference established for the children who participate.

CALVARY BAPTIST: A "21ST-CENTURY" AFRICAN AMERICAN CHURCH

Calvary Missionary Baptist Church is a 21st-century church that has reaped the benefits of its forefathers' efforts, described earlier. It is an active member of the largest African American organization in the world—the National Baptist Convention, USA, Inc., which has 8.7 million members (Billingsley, 1992). Calvary Baptist has a long history of involvement with the convention and its affiliates. The previous pastor was president of the local Sunday School and Baptist Training Union Congress of Christian Education (the educational arm of the convention), worship leader for the state convention, and president of the local ministerial alliance (an association of ministers from various denominations). The current pastor of Calvary Baptist is the moderator of the local Baptist district association of 39 churches and a vice-president of the state convention (affiliates of the National Baptist Convention). Several members of the church hold offices in the conventions, including President of the Laymen's Department and Registrar Assistant.

Calvary Missionary Baptist Church serves approximately 250 members from a range of socioeconomic backgrounds. The membership includes single-parent families, families with two incomes, and well-educated professional couples. The church is located in an impoverished urban neighborhood adjacent to a government-subsidized housing project and an elementary school. Many of the tenants at St. Thomas Apartments are familiar with Calvary Baptist Church. Most of the children living in St. Thomas Apartments attend Saffron Elementary School, which serves approximately 165 predominantly African American students, with 91% of them receiving a free or reduced-price lunch.

Saffron Elementary School and Calvary Baptist Church have an established relationship that has lasted over several generations. Several of the current leaders in the church attended Saffron as children. Most of Saffron's students live in the neighborhood and have participated in Vacation Bible School, the Summer Free-Lunch Program, the annual church picnic, or the afterschool tutoring program. The head cook at Saffron is also the bus driver at Calvary Baptist Church. Mrs. Stenson lives about three blocks from the church and faithfully evangelizes in the neighborhood. Her daughter, Mrs. Luther, who lives next door to her mother and father, attended Saffron as a child. She is currently the Directress of the Youth Department at Calvary Baptist Church.

A city park located across the street from the church is the site of an annual neighborhood "Family Reunion," in which many people from surrounding neighborhoods, including St. Thomas Apartments, participate. Mrs. Stenson and Mrs. Luther play critical roles in organizing the event. Adults who grew up in the neighborhood and moved to various parts of the country return each year for the festivities, during which Calvary Baptist Church, and other churches in the area, collaborate with neighborhood organizations to enjoy food, fun, and entertainment. They appeal to neighborhood gangs and drug dealers to change their lives and join them in stopping crime and violence.

Although some families live in the nearby neighborhood, most of Calvary's members commute from other, less impoverished parts of the city. A number of the commuting members attended Calvary Baptist as children and are very proud to have an opportunity to share their heritage with their children. Some families have as many as five generations attending church together. In some cases, three generations have had the same Sunday School teacher. These intergenerational relationships provide exceptionally close bonds among teachers, parents, and students. Teachers are very well respected by students and adult members of the church.

Calvary Missionary Baptist Church (a pseudonym) provides several programs that can influence children's literacy development, including Sunday School classes, midweek Bible study, and Children's Church for ages 2–6 (Sunday mornings during worship service). Additionally, on the second Sunday of every month, children and youth are in charge of the morning worship service. At that time, they fulfill all of the important responsibilities, such as singing, directing the choir, playing the instruments, ushering, reading the announcements, welcoming the visitors, praying during altar call, and sharing meditational thoughts with the audience.

THE STUDENT–TEACHER RELATIONSHIPS
OF CALVARY BAPTIST CHURCH

One of the most significant recurring themes in our study of literacy practices was the caring concern and support that members of the church provided for each other. Fordham (1988) asserts that the relationship orientation of African Americans (which she labels a *fictive kinship system*) is a complex social network system based on foundational African American cultural beliefs that emphasize the importance and value of relationships. She further contends that this relationship orientation could be a source of disconnection for African American students, if their classroom teacher is unfamiliar with, or insensitive to, the importance of relationships in African American culture.

The relationship orientation of African Americans is manifested in the African American church, where helping others succeed is considered a responsibility (Edwards et al., 2001). However, the perspectives that African American students develop from the cultural/social capital provided within the context of the African American church may be in conflict with perspectives that are valued in the context of other American, nonminority institutions, such as public schools, where competition is encouraged and being at the "top of the class" is rewarded. In school, there is no incentive for students to assist other students, because the farther one is ahead of others, the more recognition he or she receives. This is in stark contrast to the values African American students are taught in church.

In the African American church environment, the "human side" of literacy development (Edwards et al., 1999) is often emphasized through the establishment of meaningful relationships in which adults are addressed as *Brother, Sister,* or *Mother,* and are respected for wisdom acquired from life experiences regardless of social status or educational background (Proctor, 1995). These relationships help create a trusting, nurturing environment in which students have rich literacy experiences, while participating in classroom activities, helping peers, and sometimes sharing the teaching role (McMillon & Edwards, 2000). Teachers often enjoy intergenerational relationships with parents and hold high expectations for student performance (Edelman, 1999). Based on a *positive* self-fulfilling prophecy, most of their students achieve (Edwards et al., 2001). At Calvary Baptist, all of the church teachers express excitement about the exceptional growth shown by their students. Mrs. Nettles, a Sunday School teacher for 35 years, stated:

> "Students can learn anything. We just have to challenge them and have high expectations. I believe that my students are capable of un-

derstanding the most difficult biblical concepts. If you talk to my students, you will see for yourself that they understand a lot of things that many adults have trouble with. Their [the students] only limitations are the ones placed on them by adults."

During data collection in Sunday School, midweek Bible study, and Children's Church, where great emphasis is placed on oral language-development skills, we found numerous examples of the high expectations that teachers have for their students. In the tradition of the African American church, students are expected to speak clearly and articulately, with voice inflection and emotion (McMillon, 2001). The oral tradition of the African American church often requires members to give extemporaneous prayers, testimonies, and speeches (Edwards et al., 2001). Sunday School, midweek Bible study, and Children's Church are utilized as a type of "training ground" to develop and refine oral-language skills to prepare students to participate in the worship services with the adults.

We believe that several of the literacy practices utilized in Sunday School, midweek Bible study, and Children's Church enhance oral-language skills. In school, many students participate in Circle Time to develop oral-language and other skills. They also become familiar with storybook concepts by memorizing and retelling children's stories and poems, such as "The Three Little Pigs" and "Little Miss Muffet" (Edwards, 1995). Similarly, students who participate in classes in the African American church practice oral-language skills in their classes. For example, in the African American church, the importance of memorization is emphasized (McMillon & Edwards, 2000). Bible stories are frequently retold, and students memorize the stories after hearing them repeatedly.

One of the Sunday School teachers in this study also utilized storytelling as a way to help students understand abstract concepts, and as a means to assess student comprehension. Jesus's dying on the cross to the save the world (John 3:16), and Jesus's return for His people—also called the "Rapture" (I Thessalonians 4:16, 17; Revelations 21, 22)—are very difficult concepts to understand. To scaffold student learning and comprehension, Mrs. Nettles (the Sunday School teacher for children ages 4–6 years) involved students in an ongoing project in which she required them to learn the "Story of Jesus Dying on the Cross" and the "Story of the Rapture." Students were asked to retell these two stories utilizing a poster board and "heaven box" as mnemonics to assist with details of the stories (McMillon & Edwards, 2000). Regular class members were expected to remember these stories and be prepared to share them with younger students and new students, until they learned them also.

Requiring students to memorize and retell stories helps develop oral language as a bridge to reading (Searfoss & Readence, 1985) and fosters the beginning of metacognitive strategies for reading comprehension (Mason, McCormick, & Bhavnagri, 1986). Students are able to ask questions that address specific issues about the story. Teachers provide clarification on these issues and help students think about ways to apply the story to personal circumstances. Storytelling activities also build confidence by giving students opportunities to share "their knowledge" with others.

During the storytelling activities, students utilize "storybook terms" that are a part of the "teacher-talk register," (Cazden, 1988) the unique words and terms that teachers use to communicate with their students during specific activities. For example, when telling students "The Story of Jesus Dying on the Cross," Mrs. Nettles, the Sunday School teacher, uses terms that encourage interaction: "Now let me tell you 'The Story of Jesus Dying on the Cross'; when they put the thorny crown on Jesus' head, did they smash it hard? . . . or did they smash it soft? Did Jesus deserve to be whipped? . . . No! Jesus had never done anything wrong!" Similarly, when sharing "The Story of the Rapture," she says: "When Jesus comes back, he's coming back for a church without spot or wrinkle! Does that mean we never sin? When we get to heaven there will be no more pain and no more sorrow, no more sickness and no more dying! Won't that be a glorious day?" When students retell the story, they use the same terms and voice inflection that they often hear the teacher using. Appropriate use of the teacher-talk register indicates students' advanced familiarity with classroom discourse (Cazden, 1988; McMillon & Edwards, 2000).

One of the most unique aspects of literacy practices within the context of the church is that they take place in a *natural environment*. Students develop a number of literacy skills in the African American church environment, where they are explicitly and implicitly taught to value and utilize literacy skills, while engaging in "authentic" literacy practices. The most valued artifact and important learning tool in the African American church is the *Holy Bible*, which is considered "God's Word"— the roadmap for life. Students are taught that it is the most important book that they will ever read and are admonished to read it frequently, and obey (apply) what they read. Literacy practices within this context are based on religious beliefs taught from birth and reinforced continuously throughout adulthood. We found that, based on these beliefs, the students understand the importance of learning the "lessons" that they are taught each week. They understand that biblical knowledge acquired will be applicable throughout their lives. In this way, we believe that teachers' use of authentic print helps students understand the value of learning in the church environment, by teaching explicitly the purpose and relevance of the learning.

One way that students learn the purpose and relevance of Bible stories and scripture memorization is through listening to teachers and other adult role models share their personal stories. For example, during a Children's Church class, the teacher, Mrs. Jackson (who is a teacher assistant at a public elementary school) shared a testimony about a recent experience—suffering the loss of her mother. One of the students immediately put his head down, and the following conversation ensued:

MRS. JACKSON: What are you doing, David?

DAVID: (*looking up*) Prayin' for yo' mama. I been prayin' for her a long time. I been prayin' that she get well.

MRS. JACKSON: (*Smiles.*) Oh, thank you so much, David! I really appreciate you prayin' for my mom.

DAVID: I missed you and didn't think you were comin' back.

MRS. JACKSON: I was gone a long time, wasn't I, David? (*Looks at the other students.*) You see, David is in my class at school. I knew he was prayin' for me and my mother. (*Looks at David.*) I missed you too, David; but I'm back now. OK? And I want you to know that you can stop prayin' for my mother because God has answered your prayer. She had been sick a long time, but she's healed now. She's gone on to heaven to be with the Lord. She won't feel any more pain or have any more worries. You see, when someone dies who loves the Lord, we're supposed to celebrate! They're in heaven with God!

DAVID: (*Perks up and smiles.*) Yo' mama in heaven?

MRS. JACKSON: Yes, David, she's in heaven. (*Smiles.*)

DAVID: God answered my prayer?

MRS. JACKSON: Yes! God definitely answered your prayer. My mom is in a much better place.

During this interaction, David (age 4) displayed a keen understanding of the importance of praying for the sick to be healed by God. Mrs. Jackson skillfully utilized the moment to teach that the death of a Christian should be celebrated (a religious value) (II Corinthians 5:8). She also helped David understand that "healing" has multiple meanings: One definition for "healing" is death; however, this "death" is the beginning of "life" in heaven with Jesus, which should be a "happy time." Through her testimony, she also reassured David that his prayer was answered.

Teachers in the classes address many "difficult to talk about" issues, such as death, chronic illness, and single parenthood. The teachers feel that it is their responsibility to prepare their students for all circumstances in life. They discuss these issues and share Bible verses to support their comments. Students are expected to remember the scriptures and apply them, when necessary. The memorized scriptures provide students with standards of reference (values) to live by, and equip them with an arsenal of admonishments and encouragements to recall, when needed.

Cultural Capital Provided by the African American Church

Many Sunday School teachers and other adult role models in the church setting attempt to provide students with viable coping skills to help them succeed in school, and in their adult lives (Edwards et al., 2001). Some of these students come from homes with parents who may not be able to provide their children with the cultural capital needed to negotiate successfully the cultural boundaries between home, church, and school (Freedman, 1993). Although some parents may not have successful educational histories (Edwards et al., 1999), and some of their occupations may not be professional positions that positively influence their children's study habits (Lareau, 1989), the African American church has historically provided cultural capital for its members through adult and peer role models (Edelman, 1999; Proctor, 1995). This *community* consists of people from varied social classes, whose common beliefs, values, experiences, and histories bind them together in multiple ways, resulting in a complex social network system within the African American church environment. It is within these social interactions that learning and development take place for many African Americans (Van Dijk, 1997). Within the context of the African American Church, the connection among learning, development, and close relationships creates a nurturing environment in which students acquire cultural capital, while they simultaneously learn literacy skills. However, in the alienating context of classrooms at school, the connection among learning, development, and close relationships to which African American students become accustomed at church may be a source of cultural interference/incongruence (Edwards et al., 2001; Fordham, 1988; McMillon, 2001; McMillon & Edwards, 2000).

In our opinion, "cultural capital" can be defined as the beliefs, values, and lessons learned from one's culture that provide ways to think about, address, cope with, and/or overcome various issues and obstacles in life. We believe that our definition is similar to that of Frank and

Yasumoto (1998): the "resources that actors may access through social ties . . . which may affect one actor's action directed toward another based on the social structure in which the action is embedded in the history of transactions between the actors" (p. 645). Based on these definitions of cultural and social capital, the terms can be used interchangeably for the purposes of this study.

The perpetuation of the social ties within the context of Calvary Baptist Church was illuminated by Ms. Harris's (a Sunday School teacher) relationship with her previous pastor and his grandson, B. J. She often shares her testimony concerning how the "human side" of the church made a difference in her life at a critical time.

> "When I first came to Calvary Baptist, I was troubled and pregnant. One of my coworkers invited me to church. She often talked about the wonderful things that were going on at her church. Although I had a successful career, my personal life was a mess. I was living with a man whom I thought I loved, but did not want to marry. When I walked down the aisle and joined the church, I didn't know how people would treat a person like me, but I knew that something was missing in my life. Reverend Thompson [the previous pastor] embraced me and told me that he was going to baptize me as soon as possible. When I got baptized, I was pregnant with my beautiful daughter, and I believe she's the person that she is today because I gave my life to Christ before she was born. Reverend Thompson was so kind and inspirational! I was not ostracized for being a single mom. On the contrary, I felt at home. I was treated like a daughter by my pastor, and my church family loved me, and helped me raise my daughter. Now, I just want to help somebody else who needs to know that Jesus loves them."

Since her initial experience with the Calvary Baptist Church family, Ms. Harris has offered her assistance to many of her fellow members. She is a social worker by profession and has frequently utilized her professional skills to assist her students and other members of the church. B. J. (Reverend Thompson's grandson), was one of her students when she taught the Junior Class. When B. J. was 9 years old, his father decided to send him to a predominantly white, private school, because it was supposed to be "the best school in the city." It was a very difficult time in B. J.'s life, because his dad had recently remarried. He was living with his dad, stepmother, and older stepsister, experiencing all of the stress from living within a complex family structure, and he missed his "real mom," who lived in another city. B. J. reminisces:

"That was the worst year of my life. Nothing was going right! I hated every day that I had to go to that place. The teachers were prejudiced. The kids were prejudiced. I was one of three black kids in the school. One was half-white and the other one was black, but thought she was white. I was all alone. Kids would take my ideas for projects. I didn't have any friends. They would hide my papers . . . and nobody would believe me. My dad would punish me because he thought I wasn't tryin'. . . . They were tryin' to make me into something that I wasn't. I set one goal for myself that year—to do whatever it took to get out of that place [school]. There was only place where I felt good about myself . . . that was at church. My Sunday School teacher was Ms. Harris at the time, and she looked out for me big time! She showed me love and let me be me. I would tell her stuff, and she would try to help me out. She taught me how to deal with all the anger that I was feeling. That was the worse time of my life! If it hadn't been for her and some of the other people at church, I don't know what I would've done. It was hard!"

The relationship between B. J. and Ms. Harris exemplifies the positive influence that a teacher can have on a student. Because she recognized that some of her students were having problems, Ms. Harris adjusted her instructional time to meet their needs. By providing a forum for students to talk openly about family and school problems, she was able to facilitate sessions, during which they learned to listen to each other and suggest solutions. She simultaneously used her professional skills and biblical knowledge to teach coping strategies and help her students understand the relevance of their Christian and cultural beliefs in their daily lives.

Characteristics manifested in the empowering student–teacher relationships between David and Mrs. Jackson, Ms. Harris and Reverend Thompson, and B. J. and Ms. Harris include honesty, trust, understanding, time, compassion, knowledge, wisdom, commitment, and willingness. Because many African American students experience these powerful relationships in the African American Church environment, they may not be comfortable with the alienating, distant way that they are treated by some schoolteachers. Noddings (1984), Foster (1997), and Ladson-Billings (1994) have made critical contributions to the field concerning ways the ethics of caring transform students' lives. Pepper (1999) emphasizes this point when she asserts, "When students believe you care about them and how well they do in class, and they trust you to treat them fairly in every situation, you have won half the battle in helping them succeed in school" (p. 7). Educators must not underestimate the influence that a caring student–teacher relationship can have on teaching and learning.

OPPORTUNITIES TO PRACTICE LITERACY SKILLS

We believe that one of the most important aspects of the African American church is its commitment to children. The value of children and emphasis on their development is illuminated in a traditional cliché often utilized in the African American church environment when discussing children's issues: "Our children are the *Church of Tomorrow.*" Church teachers and adult role models spend a tremendous amount of time training and preparing students to become leaders in the church community. Biblical training and explicit instruction of cultural values (e.g., emphasis on oral development to prepare for extemporaneous prayers and testimonies and peer tutoring to teach the importance of sharing one's knowledge with others) are integral parts of all church activities organized for students. As previously stated, Sunday School, midweek Bible study, and Children's Church are considered *training grounds* to prepare students to participate in the adult worship services. In addition to these classes, students are given an "authentic" opportunity to display their talents and utilize their literacy skills during the regular worship service on the second Sunday of every month. This monthly worship service is traditionally called "Youth Sunday" or "Children's Sunday" at many churches, and is set aside so that children and youth can participate in every aspect of Sunday morning worship.

To prepare for their Youth Sunday worship service, the children and youth at Calvary Baptist attend several practice sessions. The choir and praise team learn the words of their songs, often in rhythmic patterns, similar to those used to memorize scripture verses. Repetition plays a critical role, because the choir members sing their songs several times during rehearsal, until their supervisors feel that they can sing them perfectly. The persons chosen to read the announcements, welcome the visitors, and share a thought for the day, are also expected to practice their parts. Junior ushers meet with their adult supervisors to go over their "drills" (practice collecting the offering, seating guests, etc.). The children at Calvary Baptist are told that "practice makes perfect," and they are expected to show their commitment to God and to their church by attending practices and cooperating when they are asked to repeat a song, reading, or drill. Adult supervisors encourage the children to do their best, and when Youth Sunday arrives, they expect the students to remember everything they learned during practice.

During our observations, Youth Sunday service began with the Children's Choir walking in, enthusiastically singing:

> Oh, it's a highway to heaven.
> None can walk up there,
> but the pure in heart.
> Oh, it's a highway to heaven.
> I am walking up the King's highway.

Members of the Children's Choir were dressed in black and white—starched white blouses and shirts, with fancy black skirts and dress pants. The pastor and ministers led the procession down the aisle, with Bibles in hand, and took their places on the dais. The Children's Choir (approximately 35 children), continuously singing, filled the choir stand and turned to face the audience. Their faces were beaming with excitement—it was *their time to shine.* Adults responded by returning smiles, nodding their heads in approval, swaying, clapping, and singing along with the choir.

After a few other preliminary activities, the Praise Team—three children and three teenagers—led the audience in praise songs. They encouraged audience participation and used hand movements or other gestures to accompany the words of the song. Some adults and children in the audience stood up during the Praise Period—a sign of their desire to "praise the Lord" and/or a cultural expression indicating personal enjoyment of that particular song.

Every month, a different student was responsible for welcoming the visitors. They stood at the small podium by the dais and spoke clearly, with a smile: "It is now time to welcome our visitors. Would all of our visitors please stand?" After the visitors stood, the audience gave welcoming applause, followed by special words of welcome and an invitation to join the church "if you are looking for a church home." The Thought for the Day was usually shared by a younger child (age 3–8), after the visitors were seated. The child pulled the microphone down to his or her level and articulately shared a memorized message with the audience. Again, the audience applauded with encouraging approval. Several students have been given opportunities to share the "memory verses" they learned in Sunday School or Bible study as a Thought for the Day. With great self-esteem and dignity, the young students articulately share their newly acquired knowledge with over 200 people, who immediately provide praise and encouragement.

After the pastor's comments, members of the audience are invited to come to the altar for prayer. During our observations, the children prayed "heart-wrenching prayers." Morgan, a 12-year-old musician for the children's choir, wrote two "lists" on a sheet of paper to help him remember what he wanted to say during his prayer. One list contained "things to thank God for," and the other included "things to ask God for." Danielle asked God to help all of the children to do well on their state assessment tests (which were being given at that time in many schools):

> We all need your help, God, to help us pass our tests.
> We can't do it without you . . . at least, I know I can't.
> And so, I'm asking you to bless us at our schools.

She had tears in her eyes and displayed signs of great emotion and sincerity. Both prayers indicated that the students had an in-depth understanding of "prayer." They did not repeat a general prayer that they had memorized, but thanked God for specific things pertaining to their personal lives and asked for blessings in detail. The emotion displayed and the voice inflection indicated a strong belief in God and a commitment to advocate for themselves and others. During this time, prayers were usually offered extemporaneously, but children could choose to write a few notes to help them remember what they wanted to say. Children as young as 3 years old have an opportunity to pray before the church audience during Youth Sunday worship service.

In addition to these activities, children also participate on the Junior Usher Board, which is responsible for opening and closing the sanctuary doors, seating the audience, disseminating church literature (e.g., bulletins and envelopes), directing the audience, and holding the collection baskets during the tithes and offering period. Children as young as 5 years old participate in this activity. Ushers have "signs" or codes that they must know to fulfill their responsibilities. Children are given handouts to help them learn the signs, and their parents are expected to assist them. Adults have high expectations of children who serve as ushers, because not fulfilling their responsibilities will interrupt the worship service. For example, they must know the appropriate times that people in the audience are allowed to enter and exit. At certain times, walking is not allowed (e.g., during prayer and scripture readings). Ushers must know when they can allow others to be excused. Additionally, they must understand the logistics of moving the audience from one place to another in a timely manner. Ushers plan the best routes for various activities (e.g., offering and Communion), and the Junior Ushers are responsible for carrying out these tasks during the Youth Sunday worship service.

When participating in the Youth Sunday services, children display many literacy skills and a tremendous amount of courage. By providing this forum, the African American church is authentically supporting student literacy development and perpetuating religious and cultural values. Additionally, the importance and relevance of many skills and concepts taught in students' church classes are reinforced.

CONCLUSIONS

African American students have historically struggled in the U.S. educational system. Despite the efforts of many educators, these problems have persisted. For too long, educators have overlooked the importance of out-of-school literacy experiences—specifically, considering how they might influence in-school literacy learning. It is important to investigate students' cultures to identifying possible points of connection among their home, community, church, and school learning environments. Although it has long been respected as a viable institution in the African American community, the African American church has not been invited into the conversation addressing the education of African American students. The time has come to examine the literacy practices of the African American church—a learning environment that has successfully taught African American students for many years. Conducting research in the context of the African American church allows us to observe African American students in a learning environment in which they are successful. By becoming familiar with the literacy practices in the context of the African American church, educators can become more knowledgeable about ways that many African American literacy learners may connect or disconnect with certain in-school literacy practices.

As African American researchers, we were excited to conduct a study in an environment in which we learned and developed as young children. We were given ample opportunities to develop and practice literacy skills that continue to be useful today. From a personal perspective, we understand the importance of the African American church in the lives of many African Americans. The teachers in this study agree that we do not live compartmentalized lives. Church and state may be separate institutions according to governmental regulations, but in African American culture, the African American church and the values learned in that context are connected with every part of one's life. Because many African American children are explicitly taught this cultural value, it is important to become familiar with the literacy practices of the church. We need to understand the historical and cultural context on which the church was founded, and on which it continues to build. Educators must become knowledgeable about the types of literacy skills students are learning, how they are being taught these skills, and how this teaching and learning might influence their thinking about literacy.

The African American church has much to offer in terms of time-tested, proven ways to teach and reach African American students effectively. It is crucial for all teachers of African American students to become knowledgeable about the African American church—a cultural context within which many African American children acquire and develop literacy skills. Classroom teachers can use this information to develop innovative ways to build on the knowledge acquired from literacy practices within the context of the African American church, thereby improving the literacy learning experiences of African American students in their classrooms. Educators can develop programs that use the African American church as a valuable resource.

By focusing on the historical context, student–teacher relationships, and authentic opportunities to practice literacy skills in the African American church learning environment, we hope that this chapter motivates educators to consider possible ways to use this information creatively, especially in their classrooms. Students who participate in African American Sunday School and other church activities develop specific values and beliefs about literacy and learning that must be explored and understood to develop effective teaching strategies to improve their academic achievement in the school setting, and assist them to negotiate successfully the cultural borders between church and school learning environments.

REFERENCES

Baldwin, L. V. (1991). *There is a balm in Gilead: The cultural roots of Martin Luther King, Jr.* Minneapolis, MN: Fortress Press.

Billingsley, A. (1992). *Climbing Jacob's ladder: The enduring legacy of African-American families.* New York: Touchstone.

Burkett, R. K. (1978). *Black redemption: Churchmen speak for the Garvey movement.* Philadelphia: Temple University Press.

Cazden, C. (1988). *Classroom discourse: The language of teaching and learning.* Portsmouth, NH: Heinemann.

Cone, J. H. (1989). *Black theology and black power.* San Francisco: HarperCollins.

Cone, J. H. (1997). *God of the oppressed.* New York: Orbis Books.

Copher, C. B. (1993). *Black biblical studies: Biblical and theological issues on the black Presence in the Bible.* Chicago: Black Light Fellowship.

Cornelius, J. D. (1991). *When I can read my title clear: Literacy, slavery, and religion in the antebellum South.* Columbia: University of South Carolina Press.

Delpit, L. (1995). *Other people's children: Cultural conflict in the classroom.* New York: New Press.

Edelman, M. W. (1999). *Lanterns*. Boston: Beacon Press.

Edwards, P. A. (1995). Connecting African-American parents and youth to the school's reading curriculum: Its meaning for school and community literacy. In V. L. Gadsden & D. Wagner (Eds.), *Literacy among African-American youth: Issues in learning teaching and schooling* (pp. 263–281). Creskill, NJ: Hampton Press.

Edwards, P. A., Danridge, J., McMillon, G. T., & Pleasants, H. M. (2001). Taking ownership of literacy: Who has the power? In P. R. Schmidt & P. B. Mosenthal (Eds.), *Reconceptualizing literacy in the new age of pluralism and multiculturalism: Vol. 9. Advances in reading and language research* (pp. 111–134). San Francisco: Jossey-Bass.

Edwards, P. A., Pleasants, H. M., & Franklin, S. H. (1999). *A path to follow: Learning to listen to parents*. Portsmouth, NH: Heinemann.

Elder, G., Modell, J., & Parke, R. D. (1993). Studying children in a changing world. In G. Elder, J. Modell, & R. D. Parke (Eds.), *Children in time and place* (pp. 3–21). New York: Cambridge University Press.

Felder, C. H. (1991). *Stony the road we trod: African American biblical interpretation*. Minneapolis, MN: Augsburg Fortress.

Fordham, S. (1988). Racelessness as a factor in black students' school success: Pragmatic strategy or pyrrhic victory? *Harvard Educational Review, 58*(1), 54–84.

Foster, M. (1997). *Black teachers on teaching*. New York: New Press.

Frank, K. A., & Yasumoto, J. Y. (1998). Linking action to social structure within a system: Social capital within and between subgroups. *American Journal of Sociology, 104*(3), 642–686.

Franklin, R. M. (1997). *Another day's journey: Black churches confronting the American crisis*. Minneapolis, MN: Fortress Press.

Frazier, E. F. (1963). *The Negro church in America*. New York: Schocken.

Freedman, S. G. (1984). *Upon this rock: The miracles of a black church*. New York: HarperCollins.

Gilbert, S. E., & Gay, G. (1989). *Improving the success in school of poor black children*. In B. J. Shade (Ed.), *Culture, style and the educative process* (pp. 275–283). Springfield, IL: Thomas.

Hale, J. E. (1982). *Black children: Their roots, culture, and learning styles*. Baltimore: Johns Hopkins University Press.

Hale, J. E. (1994). *Unbank the fire: Visions for the education of African American children*. Baltimore: Johns Hopkins University Press.

Heath, S. B. (1983). *Ways with words: Language, life, and work in communities and classrooms*. New York: Cambridge University Press.

Hopkins, D. N. (1994). *Shoes that fit our feet: Sources for a constructive black theology*. New York: Orbis Books.

Hopkins, R. (1997). *Educating black males: Critical lessons in schooling, community, and power*. Albany: State University of New York Press.

Irvine, J. J. (1990). *Black students and school failure: Policies, practices, and prescriptions*. New York: Greenwood Press.

Kunjufu, J. (1984). *Developing positive self-images and discipline in black children*. Chicago: African American Images.

Ladson-Billings, G. (1994). *The dreamkeepers: Successful teachers of African American Students.* San Francisco: Jossey-Bass.

Lareau, A. (1989). *Home advantage: Social class and parental intervention in elementary education.* Philadelphia: Falmer Press.

Lee, C. (1991). Big picture talkers/words walking without masters: The instructional implications of ethnic voices for an expanded literacy. *Journal of Negro Education, 60*(3), 291–304.

Lincoln, C. E., & Mamiya, L. H. (1990). *The Black church in the African American experience.* Durham, NC: Duke University Press.

Luria, A. R. (1976). *Cognitive development: Its cultural and social foundations.* Cambridge, MA: Harvard University Press.

Mason, J. M., McCormick, C., & Bhavnagri, N. (1986). How are you going to help me learn?: Lesson negotiations between a teacher and preschool children. In D. B. Yaden, Jr. & S. Templeton (Eds.), *Metalinguistic awareness and beginning literacy: Conceptualizing what it means to read and write* (pp. 159–172). Portsmouth, NH: Heinemann.

McMillon, G. M. T. (2001). *A tale of two settings: African American students' literacy experiences at church and at school.* Doctoral dissertation, Michigan State University, East Lansing.

McMillon, G. M. T., & Edwards, P. A. (2000). Why does Joshua hate school? . . . but love Sunday school? *Language Arts, 78*(2), 111–120.

Meltzer, M. (1964). *In their own words: A history of the American Negro, 1619–1865.* Chicago: University of Chicago Press.

Montgomery, W. (1993). *Under their own vine and fig tree: The African-American church in the South, 1865–1900.* Baton Rouge: Louisiana State University.

Moyd, O. P. (1995). *The sacred art: Preaching and theology in the African American tradition.* Valley Forge, VA: Judson Press.

Mukenge, I. R. (1983). *The black church in urban America.* Lanham, MD: University Press of America.

Myers, W. R. (1991). *Black and white styles of youth ministry: Two congregations in America.* New York: Pilgrim Press.

Nelsen, H. M., & Nelsen, A. K. (1975). *Black church in the sixties.* Lexington: University of Kentucky Press.

Nelsen, H. M., Yokley, R. L., & Nelsen, A. K. (1971). *The black church in America.* New York: Basic Books.

Noddings, N. (1984). *Caring: A feminine approach to ethics and moral education.* Berkley: University of California Press.

Pepper, K. (1999). Managing today's classrooms. *New Teacher Advocate, 6*, 5–9.

Ogbu, J. (1995). Literacy and Black Americans: Comparative perspectives. In V. L. Gadsden & D. Wagner (Eds.), *Literacy among African-American youth: Issues in learning teaching and schooling* (pp. 263–281). Creskill, NJ: Hampton Press.

Proctor, S. D. (1995). *The substance of things hoped for: A memoir of African American faith.* New York: Putnam's.

Purcell-Gates, V. (1997). *Other people's words: The cycle of low literacy.* Cambridge, MA: Harvard University Press.

Resnick, L. B. (1990). Literacy in school and out. *Daedalus, 199*(2), 169–186.

Scribner, L. (1985). Vygotsky's uses of history. In J. V. Wertsch (Ed.), *Culture, communication, and cognition: Vygotskian perspectives* (pp. 119–145). New York: Cambridge University Press.

Searfoss, L. W., & Readence, J. E. (1985). *Helping children learn to read.* Englewood Cliffs, NJ: Prentice-Hall.

Sernett, M. C. (1975). *Black religion and American evangelism: White protestants, plantation missions, and the flowering of Negro Christianity, 1787–1865.* Metuchen, NJ: Scarecrow Press.

Shade, B. J. (1989). Culture and learning style within the Afro-American community. In B. J. Shade (Ed.), *Culture, style and the educative process* (pp. 16–32). Springfield, IL: Thomas.

Smith, E. D. (1988). *Climbing Jacob's ladder: The rise of black churches in eastern American cities, 1740–1877.* Washington, DC: Smithsonian Institution Press.

Taylor, D., & Dorsey-Gaines, C. (1988). *Growing up literate: Learning from inner-city families.* Portsmouth, NH: Heinemann.

Thurman, H. (Ed.). (1973). *A track to the water's edge: The Olive Schreiner reader.* New York: Harper & Row.

Van Dijk, T. A. (1997). *Discourse as social interaction.* Thousand Oaks, CA: Sage.

Vygotsky, L. S. (1978). *Mind in society: The development of higher mental processes.* Cambridge, MA: Harvard University Press.

Ward, V. (1998). The African American Sunday school: Reclaiming its role as moral teacher. *Direction*, pp. 1–2.

Washington, J. R. (1984). *Black religion: The Negro and Christianity in the United States.* Baltimore: University Press of America.

Weems, R. J. (1991). Reading her way through the struggle. In C. H. Felder (Ed.), *Stony the road we trod: African American biblical interpretation* (pp. 57–77). Minneapolis, MN: Augsburg Fortress.

Wertsch, J. V. (1985). *Vygotsky and the social formation of mind.* Cambridge, MA: Harvard University Press.

Chapter 16

Family Literacy

Learning from an
Asian Immigrant Family

GUOFANG LI

More children from many diverse linguistic, cultural, religious, and academic backgrounds are attending North American schools (Garcia, 1999; Moll & Gonzalez, 1994). In fact, the changing demographics in today's schools pose an unprecedented need for literacy educators to understand children's outside-of-school literacy experiences (Au, 1993; Valdes, 1998). Important questions arise when many classroom teachers try to understand children from diverse cultural and linguistic backgrounds better to facilitate learning in their classrooms. For example, how is the literacy learning of children from diverse backgrounds supported at home? How do home literacy learning experiences differ from school experiences? How might children's home experiences inform us about fostering literacy learning in school? To address these questions, I studied a Chinese immigrant student's (i.e., Yang Li's) home literacy practices and explored ways his family supported his school learning as he made cultural and literacy transitions to North American society. Here, I provide a brief biography of Yang Li's family.

YANG LI AND HIS FAMILY

Six-year-old Yang Li was a first-grade student. He moved to Canada, in 1997, with his mother to join his father, a student at a Canadian university. Yang Li's father, Li-yong, a former engineer in China, was pursuing his master's degree in chemistry. His mother, Nie-dong, also a former engineer, was a lab assistant at the university.

Yang Li and his family lived in a crowded, one-bedroom, second-floor apartment above a Chinese café. There were five apartments on the second floor, including two one-bedroom apartments and three single rooms. Seven people (including the Li family) lived in five apartments and shared two bathrooms. All adults were university students, including four Chinese, two East Indians, and one Canadian. I visited the Li family at their apartment weekly for 8 months to explore their home literacy practices, interactions, and routines related to literacy events in their home. I also asked Yang's parents about their beliefs about literacy and Yang's learning in cross-cultural contexts. Additionally, I collected samples of Yang's writing and drawing, and participated in some of his games and activities with his parents. I describe in detail Yang's home literacy practices.

FOUR FACETS OF HOME LITERACY PRACTICES

To better present Yang Li's home literacy practices and how they differ from school practices, I used Leseman and de Jong's (1998) four, inter-related facets of home literacy practices as themes to categorize Yang's experiences at home: (1) literacy opportunity, (2) instruction, (3) cooperation, and (4) socioemotional quality. Literacy opportunity refers to children's interactions with literacy of whatever kind, in whatever form, in the home milieu. These interactions include children's direct contact with print, chances to observe parents' reading and writing activities, exposure to media, and opportunities for joint reading and writing practices. Literacy instruction refers to direct or indirect guidance provided by parents to the child through literacy activities. Leseman and de Jong's concept of instruction only includes parental guidance of a child during shared storybook reading, such as their procedural utterances, pointing, labeling, repeating and completing, explaining, evaluating, and extending. I extend the concept of instruction to more explicit and deliberate teaching with the use of different texts and strategies in literacy-related activities at home. Literacy cooperation involves active participation of the child in literacy-related events, which is reflected in the child's understanding and acceptance of the role he or she plays in activities and how he or she responds to parental literacy instructions. Socioemotional quality is an affective factor that includes indicators such as the bond between the parents and the child. In this study, I extended the notion of socioemotional quality to include the pressures from home and school that affected Yang's emotional well-being.

In the following section, I illustrate Yang's literacy learning at home and how his parents supported his literacy development relative to the four facets described earlier. Although I discuss each facet as a separate category, as Yang's story indicates, these four facets are interrelated and sometimes overlap.

YANG'S LITERACY OPPORTUNITIES IN THE HOME MILIEU

Yang's home environment was characterized by a rich presence of print, media, and other literacy materials, such as books and maps. In this positive literacy environment, Yang had opportunities not only to have direct contact with reading and writing but also to observe his parents' reading and writing in both English and Chinese. In addition, Yang's interaction with literacy also occurred in a variety of settings, such as shopping centers, the library, bookstores, and through a variety of media, such as flyers and computers.

Literacy Opportunities inside the Home

Yang's parents, Nie-dong and Li-yong, made use of the limited space in their one-bedroom apartment to provide Yang with different learning opportunities. There were bookshelves along one side of the wall, where Yang had his own book section. His section included several books written in English, borrowed from the public library, such as *Are You My Mother?* by P. D. Eastman (1967), *One Day at the Supermarket* by Donna Bryant (1989), *I Want to Be an Astronaut* by Byron Barton (1988), and other books written in both Chinese and English. The Chinese books included language arts and math textbooks, and some storybooks, such as *Collections of Children's Fables* (1993). Books in English included *Elephant Family* by Jane Goodall (1991), *Disney's Mulan* by Gina Ingoglia (1998), and *I Can Read about Seasons* by Robyn Supraner (1999). Additionally, Yang subscribed to a magazine called *Owl* (Young Naturalist Foundation). Yang's parents also used the space on the wall of their bedroom to help Yang's learning. One side of the wall displayed a large world map, where Yang was taught about world geography when time permitted. Beside the map, Yang's parents hung an English alphabet, both lower and uppercase, and illustrations of the letters, so that Yang could look at the chart any time he wanted.

Yang also had multiple opportunities to use paper and pencils. He often sat at the desk in one corner of their bedroom drawing pictures, copying textbooks, or studying math. Sometimes he just lay on his bed to draw or write. His finished and unfinished drawings were lying everywhere on the desk and on the beds. Yang was accustomed to reading and writing, because his parents often wrote and read a variety of materials at home. For example, his father read the Chinese newspaper, *China Daily Overseas Edition,* almost daily. He often brought his textbooks, lab manuals, and research papers from school to read at home. Whenever he had time, he studied English using TOFEL and GRE workbooks and Chinese–English dictionaries. To improve his listening comprehension, he used a Walkman to listen to English tapes. Yang's mother read some Chinese magazines borrowed from friends or downloaded from the Internet, and sometimes English newspapers, such as the *National Post.* The English materials she read to improve her English included the Jehovah's Witnesses monthly publications: *The Watchtower: Announcing Jehovah's Kingdom* and *Awake!* Like her husband, she sometimes read chemistry lab materials and wrote lab reports at home. Therefore, for Yang, reading and writing were inseparable parts of his family's daily life.

Exposure to Western media was also an important part of Yang's home experiences. Yang watched lots of cartoons and movies, such as *Mulan, Air Force One,* and *Speed,* and different television programs, such as the animated Eddie Murphy show *The PJs, Bugs Bunny, CBC Playground,* and *The Simpsons.* Watching television and videos was considered a learning tool for Yang. The television was always on, with closed captioning, so Yang could listen and see the words simultaneously. Sometimes, Yang mimicked long English sentences for his mother, without understanding what they meant. In Chinese, Nie-dong would ask, "What are you talking about? Say it again?" Yang just smiled. "I just learned from TV." Sometimes, after watching television programs, he drew pictures of cartoon characters, such as Chippy, Road Runner, Penguin, Tweety, and Puddy Cat.

Literacy Opportunities outside the Home

Yang's exposure to reading and writing was not limited to the boundaries of the apartment. Li-yong and Nie-dong made an effort to take Yang to a variety of places where he could learn more English. They treated outings as important learning opportunities and made use of whatever "teachable moments" were available. For example, they took Yang shopping with them and showed him how to read flyers. Yang's dream was to become president of a country and have a huge house, with big computers. Whereas his parents read flyers for groceries, Yang read about furniture and computers for his future house and office. He liked to look through the flyers of Future Shop or Home Hardware. "I like this one. This is for my office. That one is for Mom. Mine is the biggest!" he said in Chinese. "But mine costs a lot of money, lots lots of money. I need to make money first!"

Li-yong and Nie-dong also took Yang to his favorite downtown library to borrow storybooks. Yang learned how to find books he wanted on the computer, then locate them in the shelves. Once, when I was with him in the library, Yang sat in front of the computer and entered the book title he wanted, with my help. He scrolled down and selected the book, copying the call number on a piece of paper. Then, we went together to find the book. When we were ready to go, Yang handed the librarian his card and checked out all his books.

Besides the library, Yang also visited some bookstores in town, where his parents bought workbooks to enhance Yang's academic development in either English or math. Whenever there was a book sale somewhere, Yang's parents tried to buy books and magazines to cultivate his interests in science and geography. For example, Yang was first introduced to the children's magazine *Owl* at one of the book fairs, where his parents bought several issues for a nickel each.

Some evenings, when both of his parents were busy with their work, Yang went with them to their lab, where they could work on their experiments and supervise Yang at the same time. Yang sat for hours in front of a computer playing games. He often shouted and repeated voices from the games: "Game over, Man! Game Over!" or "Oops! You missed!"

Although Yang was provided with many different literacy opportunities in a variety of settings inside and outside the home, and his English was improving, his parents did not stop at merely exposing him to the English language. Instead, they took active measures to teach him English and prepare him for Canadian schooling. In the next section, I illustrate the various instructional strategies Yang's parents used to help him learn English.

LITERACY INSTRUCTIONS IN THE HOME MILIEU

Yang's parents used the instructional strategies specified by Leseman and de Jong (1998), such as procedural utterances, pointing, and explaining during parent–child shared story reading. Because these strategies are the same as mainstream practices, I do not discuss them in this section. Instead, I focus on Yang's parents' unique instructional practices, rooted in their Chinese cultural background, including explicit instructions using bilingual word lists, worksheets, and rote-learning approaches.

Yang attended kindergarten only briefly in China before moving to Canada. When Yang first moved to Canada, he was placed in first grade, without knowing English. He did not understand what the teacher and students said, and, frustrated, he cried in class almost every day the first month. The other children called him "Cry-boy." Even when Yang knew a lot about a topic (e.g., animals), he could not make the teacher recognize his ability because of his language difference. His teacher called on other, bilingual children to help him. Yang often came home and asked his mom if he was stupid, and he told her that it was not very good to be Chinese.

Yang's English has been a concern for Li-yong and Nie-dong since he began school. They used many methods to teach English to Yang and prepare him for school. They made flash cards to teach him the English alphabet. After Yang learned the basic alphabet, his parents made bilingual word lists in both Chinese and English from some children's books they borrowed from the public library. Yang read, memorized, recited, and copied (at least twice) all the words every day. For example, Yang's parents made a bilingual word list based on several children's books, such as *Daddy* and *Mr. Mugs*, from the library. They broke the sentences down into words and listed the Chinese words beside the English words. Sometimes, they made bilingual word lists using themes, such as animals and household items (see Figure 16.1). This approach Nie-dong and Li-yong had used to learn English, especially English vocabulary. They had observed that by having the Chinese meaning of the words on the list, it was easier for Yang to understand English word meanings. Yang's mother explained:

> "Yang learns the meaning of words in Chinese first, unlike English as first language learners who, once they learn how to read a word, understand the meaning. For Yang, the procedure is more complicated: He has to internalize the meaning in Chinese after learning a new English word, then he can get the meaning of the English words."

Because Yang attended kindergarten for a short time in China, to give him a sense of language continuity, Yang's parents continued to teach him Chinese characters, using simple Chinese poems and stories they downloaded from the Internet in the first couple of months, so that he could make a transition to English. As Yang progressed with his English, Li-yong and Nie-dong gradually reduced the teaching of Chinese. They thought that learning Chinese would negatively influence his progress in English, and they had already identified strong Chinese interference in his spoken English. For example, Yang had little sense of plural forms or the change of tense in English, because there is no tense change

horse	马
sheep	羊
bird	鸟
chiken	鸡
duck	鸭
dog	狗
cat	猫
pig	猪
monkey	猴
fox	狐狸
rabbit	兔
bear	熊
panda	熊猫
insect	虫
fish	鱼
elephant	大象
tiger	老虎
giraffe	长颈鹿
ox	牛
mouse	鼠
frog	青蛙

FIGURE 16.1. A sample of Yang's bilingual list by themes.

in Chinese. His parents decided not to send Yang to learn Chinese, or to teach him Chinese themselves, until he was fluent in English. Nie-dong admitted that it was not a good thing to stop his training in Chinese: "But we have no choice. Right now, his English is not good enough. If we add Chinese, it is not good for his English."

When Yang could read more words, Li-yong and Nie-dong progressed, using all-English materials instead of bilingual word lists. They made worksheets from some of the workbooks they found in the library, so Yang could practice his English. Unlike the previously used bilingual word lists, these worksheets focused on individual words (see Figure 16.2 for an example of the worksheets). When Yang could read a simple book without difficulty, his parents did not type the words from the book into a word list; rather, they asked him to read the words several times under their supervision. They made sure that he did not omit reading some of the letters and sounds, especially the ending |t| and |s| sounds. However, they continued to make Yang copy the books, word by word, because they firmly believed that copying could help Yang learn the words by heart. Li-yong told me, "It [copying] is based on how I learned Chinese when I was in elementary school. Copying is good for memory. If you read without memorizing, it is no use." Yang read, copied, and memorized over 80 books at home.

The little people study:

Red

See the red wagon.
See the red flowers.

Practice
red
_____
_____
_____
_____
_____

A red apple.

Fill in:

A bug can be _____
An apple can be _____
A berry can be _____

FIGURE 16.2. A sample of Yang's worksheets.

Although they focused a lot of effort on reading, Li-yong and Nie-dong did not deliberately teach Yang creative writing skills. They held the traditional Chinese belief that one's writing ability could be improved through continued exposure to texts and through reading/memorizing English texts. As the Chinese saying goes, "If one can memorize 300 Tang Dynasty poems, he or she who did not know how to write poetry can now write poetry." If Yang increased his vocabulary through reading and copying English story texts, and could speak fluent English, he would be able to write. Yang often wrote them notes, saying things such as "Mom and Dad, I love you," which proved to them that if he could speak and read English, he could write it, too. Occasionally, they created opportunities for him to write. For example, they modeled a letter in English to Yang's grandmother in China, and asked Yang to copy it. After Yang learned to write, they encouraged him to write letters by himself (see Figure 16.3 for one of these letters).

Besides teaching English, Nie-dong and Li-yong also taught other subjects, such as geography and math, to Yang at home. Therefore, Yang had a very busy schedule at night. However, Yang demonstrated a zest for learning and seldom expressed resistance to his parents' instructions. He understood his role in the literacy activities and was always an active participant. In the next section, I describe how Yang, as a young learner, participated and sometimes initiated interactions in joint literacy activities with his parents.

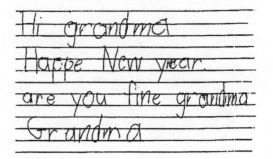

FIGURE 16.3. Yang's English letter to his grandma during Chinese New Year.

HOME LITERACY COOPERATION

Yang's cooperative efforts were reflected not only in his active response to his literacy role and the stories during shared book reading with his parents, particularly with his mother, but also in his constant enthusiasm to retell stories read to him, and his ability to initiate new play, such as a daily "mother–son" talk. He read books with his mother after supper. Usually, Yang read the books first, and Nie-dong listened. If they ran into any new words, Nie-dong checked the dictionary to figure out the meaning in Chinese. Then to have fun, they took turns reading, with Yang reading a page and Nie-dong reading a page. This way, both were reading and learning. For example, one evening before Halloween, they read *Halloween Storybook*, which Li-yong had retyped and printed from the computer for Yang. Yang started to read, but he and his mother did not know the word *pumpkin*, so they checked in an English–Chinese dictionary to find out the meaning of *pumpkin* in Chinese. As Yang read, Nie-dong underlined the words that they had problems pronouncing; she later asked Yang to repeat the words. After Yang read the story a couple of times, they began to take turns reading:

YANG: See the big pumpkin.

NIE-DONG: Gai wo le [My turn]. The pumpkin is orange.

YANG: It is round, round, round, round, round . . .

NIE-DONG: (*signaling him to stop*) Yang!

YANG: (*stops and makes faces at her*) Gai Mama le [Mom's turn]!

NIE-DONG: It is a Jack-o-latong.

YANG: Bu shi de, Mama [no, Mom]. Shi [It's] jack-o-lantern, lantern, bu shi [not] latong!

This kind of mother–child cooperation during their story reading in English also occurred during their story reading in Chinese. Yang asked his mother to read him a Chinese story every night before he went to bed. Nie-dong told me that Yang had already figured out different functions of English and Chinese: "It is so strange that he knows the difference. It is clear to him that English is something he has to learn, a necessity for school, and for talking with other non-Chinese people. But to listen to Chinese stories is a pastime, a relaxing moment." She borrowed some Chinese children's stories from friends, stories from Chinese classics such as *The Monkey King* and *The Three Kingdoms*. When they ran out of Chinese stories, Yang and his mother read the Chinese textbooks they brought from China. Yang was also keen on retelling stories his mother told him. He was interested in space and big animals, such as dinosaurs, and was able to retell information about planets and make up stories about them. One evening, he told me a story about a spaceship, a UFO, in Chinese, which he later also illustrated. The story (translated from Chinese) is as follows:

"In space, the stars crashed. One UFO did not fly away. The UFO shined with light. The light was so hot that it melted all the other stars around it and they exploded."

Yang initiated some of the mother–son shared activities, such as their routine "mother and son" talk, in which Yang took out a piece of paper and a pencil and requested that his mother have a little conversation with him and take notes on their talk, if necessary. Yang reported what he did and learned at school that day. This talk was how Nie-dong learned what Yang's school was all about, because the work Yang did at school was seldom sent home. Yang often used "Sandwich English," that is, English words preceded and followed by Chinese words. A typical talk went as follows:

NIE-DONG: Ni men you mei you zuo [Did you do] Pink Book?

YANG: Mei you [No, we didn't]. Wo men zuo le [We did] snowglow, two snow man, yi ge [one] Christmas tree. Ben lai yi ge [We only needed to do one] snowman, wo zuo le liang ge [I did two].

NIE-DONG: What is snowglow?

YANG: Wo hai hua le yi ge [I also drew] snowman picture! (*Indicates to his mom that this is important.*) Xie xia lai [Write this down]!

NIE-DONG: Ni xie [You write].

YANG: (*writing on a piece of paper*) Snow pict . . . Zen me pin [How to spell]?

NIE-DONG: P-I-C-T-U-R-E.

YANG: Picnic!

Yang appeared to enjoy this kind of literacy play with his parents, especially his mother. Through these activities, he established a strong bond with his parents. He appeared to be a cheerful, outgoing, and talkative child. However, his life in Canada was far from burden-free. As indicated in his home literacy practices, he not only had daytime school but also nighttime school at home. This double burden had a great impact on his socioemotional quality at home and at school. In the next section, I explain how Yang's life was influenced by the cultural and educational differences between home and school practices.

SOCIOEMOTIONAL QUALITY IN HOME LITERACY

Several factors influenced Yang's socioemotional well-being inside and outside the home. When he started school in Canada, Yang's main barrier was his limited English-language ability. As he progressed in English and his school performance, other factors, such as his family's social integration, the relationship between Chinese and English, and more significantly, the cultural differences between home and school became more prominent indicators of his socioemotional disposition relative to his literacy learning.

Yang's mother considered him a lonely boy, who had no siblings or friends with whom to play. Yang was used to playing with toys—a plane or a motorcycle—or other things in sight, such as a dictionary to help him imagine his journey of encountering aliens in outer space. He made continuous "wuuuuu" sounds and totally immersed himself in his imaginative worlds. Yang did not have much contact with other classmates after school. His only occasional playmate was a Chinese girl, Amy, daughter of the downstairs Chinese café owners.

Yang lived predominantly in a Chinese world. He went to family friends' homes to visit on weekends or to borrow Chinese books and videos. Sometimes, he went to the Chinese festival parties sponsored by the Chinese Students' and Scholars' Association at the university. These activities helped Yang adapt to a new life in a new country, although he still missed his Chinese classmates, his grandparents, and the things they used to do together. He even tried to write to his grandma and grandpa in Chinese. He told his mom what he wanted to say to his grandparents, and she wrote it in Chinese. He then copied it down and sent the letter to China. It was hard for him to write this way; he said, "I forgot most of my Chinese!"

Losing his Chinese began to affect Yang's ability to express himself. His parents noted that he was very eloquent in Chinese, but as his English rapidly progressed, his ability in Chinese receded. Nie-dong told me during one of our telephone conversations, "He [Yang] could not express himself as well as before. He got very frustrated sometimes because he could not remember some Chinese words. Now he uses some English words to replace them. But sometimes he does not have English words either."

Yang became more confident in his ability to succeed in school as his English progressed. His father, who had had a harsh childhood in China, set a high standard for his son. He deliberately guided Yang to have high ambition for the future. "Harvard medical school is the best!" he told Yang. To meet this goal, Li-yong expected Yang to be independent, successful, and strong, because he was going to be a man carrying the family name. To achieve this, Yang should be able to discipline himself to do homework or housework assigned to him; he should be able to get dressed and get ready for school without being reminded; he should follow a routine, doing his homework, and going to bed at 9:00 P.M. Therefore, at the age of 6, Yang was already under a lot of pressure to excel.

Because his parents came from a very traditional Chinese background, Yang was often caught between the different cultural practices of the school and his home as he became more and more involved in school life in Canada. The Western approach to schooling, as Li-yong understood it, was that students finished all their exercises in class, and the teachers corrected them right away in class; teachers emphasized afterschool play and did not assign homework. Not only was there no homework, there were no textbooks or examinations, unlike in China, where students are tested regularly in every subject. In order to help Yang, Li-yong and Nie-dong asked the teacher to send Yang's work home. The teacher sent Yang's work home that day, but did not send any work home again. No textbooks, no homework, and no exams made the Li's feel uncertain how best to help Yang. So they continued every day, teaching Yang math and supervising his reading and copy work. In Yang's parents' opinion, the no-textbook, no-homework, no-exam kind of schooling did not seem challenging enough for Yang's academic development:

> "They [the Canadian schools] do not have much training in basics.
> School is too light and relaxed for them [students]. They do not have

strict requirements for the academics. . . . Here, is the kind of relaxed style of teaching. Of course, you do not learn as much as you do in China."

Li-yong and Nie-dong discovered that the differences they experienced between Chinese and Canadian schooling lay not only in subject matter but also in extracurricular activities. For example, a school-sponsored activity, Readathon, called for parents and friends to encourage children to set aside time for recreational reading and to raise funds for the school. It was a contest among all students, and those who pledged the most money for their reading won. Li-yong and Nie-dong thought this was unorthodox. They believed it was a student's obligation to read books and to improve their literacy. If parents or friends were to pay children to read books or study, they would create a bad influence on children's morality and sense of responsibility. Yang did not want to feel left out; he wanted to participate in the activity, so Nie-yong and Li-dong filled in the forms and sent in some money. But at home, the rule remained the Chinese way: Yang did not get any money for reading books; he read the books as an obligation, as a student.

Yang also experienced cultural discontinuity during other school activities that were different from Chinese cultural practices. He was always enthusiastic about school activities, and Nie-dong and Li-yong tried their best to support those activities. When they did not agree with what the school did, they had to work out ways to compromise. These moments put both parents and child in a difficult situation. Li-yong explained how he felt, and how it was more important for Yang to assimilate than for him to do so:

"Those activities, for example, Halloween, do not accord with our own cultural values and traditions. But if they hold these kinds of activities and Yang does not participate, it is not good. I am too old to melt into their culture. I am who I am, and how I am. For Yang, it is different. He needs to mingle with the children here. So sometimes I explain to Yang that we need to keep our own traditions, although they [the school] emphasize that you have to speak English and adapt to their traditions."

Although Li-yong and Nie-dong realized that Yang was experiencing these cultural differences, they never went to the school to express their feelings. In fact, they had little communication with the teachers except for parent–teacher conferences. They regarded the teachers as the authorities and would not challenge them; therefore, they did not initiate communication about the activities with which they disagreed. Rather, they compromised based on their own understanding of the school activities, and educated their child in their own ways.

CONCLUSIONS: LEARNING FROM THE LI FAMILY

I have described Yang's home-related educational experiences in light of Leseman and de Jong's (1998) four facets of home literacy practices: (1) literacy opportunities, (2) instructions, (3) cooperation, and (4) socioemotional qualities. Yang's home experiences demonstrate that he had a bilingual, literate home environment, where he was engaged in a wide range of literacy activities. His parents were highly supportive of his learning English to successfully adapt to Canadian schools. They drew heavily on the instructional and learning techniques of their native country and utilized resources available in their new country to help Yang master English-language literacy. In many ways, Yang had a Chinese-style school at home after his regular Canadian school experiences during the day. His parents were his teachers of reading, writing, math, and science at his home school (Rasinski & Fredericks, 1988). They used a variety of methods of instruction—flash cards, bilingual word lists, copying, independent and joint reading, and use of visual aids. Li-yong and Nie-dong's teaching may also be characterized as direct teaching of literacy skills and attitudes that reflected their traditional Chinese perceptions of literacy learning (Anderson, 1995; Chao, 1996).

Li-yong and Nie-dong placed high expectations and values on Yang's education and academic success. Their influence on Yang's learning is highly *cultural*, embedded in their Chinese ways of learning and living (Zhang & Carrasquillo, 1995). Education, historically, has been regarded as the only path toward upward social mobility in China, and pressures to succeed in education are exerted on children early in life, and this continues throughout their school years, until they enter higher education institutes (Lin & Chen, 1995). For Yang, living in a new country, his journey to success in education added another new layer of complexity; that is, he had to succeed in a new language and culture, with a whole array of adjustment needs, such as lifestyle, economic change, social adaptation, and separation from his grandparents (Yao, 1985). These pressures, as Lin and Chen (1995) point out, may inevitably have a negative impact on students' intellectual, psychological, and physical development.

Given this very traditional Chinese background, Yang's learning was therefore shadowed by apparent incongruencies between the school and home. He was often affected by the cultural conflicts reflected in school activities and practices. Characteristics of Western schooling, such as emphasis on play, flexibility, creativity, and autonomy (e.g., overemphasis on drawing, no homework, no standardized textbooks) were considered drawbacks to students' learning by Yang's parents (Zhang, Ollila, & Harvey, 1998). This was one reason that Li-yong and Nie-dong "operated" a Chinese school at home, to ensure that Yang learned in depth and lay a good foundation for his future. Their concerns and cultural values, however, were not communicated to the school because of the lack of communication between teacher and parents. This lack of communication also made it difficult for them to align with the teachers to support Yang's further academic learning.

Despite the high pressure from his parents and the cultural incongruency between school and home, Yang actively participated in family learning activities, such as shared reading and "mother–son" talks. He was, under the influence of his parents, determined to learn English well and succeed in school. His success in English, unfortunately, was at the cost of his native language—Chinese. When he first started school in Canada, Yang developed negative attitudes toward the Chinese language and the concept of being Chinese, because he could not speak English within 6 months of starting school. As he became more proficient in English and more involved in schoolwork, he was losing his Chinese language ability. Yang's story of "losing one language while acquiring another" is representative of many immigrant children documented in research (Jiang, 1997; Thomas & Chao, 1999; Townsend & Fu, 1998).

Learning about Yang's home literacy practices provides us with valuable insights for teachers. Because cultural values played a central role in Yang's home literacy practices, I advocate a culturally relevant pedagogy when teaching children like Yang. Ladson-Billings (1992, 1994) suggests that the notion of cultural relevance needs to move beyond just knowing students' culture to transcend the negative effects of the dominant cultural practices in the classroom. Teachers of children like Yang can use students' cultural background as a strength to help students construct positive school experiences. This way, this pedagogy becomes one that "empowers students intellectually, socially, emotionally, and politically by using cultural referents to impart knowledge, skills, and attitudes" (Ladson-Billings, 1994, p. 17). For example, teachers can use children's knowledge in their first language as a strength in the classroom by creating situations in which the Chinese language can become uniquely meaningful and valuable (Jiang, 1997). Yang's pride in Chinese culture and ability in the Chinese language might have been maintained if he had had more support from the teacher in the early stage of his Canadian schooling.

For a culturally relevant approach, the teacher needs to become adept at collecting information about students' sociocultural backgrounds and interpreting, and making instructional decisions, based on the data to maximize the individual student's learning (Au, 1993; Davidman & Davidman, 1997); that is, to build cultural continuity between students' home and school learning experiences, teachers need to get to know their students and how they live. One of the most effective ways to collect information is a home visit (McCarthey, 1997). Though teachers may have practical challenges in entering students' homes, looking at students' lives outside the classroom nevertheless yields valuable insight in their literacy learning in different settings, which in turn informs teaching in the classroom. In Yang's case, he did not need to have two discrepant schools—a Canadian school during the day and a Chinese one at night. His home and school learning could have complemented to each other, according to his learning needs, rather than being two dichotomous operations that conflicted with each other. Therefore, learning about student home literacy practices such as Yang's can help teachers constantly adapt and adjust instructional approaches that match students' cultural and individual development needs (Au, 1993). Teachers who work with students like Yang, for example, can find information about the Chinese culture and its traditional practices through reading about existing literacy practices; they might call on parents to learn more about Chinese literacy practice in their homes. By understanding minority students' (such as Yang's) literacy opportunities, instructions, cooperation, and socioemotional qualities at home, teachers can adjust their instructional approaches and work with parents to meet these students' academic, social, and socioemotional needs.

In conclusion, I note that although Yang's story has demonstrated the distinct cultural practices in his home, generalization of Chinese or Asian immigrant children's home literacy experiences should be avoided. Research shows that the nature of immigrant children's home literacy practices is complex and diverse; different factors, such as parents' educational background, socioeconomic status, parenting styles, and English-language proficiency may yield qualitatively different home experiences (Choi, 2000; Li, 2002; Xu, 1999). Therefore, each child needs to be recognized as a unique individual from a unique home environment, with different levels of proficiency in English and in the native language, and different funds of knowledge (Moll, 1994; Xu, 1999).

REFERENCES

Anderson, J. (1995). Listening to parents' voices: Cross cultural perceptions of learning to read and to write. *Reading Horizons, 35*(5), 394–413.

Au, K. H. (1993). *Literacy instruction in multicultural settings.* Fort Worth, TX: Harcourt Brace.

Barton, B. (1988). *I want to be an astronaut.* New York: Crowell.

Beijing Children's Press. (1993). *Collections of children's fables* [in Chinese]. Beijing: Author.

Bryant, D. (1988). *One day at the supermarket.* Nashville,TN: Ideals Publications.

Chao, R. (1996). Chinese and European American mothers' beliefs about the role of parenting in childrens' school success. *Journal of Cross-Cultural Psychology, 27*(4), 403–423.

Choi, B. C. (2000, October). *Planning integration education for newly arrived children from mainland China in Hong Kong and Macau.* Paper presented at the International Society for Educational Planning, Port-of-Spain, Trinidad.

Davidman, L., & Davidman, P. T. (1997). *Teaching with multicultural perspective: A practical guide.* New York: Longman.

Eastman, P. D. (1967). *Are you my mother?* New York: Beginner Books.

Garcia, E. (1999). *Student cultural diversity: Understanding and meeting the challenge.* Boston: Houston Mifflin.

Goodall, J. (1991). *Elephant family.* Toronto: Madison Marketing.

Ingoglia, G. (1998). *Disney's Mulan.* New York: Golden.

Jiang, N. (1997). Early biliteracy: Ty's story. In D. Taylor, D. Coughhin, & J. Masasco (Eds.), *Teaching and advocacy* (pp. 143–159). Yorke, ME: Stenhouse.

Ladson-Billings, G. (1992). Reading between the lines and beyond the pages: A culturally relevant approach to literacy teaching. *Theory Into Practice, 31*(4), 312–320

Ladson-Buildings, G. (1994). *The dreamkeepers: Successful teachers of African American children.* San Francisco: Jossey-Bass.

Leseman, P. P. M., & de Jong, P.F. (1998). Home literacy: Opportunity, instruction, cooperation and social-emotional quality predicting early reading achievement. *Reading Research Quarterly, 33*(3), 294–318.

Li, G. (2002). *"East is east, west is west"?: Home literacy, culture, and schooling.* New York: Peter Lang.

Lin, J., & Chen, Q. (1995). Academic pressure and impact on students' development in China. *McGill Journal of Education, 30*(2), 149–167.

McCarthey, S. J. (1997). Connecting home and school literacy practices in classrooms with diverse populations. *Journal of Literacy Research, 29*(2), 145–182.

Moll, L. C. (1994). Literacy research in community and classroom: A sociocultural approach. In R. B. Ruddell, M. R. Ruddell, & H. Singer (Eds.), *Theoretical models and processes of reading* (pp. 179–207). Newark, DE: International Reading Association.

Moll, L., & Gonzalez, N. (1994). Lessons from research with language minority children. *Jounal of Reading Behavior, 26*, 439–456.

Rasinski, T. V., & Fredericks, A. (1988). Sharing literacy: Guiding principals and practices for parental involvement. *Reading Teacher, 41*, 508–513.

Supraner, R. (1999). *I can read about seasons.* Mahwah, NJ: Troll.

Thomas, L., & Chao, L. (1999). Language use in family and society. *English Journal, 89*(1), 107–113.

Townsend, J., & Fu, D. (1998). A Chinese boy's joyful initiation into American literacy. *Language Art, 75*(3), 193–201.

Valdes, G. (1998). The world outside and inside schools: Language and immigrant children. *Educational Researcher, 27*(6), 4–18.

Xu, H. (1999). Young Chinese ESL children's home literacy experiences. *Reading Horizons, 40*(1), 47–64.

Yao, E. L. (1985). Adjustment needs of Asian immigrant children. *Elementary School Guidance and Counseling, 19*(3), 222–227.

Young Naturalist Foundation. *Owl.* Toronto: Author.

Zhang, C., Ollila, L. O., & Harvey, C. B. (1998). Chinese parents' perceptions of their Children's literacy and schooling in Canada. *Canadian Journal of Education, 23*(2), 182–190.

Zhang, S. Y., & Carrasquillo, A. L. (1995). Chinese parents' influence on academic performance. *New State Association for Bilingual Education Journal, 10,* 46–53.

Conclusions

Improving Literacy Instruction for All Children

Current Concerns
and Future Directions

CYNTHIA H. BROCK

I draw on the work of the authors of the chapters in this book, as well as other scholarly literature, to discuss and explore current concerns and future directions in our work with children from diverse cultural and linguistic backgrounds. Making progress in our efforts to provide quality literacy learning opportunities for children from diverse backgrounds is a complex undertaking that must involve efforts by many on numerous fronts, including the daily work of classroom teachers in schools, administrators at the school and district levels, families, community leaders, university educators, and state and national policy makers. How might we work together, as stakeholders, to improve literacy instruction for *all* children in American schools? We don't have definitive answers, but we do have some ideas. In this concluding section, I discuss what we *have* learned and what we have *yet* to learn as stakeholders in various capacities, who can play a role in improving literacy education for children from diverse backgrounds.

CLASSROOM TEACHERS AND LEARNERS
FROM DIVERSE BACKGROUNDS:
WHAT WE NEED TO KNOW AND DO

Like Wallis and Rosado-McGrath, Chapter 14, I place teachers working with children at the heart of this discussion because the nature and quality of teacher–student and student–student interactions are perhaps the most significant contributors to children's learning in schools (Cummins, 1996). Teachers' beliefs and knowledge about children's languages and cultures, and about literacy and pedagogy, play a central role in children's classroom learning opportunities (Cummins, 1996; Florio-Ruane, 2001). McVee, Chapter 6, drew on the work of Delpit to remind us that "we do not really see through our eyes or hear through our ears, but through our beliefs" (Delpit, 1988, as quoted in Abt-Perkins & Gomez, 1993, p. 193). Our beliefs, as educators, drive our instructional decisions. Thus, our beliefs merit serious consideration.

If we, as educators, believe that children's languages and cultural backgrounds are valuable resources upon which to draw as we work with them, we can create "additive classroom environments" that are "nurturing and effective environments" in which to foster children's literacy learning rather than "subtractive" contexts that are punitive and emotionally distressing for children (Gutierrez et al., 2002, p. 339). Gutierrez and her colleagues (2002) argue that it is "impossible to have an additive context if the child's first language is not valued—if both or all of the languages are not highly valued or reflected in the curriculum" (p. 337). Clearly, teachers' beliefs about children play a central role in the ways they design curricula and foster learning opportunities in their classrooms.

Teachers also need a great deal of knowledge about language and culture. Jimenez, Moll, Rodriguez-Brown, and Barrera (1999) argue that teachers who work with children from diverse linguistic backgrounds must understand the principles of second-language acquisition and multiculturalism. And, unfortunately, there isn't a serious enough effort by mainstream educators, researchers, and administrators to ensure that all U.S. teachers develop these important understandings (Valdes, 2001). This situation is distressing, indeed, when research illustrates that teachers' knowledge of cultural and linguistic diversity can impact significantly children's literacy achievement (Au, 2000).

In addition to developing knowledge about language and culture, teachers need to develop knowledge about literacy and pedagogy. By knowledge of literacy, I do not mean merely knowledge of skills and strategies associated with reading and writing; although, I acknowledge that this kind of knowledge is important. Rather, drawing on work by

Gutierrez and colleagues (2002), I argue that teachers need knowledge such as "what dimensions of social life enter into meaning making and comprehension" (p. 335); that is, literacy is much more than a narrow set of discrete skills; rather, literacy involves the ability to read, write, and use language in powerful ways as complex social and cultural endeavors. More complex understandings of language, literacy, and culture can help teachers to engage in rich pedagogical practices in light of repressive policy mandates (e.g., Proposition 227, in California, and the state reading exams described by Pennington in Chapter 13). As Pennington illustrates in this volume, as do Gutierrez and her colleagues elsewhere, without conscious and thoughtful effort, teachers can resort to reductionist teaching practices that mitigate against complex literacy learning when they are teaching in contexts that mandate repressive reform or testing practices.

Various scholars (e.g., Au, 2000; Jimenez et al., 1999) propose changes to teacher education programs in universities, as well as professional development programs in school districts, to prepare teachers to work better with children from diverse backgrounds. First, we need to do a better job of recruiting teachers from diverse cultural and linguistic backgrounds to teach in U.S. schools (Jimenez et al., 1999). Second, preservice and inservice teachers need to learn more about the complex second-language acquisition process as it relates not only to literacy teaching and learning, but also to content area teaching and learning (Berg, 2003; Cummins, 1996). Third, we should encourage preservice and inservice teachers to work toward becoming multilingual readers, writers, and speakers themselves (Berg, 2003). Acquiring literacy competencies in a second language can help educators (pre-K through university) to develop an understanding of, and empathy for, the language and literacy acquisition process that English language learners' (ELLs) experience (Berg, 2003). Fourth, as an educational community, we need to recognize, value, and build on the different linguistic and cultural backgrounds that children and their families bring to communities and schools (Au, 2000; Moll, 1998).

CRITIQUING OUR WORK WITHIN SCHOOL DISTRICTS AND UNIVERSITIES

In the previous section, I discussed individual teachers' beliefs and knowledge about the children they serve in their classrooms, as well as culture, language, literacy, and pedagogy. I now move to broader circles of influence in our work with English language learners. School districts and universities influence, and are influenced by, teachers and children in classrooms. Teachers' beliefs and understandings shape their daily actions in classrooms. Also, societal and institutional beliefs and norms—and the kinds of stories that institutions and groups tell and enact—impact the ways that institutions function to serve, or fail to serve, the individuals that inhabit them (Cherryholmes, 1988). Hence, in this section, I shift to an exploration of the stories told and experiences enacted at the broader community/institution level, with an eye toward exploring how institutional beliefs, and the stories that reveal them, may mitigate against helping children from diverse linguistic and cultural backgrounds succeed in schools.

Berg (2003) suggests that, unfortunately, "linguistic diversity is seen as one of the distressing problems with which schools have to cope" (p. 105). Moreover, "education for multilingual people is almost always seen in the light of costs and burdens" (p. 105). Additionally, in Berg's estimation, there are precious few success stories from which to draw as examples of positive systematic action taken to embrace the linguistic and cultural diversity of the children served by school systems. We suggest that the work of Wallis and Rosado-McGrath (Chapter 14, this volume) illustrates a success story in the making. Wallis, Rosado-McGrath, and their colleagues are intelligent, competent educational administrators and scholars, who seek to structure meaningful systemic reform to educate effectively *all* of the children in their school district. Their work has the potential to inform other educators in other school districts as they take on the important task of interrupting deficit stories of children from diverse cultural and linguistic backgrounds and crafting new and positive stories about the strengths and rich backgrounds that these children bring to U.S. schools (Moll, 1998).

Universities and the broader literacy research community both have much progress to make on a host of different fronts in their efforts to help craft positive and powerful learning contexts for ELLs in U.S. schools. Examples abound. First, there is much that we still do not know as a research community about the impact of first language and culture on children's literacy development in a second language (Bernhardt, 2003). Moreover, there is much to be learned about relationships between the development of multilingual and monolingual literacy processes (Berg, 2003; Bernhardt, 2003; Fitzgerald, 2003).

Second, too few scholars of literacy, such as Flores-Dueñas (Chapter 10) and Li (Chapter 16) in this volume, know other languages and understand other cultures, and can, thus, conduct rigorous cross-linguistic and cross-cultural research in literacy (Bernhardt, 2003; Garcia, 2000). As a result, according to Bernhardt (2003), the majority of literacy scholars are "imprisoned figuratively in an English-language mindset" (p. 113). This is problematic for many reasons. Being trapped in one "mindset" closes us to possibilities of engaging in "alternative views and conceptualizations" about language, literacy learning, teaching, and scholarship (p. 113). For example, Bernhardt suggests that models of reading have always been based on English. She asks us to consider how models of reading that take other languages and cultures into account might help us to think differently about literacy teaching and learning.

Third, much literacy research itself has been conducted with populations of European American, middle-class children, with the use of methods and approaches that don't take into account the powerful roles of language and culture. For example, "Ann Haas Dyson (1990) has said that emergent literacy research in the U.S. tells a mainstream story; that is perhaps the case for reading/literacy research overall" (Jimenez et al., 1999, p. 220). Moreover, historically, many research methods employed in educational research (including literacy research) have been conceptualized from a perspective that is reductionist and positivist, ignoring the complex ways culture and language shape and inform human experience (Clandinin & Connelly, 2000). Gutierrez and her colleagues (2002, p. 341) challenge us, as a research community, to continue to conduct "research that concerns itself with culture and its relationship to literacy learning, or that examines how the social organization of learning influences learning outcomes." Obidah (1998) challenges educators to consider the literate currency that students and teachers bring into classrooms. Literate currency refers to "the bodies of knowledge that are in general use among and between groups of people" (p. 52). Although Obidah examined the literate currency of African American students, her work is applicable to all students from diverse cultural and linguistic backgrounds. The research of scholars such as Obidah and Gutierrez and colleagues helps all of us in the educational community to understand better the complex storied lives of children and their families, whose cultural and linguistic backgrounds differ from those of mainstream European American, middle-class children.

STATE AND NATIONAL POLICY

School literacy practices in the United States are informed by particular networks of cultural discourses, including, but not limited to, public discussions of literacy and accountability, state department of education guidelines, standards from professional organizations, mandates from legislatures, family language and literacy beliefs and practices, debates about methodology from higher education, and personal narratives of teachers and other educators. "All of these discourses have their own histories and trajectories that are themselves infused with discourses of communication, success, lifelong learning, risk, survival, method, proficiency, and deficiency, that are often replete with references to creating graduates who can compete in a global society" (Rogers, 2000, p. 420).

In the previous quotation, Rogers (2000) aptly notes that many parties are involved in the overall process of considering what should occur between teachers and children in classrooms. Although I maintain that teachers and their students are the most important parties directly involved in the public education of children, I concur with Rogers that other stakeholders, and their voices, play important roles in the shaping of school literacy practices. Fitzgerald and Cummins (1999) also acknowledge that many stakeholders influence the ways we, as an educational community, construct literacy learning opportunities for children from diverse backgrounds in U.S. schools. They emphasize, however, that there is precious little meaningful cross talk among the many different stakeholders who play roles in constructing the ways that children from diverse backgrounds will be schooled, and they call on all stakeholders to engage in such talk.

Many of the chapters in this volume provide important contributions to this conversation. For example, as discussed in Chapter 16, Guofang Li went into the home of a Chinese family to explore their family literacy practices, and Gwendolyn and Vincent McMillon looked at the rich literacy traditions in an African American church community (Chapter 15). Judy Wallis and Elizabeth Rosado-McGrath created a conversational space in their school district that brought together administrators and educators who had never before talked and planned together for the literacy instruction of children from diverse backgrounds (Chapter 14). Laura Klenk, a university professor, taught a kindergartner to examine how she, and other educators, might provide more effective literacy instruction for young children from diverse backgrounds (Chapter 12). All of these chapters, and many others in this volume, illustrate the powerful insights that can be gleaned from rich cross talk among different parties involved in the literacy education of children from diverse backgrounds.

Notably absent from the conversation in this volume, however, are the voices of public policy makers who play an important role in the kinds of public schooling that children from diverse backgrounds receive. As scholars (e.g., Gutierrez et al., 2002; Pennington, Chapter 13, this volume; Valdes, 2001) emphasize, the laws and mandates created by public policy makers can have devastating and profound implications on the education of children from diverse backgrounds. For example, speaking about the effects of Proposition 227 in California, Gutierrez and her colleagues (2002) argue that "these policies and related practices have spawned new and continued negative effects on Latino students.

They are subtractive in nature and ignore the linguistic resources these students bring to the classroom, and they are out of alignment with responsive learning attributes of programs that work well for these students" (p. 330). Valdes (2001) concurs, suggesting further that repressive public policies are the result of existing ideologies in this country that perpetuate current structures of dominance. How do we interrupt these repressive societal conversations? Valdes suggests that we begin by clearly identifying the problems we face.

Valdes (2001) maintains that effective and adequate policies for the education of children from diverse backgrounds can only be developed if policy makers and the public truly understand the complexities of second-language acquisition and how children from diverse backgrounds *are* educated, and how they *should be* educated. In spite of the fact that policy makers and the general public know little about second-language acquisition, and the social and political realities of schooling for children from diverse cultural and linguistic backgrounds, they make "far-reaching" decisions about how these children should be educated.

Valdes (2001) suggests, and I agree, that adequate policies and practices can only be created and implemented if policy makers and the public are better educated. Here's the dilemma, however. No one I've read or spoken to is quite sure how to do this; neither am I. One thing I am sure about, however, is that the conversation needs to extend beyond educators (at all levels) and public school administrators. You have undoubtedly noticed that the contributors to this volume are educators (at all levels) and administrators. I realize now, as this volume is about to go to the publisher, that we, too, have inadvertently fostered talked just among ourselves. Although we acknowledge that there is far too little cross talk even among ourselves (and this volume does help in that regard), we, too, need to start talking in wider circles of influence, with wider audiences. Although we don't have a definitive plan for doing this, we think that scholars such as Gutierrez and her colleagues (2002), Pennington (Chapter 13, this volume), and Valdes point us in an important direction. We need to raise the consciousness of members of our educational community about the problems and issues we face as we try to sort out how to provide effective literacy learning opportunities for children from diverse cultural and linguistic backgrounds. While we are doing this, we must also engage in cross talk with the various constituencies in our own educational communities about effective ways to talk with and educate the public and policymakers.

An important theme in our collective conversations should be the exploration of ways to interrupt deficit stories, and stories that render children and their families from diverse backgrounds as "voiceless" and "storyless." We should insist that the policymakers who represent us do the same. There are models on which we can draw in this work. For example, by including the voices and stories of African Americans in his discussion of the formation of America, Roger Wilkins's (2002) powerful and provocative book asks readers to rethink and reexamine the sanitized U.S. history curriculum that most of us experienced in school. Why does work such as that of Wilkins matter so much, and why should we engage in similar work? When stories are told *and heard*, when voices are heard, people matter. All of the children in our schools matter. Their stories and voices deserve to be told, heard, and heeded. Can we play a role in making this happen in our educational community, and with the public and policymakers? I think so. I end with a quotation from Wilkins that offers some useful ideas for proceeding:

> I tell my black students that they are far more than the sum of their pain and their grievances, my white students that they are more than the sum of their privileges and their resentments. And finally, I tell them all that it is a lie that "there's nothing certain but death and taxes." Nothing is certain but death, taxes, and *change*. We can either effect the change that is sure to come or stand immobile and be swept away by the change that others have shaped. (p. 143)

REFERENCES

Abt-Perkins, D., & Gomez, M. L. (1993). A good place to begin—examining our personal perspectives. *Language Arts, 70*(3), 193–202.

Au, K. H. (2000). A multicultural perspective on policies for improving literacy achievement: Equity and excellence. In M. L. Kamil, P. B. Mosenthal, P. D. Pearson, & R. Barr (Eds.), *Handbook of reading research* (Vol. III, pp. 835–852). Mahwah, NJ: Erlbaum.

Berg, C. (2003). The role of grounded theory and collaborative research. *Reading Research Quarterly, 38*, 104–141.

Bernhardt, E. (2003). Challenges to reading research from a multilingual world. *Reading Research Quarterly, 38*, 104–141.

Cherryholmes, C. H. (1988). *Power and criticism: Poststructural investigations in education.* New York: Teachers College Press.

Clandinin, D. J., & Connelly, F. M. (2000). *Narrative inquiry: Experience and story in qualitative research.* San Francisco: Jossey-Bass.

Cummins, J. (1996). *Negotiating identities: Education for empowerment in a diverse society.* Ontario: California Association for Bilingual Education.

Fitzgerald, J. (2003). Multilingual reading theory. *Reading Research Quarterly, 38*, 104–141.

Fitzgerald, J., & Cummins, J. (1999). Essay book reviews: Bridging disciplines to critique a national research agenda for language-minority children's schooling. *Reading Research Quarterly, 34,* 378–390.

Florio-Ruane, S. (2001). *Teacher education and the cultural imagination: Autobiography, conversation, and narrative.* Mahwah, NJ: Erlbaum.

Gutierrez, K. D., Asato, J., Pacheco, M., Moll, L. C., Olson, K., Horng, E. L., Ruiz, R., Garcia, E., & McCarty, T. L. (2002). Conversations: "Sounding American": The consequences of new reforms on English language learners. *Reading Research Quarterly, 37,* 328–347.

Jimenez, R. T., Moll, L. C., Rodriguez-Brown, F., & Barrera, R. B. (1999). Conversations: Latina and Latino researchers interact on issues related to literacy learning. *Reading Research Quarterly, 34,* 217–230.

Moll, L. C. (1998). Turning to the world: Bilingual schooling, literacy, and the cultural mediation of thinking. In T. Shanahan, T. & F. Rodriguez-Brown (Eds.), *National Reading Conference yearbook 47* (pp. 59–76). Chicago: National Reading Conference.

Obidah, J. E. (1998). Black-mystory: Literate currency in every day schooling. In D. E. Alvermann, K. A. Hinchman, D. W. Moore, S. F. Phelps, & D. R. Waff (Eds.), *Reconceptualizing the literacies in adolescents' lives* (pp. 51–71). Mahwah, NJ: Erlbaum.

Rogers, T. (2000). What will be the social implications and interactions of schooling in the next millennium? *Reading Research Quarterly, 35,* 420–425.

Valdes, G. (2001). *Learning and not learning English: Latino students in American schools.* New York: Teachers College Press.

Wilkins, R. (2002). *Jefferson's pillow: The founding fathers and the dilemma of black patriotism.* Boston: Beacon Press.

Index

Page numbers followed by an *f* indicate figure, *t* indicate table.

Literate currency
  of African American students, 2–3
  research on, 327
Literature-based programs, 37

M

Multiculturalism, 131–133, 141–
    142

N

Narratives
  description, 106–107, 126–127
  different ways of experiencing,
    149–150
  regarding cultural awareness, 110–
    115, 116t, 117–125
  regarding stereotyping, 136–141
  writing development and, 224–
    227
NEARStar program
  cognitive load of, 48–50
  description, 33–34, 35t–36t, 37–
    38, 50–51
  linguistic content of, 46–48, 47t
  See also Textbook programs
New Basic Reading Program of Scott
    Foresman, 44–45
No Child Left Behind Bill of 2001
  description, 153–154
  literacy learning and, 259
  Spring Branch Comprehensive Pre-
    K–12 Literacy Process and,
    274

P

Phonemic awareness, 42
Phonetically regular words
  description, 42–44
  in NEARStar program, 48
Poverty, 153–154
Preschool education, 269
Proposition 227, 155, 328–
    329

Q

Questioning, 100–103

R

Rapport, establishing, 220–224
Read-aloud books, 55–59. *See also*
    Books
Recitation script, 64–66t
Resources, 155–156
Responsiveness
  to culturally unfamiliar books,
    185–186
  of Latina(o) students, 188–189,
    204–205
  in teaching, 147–149
  See also Aesthetic responses to
    literature; Efferent responses
    to literature
Rimes
  cognitive load and, 45
  in NEARStar program, 47–48
  phonemic awareness and, 43

S

Scaffolding
  in Sunday School, 290
  use of drama and, 62–63
School environment
  administrators, 90, 271
  communication in, 96–99
  conversations in, 70
  instructional conversations within,
    64–69, 66t, 67t, 68t
  language in, 55, 93–94, 95–
    96
  reading aloud and, 57–59
  theory and practice, 103–
    105
  use of drama and, 60–64
Self-assessment
  description, 176
  example of, 179
  See also Assessment